American
Labor &
American
Democracy

American Labor & American Democracy

William English Walling

With a new introduction by Richard Schneirov

Transaction Publishers
New Brunswick (U.S.A.) and London (U.K.)

Library of Congress Catalog Number: 2004058816
ISBN: 1-4128-0472-8
Printed in the United States of America

Library of Congress Cataloging-in-Publication Data

Walling, William English, 1877-1936.
American labor and American democracy / William English Walling ; with a new introduction by Richard Schneirov.
    p. cm.
Originally published: New York and London : Harper & Brothers, 1926. With new introd.
Includes bibliographical references and index.
ISBN 1-4128-0472-8 (pbk. : alk. paper)
   1. Labor movement—United States—History—20th century. 2. Labor movement—United States—Political activity. I. Schneirov, Richard. II. Title.

HD8072.W22 2004
331.88'0973—dc22   2004058816

CONTENTS

TRANSACTION INTRODUCTION   xi

EDITOR'S INTRODUCTION   xlix

FOREWORD   1

INTRODUCTORY   7

The Old Democracy—The Heritage from Jackson and Lincoln—The New Economic Revolution—Business Consolidation—Organized Labor and Other Democratic Forces—Growth of the American Movement—Legal Status and Rights of Labor—Social Philosophy of American Labor

Volume I: LABOR AND POLITICS

PREFATORY NOTE   25

I   LABOR ENTERS POLITICS IN ITS OWN WAY   27

Early Doubts as to the Efficacy of Political Action—Labor's Magna Charta—The Bill of Grievances of 1906—The Initiation of the Non-partisan Policy—The Non-partisan Policy Successfully Applied to Congressional Elections

II   POLITICAL RESULTS—THE FIRST CROP   43

The Clayton Anti-Trust Amendment—Woodrow Wilson and Labor—Reaction Following the World War—The Non-partisan Political Policy Re-affirmed

III   LABOR TURNS FROM PARTIES TO THE PUBLIC   53

The Presidential Campaign of 1920: Harding's Election—Principles versus Parties—Measures Indorsed by Labor—Labor Disappointed in Election

CONTENTS

CHAPTER   PAGE

IV THE FARMER-LABOR ENTENTE   66

    The Farmers' Non-partisan League Experiment—
Non-partisan Participation in Primaries of Both
Parties—The Farmer-Labor Movement of 1920 and
1922—Agricultural and Industrial Workers' Status
Similar

V A NON-PARTISAN PROGRESSIVE CONGRESS   95

    The Renomination of La Follette and Other Pro-
gressive Senators in 1922—The Conference for Pro-
gressive Political Action

VI THE LA FOLLETTE CANDIDACY—A LABOR-PROGRESSIVE
EXPERIENCE   110

    Labor Not Headed Toward a Third Party—Labor's
Fifteen Points and What Happened to Them—The
Socialist Supporters of La Follette Drive Away
Labor Conservatives

VII THE NON-PARTISAN POLICY MEETS A SEVERE TEST SUC-
CESSFULLY   121

    Progressive Republicans and Progressive Democrats
—The Labor Bloc in Congress—The Two Bi-par-
tisan Blocs—Conservative and Progressive—Conflict
Between the Executive and the Legislative at Wash-
ington

VIII THE NON-PARTISAN POLICY IN ITS LATER DEVELOPMENTS   137

    The Old Slogan: "Reward Friends and Punish
Enemies"—Project for Capturing Both Major Par-
ties—Independent Candidatures Frowned Upon—
The Prospects of a Realignment of the Two Parties—
The Future of the Non-partisan Policy

IX BLOC VERSUS PARTY GOVERNMENT   154

    Labor Accepts and Defends the Two-party System
as Moderated by the Bloc—Partisan Politics and
Privilege—A Progressive Majority within the Op-
position Party

CONTENTS

CHAPTER   PAGE

X THE LABOR PROGRESSIVE PROGRAM: THE APPEAL TO THE CONSUMER   170

Liberalism and Progressivism: Are They in Conflict?—The Appeal to the Consumer—The Consumer's Chief Protection: Publicity—The Consolidated Profiteers Fight Publicity and Investigation—The Need for Some Measure of Governmental Control Over Necessities

XI THE LABOR-PROGRESSIVE PROGRAM: THE APPEALS TO THE PRODUCER AND THE CITIZEN   190

Conservation of National Resources—The Farmer-Labor Platform—Reforms That Benefit All Citizens—Democratic Taxation: for Graduated Income and Inheritance Taxes—For Federal Subsidies to States for Social Purposes

XII RISING WAGES AS PART OF A SOCIAL PROGRAM   212

Labor Rejects Fixed Wage Status—Labor Insists upon a Fair Division of the Product for All Producers—The Revolutionary Effects of Immigration Restriction—The New Wage Policy

Volume II: LABOR AND GOVERNMENT

INTRODUCTORY   3

I IS AMERICAN LABOR BECOMING CAPITALISTIC?   11

Labor Banking and Labor Insurance—"Employee Ownership" as Labor Sees It—Labor Capitalism an Illusion—Profit-sharing, Real and Nominal

II LABOR CO-OPERATES WITH CAPITAL, BUT REFUSES COMBINATION   29

"Employee Representation" and Company Unions—Union-Management Co-operation—The Baltimore and Ohio Plan

III LABOR CHALLENGES THE DOMINATION OF CAPITALISM   48

Does American Labor Accept the Capitalist System?

vii

CONTENTS

CHAPTER   PAGE

—Financial Domination Injurious to Production—Industrial Democracy Through Evolution: A Step at a Time

IV   THE SOCIAL STRUGGLE   58

American Labor Opposed to the Class-struggle Doctrine—American Labor Takes Its Stand with All Who Perform Useful Social Functions

V   PROFITS—SOCIAL AND ANTI-SOCIAL   70

Our Industrial Autocracy—Labor's Attack on Illegitimate Profits—The Struggle Against the Financial Oligarchy

VI   THE GOVERNMENT OF INDUSTRY   82

Labor's Demand for a Voice in Industry—Self-determination for Industry—The New Social Structure

VII   ATTEMPT TO ISOLATE LABOR FROM GOVERNMENT   103

The Competence of Government in Industry Questioned—Simultaneous and Related Changes Contemplated in Industry and Government—Labor Refuses to Condemn Economic Functions of Government

VIII   LABOR DEMANDS ITS SHARE IN THE BENEFITS OF GOVERNMENT   112

Capitalist Attempts to Restore Competition in Industry by Government Action—Labor's View of the Scope and Limits of Government Intervention—Capitalist Opposition to Government Control of Monopoly—Organized Business and Government

IX   GOVERNMENT OPERATION WEIGHED AND FOUND WANTING   132

Labor Favors Government Operation of Certain Public Utilities Only: The Water Power Question—The Plumb Plan for the Democratic Operation of Railroads—The Coal Miners and Governmental Intervention in the Coal Industry

CONTENTS

CHAPTER   PAGE

X   THE SOLUTION: SOCIAL SUPERVISION AND CONTROL . . 150

The Movement to Democratize and Industrialize the Economic Boards—Labor and Big Business—Economic Decentralization versus Political Decentralization

INDEX   167

TRANSACTION INTRODUCTION

William English Walling: Socialist and
Labor Progressive

American Labor and American Democracy, William English Walling's classic portrayal of the beliefs, practices, values, and aims of the American Federation of Labor (AFL) in the 1920s, remains worthy of close study by anyone interested in understanding the American labor movement. It was perhaps the first work to portray the AFL as an outgrowth of American democracy rather than as a strictly economic movement. Walling was also among the earliest socialists to recognize that rather than being "a return to normalcy," the 1920s witnessed a vigorous resurgence of the Progressive movement, and the labor movement had become its leading force. In this sense, the book is in line with recent scholarship that explores the origins in this period of "industrial democracy."[1] In addition, *American Labor and American Democracy* is important because it encourages readers to move beyond the stereotype of organized labor of this period as narrow, conservative, and overly accommodating to capital. Walling's work points the way toward a more complex and nuanced understanding of the AFL's aims and practices.

John R. Commons, the founder of the study of American labor history, wrote in his introduction that "This book is as nearly an authoritative statement of the principles and polices of the American organized labor movement of the past forty years as any statement that could be issued by any person not an active official or working member of an American union." As Commons implied, *American Labor and American Democracy* was far from a disinterested or aloof depiction of the AFL. In fact, Walling wrote it as a polemical defense of the American labor movement, less in response to labor's external enemies, and more to the criticisms of its erstwhile friends. Walling's most important audience consisted of those leftwing intellectuals—he called them "Europeanized intellectuals and liberals" (II, 4)*—who viewed the AFL as organizationally complacent, politically conservative, and representative of the narrow interests of an "aristocracy" of craft workers at the expense of the larger American working class. Because this view is again prevalent among labor historians and intellectuals, this book can be a vital contribution to a renewed contemporary dialogue over the relationship of labor and progressive democracy.[2]

William English Walling's background as activist, journalist, and iconoclastic socialist intellectual together with his steadfast loyalty to the American labor movement left him well equipped to mediate between the AFL and its left critics.[3] Walling was born into a well-to-do family of Southern gentry, his father-in-law, William Hayden English, having won fame as a pro-Southern Democratic politician in the antebellum era and vice-presidential candidate under Winfield S. Hancock in 1880. Walling, however, grew up in Indianapolis and in 1893 entered the University of Chicago, where he studied under Thorstein Veblen, among other faculty. He soon assumed socialist leanings, which further developed when Hoosier socialist, Robert Hunter, asked him to come to New

---

* Roman numerals refer to the two parts or volumes into which *American Labor and American Democracy* is divided.

York City in 1902 to work with the largely immigrant lower classes at the University Settlement, a social settlement house.

While in New York, Walling's talent and instinct for participation in movements at the cutting edge of social change became evident when he helped form the New York branch of the Women's Trade Union League and assisted in plans for the Intercollegiate Socialist Society. Later in the decade, he would assemble a group of antiracist socialists to found the National Association for the Advancement of Colored People, and pulled in W.E.B. Du Bois to be editor of its new journal, *The Crisis*.

Combining his activism with journalistic interpretation of social trends, Walling began to write articles for *The Independent* and *World To-Day*. His interests also broadened into serious social analysis. Drawing on ties with AFL union organizers and leaders, including Samuel Gompers, Walling wrote two first-rate scholarly pieces for the *Annals of the American Academy of Political and Social Science* on hopeful and progressive trends among the AFL craft unions.

In these pieces, as in *American Labor and American Democracy*, Walling did not try to hold the labor movement to ahistorical standards derived from already existing socialist ideology, which dictated the industrial form of unionism as superior to the occupational or craft form, but rather sought to discern the progressive potential in prevailing economic and social trends. Like many observers, he noted the increasing use in industry of unskilled labor and the decline of sharp skill lines within the working-class due to the advent of skill-displacing technology and a developing division of labor. But unlike those who identified this trend only with the rise of industrial unionism, he called attention to the transformation of practices *within* American craft unions. The resulting "new unionism"—what scholars have called "craft-industrial unionism"—abandoned or modified restriction of output, opposition to the subdivision of labor, apprenticeship limits, and high dues and benefits, and instead facilitated the joining together within a single union of workers of diverse trades and no trade at all, both within particular industries and across industrial lines. The trend toward craft-industrialism continued into the 1910s. In 1911, the AFL convention abandoned the principle of craft autonomy and instead opted for the principle of the organization of all workers in an industry by the paramount craft. By 1915, the academic observer Theodore Glocker, pointing to a "gradual evolution," estimated that only twenty-eight of the 133 unions active in the labor movement could still be classified as craft unions.[4]

In an illuminating comparison with British unions, Walling noted that the British craft unions had maintained the old craft monopoly policies and were unwilling to include the unskilled, forcing them to create parallel organizations composed solely of common laborers. By contrast, American unions were more democratic and adaptable, though they retained their craft form. For example, the carpenters' brotherhood organized factory operatives making wood products and related trades in the construction industry, as well as traditional carpenters. Rather than call for the victory of industrial unionism over craft unionism as did the partisans of the Industrial Workers of the World (IWW), Walling advocated the closer cooperation of both craft-industrial and industrial forms within the confines of the AFL.[5]

In 1905-06 Walling made two trips to Europe as a kind of roving sociologist-foreign correspondent. During the second he visited Russia, which was in the midst of a tumultuous revolution, and married the Jewish-American novelist Anna Strunsky. When the revolutionary couple returned, Walling published *Russia's Message to the World* (1908), a passionate report and commentary on Russia's upheaval and its future prospects based on hundreds of interviews with peasants and workers, government officials, revolutionaries, and notables. Walling presented the abortive revolution as the forerunner of a new world civilization and anticipated the Bolshevik belief that it was possible to leapfrog capitalist development and begin immediately the construction of a socialist society. The book was a hit and propelled Walling to public acclaim.[6]

Despite his new revolutionary credentials, Walling was far from being a conventional Marxist. This was evident in a 1905 article in *International Socialist Review* contrasting Veblen with Marx and Hegel to the latters' disadvantage.[7] In a short credo he wrote in 1910 Walling presented socialism not as a simple outgrowth of modern capitalism, but as a further development of the "sacred rights of the individual" rooted in the Protestant Reformation and the great democratic and republican revolutions of the eighteenth century:

> We Socialists have no quarrel with the doctrine of the Rights of Man. On the contrary, we are its only true and loyal defenders today. We propose to convert the political and civil rights of the individual into social rights. To the negative rights of freedom from every form of oppression and to the empty political rights, we propose to add the right of a decent livelihood, the right of a thorough education, the right to an equal share in all the material goods of the earth, and the right to an equal opportunity to compete for that line of occupation that most suits our individuality.[8]

Walling's implicit rejection of the idea that socialism was essentially a sectarian undertaking by a party or movement with a special ideology and his understanding of it as rooted in the mainstream trends of American history would remain at the core of his thinking throughout his intellectual career.

Still, notwithstanding this broader conception of socialism, Walling, in his enthusiasm for revolution, initially believed that the Socialist Party (SP) of Eugene V. Debs, Morris Hillquit, and Victor Berger could serve as its political embodiment. In 1909, a year before he would join the SP, Walling precipitated an open rift within the party between its gradualist and revolutionary wings. Identifying himself as a left-winger, he claimed to detect (incorrectly, as it turned out) a conspiracy to transform the SP into a labor party, a shift that revolutionaries feared would subordinate ultimate aims to day-to-day concerns. Walling's stance was a deceptive mixture of revolutionary sectarianism and electoral prudence derived from the experience of the AFL. Like Gompers, Walling did not believe that third party electoral politics were viable in the American context. Moreover, he feared that the AFL's natural evolution in response to developing historical conditions, which he had delineated in his two *Annals* articles, would be arrested by entering politics as a labor party. On the other hand, he wanted to preserve socialist purity by keeping it from becoming entangled with the immediate demands of the trade unions. Above all, he feared that Americans would follow the path of the British Independent Labour Party, which he identified with state socialism. Walling's position was almost identical to the revolutionaries' bet noir, Victor Berger, who believed that the labor and socialist movements should be kept separate to maintain the integrity of each.[9]

While Walling was at the height of his influence within the socialist movement he embarked on an ambitious project to rethink the philosophical and political foundations of socialism. The resulting three books, consisting of over 1216 pages of text and published over a period of three years, cemented his claim to be the most original and provocative American socialist thinker of the early twentieth century.

The first volume in Walling's trilogy, *Socialism As It Is: A World-Wide Survey of the Revolutionary Movement*, was not simply a survey, but a critical assessment of state capitalist reforms from the point of view of the revolutionary socialist orthodoxy that still ruled the Third International. Contrary to "revisionist" socialists associated with Edward Bernstein in Germany and the Fabian Society in Britain, Walling argued that state-expanding reforms such as the nationalization of private industry and ground rent, social insurance, the use of government services and regulatory commissions to improve working and living conditions, and compulsory arbitration of labor disputes were not identical to socialism, nor did they even pave the road toward socialism. Taking these "progressive" reforms one by one, Walling argued that where they had been implemented—largely in the English-speaking world—they left capitalist relations of production intact, strengthened large-scale capital by socializing its costs of production thereby making it more profitable, augmented the size of the existing class of small proprietors, and hamstrung unions' freedom to strike. In short, it seemed to Walling that such reforms were more in the long-term interests of what he recognized as "the new [monopolistic] capitalism" than the working class.

State collectivism, according to Walling's survey, was largely rejected by socialist theoreticians and by the bulk of socialist delegates to international congresses. Only in Britain, Australia, and New Zealand did such reformist thinking dominate. In the United States, fortunately, electoral-based reform politics characterized only the Milwaukee Social Democratic

Party led by Victor Berger. Embracing a quasi-syndicalist view-point consistent with his fear of statism, Walling urged socialists to avoid taking part in elections except where necessary for defensive or educational purposes. Instead, socialists should rely on direct action through class-wide action by labor unions.

But as Walling himself would later recognize, his belief that the trend toward reformism in the international socialist movement had been cut short was mistaken. As labor unions with their immediate demands grew larger and more effective, socialist parties everywhere accommodated labor and entered elections to win reforms in the immediate interests of workers. The experience of the English-speaking world, which Walling had derided, would become the norm among the parties of the Second International. In the United States, however, the Socialist Party, except in cities like Milwaukee, Reading, and Minneapolis, stayed aloof from the labor movement. Even at the height of its voting strength, the SP never came close to the membership strength of the socialist parties in Europe and the other English-speaking countries because of its unwillingness to accommodate the needs of American trade unions. Ultimately, the inability to develop mutually supportive links with the unions reinforced the tendency toward sectarianism and would doom the party to marginality and futility.[10]

In *Socialism As It Is* Walling had defined his political beliefs by his opposition to state socialism and reformism. In his next volume, he offered up a positive and creative reformulation of socialism based on the pragmatism of John Dewey that diverged from his earlier revolutionary orthodoxy. Pragmatism, the philosophical belief that truth emerges from, and is continually revised by, the human attempt to engage the world and mold it to humanity's developing aims, was influential among the American intelligentsia of the early twentieth century. Much like the scientific worldview, which inspired pragmatism and grounded knowledge in the testing of hypotheses, Walling argued that socialism had to dispense with its dogmas, in particular, its faith in the Hegelian dialectic and the class struggle. The former served socialists as an immutable logic or law mandating an inexorable evolution culminating in a socialist society, while the latter led socialists to give priority to the needs of a single class over a broader commitment to democratic governance and freedom of the individual. Instead of a set of immutable laws, socialism should be an open-ended inquiry rooted in the most advanced democratic and social practice.

The other strength of pragmatism was that it dissolved the ultimately false opposition between the individual and society. Rather than setting individualism against various forms of sociality, from transcendent conceptions of humanity to state socialism, Walling, along with the pragmatist Max Stirner and philosopher Friedrich Nietzsche, both of whom he quoted freely, sought to liberate the individual from all conceptions of duty, self-sacrifice, and service to social institutions. When the new morality was widely adopted, according to Walling, the bourgeois principle of free exchange among equals could be disengaged from capitalism and become the core principle of a new socialist society. "It is through self-development that we can mean most to others," wrote Walling, "rather than through the relatively petty occasion for pity and for interfering as 'benefactors' in other people's lives. This is true to-day and it will be still more true in the better organized society of the future."[11] Thus in *Larger Aspects of Socialism* Walling endorsed a version of socialism that lacked any role for the state. It also appeared distinctly utopian given Walling's inability to anchor his vision in existing social trends.

Progressivism and After, Walling's third installment in his trilogy, represented a distinct cooling of his revolutionary ardor. It was also the only book to engage directly with the Progressive reforms then transforming American governance at the national level during the presidencies of Theodore Roosevelt, William H. Taft, and Woodrow Wilson. Walling depicted Progressivism as a movement of America's middling strata, especially farmers, rather than of corporate capitalists or organized workers. He saw it as the first of a three-stage process that would result in all the less-privileged groups ascending to power. Once the less privileged *propertied* groups had been absorbed into governance, skilled workers would follow. The first stage would establish state capitalism, the second, state socialism. Only when unskilled workers had ascended to power would the socialism he had described in *Larger Aspects of Socialism* arrive. The critical test as to whether a stage had been completed was whether the less-privileged group in question had significantly increased its income and life opportunities relative to the group above it in the social hierarchy.[12]

Progressivism and After was highly speculative and prophetic. More to the point, it offered up an implicit and unmistakable challenge to the dominant principles and philosophy of the Socialist Party. Not only did it reject the idea of class struggle undertaken by a unified working class leading to socialism, but it reinterpreted the party's immediate demands as new forms of oppression for the less privileged. The book sparked controversy that spread beyond socialist circles. The great American political commentator

and former socialist, Walter Lippmann, author of the pragmatist classic *Drift and Mastery* published the same year, paid
Walling high compliment when he wrote:

> When all is said, Walling is perhaps the only American Socialist of
> standing who keeps inquiry alive, the only one who doesn't rewrite
> the same book every year or two. And if honest inquiry happens to
> produce results very damaging to the existing pretensions of the
> Socialist movement, that is nothing against the inquirer.[13]

But, Lippmann also discerned grave flaws in Walling's work,
flaws that are worth considering because they would soon
impel Walling to leave the party and embark in a new intellectual direction. First, Lippmann pointed out that the typical worker's concern with relative income shares—Walling's
test for each stage—declined in importance insofar as the
worker achieved a decent and comfortable standard of living.
In different words, insofar as workers achieved strong unions
and Progressives established a welfare state, the motivation
for further progress along the evolutionary path toward
Walling's final goal would weaken proportionately. Second,
Lippmann recognized that if Walling's diagnosis and prescrip-
tion were accepted, he "had cut away the ground from under
[the Socialist Party's] feet." However, Walling "shirks that conclusion," and "that is why his book contains no programme on
which any Socialist Party can act. He has, however, prepared
the ground for two forms of social actions. He has justified
political progressivism and industrial action." Finally,
Lippmann criticized Walling's three-stage theory as overly
speculative—a "child of abstraction"—and the opposite of the
pragmatic evolutionary view he had championed earlier.[14]

Walling would tacitly accept the truth of his criticisms by
his own actions in the next few years of his life when he quit
the Socialist Party over the issue of America entering World

War I on the side of the Allies and moved into a close cooperation with the Woodrow Wilson administration and the
leadership of the AFL.

When fighting in Europe began in 1914, Walling immediately criticized the official SP position, which at first was
conventionally pacifist and soon afterwards, conventionally
Marxist. He developed these criticisms further in a spate of
articles in *New Review* and in another book. To the argument
that modern wars were caused by capitalism, Walling replied
that the real cause of the war was the rise of worldwide nationalism. Extending his earlier analysis of Progressivism as
facilitating state capitalism, he predicted that nationalism
would become immeasurably stronger as the state brought
industry under its control and as workers achieved a direct
interest in the state. The only realistic alternative was internationalism; but it was not the internationalism of the proletariat to which Walling turned for succor, but that of the
financiers. He built his analysis in large part on a 1914 article by socialist theoretician Karl Kautsky, which argued that
competitive "imperialism" among nation-states was evolving into a cooperative imperialism in which capitalist nations could transcend their rivalry and cooperate to export
capital to the less developed nations. As Walling put it,
"[I]n the period that is approaching, competitive imperialism, like competitive industry, is doomed to be replaced
by combination. Imperialism, which is now militarist and
nationalist, may then become pacifist and international
through a combination of empires, through ultra-imperial-
ism."[15]

Walling's new analysis, unique among American socialists, contrasted sharply with that of the Bolshevik Vladimir
Lenin, who believed that imperialism and imperialist rivalry

were structural imperatives of capitalism. While Lenin's analysis justified revolution as the only answer to war, Walling's led toward association with the governments of the advanced democratic states, notably the United States and Britain, in creating an international framework to secure economic and political cooperation. Thus, in an important article in *Annals*, Walling suggested that a British and French proposal for a low tariff zone among allied countries had the potential to become the basis for a permanent solution to inter-capitalist wars. When the United States entered the war in 1917 for just such a program, Walling left the party and began cooperating with the Wilson administration and the AFL in support of the war effort. With other pro-war defectors from the party, he formed the Social Democratic League to woo American immigrants away from the SP's antiwar stance and support the cause of the Allies, which Walling viewed as the only bulwark against the expansionism of reactionary and authoritarian Germany.[16]

The Russian Bolshevik Revolution of 1917 further cemented Walling's new political loyalties to progressive democracy. Bolshevism was doubly repellant to Walling. It threatened to pull Russia out of the war against Germany, allowing Germany to swing its Eastern armies back to France to use against the Allies. It also promised to hijack the worldwide democratic socialist movement and turn it into one bent on violent revolution and a single party, statist dictatorship. Accordingly, Walling warned Wilson against recognition of the new Russian government, and agreed to serve as Wilson's emissary to visit the European socialists to prop up their failing support for the Allied war effort. Back in America, the Socialist Party, already reeling from government repression brought on by its antiwar stance and the replacement of its native-born members by newly arrived immigrants prone to revolutionary enthusiasm, found itself irreconcilably divided. Eventually, a large faction joined the new communist parties, while the socialist remnant in self-defense adopted key aspects of the communists' new political philosophy.[17] In response, Walling authored one book and co-authored with Gompers another condemning Bolshevism's methods, values, and program. Meanwhile, he bitterly and rancorously assailed his former party colleagues in the press. From this point forward, Walling was an irreconcilable enemy of the American Socialist and Communist parties.[18]

Walling's wartime departure from the SP occurred at a time when the AFL was also at a crossroads. The labor movement had become more confident that the nation-state could be used for progressive purposes without inviting excessive state control. At the same time, craft-industrial unions were finally coming to terms with the managerial practices of the large industrial corporations, opposition to which had hitherto inhibited any kind of enduring cooperation. The turning point occurred before America's entry into the war with the formation of the United States Commission on Industrial Relations.

Chaired by the pro-labor Democrat Frank Walsh, the USCIR exposed in dramatic hearings the anti-labor practices of large corporations like John D. Rockefellers's Colorado Fuel and Iron Company and publicized the need for workers to have a "a compelling voice" in industry. The Commission's report, issued in 1915, called for a progressive income tax to fund education and unemployment relief and for the federal government to protect workers' right to organize. "Industrial democracy," the rubric used by Walsh and Progressive intellectuals to designate this new role of government, quickly became a catch-phrase for the argument that to secure labor peace, corporations must win workers' consent to managerial prerogatives by acceding to collective bargaining with independent unions; the results of such bargaining would be analogous to the rule of law in civil society. By the time Wilson ran for reelection in 1916, the budding alliance between the AFL and the Wilson administration, evident in the passage of a spate of pro-labor legislation, had evolved into a cross-class movement for industrial democracy that owed as much to Progressive intellectuals as to labor leaders.[19]

When the war began, the alliance of Progressive intellectuals and the AFL flowered. Gompers wheeled the AFL into line in support of the administration, and Wilson appointed Frank Walsh together with William Howard Taft as co-chairs of the National War Labor Board (NWLB). Several conditions combined to tip the balance of class forces in labor's direction during the war. The tight labor market, the need of mass production industries to avoid high turnover, and the Wilson administration's threat to nationalize businesses that resisted the decisions of the NWLB created unprecedented opportunities for activists to mount new demands for union recognition in war-related industries. In response, the NWLB adopted the policy of outlawing strikes and lockouts and protecting the right of workers to organize and bargain collectively. Where unions did not exist, workers could organize in shop committees. All workers were to be guaranteed an eight-hour day, equal pay for equal work (for women), and a living wage. In return, however, unions or shop committees were not allowed to limit production or engage in jurisdictional warfare. By 1920 the nation's unions had over two million more members than in 1917, a gain of 70 percent. The growth was greatest in the new industries where craft distinctions were falling away or were non-existent, as in textiles, coal, railroad shops, metal trades, electrical appliances, and the packinghouses.[20]

But, when the war ended, labor's gains could not be consolidated. During the 1919 strike wave involving four million workers, which followed the armistice, corporate employers fiercely resisted the demands of shop committees and unions for formal recognition. Opposition to bargaining with independent unions caused the breakup of the 1919 national industrial conference created by the Wilson administration to restore labor peace. When the economy went into recession in 1920, corporate employers and other business leaders used the occasion to launch an open shop drive across the nation. Aided by the return of the federal labor injunction that made most picketing illegal and enfeebled the labor boycott, employers were able to defeat two large strikes in 1922, and thereafter, work stoppages declined dramatically. Concurrently, corporate leaders adopted their own version of industrial democracy, which involved job ladders, seniority rights, profit sharing, sick and death benefits, and bargaining with a watered down version of shop committees (company unions) in place of independent unions. Growing real wages—26 percent higher in 1928 than in 1919—helped cement the new "corporate welfare" approach in place. So successful was it that by the end of the decade union membership had dropped from 5.1 million members in 1920 to 3.44 million in 1929, the greater part of the decline occurring before 1923.[21]

Despite the lack of labor militancy and the decline in union density in the 1920s, capital and labor showed important signs of reaching a new accommodation within the confines of the corporate economy, creating precedents for the "postwar accord" that the CIO accepted in the 1940s.[22] The leading figure in this new version of industrial democracy was Secretary of Commerce Herbert Hoover. Hoover, who had become a convert to the old labor idea of a "high wage economy" as a way of absorbing the output from mass production, was willing to support collective bargaining with independent unions. But for their part unions must tolerate the open shop and the existence of nonunion competition within each industry to protect the nation against union monopolies; unions would also be expected to eliminate wasteful practices and any opposition to productivity improvements.[23]

Though Hoover's conditions, especially his opposition to the closed shop, were not acceptable to labor, they were important in establishing new terms for public discussion of industrial democracy in the 1920s. Indeed, even before the twenties a "progressive bloc" of unions had decided to cede craft control of the workplace and accept scientific management in return for union recognition and a share in the managerial decision-making. This was the gist of the proposals made by the coal miners, machinists, and needle trades unions during and immediately following World War I.[24] By the mid-twenties, the AFL also accepted scientific management in a declaration by President William Green (successor to Gompers after the latter's death in 1924) and its endorsement of the Baltimore and Ohio Railroad Plan. But, in return employers were expected not only to recognize unions, but to allow workers increases in real wages virtually equivalent to the value produced by the rise in productivity. In fact, the idea had strong socialist implications, as it called for a wage that would prevent an increase in the share of capital in national income. Not coincidentally, the new AFL doctrine was composed by a German-trained Marxist who drew on Karl Marx's idea of "relative wages" being more important than real wages.[25]

Still, the hampering of strikes and boycotts by the courts and the federal government severely limited the AFL's ability to challenge the terms of Hoover's accommodation, much less maintain labor's national income share in the midst of rising productivity. Thus, just as it had done in earlier periods when its economic struggles had been thwarted, the AFL turned to politics to restore the power of its voice. This time, however, it entered politics as part of a progressive coalition with farmers, consumers, and leftwing groups. Calling itself the Conference for Progressive Political Action (CPPA), the coalition turned its back on third party politics and supported pro-labor politicians in the primaries of each party. The CPPA was an unprecedented success, electing twenty-three of the twenty-seven candidates it endorsed for the U.S. Senate and 170 members to the House. In 1924, faced with two anti-labor presidential candidates, it ran longtime Progressive Senator Robert LaFollette for president on a third party ticket, winning 16.6 percent of the presidential vote and running ahead of the Democrats in twelve states. But, the AFL had no intention of committing itself to party building as SP leaders hoped, and thereafter contented itself with support for the new progressive bloc of legislators from both parties it had helped establish in Congress.[26]

It was at this point that Walling returned to writing with his *American Labor and American Democracy* (ALAD), a defense of the AFL's policies in the 1920s. At first glance, Walling's book can be viewed as an institutional study, the sort of history that labor historians abandoned beginning in the 1960s.[27] Since that time, labor and working class historians have focused their efforts to understand the rank and file of unions rather than labor's leadership and its formal pronouncements and have used the tools of the new social and cultural history to study the working class in all its variety and in its diverse settings. Indeed, the three most recent and influential studies of the American labor movement in World War I and the 1920s identify a progressive movement within the AFL for industrial democracy, but limit this movement to rank and file militants and particular unions. Gompers and the AFL leadership are viewed as conservative, even reactionary, a barrier to the tide that would eventually engulf the labor movement during the 1930s depression and New Deal.[28]

Walling's ALAD is a valuable corrective to this prevailing view. His book can be considered an extended argument for the position that the AFL and its leadership were in the mainstream not only of an updated progressive movement, but of the most advanced thinking on many questions. ALAD is actually a history of the AFL as a social movement; in different words, it is a social history of an institution.

ALAD is divided into two volumes, the first dealing with the AFL's accession to the Progressive movement. *In Socialism As It Is* and in *Progressivism and After* Walling had viewed America's Progressive movement as the creature of the middle classes and instigator of state capitalism. In ALAD, he revised his analysis, portraying progressivism as a multi-interest outgrowth of American democracy in the post-frontier era. During the first fifteen years of the new century when it had been forced to enter national electoral politics, labor, according to Walling, had begun to transcend its narrow interests by being forced to take positions on issues not of direct economic concern. In doing so it came to stamp Progressivism with its own outlook. The turning point came in 1919 when the AFL joined the broad movement for industrial democracy.

Prior to this date, according to Walling, the AFL opposed the small producer demand that government use the Sherman Act to break up the trusts, but didn't yet trust the state to step in to regulate large corporations because government was still seen to be in the hands of the capitalists. From 1919 forward, the AFL believed that a powerful progressive movement *could* democratize government enough to allow state regulation to serve democratic ends. To avoid an oppressive state bureaucracy, the AFL, according to Walling, supported the democratization of government boards and commissions that had been set up under presidents Theodore Roosevelt, William Howard Taft, and Woodrow Wilson. Such democratization meant the direct representation of all interests on boards and the fullest publicity possible to educate public opinion. In this way American labor sought to reconcile its older commitment to the primacy of the economic struggle—still evident in many of its pronouncements—with the new progressive demand for government regulation of the economy.

By the 1920s, in Walling's analysis, Progressivism had evolved into a bipartisan bloc of organized interests led by labor. Walling explicitly rejected the Socialist Party's newfound support for a labor party or even liberals' hope that a realignment of the two major parties would make the Democratic Party into a progressive party. Such a solution would circumscribe too narrowly labor's influence and put unions under the spell of party politicians or intellectuals. The way to conserve and maximize labor's power, as the experience of the CPPA had shown, was to operate within the dominant political party in each state or locality by supporting pro-labor candidates within that party's primary. Walling noted that America's political parties represented principles with great difficulty; it was better to leave the legislative task to blocs of

interests represented by individual legislators, while assigning the job of administering laws to the party. Walling made
clear that this new policy, which he called "bi-partisanship,"
differed from the older one of rewarding labor's friends and
punishing its enemies. Rather than being reactive, it put a
premium on carefully formulated principles and programs.
The new interest group governance that Walling viewed as
emerging in the 1920s was far from anti-democratic as conservatives then (and now) argued, but should be construed as
the first great accession to power of the popular movements
that had arisen in the Progressive Era.[29]

Those 1920s readers familiar with Walling's earlier commitments to socialism and revolution must have wondered
on picking up this book whether he had given up on his aspiration of socialist transformation. Walling addressed this
question in the second part of ALAD, and in an article in
Bankers Magazine the same year. Walling denied that American society was monolithically capitalist; rather it was a complex evolutionary development of three major forces:
democracy, capitalism, and nationalism. The mix was dy-
namic and sometimes contentious, at other times mutually
reinforcing. Walling believed that the world was moving away
from capitalism, but "not toward socialism, at least not in
the accepted sense of government industry." Rather, government was becoming more democratic and seeking to control
capital without destroying it or the principle of private profit.[30]

What Walling called "economic democracy" was deeply
rooted in a doctrine central to American labor's thinking dat-
ing to the 1860s. Ira Steward, a Boston-born machinist had
originated in that decade a theory in which shorter hours
and higher wages would accelerate a transition to a cooperative society, the nineteenth-century term for socialism. Ac-

cording to Steward the standard of living, not supply and demand, determined wages. Shortening hours would afford workers the social and cultural opportunities necessary to encourage new wants and desires; eventually higher wages would follow. Rising wages would be good for industry because it would raise consumers' purchasing power and allow manufacturers to take advantage of labor saving machinery. Rising consumer purchasing power would also counteract crises of overproduction, which bedeviled the late nineteenth-century economy. Over the long run, however, profits would decline as a share in national income and wages and consumption would rise until profits would disappear and producers' cooperation become the norm.[31]

Suitably modified to take account of the need for trade union action to achieve higher wages, Steward's theory became official AFL doctrine by 1889.[32] This equation of socialism with an upward shift of income shares and hence life opportunities for workers recurred in all of Walling's works, making it one of the most important threads of continuity in his intellectual career. What was new in ALAD was that instead of being tied to shorter hours and the rising standard of living, the AFL's new wage doctrine, according to Walling, linked wages directly to productivity increases, such that labor's income share should not decline relative to the returns to capital. Walling himself went further. In his one major dissent from AFL thinking, Walling reiterated his older socialistic belief that wages should be governed by a "higher standard," that is, in order to decrease social inequality wages should rise *faster* than productivity.

Economic democracy resembled socialism in yet another way. In ALAD Walling argued that class rule and the primacy of private profit could be reduced to a secondary role in the governance of industry without abolishing private property, the profit motive, or creating a state command economy, the demand of orthodox socialists of the early twentieth century and the communist parties of the 1920s. The key element in transacting this nonstatist transformation was the modern business corporation. By separating ownership from control through the dispersal of stock to the public and the operation of the company by salaried, professional managers, the corporation blurred the line between public and private spheres and raised the possibility of democratizing the operation of the economy. It was this possibility that Walling seized on in ALAD.

Walling did not for a moment believe as did 1920s advocates of "people's capitalism" that widespread stock ownership had given workers and the middle class control over the economy. Rather, as he made clear in ALAD, he believed that a powerful multi-class progressive movement was necessary to accomplish that goal under the leadership of the labor movement. Quoting from Gompers' testimony, Walling argued that the AFL sought to keep those aspects of the corporation that were of a public nature—"superintendence, the creation of wants, administration, [and] return for investment in so far as it is honest investment"—from being distorted by the interests of large bond holders, bankers, and others who controlled credit (II, 72). In short, labor sought to disengage the corporation and its profit claims as much as possible from the control of capitalist interests and place them in the service of the broad interests of a progressive public.

Accordingly, it was not necessary to make a working-class revolution to establish a postcapitalist society. It was only necessary to build and bring to power a progressive move-

TRANSACTION INTRODUCTION

ment for economic democracy. It seems hard to argue as some
have that Walling had abandoned his old commitments; rather
he had only updated and modified them. As he noted in several places, this thinking was close to that of "[a]lmost all
factions of organized labor throughout the world [who] are
now standing for mixed control in which labor shall play an
important part" (II, 143).[33] This "postcapitalist vision" or "mix"
was also the policy of many European socialists, including
the Germans and British, whose views in the 1920s on the
mixed economy now closely approximated labor thinking.
Indeed, Walling's labor- and progressive-based version of socialism may be viewed as the closest American counterpart to
that of the era's European social democratic parties, which
had supported their governments' entry into World War I,
taken part in national governments, and remained closely
tied to the trade unions and their emphasis on incremental
improvements. This political vision, which affirmed a blend
of profit and non-profit principles, labor and capitalist class
rule, and socialism and capitalism was the core of the new
outlook that Walling prophesied for the future. By the end of
the decade, Walling confidently looked forward to a "new *democratic* internationalism" to replace the old proletarian one.[34]

Walling's vision of labor elaborated in ALAD anticipated
future developments in two important ways. First, the book
closely resembled the first great and still influential interpretation of American labor history, *A Theory of the Labor Movement*, published two years later, by Selig Perlman. In 1907
Walling had brought Perlman, then a young Marxist revolutionary, to America from his native Poland and funded his
studies at the University of Wisconsin, where he apprenticed
under the dean of American labor historians, John R. Commons. Both Perlman's and Walling's works were attempts to

understand the philosophy and practices of the American labor movement outside the concepts of Marxism as then understood. In particular, they rejected the secular faith that the growth of the unions and the intensification of the class struggle would eventuate in a socialist revolution. Both also agreed that what made American labor different from European labor was that it had developed outside the tutelage of revolutionary intellectuals, and that was a good thing. Perlman recalled a 1934 meeting with Walling in which they "marveled with mutual delight at each of us having arrived independently at an identical analysis of the labor situation—even to the point of employing the same expressions."[35]

But in other ways, the two works differed markedly. To Perlman, still to a degree under the grip of Leninist thinking in which socialism had to be brought *to* the workers by professional revolutionaries, the natural expression of working class consciousness was "scarcity" rather than abundance, which led unions toward a narrow and defensive "job consciousness." Walling, on the other hand, viewed labor's policies and practices as the outcome of applying the principles and goals of American democracy to labor's class situation. The labor movement was therefore a branch of American democracy, and the spontaneous ideas of American workers were not narrow, but were limited only by the aspirations and possibilities of American democracy. Walling's reformulation of socialism as economic democracy and a mix of capitalist and working class control over the industrial system followed from this shift in perspective. As a self-consciously democratic history of labor, ALAD represented perhaps the first break from the early twentieth-century scholarly practice of studying labor from within the discipline of labor economics. Since that decade many treatments of labor history, particularly with the advent of the new labor history, have been conceived within the democratic framework.[36]

ALAD was anticipatory of future developments in a second important way. Walling may not have seen the coming of industrial unionism and the political split that rent the House of Labor from 1936 to 1955; nor did he tackle the tough question of discrimination within unions against blacks and women. These ignored issues point to limitations of the AFL and labor in general in this decade as well as ALAD.[37] In other ways, however, Walling appears remarkably prescient. It has already been noted that Walling's depiction of AFL policy looked forward to the postwar accord between labor and the large industrial corporation in which labor ceded shop floor control to the "workplace rule of law" embodied in the grievance procedure and accepted a formula of wage increases linked to the cost of living and productivity increases. Walling's understanding of the social implications of labor's wage policy also became the basis for a book he wrote with AFL vice-president Matthew Woll during the 1930s depression. *Our Next Step* argued that the depression had been caused by a lack of consumer purchasing power and that government policies limiting the share of profits and aiding unions in raising wages in relation to profits would be necessary to sustain recovery.[38] In short, Walling's wage doctrine had by 1934 evolved from chief mechanism for ensuring socialist transformation to a functional element of Left-Keynesian, social-welfare politics, the mainstay of postwar labor policy. Finally, Walling's own powerful opposition to totalitarianism combined with a strong commitment to liberal internationalism anticipated labor's foreign policy of the 1940s and beyond with its support for strong American action against the Axis powers before and at the start of World War II and in its anticommunist internationalism during the Cold War.[39]

William English Walling's *American Labor and American Democracy* remains relevant not only to an understanding of the origins of the polices of the modern American labor movement and the Progressive movement of the1920s, but to the enduring questions that are still current in American public life, notably the relationship of socialism, capitalism, and democracy in American society.

RICHARD SCHNEIROV

Notes

[1] Howard Dickman, *Industrial Democracy in America: Ideological Origins of National Labor Relations Policy* (La Salle, IL: Open Court Press, 1987); *Industrial Democracy in America: The Ambiguous Promise* ed. Nelson Lichtenstein and Howell John Harris (New York: Cambridge University Press, 1993); Joseph A. McCartin, *Labor's Great War: The Struggle for Industrial Democracy and the Origins of Modern American Labor Relations, 1912-21* (Chapel Hill: University of North Carolina Press, 1998).

[2] For an example of this view see the review, "Fifty Years Behind," *The Nation* 125 (July 15, 1927); more recently see James Gilbert, "William English Walling: The Pragmatic Critique of Collectivism" in *Designing the Industrial State: The Intellectual Pursuit of Collectivism in America, 1880-1940* (Chicago: Quadrangle Books, 1972), 200-39.

[3] For narratives of Walling's life and politics see Jack Meyer Stuart, "William English Walling: A Study in Politics and Ideas" (Ph.D. diss., Columbia University, 1968) and James Boylan, *Revolutionary Lives: Ann Strunsky & William English Walling* (Amherst: University of Massachusetts Press, 1998). For recent interpretations of Walling's intellectual career see Gilbert, "William English Walling"; Leon Fink, "Joining the People: William English Walling and the Specter of the Intellectual Class," in *Progressive Intellectuals and the Dilemmas of Democratic Commitment* (Cambridge, MA, 1997); and Richard Schneirov, "The Odyssey of William English Walling: Revisionism, Social Democracy, and Evolutionary Pragmatism," *Journal of the Gilded Age and Progressive Era* 2 (October. 2003): 403-30.

[4] "The New Unionism—The Problem of the Unskilled Worker," *Annals of the American Academy of Political and Social Science* 24 (July-December

TRANSACTION INTRODUCTION

1904): 296-315; Theodore Glocker, "Amalgamation of Related Trades in American Unions," *American Economic Review* V (Sept. 1915): 554. Notwithstanding the evidence of craft-industrialism, many labor historians continue to contrast "craft" to "industrial" unionism. Among scholars who have recently called attention to the importance of craft-industrialism are Christopher L. Tomlins, "AFL Unions in the 1930s: Their Performance in Historical Perspective," *Journal of American History* LXV:4 (March 1979): 1021-42 and Dorothy Sue Cobble, "Organizing the Postindustrial Workplace: Lessons from the History of Waitress Unionism," *Industrial and Labor Relations Review* 44 (Apr. 1991): 419-36.

⁵ William English Walling, "British and American Trade Unionism," *Annals of the American Academy of Political and Social Science* 26 (November 1905): 721-39; the same contrast is made by Walter Galenson, *The United Brotherhood of Carpenters, The First Hundred Years* (Cambridge: Harvard University Press, 1983), 98-99.

⁶ *Russia's Message; The True World Import of the Revolution* (New York: Doubleday, 1908).

⁷ "An American Socialism," *International Socialist Review* V (Apr. 1905): 577-84.

⁸ Anna Strunsky Walling et al., *William English Walling, A Symposium*, (New York: Stackpole Sons, 1938), 98-100.

⁹ For a summary of this affair see David A. Shannon, *The Socialist Party of America: A History* (New York: Macmillan, 1955), 62-69; see also Sally M. Miller, *Victor Berger and the Promise of Constructive Socialism, 1910-1920* (Westport, Conn.: Greenwood Press, 1973), 27-28, 54-58 and William English Walling, "Laborism versus Socialism," *International Socialist Review* IX (March 1909): 683-89.

¹⁰ Seymour Martin Lipset and Gary Marks, *It Didn't Happen Here: Why Socialism Failed in the United States* (New York: W.W. Norton & Co., 2000), chaps. 3 and 5.

¹¹ William English Walling, *The Larger Aspects of Socialism* (New York: Macmillan, 1913), 191-227, quote at 215.

¹² *Progressivism and After* (New York: Macmillan, 1914).

¹³ *New Review* (June 1914): 349.

¹⁴ Walter Lippmann, "Walling's 'Progressivism and After'" *New Review*, (June 1914): 344; 348 (child of abstraction); Lippmann, "Why a Socialist Party," *New Review* (November 1914): 658-59.

¹⁵ William English Walling, "British and American Socialists and the War," *New Review* (September 1914): 512-18 and "The New Map of Europe," *New Review* (December 1914): 698-702; William English Walling, *The Socialists and the War: A Documentary Statement of the Position of the Socialists of All Countries; With Special Reference to Their Peace Policy* (New York, 1915), 16 (quote); Carl Parrini, "Theories of Imperialism," in *Redefining the Past: Essays in Diplomatic History in Honor of William Appleman Williams*, ed., Lloyd C. Gardner (Corvallis, OR: Oregon State University Press, 1986): 65-83 and Martin J. Sklar, "The Open Door, Imperialism, and

TRANSACTION INTRODUCTION

Postimperialism: Origins of U.S. Twentieth-Century Foreign Relations, Circa 1900," in *Postimperialism and World Politics*, eds., David G. Becker and Richard L. Sklar (Westport, Conn: Greenwood, 1999): 317-36.

[16] Kenneth E. Hendrickson, Jr., "The Pro-War Socialists, the Social Democratic League, and the Ill-Fated Drive For Industrial Democracy in America, 1917-1920," *Labor History* 11 (Summer 1970): 304-22; William English Walling, "The Prospects for Economic Internationalism," *Annals of the American Academy of Political and Social Science* 157 (November 1916): 10-22; Walling's economic internationalism continued after the war; see "Will Public Opinion Abdicate?" *American Federationist* (November 1921): 932-34.

[17] Ronald Radosh, *American Labor and United States Foreign Policy* (New York: Random House, 1969), 30-303; Hendrickson, "The Pro-War Socialists, the Social Democratic League"; Boylan, *Revolutionary Lives*, 209-55; Stuart, "William English Walling," 105-73.

[18] Boylan, *Revolutionary Lives*, 237-55; William English Walling, *Sovietism: The A B C of Russian Bolshevism—According to the Bolshevists* (New York: Dutton, 1920); Samuel Gompers with the collaboration of William English Walling, *Out of Their Own Mouths: A Revelation and an Indictment of Sovietism* (New York: Dutton, 1921).

[19] McCartin, *Labor's Great War*, chap. 1.

[20] Ibid., chaps. 2-6; David Montgomery, *The Fall of the House of Labor: The State and American Labor Activism, 1865-1925* (Cambridge: Cambridge University Press, 1987), chap. 8.

[21] Ibid., chap. 7; Melvyn Dubofsky, *The State and Labor in Modern America* (Chapel Hill: University of North Carolina, 1994), 76-81; George Soule, *Prosperity Decade: From War to Depression: 1917-1929* (New York: Rinehart & Co., 1947), 221, 227-28.

[22] David Montgomery, "Thinking about American Workers in the 1920s," *International Labor and Working Class History* 32 (Fall 1987): 4-24; David Brody, *Workers in Industrial America: Essays on the Twentieth Century Struggle* (New York: Oxford University Press, 1980), 173-257.

[23] Dubofsky, *State and Labor*, 101-02; Robert H. Zieger, "Herbert Hoover, the Wage-earner, and the 'New Economic System', 1919-1929," *Business History Review* 51 (Summer 1977): 161-189; on the acceptance during this period of the idea of the economy of high wages see Dickman, *Industrial Democracy in America*, chap. 6.

[24] Montgomery, *Fall of the House of Labor*, 385-99; 419-24; Steve Fraser, "Dress Rehearsal for the New Deal: Shop-Floor Insurgents, Political Elites, and Industrial Democracy in the Amalgamated Clothing Workers," in Michael H., Frisch and Daniel J. Walkowitz, *Working-Class America: Essays on Labor, Community, and American Society* (Urbana: University of Illinois Press, 1983), 212-55; David Montgomery, "Whose Standards? Workers and the Reorganization of Production, 1900-1920," in *Workers Control in America* (Cambridge: Cambridge University Press, 1979), 113-38.

[25] Soule, *Prosperity Decade*, 218-22; Montgomery, *Fall of the House of Labor*, 422-24; Marc Linder, *Labor Statistics and Class Struggle* (New York: International Publishers, 1994), 6-25.

TRANSACTION INTRODUCTION

[26] Montgomery, *Fall of the House of Labor*, 406-07, 434-37; Lipset and Marks, *It Didn't Happen Here*, 68-71.

[27] For an introduction to the new labor history and its critique of institutionalism see David Brody, "The Old Labor History and the New: In Search of the American Working Class," *Labor History* 20 (Winter 1979): 111-26; for a an attempt at synthesis see Howard Kimmeldorf's round table discussion, "Bringing Unions Back In (Or Why We Need a New Old Labor History," *Labor History* 32 (Winter 1991): 91-129.

[28] Montgomery, *Fall of the House of Labor*; Dubofsky, *The State and Labor*; McCartin, *Labor's Great War*.

[29] William English Walling, "Labor's Attitude Toward a Third Party," *Current History*, (October 1924): 32-40; on the causal relation between Progressive Era social movements and the rise in the 1920s of interest groups see Daniel J. Tichenor and Richard A. Harris, "Organized Interests and American Political Development," *Political Science Quarterly* 117 (Winter 2002-03): 587-612; for the contemporary conservative criticism of interest group pluralism see Theodore J. Lowi, *The End of Liberalism: Ideology, Policy, and the Crisis of Public Authority* (New York: W.W. Norton and Co., 1969).

[30] William English Walling, "Capitalism-Or What?" *Bankers Magazine* 113 (September 1926): 309, 310, 311.

[31] Ira Steward, "A Reduction of Hours an Increase of Wages," in *A Documentary History of American Industrial Society in the United States*, vol. IX, eds., John R. Commons et al. (1910; reprint, New York: Russell & Russell, 1958), 284-301.

[32] Geo. E. McNeill, *The Eight Hour Primer: The Fact, Theory and the Argument. Eight Hour Series No. 1* (Washington D.C.: AFL, 1889); George Gunton, *The Economic and Social Importance of the Eight-Hour Movement, Eight-Hour Series, No. 2* (Washington D.C.: AFL, 1889); Lemuel Danryid, *History and Philosophy of the Eight-Hour Movement, Eight-Hour Series, No. 3* (Washington, D.C.: AFL, 1899). It is likely that Walling picked up the doctrine from the United Mine Workers' leader John Mitchell who had written in his 1903 book that over time with strong trade unions, "[t]he remuneration of labor will increase relative to the reward of capital," though by this time Mitchell and other labor leaders denied that the establishment of a socialist society would mark the end of labor's upward march. See John Mitchell, *Organized Labor; Its Problems, Purposes and Ideals and the Present and Future of American Wage Earners* (Philadelphia: American Book and Bible House 1903), 432.

[33] Martin J. Sklar contends that the modern corporation is managed as a mix of capitalist and socialist operating principles; see *The United States as a Developing Country: Studies in U.S. History in the Progressive Era and the 1920s* (Cambridge: Cambridge University Press, 1992), 20-36 and chap. 7; on postcapitalist thought in this period and more generally see Howard Brick, "The Postcapitalist Vision in Twentieth Century American Social Thought," in *Imagining Capitalism: Social Thought and Political Economy in*

TRANSACTION INTRODUCTION

20th Century America, ed. Nelson Lichtenstein (Philadelphia: University of Pennsylvania Press, 2005).

[34] William English Walling, "Economic Democracy," *New Republic* (July 31, 1929): 292-93 (quote at 293). Lipset and Marks contend that the "right" or constructivist wing of the SP led by Morris Hillquit and Victor Berger was in fact much closer politically to the revolutionaries on both continents than to the revisionist wing of the European Social Democrats and the labor parties of Britain, Australia, and New Zealand. See *It Didn't Happen Here*, 115, 117, 176, 179, 185, 198-99; also see James Weinstein, *The Decline of Socialism in America, 1912-1925* (New York: Vintage, 1969) and Irving Howe, *Socialism and America* (San Diego: Harcourt Brace, 1985), 3-48. If this point is accepted, Walling's postwar political stance emerges as the closest counterpart to that of European social democracy and overseas labor parties.

[35] Selig Perlman, *A Theory of the Labor Movement* (New York: Macmillan, 1928), Preface; Strunksy et al., *William English Walling: A Symposium*, 89-91, quote at 90.

[36] Among the many works that treat American labor in a democratic framework see Norman J. Ware, *The Labor Movement in the United States, 1860-1895: A Study in Democracy* (New York: Vintage Books, 1929); David Montgomery, *Beyond Equality: Labor and the Radical Republicans, 1862-1872* (New York: Vintage Books, 1967); Sean Wilentz, *Chants Democratic: New York City & the Rise of the American Working Class, 1788-1850* (New York: Oxford University Press, 1984); Leon Fink, *Workingmen's Democracy: The Knights of Labor and American Politics* (Urbana: University of Illinois Press, 1983); Richard Schneirov, *Labor and Urban Politics: Class Conflict and the Origins of Modern Liberalism in Chicago, 1864-97* (Urbana: University of Illinois Press, 1998); and McCartin, *Labor's Great War*.

[37] On the other hand, Walling's unwillingness to deal with these issues in ALAD may partially be excused because his stated topic was the AFL leadership not the state of the labor movement as a whole. On the origins of the CIO and racial and gender discrimination in the American labor movement the reader may consult the following: Lizabeth Cohen, *Making a New Deal: Industrial Workers in Chicago, 1919-1939* (Cambridge: Cambridge University Press, 1990); Robert H. Zieger, *The CIO, 1935-1955* (Chapel Hill: University of North Carolina Press, 1995); William H. Harris, *The Harder We Run: Black Workers since the Civil War* (New York: Oxford University Press, 1982); Jack Stuart, "William English Walling's Enduring Vision of Racial Reconciliation," in *American Socialist Visions of the Future: Expectations for the Millennium*, ed. Peter H. Buckingham (Westport. Conn.: Greenwood Press, 2002); Ruth Milkman, *Women, Work and Protest: A Century of U.S. Women's Labor History* (London: Routledge, 1985); Ava Baron, ed., *Work Engendered: Toward a New History of American Labor* (Ithaca, New York: Cornell University Press, 1991).

[38] Matthew Woll and William English Walling, *Our Next Step: A National Economic Policy* (New York: Harper & Bros., 1934).

TRANSACTION INTRODUCTION

[39] Walling's end at the age of fifty-nine was in keeping with his lifelong commitments. In 1936 as executive director of the Labor Chest for the relief and liberation of the workers of Europe, he visited European countries to organize relief committees. Stricken with arthritis during his visit, Walling nonetheless extended his stay in Europe so that he could meet with labor representatives smuggled out of Nazi Germany. Unable to make that vital meeting, William English Walling died September 12, 1936.

Published Writings of William English Walling

Books

The Dangerous Trades. Albany: New York State Labor Department Annual Report, 1900-01, 1902.

Russia's Message: The True World Import of the Revolution. New York: Doubleday, 1908.

Socialism As It Is: A World-Wide Survey of the Revolutionary Movement. New York: Macmillan, 1912.

Labor-Union Socialism and Socialist Labor-Unionism. Chicago: Charles H. Kerr, 1912.

The Larger Aspects of Socialism. New York: Macmillan, 1913.

Progressivism and After. New York: Macmillan, 1914.

Russia's Message: The People Against the Czar. New York: Knopf, 1915.

The Socialists and the War: A Documentary Statement of the Position of the Socialists of All Countries. New York: Henry Holt, 1915.

Whitman and Traubel. New York: Albert and Charles Boni, 1916.

State Socialism: Pro and Con. New York: Henry Holt, 1917; with Harry Laidler.

Addresses by Paul U. Kellogg, Samuel Gompers and William English Walling on the British Labor Party's Program of Reconstruction and the Stockholm Conference. March 16, 1918.

A Program of Social Reconstruction after the War. Social Democratic League of America, 1918.

Sovietism: The A B C of Russian Bolshevism—According to the Bolshevists. New York: Dutton, 1920.

Out of Their Own Mouths: A Revelation and an Indictment of Sovietism. New York: Dutton, 1921; with Samuel Gompers.

American Labor and American Democracy. New York: Harper, 1926.

The Mexican Question: Mexico and American-Mexican Relations under Calles and Obregon. New York: Robins, 1927.

Our Next Step: A National Economic Policy. New York: Harper, 1934; with Matthew Woll.

xlii

TRANSACTION INTRODUCTION

Articles

"Child Labor in the North: A Great National Evil." *Ethical Record* 4 (December 1902-January 1903): 39-42.

"The Mission of Mr. Hearst." *Wilshire's Magazine* (April 1903): 28-32.

"Building Trades and the Unions." *World's Work* 6 (August 1903): 3790-94.

"Great Cripple Creek Strike." *Independent* 56 (March 10, 1904): 539-48.

"Why Municipal Reform Succeeds in Chicago and Fails in New York." *Independent* 56 (April 14, 1904): 829-35.

"Can Labor Unions Be Destroyed?" *World's Work* 8 (May 1904): 4755-58.

"Open Shop Means the Destruction of the Unions." *Independent* 56 (May 12, 1904): 1069-72.

"New Unionism—The Problem of the Unskilled Worker." *Annals of the American Academy of Political and Social Science* 24 (July-December 1904): 296-315

"Labor Rebellion in Colorado." *Independent* 57 (August 18, 1904): 376-79.

"Labor Vote." *Independent* 57 (November 24, 1904): 1188-90.

"Children's Strike on the East Side." *Charities* 13 (December 24, 1904): 305

"Convention of the American Federation of Labor." *World To-Day* 8 (January 1905): 89-91.

"What are Factory Inspectors For?" *Charities* 13 (January 14, 1905): 375-77.

"Defeats of Labor." *Independent* 28 (February 23, 1905): 418-22.

"An American Socialism." *The International Socialist Review* 5 (April 1905): 577-84.

"Why American Unions Keep Out of Politics." *Outlook* 80 (May 20, 1905): 183-83.

"What the People of the East Side Do." *University Settlement Studies* I (July 1905): 79-85.

"British and American Trade Unionism." *Annals of the American Academy of Political and Social Science* 26 (November 1905): 721-39.

"Revolution in Poland." *Independent* 59 (November 2, 1905): 1040-42.

"Siege of Warsaw." *World To-Day* 9 (December 1905): 1304-06.

"Peasants' Revolution." *Independent* 61 (October 18, 1906): 905-10.

"Call to the Young Russians." *Charities* 17 (December 1, 1906): 373-76.

"Will the Peasants Act?" *Independent* 61 (December 6, 1906): 1315-23.

"Ominous Russian Famine." *Charities* 17 (February 2, 1907): 785-88.

"Village Against the Czar." *Independent* 62 (March 7-14, 1907): 530-38 and 587-94.

"How is it with the Russian Revolution?" *Outlook* 85 (March 9, 1907): 564-67.

"Civil War in Russia." *Independent* 62 (April 4, 1907): 774-79.

TRANSACTION INTRODUCTION

"Real Russian People at Church." *Independent* 63 (July 4, 1907): 26-32.

"Real Russian People." *Independent* 63 (September 26, 1907): 728-35.

"Power Behind the Czar." *Independent* 65 (March 19, 1908): 610-20.

"The Evolution of Socialism in Russia." *The International Socialist Review* 8 (July 1908): 42-46.

"Portrait." *Review of Reviews* 38 (August 1908): 254.

"Race War in the North." *Independent* 65 (September 3, 1908): 529-34.

"Laborism Versus Socialism." *The International Socialist Review* 9 (March 1909): 683-89.

"Science and Human Brotherhood." *Independent* 66 (June 17, 1909): 1318-27.

"Crisis in the Socialist Party." *Independent* 72 (May 16, 1912): 1047-51.

"The Socialist Party and the Farmers." *New Review* 1 (January 4, 1913): 12-20

"Industrialism or Revolutionary Unionism (Part I)." *New Review* 1 (January 11, 1913): 45-51.

"Industrialism or Revolutionary Unionism (Part II)." *New Review* 1 (January 18, 1913): 83-91.

"Government Ownership Contrasted with Collective Ownership." *Intercollegiate Socialist* (February-March 1913): 9

"Socialist Gains and Losses in the Recent Election." *New Review* 1 (February 8, 1913): 175-81.

"Woodrow Wilson and State Socialism." *New Review* 1 (March 15, 1913): 329-35.

"Woodrow Wilson and Big Business." *New Review* 1 (March 22, 1913): 364-69.

"Woodrow Wilson and Class Struggle." *New Review* 1 (March 29, 1913): 399-405.

"The Pragmatism of Marx and Engels (Part I)." *New Review* 1 (April 5, 1913): 434-39.

"The Pragmatism of Marx and Engels (Part II)." *New Review* 1 (April 12, 1913): 464-69.

"State Socialism and the Individual." *New Review* 1 (May 1913): 506-15.

"Belgian Strike." *Survey* 30 (May 13, 1913): 205-06.

"State Socialism and the Individual." *New Review* 1 (June 1913): 579-83.

"Municipal Socialism." *New Review* 1 (November 1913): 882-88.

"The New Fabianism." *Intercollegiate Socialist* (December 1913-January 1914): 11-15.

"A Socialist Digest." *New Review* 2 (February 1914): 117-28.

"The Remedy: Anti-Nationalism." *New Review* 3 (February 1914): 77-83.

"A Socialist Digest." *New Review* 2 (March 1914): 181-91.

"A Socialist Digest." *New Review* 2 (April 14, 1914): 246-55.

"Roosevelt's Socialism." *New Review* 2 (May 1914): 269-75.

"Financial Intervention in Mexico." *New Review* 2 (June 1914): 327-29.

"A Socialist Digest." *New Review* 2 (June 1914): 357-80.

"The Student's Heritage." *Intercollegiate Socialist* 2 (Spring-Summer 1914): 8-14.

TRANSACTION INTRODUCTION

"Why A Socialist Party." *New Review* 2 (July 1914): 400-03.

"A Socialist Digest." *New Review* 2 (July 1914): 418-39.

"A 'Socialist' Advocate of Plutocracy." *New Review* 2 (August 1914): 471-77.

"Socialists and the Great War." *Independent* 79 (August 24, 1914): 268-70.

"A Socialist Digest." *New Review* 2 (August 1914): 478-83.

"Socialists and the Great War." *Independent* 79 (August 24, 1914): 268-70.

"British and American Socialist on the War." *New Review* 2 (September 1914): 512-18.

"A Socialist Digest." *New Review* 2 (September 1914): 547-59.

"German Socialists and the War." *New Review* 2 (October 1914): 579-91.

"Socialists and the War." *Harper's Weekly* 59 (October 3, 1914): 319.

"Real Causes of the War." *Harper's Weekly* 59 (October 10, 1914): 346-47.

"Why A Socialist Party." *New Review* 2 (November 1914): 658-62.

"A Socialist Digest." *New Review* 2 (November 1914): 663-79.

"Are the German People Unanimously for the War?" *Outlook* 108 (November 25, 1914): 673-78.

"The New Map of Europe." *New Review* 2 (December 1914): 698-702.

"A Socialist Digest." *New Review* 2 (December 1914): 716-36.

"Nationalism and State Socialism." *Publications of the American Sociological Society* X, *War and Militarism in Their Sociological Aspects* (1915): 82-92.

"Are Socialists of the World Being Used by the Kaiser?" *New Review* 3 (January 1915): 33-36.

"A Socialist Digest." *New Review* 3 (January 1915): 41-49.

"A Socialist Digest." *New Review* 3 (February 1915): 100-19.

"A Socialist Digest." *New Review* 3 (March 1915): 163-79.

"Minority Representation." *New Review* 3 (April 1915): 199-205.

"A Socialist Digest." *New Review* 3 (April 1915): 225-40.

"Karl Liebknecht." *Survey* 34 (April 3, 1915): 18-20.

"American Progressivism." *New Review* 3 (May 1, 1915): 15-16.

"A Socialist Digest." *New Review* 3 (May 1, 1915): 17-21.

"A Socialist Digest." *New Review* 3 (May 15, 1915): 41-44.

"The Great Illusions." *New Review* 3 (June 1, 1915): 49-51.

"A Socialist Digest." *New Review* 3 (June 1, 1915): 65-69.

"A Socialist Digest." *New Review* 3 (June 15, 1915): 90-93.

"Germany's Foreign Policy Based on Her Home Policy?" *New Review* 3 (July 1, 1915): 104-05.

"A Socialist Digest." *New Review* 3 (July 1, 1915): 112-17.

"A Socialist Digest." *New Review* 3 (July 15, 1915): 148-50.

"A Socialist Digest." *New Review* 3 (August 1, 1915): 170-73.

"Trust of Nations." *New Review* 3 (August 15, 1915): 184-85.

"A Socialist Digest." *New Review* 3 (August 15, 1915): 194-97.

"Futility of Bourgois [sic] Pacifism." *New Review* 3 (September 1, 1915): 208-09.

TRANSACTION INTRODUCTION

"A Socialist Digest." *New Review* 3 (September, 1, 1915): 217-20.

"The Sure Winner: America." *The Masses* 6 (September 1915): 20.

"The Newest Socialism." *New Review* 3 (September 15, 1915): 229-32.

"A Socialist Digest." *New Review* 3 (September 15, 1915): 243-46.

"A Socialist Digest." *New Review* 3 (October 1, 1915): 265-69.

"A Socialist Digest." *New Review* 3 (October 15, 1915): 311-14.

"A Socialist Digest." *New Review* 3 (November 1, 1915): 290-93.

"Socialist Attitude Toward Peace at Any Price." *New York Times Magazine* (November 14, 1915): 19.

"A Socialist Digest." *New Review* 3 (December 1, 1915): 340-43.

"A Socialist Digest." *New Review* 3 (December 15, 1915): 368-71.

"Who Gets America's Wealth?" *Intercollegiate Socialist* 4 (December 1915-January 1916): 3-14.

"German State Socialism." *Intercollegiate Socialist* 4 (December 1915-January 1916): 10-13.

"A Socialist Digest." *New Review* 3 (January 1, 1916): 18-20.

"A Socialist Digest." *New Review* 3 (January 15, 1916): 44-46.

"Socialism and Nationalism." *Intercollegiate Socialist* 4 (February-March 1916): 8-9.

"A Socialist Digest." *New Review* 3 (March 1916): 87-91.

"A Socialist Digest." *New Review* 3 (April 1916): 129-33.

"Review of Socialism and the War." *Intercollegiate Socialist* 4 (April-May 1916): 28-29.

"New Income and Inheritance Taxes for the United States," 4 *Intercollegiate Socialist* (April-May 1916): 3-15.

"A Socialist Digest." *New Review* 3 (May 1916): 166-69.

"The German Paradise." *The Masses* 8 (June 1916): 20.

"Prospects for Economic Internationalism." *Annals of the American Academy of Political and Social Science* 68 (November 1916): 10-22.

"Socialists and the Problems of War: A Symposium." *Intercollegiate Socialist* 5 (April-May 1917): 25-27.

"A Separation." *The Masses* 9 (May 1917): 14-15.

"No Annexations, No Indemnities." *Independent* 90 (May 19, 1917): 327-28.

"Wilson-Kerensky Peace Policy." *Proceedings of the American Academy of Political and Social Science* 7 (July 1917): 316-22.

"Socialists: The Kaiser Party." *Independent* 92 (November 10, 1917): 290.

"Kaiser's Socialists." *New York Times Magazine* (January 6, 1918): 1-2.

"Internationalism and Government Ownership." *Public* 21 (January 11, 1918): 49-52.

"Sowing the Seeds of Bolshevism." *New York Times Magazine* (April 21, 1918): 3-4.

"German Shop Councils." *American Federationist* 28 (February 1921): 116-21.

"American Labor Leads the World." *American Federationist* 28 (September 1921): 740-43.

TRANSACTION INTRODUCTION

"Will Public Opinion Abdicate?" *American Federationist* 28 (November 1921): 932-34.

"British Labor's Proposed Solution of the Unemployed Problem." *American Federationist* 29 (January 1922): 26-28.

"Russia as the Chief Obstacle to European Rehabilitation; From the Labor Viewpoint." *Annals of the American Academy of Political and Social Science* 102 (July 1922): 131-37.

"European Labor at War Against the Russian Soviet." *American Federationist* 29 (September 1922): 653-56.

"League of Nations and Soviet Responsibility for the Russian Famine." *American Federationist* 30 (April 1923): 297-302.

"French Radical Support for Ruhr Policy." *Current History Magazine, New York Times* 19 (October 1923): 53-60.

"Program of the British Labor Party." *Current History* 19 (February 1924): 749-57.

"American Labor Leads the World." *American Federationist* 31 (September 1924): 738-39.

"Labor's Attitude Toward a Third Party." *Current History Magazine, New York Times* 21 (October 1924): 32-40.

"Edward Herriot, The LaFollette of France." *American Federationist* 31 (November 1924): 869-71.

"Samuel Gompers, The Great Actor." *American Federationist* 26 (February 1925): 11-12.

"Mexican Peasant Struggle for Land Reform." *Current History Magazine, New York Times* 22 (April 1925): 40-44.

"Is Labor Divided as to Political Principles?" *American Federationist* 32 (May 1925): 347-50.

"Capitalism—Or What?" *Bankers Magazine* 113 (September 1926): 309-11.

"Labor's Hope in Congress." *American Federationist* 33 (December 1926): 1457-59.

"Pan-American Conference at Havana." *American Federationist* 35 (April 1928): 428-33.

"Economic Democracy." *New Republic* (July 31, 1929): 292-93.

"President Machado's Administration of Cuba." *Current History* 32 (May 1930): 257-63.

"For Better Understanding: From a Preface to the French Edition of *American Labor and American Democracy* by A. Thomas." *American Federationist* 37 (November 1930): 1359-62.

"Program for Progressives." *New Republic* 66 (April 29, 1931): 304.

EDITOR'S INTRODUCTION

This book is as nearly an authoritative statement of the principles and policies of the American organized labor movement of the past forty years as any statement that could be issued by any person not an active official or working member of an American union. The real American labor movement, its historic and world-wide significance, its thinking, its aims, the direction of its growth, are, obviously, not to be understood without direct acquaintance with the leaders and their purposes. Mr. Walling has had this opportunity to an exceptional degree for more than two decades—but especially during the period of which he writes. He was associated with organized labor during the war, and he accompanied the American labor delegation to Europe at the personal invitation of President Gompers during the peace negotiations and later for the foundation meeting of the International Federation of Trade Unions. He afterward collaborated with Mr. Gompers in a book and has frequently worked and conferred with him and with other officers of the Federation.

JOHN R. COMMONS

August, 1926.
University of Wisconsin

xlix

FOREWORD

SAMUEL GOMPERS'S dying words were, "God bless our American institutions; may they grow better day by day." The American Federation of Labor in its memorial publication selected a longer passage from Gompers's writings: "America is not merely a name. It is not merely a land. It is not merely a country, nor is it merely a continent. America is a symbol; it is an ideal; the hopes of the world can be expressed in the ideal—America."

This faith in American democracy did not mean with Gompers—nor does it mean with the Federation—a passive acceptance of American institutions as they are, but their further development with the aid of a new power— organized labor. In addressing his last convention, a few weeks before his death, Gompers pointed out that the aim of the Federation from the beginning had been "to make the labor movement a force in the determination of national policies."

A new generation of labor statesmen has come into control of the American movement, and it is with their policies that we are now concerned. But there has been no change in the Americanism or the democratic principles upon which the movement is founded.

American labor policy has developed from the actual experience of Americans "applying the principles and methods of democracy, in an American environment."[1] American labor is not a thing apart; it is a branch of American democracy. But it brings a new experience into American society—and American democracy has become a different thing from what it was before organized labor, and similar "organizations of mutual aid," became incorporated in the body politic.

American labor does not attempt to lay out in advance what the great change that is coming over America will be—all other branches of democracy are having and will continue to have their say about that—but it does not doubt that the change will be revolutionary in the end, or that our conceptions of property and government are being and will continue to be profoundly affected. Even before the war (during the high tide of pre-war progressivism) labor found that "government and laws have developed from an institution merely by virtue of and for the protection of property, into a medium for attaining social ideals and needs beyond (the possibility of) individual realization."[2]

This is the social democracy aimed at by American labor. Industrial democracy is another aspect of the same goal. Viewed from still another angle, the aim is economic democracy—the control of government and industry by economic organizations representing not only labor, but every essential social group.

II

Some of the material in the present volume is taken from my articles in the official organ, *The American*

[1] American Federation of Labor Convention, 1922.
[2] *American Federationist*, November, 1912.

Federationist. Most of it is entirely new, however, with the exception of a few passages from signed articles appearing on the editorial pages of the New York *Evening Post* and the New York *Tribune,* and in *Current History* (published by the New York *Times*).

I have availed myself of first-hand knowledge of the movement, and my survey of its larger policies is based on that knowledge. At the same time I have aimed to avoid absolutely the injection of personal views into the discussion, and so I have followed the method of documenting every point, fully and fairly. I have not, however, leaned upon any document or quotation that I did not have good reason to believe was a sincere and accurate expression of the movement.

I think I have covered the ground laid out, with the exception of American labor's foreign policies and foreign relations. In the course of preparation of the present volume I saw that this was a large and more or less separate subject, and I have excluded the sections I had written dealing with it. Public interest may justify its treatment in a separate volume.

AMERICAN LABOR
AND
AMERICAN DEMOCRACY

INTRODUCTORY

The Old Democracy—the Heritage from Jackson and Lincoln—
The New Economic Revolution—Business Consolidation—Organ-
ized Labor and Other Democratic Forces—Growth of the Ameri-
can Movement—Legal Status and Rights of Labor—Social
Philosophy of American Labor.

I

WE must not think of the American labor movement as
existing independently of America past or present. Our
labor movement is not an importation or the result of
a theory; it is a typical and representative product of
American history. The American labor movement can
be understood only as a part of the American economic
structure—perhaps the most amazing and stupendous of
all the products of the genius and energy of man.

While the foundations of political democracy were laid
in western Europe from 1848 to 1918, they were established earlier in the United States—not so early as 1776
and 1789, as we have long been taught, but during the
Jefferson-Jackson democratic wave that reached its crest
in the 1830's and in the Lincoln democracy at the time of
the Civil War. Even in those early days organized labor,
then comparatively weak, made very decided contributions
to the shaping of American democracy, and those contributions have grown steadily.

Organized labor has always regarded itself as a product
of American democracy. There may have been times

7

when that democracy did not function to much purpose; there may have been times—like the generation just past—when the enemies of democracy were getting very much more out of our political system than were the masses of our people. But at all times, when democracy was functioning as well as when it failed to function, organized labor has been a part of the democratic movement—on the whole exploited neither more nor less than the rest of the people, conscious of that fact and not conscious of itself as a separate proletariat of outcasts or disinherited. When 90 or 99 per cent of the American people lost, organized labor lost, when 90 or 99 per cent of the people gained—or began to feel that their interest was being advanced under our government and social system—labor felt that it also was gaining, that its interest was being advanced. There were no classes within the democratic movement, nor did labor or the people as a whole feel that they were subjected to any lasting class rule. The enemies of democracy had, at times, seized the reins of power; that was bad enough, but that was all. There was no enduring class government.

During the Jackson-Lincoln period and for several decades afterward, the most important class in the community, numerically and otherwise, was that of the small farm owners who did all (or practically all) of their own labor. As there was a sufficiency of free land until 1880 (or perhaps even until 1890), it was possible for any wage-earner who had saved a comparatively small sum to become a small farm owner. This fact kept even the unskilled wage-earner on an economic level nearly equal to that of the small farmer. Other small producers and traders were in a similar economic situation and for the first century of our history as a nation the overwhelming majority of the community was practically in a single social class.

When this period came to an end, during the last quarter of the nineteenth century, it was widely held that the entire economic and social foundation of American democracy had disappeared. On the surface there seemed to be much truth in this view. Lincoln had said that the normal life of the American citizen was to be a wage-earner in his earlier years and an independent small producer and finally an employer as he grew older. Clearly that time had passed. With the rising value of the land and the increasing use of farm machinery, the farmer was becoming a capitalist, and it was no longer an easy matter for the wage-earner to take up a farm or to enter, with high average chance of success, into any other small business. Cities had become so large that the average wage-earner hardly knew what a farm was. Wage-earning employments had become so specialized that a new type of skill or semi-skill was the rule and constituted the wage-earner's principal capital. At the same time the successful operation of a farm (or small business) required not only more capital, but more specialized skill, than it had in the previous generation.

So, at the beginning of the present century it was widely held that we were developing a very sharp separation between the small capitalist and the wage-earning classes. But the quarter-century that has elapsed has shown that this was less than a half-truth. For the progress of the small farm owner has been checked in many ways. As the land has become more valuable, farm ownership has become more and more frequently separated from farm operation, the owner frequently retiring to rent his farm to a tenant; then cheap and efficient farm labor has not been forthcoming, the overwhelming majority of farmers doing almost the same proportion of their labor as they did half a century ago. At the same time a large proportion of wage-earners have improved their position through organization, and finally the restriction of immigration has brought it about that the demand for industrial labor has become as great as the demand for the products on the farm.

As a result of these and other forces the average wage-earner and the average farmer remain economically as close, perhaps, as they were half a century ago. And in the meanwhile the enormous spread of free public education has held all the clerical and minor professional and minor salaried groups at somewhat the same level.

The extraordinary economic development of the United States from 1875 to 1925 has not, therefore, destroyed the economic and social foundations of American democracy. The vast experience gained by American labor in a century of democratic progress is as valuable to-day as it ever was; and the American political system is as solid and reliable a foundation on which to build.

II

But this country has been undergoing an unparalleled economic revolution—more rapid than that of any of its European rivals—and this revolution has had the most profound influence both on the American labor movement itself and on the problems with which it is confronted.

The economic revolution through which we are passing

may be called "the consolidation of industry." Proceeding simultaneously along many lines, there is a tendency in the direction of the unified organization or integration of all industry, or at least of all the more important industries, of the country. How near (or far) we are from thoroughgoing consolidation, or whether we are at all likely ever to reach such consolidation before some new force intervenes to stop the present development, is beside the question. The absolutely vital consideration is that there is an overwhelming, irresistible, and rapid movement *toward* the consolidation of all the leading business interests—of course with a large measure of autonomy for each of the giant corporations or corporation groups—and that, leading all the nations in this development, we are already far along that road.

This movement is but the latest phase of a development that has been going on for decades. Toward the end of the nineteenth century the development of large-scale industry, which had been proceeding steadily for generations, was followed by a period (not yet ended) marked by the formation of combinations, trusts, or monopolies, the giant corporations of to-day. Early in the present century a new tendency, the interlocking directorate, was first noted by the public and the march toward the consolidation of all "big business" entered into its second stage. That development, too, has now become a commonplace. We have come to a period when it is universally recognized not only that our chief industries are in the hands of gigantic corporations, but that these corporations are increasingly interconnected by interlocking directorates, holding companies, and voting trusts—a few hundred directors controlling the vast bulk of our greatest banks, railroads, public utility and industrial corporations.

The concentration of industry has now reached its third stage. Rapidly we are passing out of the period of mere groups of colossal corporations toward a *more or less* consolidated corporation structure. There is already a decided "community of interest" throughout the whole corporation complex, and it is growing closer and stronger day by day. Practical monopolies of given articles or of local and sectional markets are common. *They are accepted by the business community as a whole,* and practically are protected by the law. A small amount of competition is often admitted for the sake of appearances, or to fix the prices at a level just high enough to give a bare profit to a few small and inefficient establishments, and so at a level high enough to afford a huge rate of profit to the efficient giant corporation. This is the well-authenticated practice, to mention only one of countless examples, among the anthracite coal corporations.

In addition we have thousands of trade associations whose purpose it is to "standardize" or "stabilize" competition, or in reality to keep it within as narrow bounds as the law will permit. So powerful is the business sentiment against effective competition, and so strong is the tendency toward organization, that often the free exchange of "information" as to production, prices, and markets suffices to produce the "co-operation" desired.

And, finally, we have the national associations of manufacturers and chambers of commerce and similar organizations whose function it is to put an end to business competition on the field of politics and public policy, or in dealing with labor questions—tasks in which they have achieved their most remarkable successes since the World War.

There is little friction as to such matters between these various types of organization or between them and the giant corporations and financial institutions. Like the giant corporations, they are tied together more and more closely every year by interlocking directors. They represent a fairly united front to the rest of the public, to labor, and to government—a front that is rarely divided or even materially weakened by any differences they may have among themselves. Such differences as do occur are, as a rule, quickly healed whenever unity is necessary to prevent other economic groups, such as organized labor or organized agriculture, from increasing their share of the national income or their economic or political power.

This consolidating business world is strengthened (1) by that part of our agriculturalists who have built up their business, or confidently count upon building it, on industrial or capitalist principles, (2) by the higher salaried employees or those who expect to draw such salaries, (3) by recipients of large unearned incomes, and (4) by those who live upon these classes.

These are the forces organized labor and other democratic elements have often to meet. They have been greatly strengthened in the last quarter-century both in organization and in their numbers in proportion to the whole population. But organized labor and the other democratic groups have also advanced rapidly in intelligence, information, organization. So that several extremely important progressive measures have been forced through in recent years *against the practically united opposition* of this consolidating business world—from the enactment of the Amendments of the Federal Constitution establishing a federal income tax and the direct election of Senators (passed by Congress in 1909 and 1912, respectively, and ratified by the States in 1913) to the so-called "soldiers' bonus," in 1924. It would seem, then, that the stupendous power of organized business in America, due to its concentration and its control of half the mobile capital of the earth, is largely, if not fully, offset by the experience in self-government that has been developing for almost a century in these United States. And this is due in part to the activities of organized labor. The same industrial society that has created our gigantic business interests has produced a variety of labor organization, as remarkable, as typically American, as the business structure itself.

III

In this favorable and unfavorable environment the American labor movement has expanded steadily— strengthened both by the forces working with it and by the resistance it has had to meet—and as the movement has expanded it has adopted new policies, taken on new functions, and entered into new fields of activity.

Even before the outbreak of the European war, labor-unionism had been spreading very rapidly in this country, the membership of the American Federation of Labor rising from half a million in 1900 to two million in 1913! The membership remained at this figure until America's entry into the war, in 1917. Within four years—that is, by 1920—it had doubled again, rising to more than four million! With the addition of the railroad brotherhoods and the clothing unions outside the Federation the total union membership was approximately five millions.

A certain setback took place after 1922, the membership dropping to approximately three millions for the Federation, with a proportionate loss for the outside unions. However, a part of the war-time gain was held—and union membership in 1925 was fully fifty per cent greater than it had been twelve years before, though the number of working people employed had not increased half so fast.

It is still asserted by those who minimize the rôle of organized labor that only a very minor part of the wage-earners of the country are organized. This is true only of wage-earners as a whole. It is not true of industrial wage-earners, the sole field where labor unionism has concentrated any considerable organizing energy. Practically no effort has been made to organize agricultural wage-earners, and comparatively little energy has been expended on clerical or office employees, school-teachers, and other salaried workers.

A very considerable part, though not a majority, of industrial wage-earners are organized. In addition to the paid-up membership roll, hundreds of thousands regard themselves and are regarded by the unions as members, though they cannot be carried on the rolls because of non-payment of dues. Other hundreds of thousands may be looked upon as intermittent members. They have been unionists whenever they felt the unions could serve them, they favor the principle of unionism, and are ready to join again whenever a promising struggle for improvement is on—as it could not be, for example, during the

financial and industrial setback of 1922 or during the
period of recovery immediately following.

But there are serious hindrances to labor-union expansion even among industrial wage-earners. Those industries where there has been a large influx of women and
children are, of course, not so well organized—as, for
example, the textile industries. This is not because
women of the same age as men are not organizable,
though the difficulty of organization is somewhat greater.
But the women workers are usually rather young and
unmarried, and a large part have not yet reached the
legal voting age. Organized labor hopes, ultimately, to
include also the great bulk of these industrial wage-earners. But the process is relatively slow and the goal will
hardly be reached in the immediate future.

In addition to such obstacles to labor-union development, which are to be met in all countries, there are some
difficulties peculiar to America, and these must be carefully noted and firmly held in mind in any study of any
aspect of labor-unionism in this country.

First there is our large foreign-born population. Many
of these are easily organizable as far as their nationality
is concerned, though there is always the difficulty that
they may be adapted to the labor movements of their own
countries under the conditions of those countries and less
easily adaptable to the American labor movement under
the conditions of the United States. But this is a minor
difficulty, almost invariably disappearing in time, and will
probably be overcome under the new restriction of immigration. The major difficulty is that the bulk of these
foreign-born workers are unskilled and that a high proportion are illiterate. Therefore those American indus-

tries that employ an unusually large proportion of unskilled or semi-skilled operatives are exceptionally hard to organize. However, this difficulty also will tend gradually to disappear with the rise of the new generation out of our public schools.

But in the meanwhile employers in all industries in which a major portion of the labor is unskilled have taken full advantage of their temporary opportunities and have evolved a highly efficient organization and machinery to prevent unionization. In the first place, nearly all the giant industrial corporations have an active anti-union policy. But, in addition, many other employers, united in the National Association of Manufacturers, in the Chamber of Commerce of the United States and in the employers' associations of each industry, are actively hostile to effective and powerful labor organization.

In a word, the efficiency of organized capital has doubled the task of organized labor in this country. And if organized labor has been defeated at certain points, or temporarily checked, by this seemingly all-powerful opposition, that does not prove the weakness of American unionism. It is a proof only of the colossal strength of the opposing forces. The fact that American labor has been able to progress as far and as fast as it has and that it has developed its present power against such unprecedented opposition shows how extraordinary are its vitality, its momentum, and its reserve force, and proves that its foundations go down into the very roots of American history and of our present economic structure.

If American labor were not developing new and special policies to meet the major problem offered by this opposition, there would be little prospect that it would fulfill

17

the great historic destiny which seems to lie before it. But American labor *has* evolved new policies aimed at overcoming this resistance, and in evolving these policies has shown itself possessed of all the energy, the originality, the resourcefulness of American business.

IV

The modern labor movement is related to about everything there is in a country; its activities and connections branch out in all directions. To summarize the leading activities of the American movement would require, perhaps, a dozen volumes. These might deal with internal structure, organization, government; with collective bargaining; with the social, economic, and political philosophy (or ideas) of the movement; with its legal status and struggle for legal rights; with labor legislation; with educational activities; with foreign policies and relationships; with political activities and public policies; with the organization of the wage-earners as consumers; and with the new economic activities outside of the workshop.

Some of these phases of labor-unionism are central and fundamental—such as collective bargaining. Though I have not treated this subject directly, in discussing wages and the government of industry I have shown how collective bargaining leads inevitably to a broad industrial and social policy.

The first object of every union is to make a sufficient number of collective contracts or agreements with employers to provide for its entire membership—agreements covering wages, hours, shop conditions, the "hiring and firing" of the employees. Labor-unionism secures and enforces such agreements mainly through its ability to withdraw either all the labor force in a given trade or industry or a large part of it. But it also reverts to the withdrawal of labor's patronage as consumers (through the boycott or denying the use of the union label) and to an appeal to public opinion—which is effective in proportion as an industry is subject to any form of governmental action.

Employers also—in resisting those demands of organized labor which they believe will have to be paid out of profits—use both their economic and their political power. Their economic weapon is either a shut-down, aimed "to starve out" the workers—or at least to reduce them by the superiority of the economic resources of employers when compared with those of employees—or the "blacklist" or so-called "open-shop," efforts to operate the industry wholly or largely by non-unionists. But employers have another form of resistance—the use against the unions of their influence, at times amounting to control, over government, accompanied by an appeal to the "public" for support. The resistance takes the form either of legislative, executive, and judicial attacks on the legal rights of labor organizations and individual wage-earners or of getting judges to declare "unconstitutional" or otherwise to nullify the legislative remedies and reforms secured by organized labor to protect its rights.

This subject of the legal status and rights of organized labor would also require, as I have said, a separate volume. That volume would deal with the effort of the unions to preserve their rights to free speech and to quit work collectively, and it would discuss judicial injunctions depriving labor organizations of legal rights and the position of the Supreme Court.

At the same time this phase of the labor movement is closely related to labor's social policies and its recent political history, as discussed in the present volume. Labor's political activity was developed largely as a defense against this legal and political attack. But such defensive and negative political action is important mainly because it has served as a bridge by which organized labor has passed from an almost exclusive preoccupation with wages, hours, and collective bargaining to a broadly constructive economic and political policy. It is true that the question of the legal status and rights of labor looms as large to-day as it ever did; the resistance to labor, if somewhat altered in character, is as strong as ever—and it is better organized. But there is this difference— to-day organized labor has found a host of new friends and associates through its newer activities and constructive economic and political policies.

When the question of the legal status of labor comes into the foreground to-day it is usually as a part of some larger social problem. For example, the rights of railroad or mine workers are publicly discussed as an organic part of the entire railroad and coal questions. And the anti-union policies of our great corporations are related in the public mind to the huge profits they draw from industry at the expense not only of labor, but also of consumers, agriculturists, salaried employees, small investors, small taxpayers, and the public generally.

Nor does the so-called "labor legislation" represent the chief legislative effort of organized labor in this country. The term labor legislation, as ordinarily used, covers "social reform" and "social justice" measures, many of which concern groups of workers who are not unionists—measures that interest organized labor as they do other citizens, largely for purely humanitarian reasons —such as the laws protecting women and children.

On the other hand, many kinds of legislation of the greatest interest to labor are not classed as labor legislation, such as the regulation of the railroads and the proposed legislation covering the coal mines. Also labor is powerfully and directly interested in still another type of legislation, such as the control of banks and corporations, and direct primary laws, that has no special reference whatever to labor. And finally, American labor proposes alternative solutions for problems commonly dealt with by what is technically called "labor legislation."

For example, the labor unions have initiated their own private insurance corporations which will cover a large part of the field provided for in Great Britain and other countries by governmental or social insurance, recognized as one of the leading branches of "labor legislation." In the same way American labor, except in a few States, prefers to unemployment insurance by the States, which is a branch of "labor legislation," certain *preventive* remedies against unemployment, both private and governmental. The preventive governmental remedy, the extension of public credit to public works in times of unemployment, since it has other equally important and altogether different objectives, is quite properly not regarded as a branch of "labor legislation."

For all these reasons, "labor legislation," though a very important branch of organized labor's activity in America as in other countries, is not so fundamental as that type of legislation which is connected with the major economic problem, the government of industry, or with the central political problem, the voice of labor in our political and social system.

Another branch of the general subject of labor-unionism, organized labor's social philosophy, its system of ideas (or its *leading* ideas, with or without system), is comparatively less fundamental in America than in other countries because our labor-unionism is based not upon ideas, but upon experience. In other countries labor organizations have been founded largely on general ideas and an effort has been made to base economic and political policies on those ideas. In America, on the contrary, general ideas have arisen exclusively out of labor's daily experience in collective bargaining and in putting into effect economic and political policies that have risen out of collective bargaining. The general ideas of the American movement are most accurately described in connection with its economic and political activities.

The internal structure, organization, and government of the American movement does not require any special treatment for our purposes. It is typified in the American Federation of Labor—the most important organizations outside of the Federation, the four "brotherhoods" of the railroad trainmen, being similar in most respects to the 120 unions that compose it.

The structure of the American Federation of Labor shows the following salient features:

The American unions, unlike the European, are not affiliated with political organizations, admission to which is open to non-labor-unionists and to non-wage-earners.

In the second place, the American Federation of Labor is a true federation—that is, the constituent unions enjoy a very large measure of autonomy.

In the third place, the state and city federations, composed of the local units of the national organizations, also enjoy a considerable measure of autonomy, especially in political affairs.

In the fourth place, American labor, having adopted neither socialism nor any other doctrine, is wholly free to co-operate with all other democratic and progressive organizations, economic, political, and educational, and does co-operate in innumerable instances.

This democratic and federal type of organization means that the American movement as a whole can move no faster than its constituent unions and the rank and file of its membership. It means, further, that the unions may often have to wait for other democratic elements of the community before they can successfully launch their own policies. But it means also a very large degree of unity and certainty once the policy agreed upon is launched. In this way policies have been developed out of daily activities, and have been tried and tested by experience. Upon these policies labor is practically united, and it is only in so far as it is united that any appeal is made, or can be successfully made, to the general public.

LABOR AND POLITICS

PREFATORY NOTE

THE larger part of the labor activities I have dealt with in the present volume, have some relation with government. How is this treatment justified when the American labor-union movement remains what it always has been, fundamentally an economic movement concerned with collective bargaining?

While it is true that collective bargaining with employers is still the chief daily activity of organized labor, and that wages and labor conditions are still its chief concern, this wage struggle, under the industrial conditions of the last two decades, has led to broader economic and political policies.

A generation ago, the organization of American capital, industry, and business into combinations, interlocking directorates, as well as voluntary associations, such as the National Association of Manufacturers and the United States Chamber of Commerce, was still in its infancy. To-day the era of organization is so advanced that it almost seems complete, and we find this more or less consolidated business world active in every direction that bears any relation to its business purposes. And it is particularly active in relation to government and to politics.

Labor organization has been under the same influences that have been molding business. It has branched out into education, book publication, banking, insurance, the employment of engineering, statistical, and legal experts, co-opera-

25

tion with other economic and political organizations, and new relations with government.

These new economic, social, and political functions have grown out of labor's economic experience. Collective bargaining has led to larger and larger activities, until "the labor movement, representing great productive forces of society, is an indispensable part not only of society's productive processes, but of society's intellectual, political, and sociological processes." [1]

In this newer and larger field American labor is not following the labor of any other country. It is acting on the basis of long experience gained through our more or less democratic political institutions, but above all it is acting as a part of the colossal and highly developed economic organism of America—an organism that all the world is studying to-day. The time cannot be far distant when the labor movements of the world also will be sending delegations to this country to study the newer activities and policies of American labor, both the goal of social, industrial, and economic democracy we have set before us and the methods we are adopting to reach that goal.

[1] *American Federationist*, November, 1912.

CHAPTER I

LABOR ENTERS POLITICS IN ITS OWN WAY

Early Doubts as to the Efficacy of Political Action—Labor's Magna Charta—the Bill of Grievances of 1906—The Initiation of the Non-Partisan Policy—The Non-Partisan Policy Successfully Applied to Congressional Elections.

WHEN the American Federation of Labor took the first step in its present political course twenty years ago (in 1906) it pointed out that "trade-unionism, in teaching the paramount importance of questions affecting the lives and homes of the labor seller, also teaches the citizen that the use of the ballot should be determined by these issues."

By the end of the European war, when American labor's political activities had entered into their second phase, the importance of politics to the wage-earner had become a truism that "no one will gainsay or deny." [1]

From its foundation the Federation and the labor organizations composing it had been engaged in politics. But the emphasis placed upon the importance of trade-union or economic action as contrasted with political action created the impression that they were against all political activity. This determination not to allow political activities to predominate over economic or trade-

[1] Convention of 1919.

union activities was due to the early experience of the movement. Until the formation of the American Federation of Labor all attempts to build up a powerful labor movement had failed because the plan had been to unite the labor unions, together with members of other social groups, in the form of a political body rather than a federation of autonomous unions. The labor-unionists who came to America from continental Europe made desperate efforts to subordinate the unions to a Socialist or Labor party. Every "new" or "third" party, from 1880 to 1924, tried to include the labor unions, subordinating labor union objectives to those of the new party. And, finally, continuous efforts were made by both of the "big" or "old" parties, Republican and Democratic, to annex organized labor. Nationally these old party efforts were rarely dangerous to the movement; locally, and in a number of States, they often came near to dividing and wrecking it.

It was to avoid these dangers of *partisan* politics, and not because of any disinclination of organized labor to enter into political activities, that the Federation so strongly emphasized economic action in contrast to political action. It is true that the reaction of labor leaders against the excesses and dangers of partisan politics at moments almost amounted to an exclusion of all political action. But this negative attitude was much more common in the first two decades of the present labor movement (1881-1901) than it has been in the last quarter century (1901-26).

While the unions were "in politics" from the first, many of their utterances in the early days were distinctly anti-political. As late as 1902 President Gompers could say, in the official organ of the Federation: "I now address myself to this question of the ballot-box. What is to be remedied—the economic or the social or political life? If it is the economic life that is to be remedied, then it should be done through the economic life and through no other medium."[1]

As the ills from which labor suffers, including nearly all of those for which political remedies are proposed, are indeed economic, this pronouncement strongly suggests, though it does not definitely propose, the abandonment of political action. As President Gompers said at the time:

The point of success and superiority which we have reached, together with the bungling which the politicians, misnamed statesmen, have made of any attempt to deal with industrial affairs, ought to be a sufficient warrant to all earnest, right-thinking Americans to insist that political jugglery ought to be kept free at least from the industrial affairs of our people.[2]

This proposition that all political intervention in industrial affairs means either political jugglery or the bungling of politicians, had the unions definitely and permanently accepted it, would have precluded any but a purely defensive political activity.

All the spoken and written emphasis was placed on economic action, in resistance to the political temptations and dangers that surrounded labor on every side. However, there was no cessation of political activity. Legislation in the interest of labor had been demanded from the beginning, and it was realized that this meant an ever-

[1] *American Federationist*, September, 1902.
[2] *Organized Labor, Its Struggles, Its Enemies, Its Fool Friends,* by Samuel Gompers.

29

increasing political action. And as early as 1887 President Gompers had declared:

It seems to me that the trade unions, apart from their work of attending to the matters of wages, hours of labor, and unjust conditions of that labor, should extend their thoughts and actions more largely into the sphere and affairs of government. We have a right to demand legislation in the interest of the wage-workers, who form so large a majority and are certainly no unimportant factor to the well-being of our country.[1]

Labor was engaged in politics, but it was invariably and consistently pointed out that labor's political power was based mainly not on its voting strength elections, but on its economic power. The 1896 convention of the Federation declared that "in the same degree that the workers master a greater influence in the conditions and regulations under which they are employed, will their associated voices be heard and heeded in the halls of legislation and be the will of the people, the will of the nation."

The year 1906 marked the end of the period of political hesitancy. But if this was the moment when a new policy began to crystallize, it was also the time when the older tactics reached their strongest formulation. It was still held that by unaided trade-union action the working people would be able not only to redress their wrongs, but to "strengthen their economic position until it will place labor in full possession of its inherent rights."

The entrance into politics was, and has continued to be, very cautious. For example, a formulation of policy made in 1910 and reprinted in 1920 advised the unions "to trust all the time to definite and time-tried trade-union

[1] American Federation of Labor Convention of 1887.

economic methods, and to the ballot only in so far as results are to be foreseen to a positive certainty." [1]

Now, results cannot always be clearly foreseen to a positive certainty either on the economic or on the political field. The Federation convention of 1919 formulated labor's political policy more boldly and positively, and based it on "the workers' necessity to secure the legislation covering those conditions of life not subject to collective bargaining with employers," thus assigning an extremely broad field to be covered by politics without specifying "positive certainty" as a prerequisite to action.

Economic action is to be given precedence, but as soon as fundamental economic needs are sufficiently provided for, increased political activity is to follow, and for the first time is expected to give big results, even to the point when "collective constructive effort will revolutionize the organization of society." "Changes in standards of living, conditions of work, and the freeing of individual will from repression will result in freeing spiritual forces that through collective constructive effort will revolutionize the organization of society. *Until* these radical fundamental changes are brought about, superficial changes coming through legislation would be without avail." [2]

In accordance with this political philosophy and policy organized labor's *first* demand on entering seriously into political life on a nation-wide scale was not so much for progressive social legislation as for such defensive legislation as might strengthen economic organizations:

[1] From *Convention Proceedings, 1910,* pp. 16, 103. Also *Forty Years of Action,* 1920.
[2] *American Federationist,* August, 1918.

LABOR AND POLITICS

One great advantage of the (political) policy the A. F. of L. has pursued is that it has in no way hampered or detracted from the economic power or effectiveness of the trade unions. Nonpartisan political activity does not subordinate the economic interests of the trade unionists to partisan interests, but our political policy has made our economic influence, our economic needs, our economic welfare of paramount importance. The paramount issue of our political campaign was the enactment into law of legislation that would assure the legal right to organize and secure for labor organizations the legal right to perform those activities necessary to carry out the purposes of the economic organizations.[1]

Labor enters into politics first of all to defend and strengthen its economic organizations, but from the moment it seeks this or any other political object it is confronted with the problem of securing outside political support. Anxious not to subordinate the economic movement to any extraneous political object, nevertheless it must at once proceed to add to its purely defensive political program in order to get political support. The precise nature of this broader program and of the inner struggle going on around it—not only between factions of the labor movement, but also within the minds of individual leaders, began to appear in the 1908 convention.

After stating that labor had been compelled to enter into the political arena in order "to acquire for our economic movement its freest and fullest development" the convention declared that it could not "obtain legislative enactment to protect the rights and interests of the organization, but it must equally include all our people,"

[1] *American Federationist,* February, 1917.

and that on this ground, the protection of the economic rights of labor organizations *ought* to appeal to the entire mass of the voters.

Defending the economic power of the unions as being desirable from the standpoint of society, the Federation contended that,

The trade-union movement, true to its history, its traditions, and aspirations, has done, is doing, and will undoubtedly do more in the interest of mankind to humanize the human family than all other agencies combined. Devoting primarily our efforts to the membership of our organizations, yet there is not a declaration which we can make, or an action we can take for their protection and their advancement, but which will have its correspondingly beneficent influence upon the unorganized workers and upon the masses of the people.

The possession of great economic power does not imply its abuse, but rather its right use. Consciousness and possession of economic power bring with them responsibility, wisdom, and care in its exercise. These have made the labor movement of our country a tower of strength inspiring the confidence and respect of the masses of our workers, as well as the sympathetic support of students, thinkers, and all liberty-loving people.

The Federation took the stand that there is no limit to what can be obtained by labor through pure economic action (aided only by these purely defensive politics), except the physical limit of what industry can produce. Provided only that the labor unions' rights are in full play, it reasoned, they will be possessed "of economic power the limits of which have never yet been reached nor with certainty foreseen by any authority however prescient."

This is doubtless true, but how were economic rights

33

to be made secure? How were the labor unions to win public sympathy in their struggle to increase their economic power unless they supported general democratic and progressive measures just as they asked support for their own? Gompers mentioned that, as late as 1908, what organized labor was asking of Congress was "amendments to the Sherman anti-trust law excluding wage-earners and farmers from its purview," anti-injunction, employer's liability, and eight-hour statutes—a program primarily of interest to labor, with one measure only that appealed strongly to farmers and none directed especially to the urban middle class.[1]

Although the Federation of Labor had been "in politics" from the day of its foundation in 1881, its political activity for twenty years was largely intermittent and confined to local elections. The Federation was too weak numerically during the first two decades of its history to hope to have any considerable influence in national elections.

In the early years of the twentieth century, when the organization was growing rapidly in numbers and in economic strength, it began to resent the failure of the dominant parties to give it political consideration corresponding to its new development.

When nation-wide political action was first put into the foreground, through the presentation to Congress of the "Bill of Grievances" of 1906, the political situation of preceding years was passed in review and a new standard was set for labor's demands. That standard is of the utmost significance. For labor gave warning at that early day that it would no longer be satisfied with a

[1] *Seventy Years of Life and Labor,* p. 258.

34

treatment at the hands of Congress less favorable than
had been given to our most powerful business interests:

We are not unmindful of the fact (the unions declared)
that laws in the interest of labor have been enacted, but these
have been fragmentary in character and of insufficient importance. When we contemplate the alacrity with which our
Congresses respond to the demands of special interests, by
the prompt granting of charters, franchises, immunities,
special privileges, and special and class legislation, that are
winged into enactment by legislative flights, while any measure in the interests of the toiling masses progresses as if
with a leaden heel; that particularly in recent years slower
progress has been made than heretofore; that the toilers'
appeals and petitions are treated with indifference and contempt, it is not surprising that the men of labor throughout
our country have become impatient and have manifested that
impatience.[1]

This statement, which was signed by one hundred and
seventeen presidents or leading representatives of national
and international unions, took a political stand considerably more advanced than that of any previous labor
declaration. In 1898 the Federation convention had declared for "the independent use of the ballot of trade-
unionists and workmen regardless of party," as well as
"the election of men from our own ranks to make new
laws and administer them along the lines laid down in
the legislative demands of the Federation and to secure
an impartial judiciary." But the 1906 Bill of Grievances
confessed that with the political method, or lack of
method, that had been in use, since 1898, leaving actual
political campaigns almost wholly to local labor bodies,
labor had failed to carry out this program:

[1] From *American Federation of Labor Convention, 1906.*

35

LABOR AND POLITICS

At times we met with partial success, yet within the past few years claims and promises made in platforms or in the hustings by political parties and politicians, and especially by the present dominant party, have been neither justified nor performed. Little attention has been paid to the enactment of laws prepared by us and presented to Congress.

Several Presidents of the United States have, in their messages to Congress, urged the passage of equitable legislation in behalf of the working people, but Congress has been entirely preoccupied looking after the interests of vast corporations and predatory wealth.[1]

What the Bill of Grievances now proposed was a nation-wide effort on the part of labor systematically to "reward friends and punish enemies." The first step in this effort was to be to present labor's grievances to Congress and to ask Congress for action, and then, if satisfaction was not obtained, to enter into the political campaign on a national scale to oppose certain Congressmen and support others—"to reward friends and punish enemies." These steps were carried out as planned, but they resulted in little more than scattered attempts "in widely separated localities to defeat conspicuous enemies of labor." [2]

The convention of 1908 reported that the new plan of campaign had as yet brought no immediate legislative results, Congress continuing deaf to labor's appeals. Now Congress was at that time in control of one of the great political parties (the Republicans), to which the overwhelming majority of labor's opponents belonged. The inevitable result was that labor's campaign aided the opposition party—the Democrats. The 1908 convention

[1] *Seventy Years of Life and Labor*, Vol. II, p. 258.
[2] *Ibid.*, p. 266.

approved Gompers's review of the political situation indorsing—for that year only—the Democratic candidate for President and the Democratic platform, while continuing to apply the usual labor tests in a non-partisan manner to Democratic as well as Republican candidates for Congress. As the same labor procedure was followed in later Presidential campaigns I shall reproduce Gompers's report at some length:

With members of the Executive Council [reported Gompers] our legislative committee appeared before the Congressional committees to argue our cause and present our claims, but all to no avail.

The leaders of the minority party in Congress [the Democrats] declared their willingness and their purpose unitedly to aid the majority or any part of the majority to enact the legislation which labor asked; but the members of the dominant party in Congress [the Republicans] had set their hearts like flint; they had no ears to hear, no patience to heed any claim, argument, or appeal involving the principles of equal rights to equality before the law, or of the liberty of the workers, on a par with other citizens of our country.

As already stated, we presented identical demands to the Republican and the Democratic party conventions. In the one instance, that of the Republican convention, the declarations adopted were for the enactment of a law that would legalize the worst abuse and perversion of the injunction writ, this in direct opposition to what we had asked. *The Democratic party, in convention at Denver, adopted labor's demands and incorporated them in its party platform.*

In view of the specific declarations of the men of labor throughout our country for many years, the repeated declarations and instructions of the American Federation of Labor at many of its conventions, some of which I have quoted, it devolves upon you, the duly constituted representatives of the men of labor of our country, you who come here and have been in immediate touch with the toilers of

America, it is for you to say whether the course pursued, to stand faithfully by our friends and elect them, oppose our enemies and defeat them, whether they be candidates for President, for Congress, or other offices, is justified, and meets with your approval, or your condemnation.[1]

Labor acted in accordance with these principles and tactics in the ensuing Presidential election. And when the election results were declared, it felt that it had been justified. But labor's successes in this first nation-wide Presidential campaign were not numerous—and labor's opponents could claim plausibly that its campaign had failed. The truth seemed to be that the Congressional campaign had been naturally overshadowed by the Presidential election.

It has been labor's attempts to apply its non-partisan policy to Presidential elections that have obscured the true character of that policy from the public. For either the policy is inapplicable to Presidential elections or it is applied to them only with great difficulty. If used in a Presidential election the policy involves the indorsement of the head of a party and of his platform and that indorsement cannot be proven to be non-partisan by the indorsement of the candidate and platform of another party for at least four years. In the meanwhile it is difficult to convince the public—including even many labor voters—that the policy has been truly non-partisan (see Chapters VI to VIII).

President Gompers and the American Federation of Labor—especially before Gompers's death—held that the non-partisan method was applicable to Presidential elections—but they admitted that it was applicable only with

[1] From Annual Report to A. F. of L. Convention, November, 1908.

38

great difficulty. Gompers, in his autobiography and in most of his public expressions was perpetually on the defensive, explaining that, in favoring the Democratic candidate and platform in each Presidential election from 1908 to 1920 and La Follette and his platform in 1924, there had been no violation of the non-partisan principle, but merely a temporary choice forced upon labor. Sometimes this policy was frankly referred to as nothing else than a choice between evils, but not always, for it is scarcely an effective way to work for a candidate, once he is preferred, to speak of him as the lesser evil.

Gompers could certainly make good his claim that he had refused to let the labor movement be annexed by a political party.[1] But as each Presidential campaign came along, especially after 1908, he and the Federation *appeared* to be acting as political partisans. That Gompers was not a political partisan was shown not only by his support of Republican Congressional candidates even during Presidential elections, but by his many complimentary references to Roosevelt, his strong attacks on Bryan, and his frequent and sweeping condemnations of the Democratic as well as the Republican party. As he says in his autobiography:

In the first four years of my citizenship I was a member of the Republican party. For years after in Presidential elections I cast a protesting vote. I believed that the Republican party had fulfilled its mission, growing out of the Civil War, and so far as the Democratic party was concerned, *it had no concept of the political and industrial problems of the times.*"[2]

[1] *Seventy Years of Life and Labor,* Vol. II, p. 88.
[2] *Ibid.,* p. 76.

Gompers did not dodge the fact, more than ever evident to-day, that political support of labor's policies had come largely from one party. But he answered that the fact "that in recent years more Democratic candidates have been favorably disposed toward the cause of labor and freedom than have Republicans" was neither his fault nor the fault of his associates.

Gompers pointed to "absolute impartiality" in his support of Senators and Representatives, in the election of whom, as he admitted, "there is better opportunity to exercise the non-partisan policy"[1]—the clear inference being that labor's impartiality has not been and could not be absolute in Presidential elections. Gompers saw clearly that during Presidential years—though just as many Congressmen are voted for then as during the intervening and exclusively Congressional elections—public interest is "focused upon the election of President, though the making of legislative decisions depends primarily upon the election of members of Congress." [2]

The Federation has repeatedly made the same distinction. For example, we read in an official pamphlet entitled "Legislative Achievements" that it is evident that "labor's non-partisan political policy *insofar as Congressional elections are concerned,* thoroughly justifies the assertion that labor has achieved signal legislative successes since 1906."

A difficulty in electing Congressmen without regard to party arose from "the firmly rooted two-party system with no traditions of independent voting" and the fact

[1] *Seventy Years of Life and Labor,* Vol. II, p. 77.
[2] *Ibid.,* p. 267.

that party organization "had jealously guarded against any tendency to non-partisanism." [1] But this difficulty was incomparably less than that which met labor in the Presidential elections—and, with the co-operation of other progressive elements, it was rapidly overcome in large sections of the country, especially where the progressives were able to introduce the system of primary elections (see Chapters V and VI).

Labor indorsed Presidential candidates and platforms in 1916, 1920, and 1924, as well as Congressional candidates in those and the intervening even years. But after 1910 there was a steadily increasing emphasis on Congressional candidates both in primaries and in elections. For example, Gompers confesses that he felt "very much disheartened at the outcome of the political conventions in the summer of 1912," [2] but notes that there was "intensive labor activity in the Congressional elections." [3]

The Congressional elections of 1910 gave the first test of labor's non-partisan political policy freed from a disturbing and overshadowing Presidential election. Labor was at once able to make a strong and plausible claim to political victories. And certainly many of its "enemies" were defeated and many of its "friends" were elected, though the Roosevelt progressive movement, which developed into the Progressive party in 1912 and was then at its height, was generally given the entire credit for the political overturn. Undoubtedly it was due in part to labor. Whatever may have been the precise weight of the labor vote in the 1910 election, it must have had

[1] *Seventy Years of Life and Labor,* Vol. II, p. 267.
[2] *Ibid.,* p. 282.
[3] *Ibid.,* p. 291.

a large influence. Here, at least, are the claims made at the Federation's convention in November of that year:

> We have curbed the sordid, self-seeking agents of predatory interests—now somewhat softened by the new title of "big business." We have seen Mr. Cannon, the most potent evil influence against the people's rights and interests, stripped of his autocratic, arbitrary power as Speaker of the House of Representatives. We have seen the Rules Committee of the House restricted and reformed so that it shall respond to the will of the majority rather than be the pliant tool of "the interests" under domination of Speaker Cannon or any future Speaker of a like caliber and make-up.
>
> A great majority of the public news venders have conspired to keep silent on our extraordinary political successes in California, Washington, Oregon, Kansas, Iowa, Minnesota, Wisconsin, New York, Maine, and elsewhere throughout the country. They ascribe a thousand and one fictitious reasons for the uprising of the people. Anything and everything in their eyes has been responsible except the one real cause.
>
> The wholesale overthrow of the legislative and political jugglers with the people's rights and interests can unerringly be traced to organized labor's appeals to the people to defend their common interests and precious rights.

From the point of view of history the great result of this campaign for labor was that *it encouraged political action*. Rightly or wrongly, as the statement just cited shows, labor had become confident of its political power.

CHAPTER II

POLITICAL RESULTS—THE FIRST CROP

The Clayton Anti-Trust Amendment—Woodrow Wilson and Labor—Reaction following the World War—The Non-Partisan Political Policy Reaffirmed.

UNTIL 1912, as Gompers admitted, labor's non-partisan policy had not yet elected enough friendly Congressmen "to put constructive legislation on the statute books." Measures hostile to labor had been defeated since 1908, but that was all that had been accomplished. The situation had become so desperate that, although all members of the Executive Council of the Federation were believers in the non-partisan policy, several of them felt that some new political method would have to be tried unless labor could show some positive legislative achievements as a result of the 1912 election.[1]

It proved not to be necessary to wait for the election. Labor and its progressive allies were so successful in the primaries (this was the year of the founding of the Roosevelt Progressive party) that an immediate effect was produced on the Congress already in session—and, of course, that effect was still more marked after the election.

By the end of 1912 labor not only had secured important political victories, but could say that, "as a result of

[1] *Seventy Years of Life and Labor,* Vol. II, p. 275.

43

the recent awakening of the workers of the United States, this growing realization of their political power and influence, more progress in remedial, constructive legislation has been made this year than in the decade previous." [1]

There can be little doubt that a part of the legislation secured from the Congress elected in 1912 was, indeed, wrung from labor's opponents by the sheer exercise of its political power. The most important achievement of this character was the Clayton Act (passed in 1914) declaring that the labor of the human being is not a commodity or an article of commerce, and so, apparently, removing the foundation of most of the judicial decisions hostile to labor organization. The strength of labor's feeling about this law cannot be overstated. President Gompers declared that it was "the most far-reaching declaration ever made by any government in the history of the world."

The American Federation of Labor won a remarkable victory (the Clayton Act) during the past year. It has brought to a successful culmination the political campaign inaugurated in 1906. The purpose of that campaign was to establish industrial freedom for the working people that they might have the right to organize and the right to activities necessary to make organization effective in human welfare. The law that accords the workers of America these rights contains the most fundamental, the most comprehensive, enunciation of freedom found in any legislative act in the history of the world. The workers of our land were able to secure that law because they represented an organized economic power [see p. 45].[2]

Not satisfied with mere assertions that the Clayton law was the most comprehensive, fundamental, and far-reach-

[1] From *American Federation of Labor Convention, 1912*, p. 13.
[2] American Federation of Labor Convention, 1914.

ing legislative or governmental act in the history of the world, organized labor explained at great length the precise grounds for this feeling. If no legal obstacles could be put in the way of labor organization, it believed there was no limit whatever to the expansion of the labor unions and similar economic organizations, and industrial democracy was assured. A speech of Gompers, indorsed by the Executive Council, after stating that the Federation was not non-political, proceeded as follows:

We have changed the control of our government from the old-time interests of corporate power and judicial usurpation. We have secured from the government of the U. S. the labor provision of the Clayton Anti-Trust law, the declaration in the law that the labor of a human being is not a commodity or article of commerce. In that law we have secured the right of our men to exercise functions for which, under the old régime our men were brought before the bar of justice and fined or imprisoned. We have secured the eight-hour work day not only as a basic principle, but as a fact. We have secured the seamen's law, giving to the seamen the freedom to leave their vessels when in safe harbor. The seamen of America are now free men and own themselves. We have secured a child-labor law, and although it has been declared unconstitutional, we are again at work to secure a law for the protection of our children.[1]

Labor's logic with regard to the Clayton Act and other legislation passed at this time was irrefutable. But it was shouting before it had got out of the woods. Little remains to-day of the supposedly friendly features of the Clayton Act (see Chapter III) and nothing of the federal child-labor law. This is not a reflection on the efficiency of labor's non-partisan political policy, for a large part of

[1] December 9, 1918.

the legislative achievements of this period (1912-20) has proven to be permanent. But the ultra-optimism that prevailed at the end of this period was later understood by labor itself not to have been justified. Such excessive optimism had led, finally, to an interpretation of the non-partisan policy and to an anti-political emphasis (further defensive politics being regarded as less necessary after the Clayton Act) that had later to be abandoned.

In 1916, however, the effects of the 1906 political policy were reaching their climax and the convention of that year claimed that "as a result of labor's non-partisan political activities a tremendous change has been wrought in the policies and in the spirit of those who make up the administrative and legislative divisions of the federal government."[1]

One of the most important results achieved had been to win the adhesion of the Democratic party to the Clayton Act. Not only had that Act been passed by the Democrats, but they were willing to make it one of the main issues of the 1916 campaign. This Democratic action was fully reported in the Federation convention of that year:

Labor's demands were presented to the Democratic party, which placed in its platform the following labor plank:
"We have lifted human labor from the category of commodities, and have secured to the workingman the right of voluntary association for his protection and welfare. We have protected the rights of the laborer against the unwarranted issuance of writs of injunction, and have guaranteed to him the right of trial by jury in cases of alleged contempt committed outside the presence of the court."[2]

[1] From *American Federation of Labor Convention, 1914*, p. 329.
[2] Gompers's Speech at New Haven, April 15, 1922.

POLITICAL RESULTS—FIRST CROP

Reviewing labor's political activities during President Wilson's administrations (1912-20), Gompers was able to make a plausible claim that there had been a very large measure of political co-operation between labor and the government: "Organized labor had a large part in the election of Woodrow Wilson to the Presidency. During his administration laws beneficial to everyone who toils were passed. This was not due to any 'pull,' but solely because Mr. Wilson had a real insight into the needs of the people."

In his autobiography Gompers remarks that the Administration (President Wilson) had recognized after the election of 1912 that "labor had been an effective agency in taking the political control out of the hands of the reactionaries." [1] All this is, undoubtedly, true, but it is equally true and equally important that labor had helped to nominate and elect to Congress not only progressive Democrats, but progressive Republicans of the La Follette as well as the Roosevelt group. This, according to labor's own position, was the main fact, and not the friendliness to labor either of President Wilson or of the Democratic party, valuable as these friendships may have been. Furthermore, President Wilson had stood against two of the most important labor measures, the Immigration Act and certain clauses of the Adamson Railway Act, and after his return to America in 1919 his public statements and administrative policies were rather hostile than friendly to labor. While the Democratic friends of labor in Congress remained friends, they were no more friendly than many Progressives and Republicans, and Democratic enemies remained numerous. In other words, labor's

[1] *Seventy Years of Life and Labor*, p. 294 ff.

achievements were not a party matter—as might have appeared from labor's relation to the Democratic party in the Presidential campaign of 1920.

During the whole of the war period—which, for practical purposes, extended from the spring of 1917 through the Armistice period until the fall of 1919—labor's political successes continued. While the Federation made no new demands during the war, it did urge and secure the concession that labor standards already widely accepted by many private employers should be adopted for the government's millions of war-time employees and that the Administration during the war should continue the friendly policy it had followed from 1913 to 1917. Labor secured full and equal representation in all the war boards fixing wages and labor conditions, such as the War Labor Board, the Shipping Board, and the Railroad Administration, and was represented in the Committee on the Taxation of War Profits, in the important Food Administration, in the Housing Bureau, on the War Industries Board, as well as other governmental war organizations.

By the fall of 1919, with the repeal of war legislation and the ending of war regulations by administrative edict, this period of labor's political history came suddenly to an end. Not only had the opposition party (the Republicans), which had opposed most of labor's contentions, become more powerful, but the national Administration had also turned against labor in the coal strike and many other instances and it was badly defeated in the Presidential campaign of 1920. But the impetus labor had gained from the political successes of a decade were not to be obliterated by the failures of a single year. Naturally, the hope and expectation remained that these successes might be repeated. Naturally, the tendency was to attribute the new setback to temporary causes, to the aftermath of the war, to the extraordinary economic depression, and to the absorption of the workmen of foreign birth and parentage (a majority of America's wage-earners) in the affairs of Europe rather than those of the United States.

As President Gompers said to me two years later:

In the convention of the American Federation of Labor in 1921 the dominating question was still the Irish question; everything was decided with reference to that. In 1922 there was no resolution on the Irish question, not one word was said about it during the entire convention. We ought to be interested in foreign questions, we are not so far from Europe as we were, but we have first the American problem to consider.[1]

That the check of 1920 was due largely to these undoubtedly temporary influences is not to be questioned. But it is also true that the opposition to labor had studied the non-partisan or bi-partisan method by which labor had secured its victories and was by this time using this method successfully. And once the anti-labor forces had secured the ascendancy, they began taking strong measures to prevent a recurrence of the labor victories of 1908 to 1916.

The 1919 convention of the Federation, held for the first time in June instead of November, was still in an optimistic frame of mind, as we may see from the following declaration—which was republished by the Federation on the cover of one of its pamphlets during the ensuing Presidential campaign of 1920:

The experiences and results attained through the non-

[1] Washington, August 3, 1922.

partisan political policy of the American Federation of Labor cover a generation. They indicate that through its application the workers of America have secured a much larger measure of fundamental legislation establishing their rights, safeguarding their interests, protecting their welfare, and opening the doors of opportunity, than have been secured by the workers of any other country.

What was the justification of this claim? We have already noted that labor's legislative achievements were considerable. But the above is strong language. Let us examine the record. Ignoring, for the moment, the new hostile legislation and hostile court decisions of this period, what results could be claimed by American labor for the era of its greatest political successes, 1912-20? In a pamphlet entitled, "Legislative Achievements," the Federation sums them up. Some of the most important enactments there referred to, such as the parcels post and postal savings bank, do not *especially* or *mainly* concern wage-earners, however greatly they may benefit them. The question arises as to the relative influence of organized labor in getting such measures passed. Among labor's achievements, besides the postal savings-bank law, are listed direct election of Senators, the parcel-post law, the Industrial Education Act, the Immigration Exclusion Act, and even the farm-loan law. The answer is that labor has every justification for mentioning these great measures, having played a prominent and, no doubt, an indispensable part in securing their enactment. But they cannot in any correct sense be called labor measures, nor does labor so term them.

Other measures listed concern labor primarily, and for the most part were passed through labor's political influence. The most important of these were the establishment of the right of organization for post-office employees, of the eight-hour law for public contracts and of the department of labor, the appointment of a labor-unionist as Secretary of Labor, and the enactment of the seamen's law, the Adamson eight-hour law for the railroads, and the Clayton Act.

To judge the value of this political achievement from labor's standpoint we should have to compare it with labor's entire political program, so that we might take note of the measures which labor failed to get enacted. As I have pointed out, President Gompers was able to state that practically the entire Bill of Grievances (of 1906) had been made into law; that is, that only one of this group of labor measures had failed.

Just before America's entry into the European War the *American Federationist* printed a summary of labor's political successes, which had culminated in the passage of the Immigration Act by Congress over the veto of President Wilson:

Without forming a political party, without forming any new organizations, without additional expenditures of trade-union funds, all except one of the demands contained in the Bill of Grievances (of 1906) have become the law of the land. The passage of the Immigration law, the last demand removed from the list, illustrates the distinctive political power which organized labor has developed since 1906. The proposal to restrict immigration was not a partisan measure.[1]

"By 1917," the Federation declared, "practically every demand set out in the petition to Congress in the Bill of

[1] *American Federationist,* March, 1917.

51

Grievances submitted in 1906 had been enacted into law. The one exception was the proposed statute to enable states to protect themselves from the competition of the products of convict labor of other states." [1]

Organized labor's leading opponents do not deny it the credit for important legislative accomplishment. For example, the *Chicago Tribune* concedes editorially that "without making the mistake of turning into a political body for political purposes, the Federation has been able to procure legislation much of which has been beneficial to labor and to the country." [1]

As the larger part of labor's legislative achievements were crowded into five years and represent the result approximately of only ten years of political activity, few persons would deny their significance, especially as the situation stood in 1920. The questions that arose were: First, were these results, obtained by the political tactics followed up to 1920, permanent? Second, did this political policy permit the development, along with progressive legislation, of a reactionary movement equally or more powerful—or at least powerful enough to counterbalance in large part the gains achieved? Third, if the gains made were largely permanent, and if the reaction proved to be temporary, could the *rate* of progress of 1912 to 1920 be continued—and could it be continued without a further development of new political method?

[1] October 7, 1925.

CHAPTER III

LABOR TURNS FROM PARTIES TO THE PUBLIC

The Presidential Campaign of 1920—Harding's Election—Principles Versus Parties—Measures Indorsed by Labor—Labor Disappointed in Election.

THE election of 1920 marked a serious setback to labor's efforts to secure legislation and to influence administration. There was no tendency in labor ranks to deny the victory of the anti-labor forces in that election; though there was a general agreement that labor's partial defeat in the final election was largely offset by the brilliant results obtained from the Federation's concentration on the primaries.[1]

It was claimed that Senator Cummins, who was chiefly responsible for the present railroad law (the Cummins-Esch Act), was almost defeated in the primaries by labor's vote; that labor nearly defeated the Senate leader of the opposite party, Senator Underwood, in Alabama, and helped to defeat Senator Hoke Smith of Georgia; that labor, together with radical farmer elements, had captured the Democratic party organization in Montana and Colorado and claimed the credit for defeating Senator

[1] The Executive and department heads had issued a special statement on February 12, 1920, declaring "this political campaign must begin in the primaries."

53

Thomas in the latter state, ex-Senator Bailey in Texas and Senator Gore in Oklahoma, as well as a number of Congressmen in Pennsylvania and other states.[1]

However, some of these victories in the primaries were of a merely negative value, insofar as labor candidates were defeated in the final election in November. The final result was that labor eliminated a number of its worst enemies, but elected few of its friends. Certainly the political machinery devised in 1906 and responsible for very considerable legislative achievements from 1912 to 1920 was far from having become useless or from being out of commission. But it was no longer carrying labor forward. President Gompers admitted that not more than fifty Representatives out of four hundred and thirty-five could be relied upon as friends of labor.

In the campaign of 1920 the labor organizations, both the Federation of Labor and the railway brotherhoods, had continued the non-partisan plan adopted in 1906. In so far as candidates for Congress and the Senate were up for re-election, labor-unionists were advised to support or oppose them according to their records in Congress. A careful tabulation had been kept by the Federation of Congressional voting on all measures of special interest to labor, and this record was sent to all the forty thousand local organizations which compose that body. The railway brotherhoods and also, to some extent, those unions of the Federation associated with the brotherhoods in its Railroad Department, adopted a simple plan, gauging the candidates mainly by their votes for or against the Cummins-Esch Railroad Act. Under this plan the overwhelming majority of the candidates supported were

[1] *American Federationist,* October, 1920.

Democrats and the overwhelming majority of those opposed were Republicans. But exceptions were numerous enough to preserve the non-partisan character of the labor campaign—as far as Congressional candidates were concerned.

During Presidential campaigns, as I have pointed out, the contest for the Presidency overshadows all other contests, and for this office labor had either to remain neutral or indorse the Republican or Democratic candidates. There was no middle ground as in the Congressional elections, when candidates could be supported from both parties. In 1920 the railroad organizations mildly indorsed the Democratic candidate for President. The American Federation of Labor came out more and more definitely as the election approached and finally advocated the Democratic candidate in as strong terms as could be conceived.

A third element of the situation was the national platforms of the two parties adopted by the conventions that nominated the Presidential candidates. The railroad brotherhoods and the Federation agreed in violently rejecting the Republican platform, as it not only opposed or ignored labor measures, but strongly indorsed the Cummins-Esch Railroad Act. The brotherhoods and the Federation agreed also in a mild indorsement of the Democratic platform, not at all as being satisfactory, but as representing a somewhat friendly attitude to labor and as being distinctly preferable to the Republican.

This is a summary of labor's position in the campaign of 1920. Did it not amount practically to a partisan indorsement of the Democrats? And if it did, was this not a violation of a non-partisan principle? To answer the

55

question intelligently we must first take into account the fact that labor's policy is in reality intended not to be non-partisan in the strict sense of the term, but rather to be bi-partisan (or even multi-partisan). This policy was most clearly stated by the 1919 convention when it declared: "Labor must learn to use parties to advance principles, and not allow political parties to manipulate us for their own advancement." [1] In other words, the temporary indorsement of one or another party, whether wise or not, was no violation of labor's so-called non-partisan policy—as then formulated.

The intention not merely to support friendly candidates, but, under certain circumstances, temporarily to support a friendly party, had been definitely expressed, years before, as follows:

> While no member of Congress or party can evade or avoid his or their own individual or party share of responsibility, we aver that the party in power must and will by labor and its sympathizers be held primarily responsible.
>
> If these, or new questions, are unsettled, and any other political party becomes responsible for legislation, we shall press home upon its representatives and hold them responsible, equally as we now must hold you.[2]

There is here no demand for a share in party power, party responsibility, or party spoils, but only a temporary indorsement, the chief weakness of the policy being, as is here admitted, that it is likely to lean always to the party that happens to be in opposition (see Chapter VIII).

Labor's attempt to measure the relative merits of the two leading political parties according to labor principles

[1] From *American Federation of Labor Convention, 1919*, pp. 32, 316.
[2] Special Conference of March 18, 1908.

(scarcely to be avoided in a Presidential election) is more clearly seen in its attitude to the two party platforms than in its support of or opposition to their Presidential candidates. The plan adopted by the Montreal convention (1920) for testing the platforms was this: from the many political measures and principles indorsed by labor some fourteen were chosen to be presented to the 1920 conventions of the leading two political parties. The number of labor's demands was cut down to this small number in order to secure the maximum labor support, labor indorsement of these fourteen measures being practically unanimous. The labor demands presented to the two conventions, briefly stated, were:

(1) The right of labor to organize to select its own representatives and to bargain collectively.

(2) An anti-injunction plank guaranteeing the right of trial by jury in contempt cases—a federal law to be enacted.

(3) No compulsory arbitration; the right of organization and political rights to be guaranteed to government employees.

(4) Freedom of speech, press, and assembly.

(5) The Seamen's Act to be vigorously enforced and liberally interpreted.

(6) No child labor under the age of sixteen.

(7) As remedies against the high cost of living (a) the legislative encouragement of co-operation, (b) the monthly issuance by the Department of Labor of statements of the cost of manufacturing staple articles, (c) the investigation of profits and prices; the income and other tax returns to be made available for inspection.

(8) The restriction of immigration.

(9) Enforcement of the federal eight-hour laws.

(10) A more comprehensive federal law for compensation accidents.

(11) The exclusion of products of convict labor from interstate commerce.

(12) The repeal of the Cummins-Esch Railroad Act.

(13) Federal courts to be forbidden by Congress to pass on the constitutionality of legislation and to be elected instead of being appointed as at present.

(14) Opposition to United States intervention in Mexico.

Only a few of these planks are of special interest to the non-labor public, and only a minority are of the first importance to labor. With important exceptions—such as the proposed measures against the high cost of living— they demand no new advance, but seek only to make secure the advances won during the previous decade. *The practical effect of this program was not so much to show whether either of the parties was progressive as to show whether either or both of them was reactionary from the labor standpoint.*

The natural result of this kind of a test was that both parties were able to give favorable answers to some of the demands, and were either ambiguous or silent as to others. Though there was sufficient divergence between the answers of the two party platforms to justify labor in favoring one as against the other, there was no such difference as could enable labor leaders to rally the overwhelming majority of the labor vote to either side—or to form a broad common platform with a strong appeal to the rest of the progressive public.

The Republican platform satisfied labor's demands completely only in regard to free speech and convict labor. On the subjects of the rights of public employees, the Cummins-Esch Railroad Act, and Mexico, it took a stand diametrically opposed to labor's demands.

58

The Democratic platform, while failing to indorse labor's demands as to convict labor, accepted the other measure indorsed by the Republicans, and in addition met labor's views as to the right of collective bargaining through representatives of labor's own choosing, and as to the Seamen's Act, the eight-hour law on federal contracts, and the federal employees' compensation law. On the matters of compulsory arbitration, injunctions, and the Cummins-Esch law, the Democratic and Republican platforms were both ambiguous.

Neither Republican nor Democratic platform responded to labor's demands as to immigration, the federal courts, or publicity for profits and costs of production.

There can be no difference of opinion as to this presentation of the result of labor's questionnaire to the two conventions. The response of the Democratic party was distinctly more friendly, or rather, less hostile and indifferent to labor than that of the Republicans. But the Democrats were very far from meeting labor's demands, even though they had been cut down to the very minimum, and the results of this branch of labor's campaign could scarcely be regarded as satisfactory.

The Federation also sought to compare the records of the two leading candidates, Harding and Cox, as a method of deciding which candidate labor should support. Harding, when a United States Senator, had voted for the obnoxious Cummins-Esch bill, though there were few other important measures by means of which to gauge his position on labor questions. But we must not forget that many Democrats had also voted for the Cummins-Esch Act and that President Wilson had signed it.

Cox, as Governor of Ohio, has done important service to labor on several occasions, though the issues arising in that state could not be compared in importance, from the labor standpoint, with the issues that Harding had to vote on in the United States Senate. The result of the test was clearly favorable to the Democratic candidate, but not sufficiently convincing to impress the voter with trade-union affiliations or sympathies very deeply.

The point is not that labor made any mistake in discriminating between the two parties, but that the record of the Democrats was not so different from that of the Republicans as to make possible such a sharp discrimination as would appeal to the great mass of labor voters, to say nothing of non-labor progressives in the Democratic and Republican ranks.

Labor conducted its political agitation during the closing weeks of the campaign in such a way as to create the impression with a large part of the public that it had merged itself in the Democratic party. This impression could not have been justified by any close study of labor's campaign. But that campaign was so shaped that it tended to appear as partisan to the average newspaper reader. Harding was represented in the official publications of the Federation as nothing more nor less than reactionary, Cox as nothing more nor less than progressive.[1] Whatever truth there may have been in this contrast, it is certain that the Democratic campaign was not conducted entirely along the lines of militant progressivism. One of the last statements of labor before the election referred to the "superiority on the part of the Democratic platform." A more correct statement,

[1] *American Federationist,* September and October, 1920.

60

though hardly suitable for campaign purposes, would undoubtedly have been that the Republican platform showed
an *inferiority* from the labor standpoint.

While it is impossible to say whether, in this particular election, other tactics would have obtained widely
different results, the methods pursued were not very effective and were at least sufficiently doubtful at points
to give a foundation for labor and progressive criticism.

The results of the 1920 election, as I have said, were
disappointing to labor. It later admitted that the Congress elected in that year was the most reactionary for
decades. Nevertheless, labor's non-partisan tactics had
won a large number of victories in the primaries and not
a few in the general election. President Gompers pointed
out that fifty members of Congress whose records had
shown hostility had been defeated. The crucial weakness of labor's political position was its limited influence
over the Presidential vote. President Gompers referred
with evident dejection to the fact that it was "still possible for a candidate allied with the forces of reaction
and with the forces that are hostile to labor to secure in
a single American city (New York) a majority of one
million votes." [1]

Certainly the results of the election were sobering from
the labor standpoint, to whatever causes they might be
attributed, and they led naturally to a re-examination
by labor of its political methods, as being at least in
some part responsible. Even before the election the
convention of 1919 had rather cautiously declared that
"there is room for improvement in the efficient exercise
of the political power of the wage earners." And the

[1] From the *National Labor Digest*, December, 1920.

61

recognition of the need for improvement in political methods was hastened by anti-labor judicial decisions and legislation in various states, such as the Kansas Compulsory Arbitration Act, which immediately followed the election—these hostile actions culminating in a decision of the Supreme Court which President Gompers confessed "practically annulled the Clayton Act." [1]

In other words, labor's proudest and greatest achievement was all but wiped out and, in the vital matter of the right to strike, labor was set back almost to its position of fifteen or twenty years before. These facts were enough to compel an effort to seek new and more efficient political tactics.

Labor was by no means in despair. Its legislative strength was far from negligible, at least negatively. While numerous measures were offered in various legislatures and in Congress (during 1920, 1921, and 1922), aimed practically to destroy the labor unions, they were nearly all defeated—with the important exceptions of the compulsory arbitration acts of Kansas, Colorado, and hostile statutes in a few other states. The main element in labor's political psychology after the campaign, however, was this, that at the time of this serious political setback labor had reached its greatest numerical strength—approximately 5,000,000 members. In other words, during the election of 1920 labor was economically more powerful and had a larger numerical following than at any time in its history. So that at a time when labor might have expected most it secured least. The consequences were, first, an extreme spirit of discontent with such political results as had been obtained, and, sec-

[1] From Mr. Gompers' Speech in New Haven, Conn., April 16, 1922.

ond, an almost universal confidence that the setback was only temporary.

Labor was not discouraged; it felt that the development of political strength is a matter of gradual evolution and had just begun. As it had declared in its reconstruction program of 1919, "this phase of our movement is still in infancy. It should be continued and developed to its logical conclusion."

The political propaganda of labor during the campaign had reflected this hopeful point of view. A pronouncement of the 1901 convention was reprinted claiming that, through the trade-union movement the workingmen and workingwomen of America would be able not only to redress their wrongs, but to "strengthen their economic position until it will control the political field."

The day had come when labor felt that its huge membership gave it the absolute certainty, if not of "control of the political field," at least of a large and growing political power. The unions had come to feel confident that, as their membership grows, they will be able to command the respect of other numerically important social elements and so obtain their co-operation. This view had been expressed as early as 1898:

Our movement is of the wage-earning class, recognizing that class interests, that class advancement, that class progress is best made by working-class trade-union action. That we shall receive the co-operation of others goes without saying; but only as the trade unions grow in numbers, in power, and in intelligence.[1]

The campaign of 1920 afforded the first nation-wide instance of this broader policy of appealing politically to

[1] From 1908 Convention of American Federation of Labor.

the entire progressive public. When the policy of 1906 had first been decided upon the main idea, on the contrary, had seemed to be labor representation secured by the un-aided vote of labor-unionists; "labor's representation com-mittee" was appointed on the British Labor party model and the election of fifty-four trade-unionists to the British Parliament was specifically referred to. However, the 1906 convention called attention to "Congressional and legislative indifference and hostility not only to the exis-tence of labor, but also to the mass of our people."

"The press for a month" (the convention continued) "has been burdened with exposures of graft in high circles. The great insurance companies, the trusts, the corporations, the so-called captains of industry, have in-deed become the owners of the legislatives of our coun-try." An appeal was then made not only to labor, but to progressives generally to rally "against reaction."

Again in 1908, the Federation had issued an appeal which was by no means directed exclusively to labor, declaring that it was "the duty of trade-unionists, their friends, and sympathizers and all lovers of freedom, jus-tice, and democratic ideals and institutions, to unite in defeating those seeking public office who are indifferent or hostile to the people's interests and the aspirations of labor." [1]

But it was not until 1919 that American labor came to regard itself primarily as a part of a great democratic and social-progressive movement:

"We call upon all those who contribute service to so-ciety in any form [the unions declared in their Bill of Grievances]. There is a great community of interest

[1] From New York *Times*, Monday, February 8, 1908.

between all who serve the world. All workers, whether of the city or country, mine or factory, farm or transportation, have a common path to tread and a common goal to gain.

"The issues herein enumerated require the action of our people upon both the economic and political field. We urge that every practical action be taken by the American Federation of Labor, with the co-operation of all other organized bodies of workers, farmers, and sympathetic liberty-loving citizens of the United States, to carry into effect the principles and purposes set forth in the declarations of this conference.

"We call upon all to join us in combating the forces of autocracy, industrial and political, and in the sublime task of ridding the world of the power of those who but debase its processes and corrupt its functions.

"We speak in the name of millions who work—those who make and use tools—those who furnish the human power necessary for commerce and industry. We speak as part of the nation and of those things of which we have special knowledge. Our welfare and interest are inseparably bound up with the well-being of the nation. We are an integral part of the American people and we are organized to work out the welfare of all." [1]

The position taken in this declaration, signed by the officers of all the unions, including the railway brotherhoods, at the end of 1919, has been that of all of the more important statements since that time. It was only very partially applied in 1920, but it was put into full effect in the campaign of 1922.

[1] From *Labor, Its Grievances, Protest and Demands. Conference of over 100 executives at Washington, D. C., December 13, 1919.*

CHAPTER IV

THE FARMER-LABOR ENTENTE

The Farmers' Nonpartisan League Experiment—Nonpartisan Participation in Primaries of Both Parties—The Farmer-Labor Movement of 1920 and 1922—Agricultural and Industrial Workers' Status Similar.

ONE of the first results of the 1920 campaign was that the American Federation of Labor decided to make its non-partisan political campaign committee a permanent body, instead of having it organized anew after each campaign. This created the first efficient framework for centralized and nation-wide political effort. The successful functioning of the new political organ depends not so much upon further change in its structure as upon the provision of funds. Whenever the national unions or the majority of the rank and file feel sufficiently interested in the political situation, this organization is able at a moment's notice to increase its activities indefinitely. In the meanwhile, even with the limited funds at its disposal, it is able to maintain, for the first time in labor's history, a continuity of political activity.[1]

This permanent political organization appeared just in time to give effective aid to the new tactics of permanent political co-operation with farmers' organizations which had developed throughout the West, from Wisconsin to

[1] *American Federationist,* August, 1921.

Washington—and as far south as Oklahoma and Texas. Labor had long endeavored to find organized progressive elements to collaborate with it politically. And labor had co-operated *intermittently and locally* with farmers' organizations, but the first movement for a nation-wide lasting political entente was concentrated mainly in the West because it was in that section only that a large *organized* body of voters was found whose views on many questions closely coincided with those of labor.

The unions had tried to bring about some form of political entente with farmers and had often met with a certain success. Results had been obtained as long ago as 1904, when the Federation noted that "in Pennsylvania, Oklahoma, Indian Territory, and Texas the organized farmers, with organized wage-earners," had been "questioning conditions as to the establishment of the people's sovereignty in place of machine rule," and that this had been accomplished "without a formal alliance."

During the whole period of the Progressive party and the related progressive movement within the old parties, 1904-12, labor co-operated not only with the farmers, but with the progressives of all parties and rightly claimed a large part of the credit for progressive victories.

The first important measure which farmer-labor co-operation forced through Congress against the resistance of organized business was the amendment of the Sherman Anti-Trust Act, so that it would not apply against labor and agricultural organizations. Labor pointed out that the debates in Congress had shown that the Sherman Act had been aimed exclusively at combinations of industrial capital and that not a single Congressman had suggested that it might strike industrial and agricultural workers.

Yet the courts had interpreted it as in large measure out-lawing the collective bargaining of labor unions and farmers' co-operatives.

Here was a common cause, involving the very existence both of organized labor and of organized agriculture. Acting separately, neither could hope to amend the law— against the bitter opposition of organized business and organized industry. Acting together, they were invinci-ble, and in 1914 succeeded in enacting the amendment known as the Clayton Act (see Chapter III). This was the first important instance of nation-wide and successful farmer-labor co-operation.

Because of the confusion of this new entente with the North Dakota experiment and the National Farmers' Non-Partisan League the public long failed to grasp its true significance. Labor's political tactics were judged by the merits or demerits, successes or failures, of that or-ganization. The Non-Partisan League was devoted primarily to certain experiments in state ownership of banks, flour mills, grain elevators, etc., and is rightly judged by the success or failure of these experiments. This program was indorsed by North Dakota labor, and in part was approved by labor nationally. But these measures did not emanate from labor, and by no means accurately represent labor's political tendency. Organized labor has no more expressed a belief in the general de-sirability of *state operation* than it has in the general feasibility of *national operation* (see Volume II, Chapter IX).

There is no general belief in labor circles that the Farmers' Non-Partisan League or the North Dakota ex-periments were a failure. On the contrary, what became clear to labor was only that the majority the League had secured for its ambitious governmental experiments in North Dakota was no majority sufficiently large or permanent to justify proceeding very far. The 1922 elections indorsed the experiments by referendum (though by a small majority) while removing from office (by a similar majority) several state officials belonging to the League, who alone could be relied upon to carry out the experiments thoroughly and with enthusiasm. However, after four years of experience, an important Eastern newspaper—a relatively conservative organ—pointed to the success of the North Dakota experiments, notwithstanding all obstacles: "These experiments were pursued in the face of a ruthless warfare by business interests. They have been widely branded as failures. As a matter of fact, the State Bank, which has made $23,000,000 in farm loans, the State elevator, which earned $143,000 profit last year, and the State insurance system are all flourishing and saving the farmers' money." [1]

But these experiments were of secondary importance to labor. The important and lasting result of farmer-labor co-operation in North Dakota was that the Non-Partisan League's political *method* secured labor indorsement. This was the policy of advising the voters to concentrate their efforts in the primary *of one only* of the two leading political parties and so to capture it for the purpose of the farmers and organized labor.

Up to this time labor had usually divided its forces by encouraging its members to work in the primaries of both parties. The new plan was based on the assumption that there is little difference, or at least no fundamental dif-

[1] New York *World*, July 2, 1926.

ference, between the two great parties nationally. The main consideration in choosing which party to operate within is the strength of that party in each state. Naturally in any states which are overwhelmingly Democratic or Republican the plan called for concentration of progressive and farmer-labor voters within the primaries of the party that was bound to win the election. But where the two parties were equally balanced the plan could take into account any differences which might exist in the degree of progressivism. Following this plan, the Non-Partisan League, which was confined practically to the Northwest, operated in most instances within the Republican party.

Utilizing the same principle, organized labor, in co-operation with progressive farmers, gained possession of the Democratic political organization in Montana and Colorado, defeating the regular Democratic "machine" candidate for the United States Senate in both states. The farmer organization with which labor co-operated in Montana was the Non-Partisan League; but the railroad brotherhoods were given the Congressional nomination in both of the state's two Congressional districts.

In Minnesota labor organized a Workers' Non-Partisan League to co-operate with the Farmers' Non-Partisan League. In that state, as in the state of Washington, the farmer-labor entente was forced to put up an independent or third party ticket—and, as a result, the Democratic party secured a smaller vote than the progressive combination—which in Minnesota failed only by a narrow margin of electing the Governor and did elect a large part of the Congressional delegation, including (at one time) both Senators.

THE FARMER-LABOR ENTENTE

In view of such results, obtained at the first trial of this new experiment, it can be truly said that in 1920 labor—co-operating with farm organization in every instance, and some cases, as in Minnesota, Washington, Montana, and Colorado having a practically equal voice— won a great victory throughout the entire Northwest.

In Nebraska the Farmers' Non-Partisan League had begun to operate only in the election of 1920. By 1922 a special organization had been formed—not by the League itself, but by a group of progressive farmers' organizations and organized labor—to put a ticket in the field for the fall election. The candidate nominated for Governor had already secured 20 per cent of the vote cast in the 1920 election. The program of this organization demanded among other things "credits to be taken over by the government, government ownership of railroads, taking over the Federal Reserve banking system, municipal ownership, and the right of collective bargaining." It also declared that *unreasonable profits should be prevented,* that the prices of farm products should not be permitted to fall below cost of production plus a reasonable profit, or wages below American standards of labor. Specifying more definitely its railroad policy, it demanded that the roads be operated by governmental agencies at cost. This progressive group supported and helped to elect a Republican Senator (Howell) and a Democratic Governor (Bryan).

In Oklahoma the progressive farmer-labor movement was inaugurated at a special convention early in March (1922); "there were present 752 delegates from the Farmer-Labor Reconstruction League, composed of the Oklahoma State Federation of Labor, the railroad employees' organizations, the United Mine Workers of America, Farmers Union, Farm-Labor Union, the Non-Partisan Leagues, and community clubs organized by the Reconstruction League." [1]

The most important demands made by the convention were for laws covering the marketing of farm products, dealing with the middleman and the repeal of the Cummins-Esch railroad law. The candidate for Governor made the following declaration for the establishment of home loan banks as demanded by organized labor:

"I believe that no community is so prosperous as that in which every worker owns the land he tills or the house which shelters his family.

"To this end banks should be established where state funds are on deposit to be loaned to home builders on approved security and at a rate of interest sufficient only to bear the costs of administration." [2]

The object of the Oklahoma movement was to capture the most powerful political organization in that state— the Democratic party—and it succeeded in the attempt.

In Iowa the progressive farmers and organized labor operated within the only party that had any chance of success in that state, namely the Republican party. The candidate supported in the primaries for Governor emphasized the most important three points of the farmer-labor program—control of credit, control of the middleman, and control of railroads. The farmers and organized labor, he said, should co-operate "to control the Federal Reserve bank":

[1] From *Labor,* March 11.
[2] *Ibid.,* March 18, 1922.

72

THE FARMER-LABOR ENTENTE

Primarily the farmers furnish about half of the bank deposits upon which the resources of the Federal Reserve Bank are built [he continued]. They should have half of the government board.

Labor furnished more than 25 per cent of such deposits and should likewise be represented upon the board.

The rest of the board should represent other business than banking. The great Bank of England has had no banker on its board for eighty-six years.

The use of Federal Reserve funds in speculation, extortionate discount rates, and profiteering earnings must be ended. Longer time credits must be provided to fit the needs of agriculture and the whole system must co-operate with the Federal Land banks.[1]

The candidate for Senator, Smith W. Brookhart, also denounced absolutely the Cummins-Esch law:

"The railroad law should never have been enacted," he said, "and it should be immediately repealed.

"It legalized the capitalization of about seven billion dollars of water. It gave legislative guarantee for a 5½ per cent return and ½ per cent bonus upon this fictitious capital." [2]

On the question of marketing and the middleman, which is also the question of the cost of living for labor as far as food is concerned, his declaration was particularly interesting to labor:

The recent report of the Congressional Agricultural Commission shows that out of the dollar paid by labor for the products of the farm, the farmer only gets 37 cents. Processing, distribution, and profits amount to 63 cents.

In the campaign of 1926, Brookhart was again renominated against the opposition of high finance, organ-

[1] From *Labor*, March 25, 1922.
[2] *Ibid.*

ized business and organized industry—and again he
attributed his nomination to organized labor as well as
organized agriculture, a view that was conceded by practically all observers. His nomination was so important
and typical that his platform and principles are worthy
of further attention. I shall exclude foreign issues, since
Iowa, like Wisconsin, is a state with an exceptionally
large population of recent foreign extraction—and American labor is entirely out of accord with the progressives
(and conservatives) of those states on these issues (see
Chapter VI).

Excluding foreign issues Brookhart's chief platform
"planks" were the Haugen bill and opposition to the Administration's railroad policy, to the Mellon tax-reduction
Law, and to the policy and control of the Federal Reserve
Board over the banks. In addition he attacked his rival,
Senator Cummins, for having voted against the investigation of Secretary Mellon's Aluminum Trust, for having
voted to confirm the Sugar-Trust lawyer Charles B.
Warren as Attorney General (a Coolidge nomination defeated by the Senate), for having favored the seating
of Senator Newberry (accused of practically purchasing
his seat) and of having voted for the "white-washing"
of Attorney General Daugherty after the Teapot-Dome
oil scandals. Every one of these planks was fully as much
appreciated by organized labor as by organized agriculture.

In addition Brookhart advocated the maximum extension of co-operation with the hope that ultimately "labor
would hire capital instead of capital hiring labor and that
farming would be considered a branch of labor." [1] As

[1] New York *Times*, June 11, 1926.

an approach to such a social system he favored "a complete co-operative credit system—a modification of the intermediate credit banks, for the benefit of labor equally with the farmers." [1]

But, like most of the other leaders of organized agriculture and organized labor, he realized that "this remedy cannot be introduced without a fight to the finish with the forces in Congress that oppose governmental aid for farmers but support such aid for railroads and other industries." [2]

The other chief farm leaders have the same conception of the opposition. As George N. Peek, leader of the North Central States Agricultural Conference, says, "Opposition developed from the start from certain people high in Administration and business circles." [3]   Representative Dickinson of Iowa, more explicit, named Secretaries Hoover and Mellon. The farmer, Dickinson says, "is told by the master mind of the Administration, Secretary Mellon, that he must continue to feed the consumers of the country as cheaply as those of bankrupt Europe are fed in order that our industries may compete in world trade.

"Evidently Secretary Mellon has taken careful stock of the situation and *is willing to array the city against the country.* We do not welcome such a contest; on the contrary, we want to avoid it if it is humanly possible. But the farmer is an American—and an American will not accept serfdom without fighting to the last ditch." [4]

The 1926 State Platform of the Republican Party of

[1] Article by Brookhart, New York *Times,* June 13, 1926.
[2] *Ibid.*
[3] New York *World,* June 14, 1926.
[4] Associated Press, June 16, 1926.

LABOR AND POLITICS

Wisconsin, under the leadership of Senator Robert La Follette, Jr., expressed the struggle as seen by organized agriculture and organized labor even more bluntly:

"The dominance and dictation of Eastern *industrial and financial interests* in the Government at Washington," says the platform, "is ruinous to the prosperity of every other section. We declare it to be our purpose to join hands with Progressives everywhere to gain fair treatment for the Middle West, West and South, and free our National Government from the control of any one class or section." [1]

While the American Federation of Labor has always followed the tactics of political co-operation with progressive agricultural organizations, that policy became a permanent foundation of its political policy only in 1920 and 1922. In the latter year the Federation not only declared that "all legislation in favor either of labor or the farmers will benefit both"; [2] it put at the head of its program this slogan: "Whatever injures labor injures the farmer. Whatever benefits labor benefits the farmer. Whatever is for the interest of labor and the farmer is for the best interest of all people except the privileged few." [3] In his last Christmas message Samuel Gompers predicted political success for American labor "with the co-operation of the great farming population." [4]

On no other policy is American labor more completely united than on this. The length to which the unions

[1] New York *Times,* June 15, 1926.
[2] Letter of American Federation of Labor National Non-Partisan Campaign Committee calling for conferences and co-operation of local labor organizations with farmers' organizations, July 29, 1922.
[3] Letter A. F. of L. National Non-partisan Campaign Committee calling for conference and co-operation of local labor organizations with farmers' organizations, August 26, 1922.
[4] International Labor News Service, December 11, 1923.

have gone is best seen in labor's loyal support of the paramount demand of organized agriculture from 1922 to the present moment, namely governmental aid for marketing, as illustrated by the McNary-Haugen bill and other similar measures. When that measure appeared before Congress, organized labor did everything in its power to get it passed. Not only the American Federation of Labor, but the railway brotherhoods, the unions represented in the railway shops, the United Mine Workers, and other unions appeared before Congress in its behalf:

Organized labor, through authorized representatives, got squarely back of farmers' relief legislation when they appeared before the Senate Committee on Agriculture as advocates of the $100,000,000 emergency loan to stabilize the prices of staple farm products.

The significance of an appeal by consumers of the bulk of farm products for more decent conditions for producers was not lost upon the members of the committee. It was in marked contrast with the impoverishing deflation demanded by middlemen and the big interests that have been exploiting both agrarian and industrial workers.[1]

Among those who supported the farmers on this occasion were Edgar Wallace, representing the American Federation of Labor, Grand Chief Stone of the Brotherhood of Locomotive Engineers; William H. Johnston, president International Association of Machinists; Sidney Hillman, president Amalgamated Clothing Workers of America; W. S. Carter, president Brotherhood of Locomotive Firemen and Enginemen; J. W. Kline, president International Brotherhood of Blacksmiths; John L. Lewis, president United Mine Workers of America.[2]

[1] *Labor*, February 18, 1922.
[2] *Ibid.*

LABOR AND POLITICS

Again in 1926, organized labor appeared before the House Committee on Agriculture in support of the Haugen bill—mainly on the ground that it was fathered by fifteen leading farm organizations.[1] The Railroad Conductors and Engineers were represented as well as the American Federation, and the labor organizations believe they brought a number of additional Congressmen to support the measure.

Congress finally defeated the Haugen bill—which led Vice-President Matthew Woll, of the American Federation of Labor, to the following comment:

Great rejoicing was manifested in circles opposed to the farmers' best interests when the Haugen bill was defeated by a bi-partisan bloc of the East and South. President Coolidge's flirtations with the Bourbon South have produced their fruit—for the moment. But this desperate effort to divide the nation along sectional lines has been undertaken without reckoning ultimate consequences. The policy of divide and conquer may have gained for the day, but other days are to follow. The consumers and workers of the cities and the farmers of the country can not longer be kept ignorant of their mutuality of interests. Big business is only hastening the day of a new regrouping of powerful economic, social and political forces.[2]

Vice-President Woll, like the great majority of observers, attributed the defeat of the Administration (Coolidge) Senatorial candidates by progressives—uniformly supported by labor—largely to the Administration's position on the Haugen bill:

The agricultural uprising that is defeating the Coolidge candidates in primary after primary is no longer a revolt; it

[1] *American Federationist*, May, 1926.
[2] International Labor News Service, June 12, 1926.

78

is a revolution. It is not merely a protest of a handful of so-called "radical" Senators; it is a political revulsion of agriculturists in general against the dominating control of the Federal administration by large financial, manufacturing and commercial interests—big business.

Coolidge "business" Senators are being voted out of office. "Political" Senators of progressive and radical tendencies are being voted into office. This may not mean undiluted progress. At least political Senators are not circumscribed by industrial and financial bosses. They do study the pulse of the electorate and follow powerful social and economic influences at work and avoid dangerous class interests.[1]

Let us now note the response of organized agriculture to all these labor overtures.

As early as 1893 the convention of the American Federation of Labor had instructed its executive "to use every effort to perfect an alliance between the unions and the farmers." Within a decade the farmers' response was highly satisfactory. By 1904 the radical farmers' unions in a number of states, such as Texas, where it had 100,000 members, secured the support of labor in their fight against the trusts and in return took a stand against the use of court injunctions in labor disputes. By 1907 the American Society of Equity and the American Federation of Labor were studying methods "to establish and maintain a working agreement." In the annual report of the convention of that year the Executive Council declared for "the most fraternal relations" and "mutual reciprocal aid between the organizations of labor and the organizations of farmers."

The Farmers' Educational Co-operative Union as early as 1910 had resolved:

[1] International Labor News Service, June 12, 1926.

79

LABOR AND POLITICS

That the officers of the Farmers' Union be and are authorized and directed to confer with the officers of the *bona fide* organized labor movement of America, with the purpose of carrying into effect the objects of our respective organizations, the protection and uplift of America's workers engaged in all fields of productive activity.

That our officers and legislative committee co-operate with similar officers and committees of organized labor to secure such relief and reformatory legislation as may be necessary to the rights, protection, and freedom to which the workers as men and as citizens are, under our constitution, entitled.

That without regard to political partisanship we join in the effort to secure larger representation in our national, state, and local lawmaking bodies, for men who are engaged in the creative industries.[1]

This declaration was indorsed by the convention of the American Federation of Labor in that same year.

The National Board of Farm Organizations, in 1921, issued the following pronouncement:

We say that in these unsettled times Congress should seek to remove the causes of strikes rather than to make strikes a felony. Our position on the strike question is in line with the position taken by various members of the General Board of Farm Organizations, who last February joined in the publicly declared statement that the right to cease work individually or collectively, for adequate reasons, is unassailable.[2]

The causes of this political co-operation lie deep. The great mass of agriculturists and labor-unionists have similar incomes, their organizations have adopted similar

[1] Declarations adopted by Farmers' Educational and Co-operative Union of America convention, St. Louis, May 2-6, 1920.

[2] Declaration by National Board of Farm Organizations in its convention held in St. Louis, May, 1921.

political programs and methods, and their underlying political philosophies are also similar at many points.

Agricultural and labor organizations alike claim a right to a direct influence on government and they both base this claim partly on the fact that capitalist, business, and industrial interests exercise such an influence. "If it was wise, on the part of Congress," declared a meeting of the farm organizations in the grain belt, "to stabilize our banking system through the Federal Reserve Act and our transportation system through the Cummins-Esch Act, then why not indulge the same solicitude for the 40,-000,000 people who live upon the farm and whose purchasing power is so vital to our myriad mills and factories?"

The agricultural organizations then referred to the benefits industry had secured from the protective customs tariff, as another illustration of business leaning upon government. They concluded that non-agricultural persons (they clearly referred to a speech of President Coolidge) had no right to "thwart a constructive agricultural program" in the formulation of which "the best intelligence of agriculture has put so many years of devoted and sincere study."

This demand for economic self-government and for "equality" in the benefits of political action is precisely the demand of organized labor (see Volume II, Chapter VIII). Like Vice-President Woll of the American Federation of Labor, Senator Capper, head of "the farm bloc" in Congress, demands that agriculture should secure something more from government than the indirect benefits of business prosperity and of legislation in behalf of "business."

LABOR AND POLITICS

Senator Capper says:

This prosperity, without parallel, has not been equitably shared by all the elements in the national community.

True it is that within the last two years the farmer's position has materially bettered. But this betterment, encouraging as it is, unfortunately is not the result of fundamental readjustment of the economic status of his industry that must be accomplished before the farmer can keep abreast of the procession.

In producing activity the farmer has kept pace. But in distribution—the sale and marketing—of his production he's at a disadvantage. In short, the farmer is not on a bargaining equality with other groups and units in the economic community.[1]

Change the word farmer into labor and these propositions are precisely those of the labor movement.

Senator Capper went on to state that the farmer demands no privileges, no special favors, no paternalistic experiments, but only equal treatment; that he is no "radical," but that he is entitled to the earnest co-operation of every thinking citizen; that "what the farmer is asking does not put the government in business in any greater sense than it is in business in many ways to-day." Although Senator Capper and the farm bloc favor the tariff, he points out that it embodies a form of price-fixing and that legislative fiat has also guaranteed the railroads a return of 5 3-4 per cent. Every word of this statement would be indorsed by the organized wage-earner as applying equally to the farmer and to himself.

A typical labor statement of Matthew Woll rests on identical principles. After pointing out that organized

[1] New York *Times*, January 24, 1926.

82

labor was co-operating with the organized farmers in every Western State, Woll continued:

Soon the whole of our body politic will be involved in political upheaval. It will have for its immediate purpose agricultural relief, for its ultimate aim the wresting away of the reins of federal administrative and legislative authority from the hands of organized business and the placing of this authority into the hands of the farmers, the workers, business and other social groups upon fair basis of equality.

The time is passing for a political policy based on the sole domination of organized business and for the selfish gain of organized business alone. There can be no justification for the doctrine that organized business should dominate and control exclusively our economic, industrial and political destinies and that all other groups should be mere dependents upon organized business and rest content with such indirect benefits as may be allowed by or be forced from organized business.[1]

But while labor and the farmers readily co-operate in many directions and especially against the economic and political powers of high finance and "organized business," undoubtedly co-operation on some questions has been difficult. Above all, there is always the interest of the farmer in high prices for food products and raw materials as against the interest of the industrial wage-earner in low prices. Obviously, if no compromise were possible on this price question there never could be any thorough-going co-operation between labor and the agricultural producer. But a compromise is possible because of the fact that labor's interest requires only relatively low *retail* prices, whereas the farmer is satisfied with relatively high *wholesale* prices—both movements being directed

[1] International Labor News Service, June 12, 1926.

83

largely against the profiteering and parasitism among middlemen (see Chapter X).

Labor has met the effort of the farmer to secure higher prices for his products more than halfway, giving full indorsement to the progressive agricultural standpoint. This indorsement has not been limited to any one section of American labor; it is not impulsive or momentary, but deliberate, and will doubtless continue. Only recently President Green once more pledged that the Federation would go along with the farmers' program even if it resulted in increasing the price of farm products:

> The question is frequently asked, "What is organized labor's attitude toward legislation in Congress for substantial relief of the farmers? Would they approve a measure that raises the price of farm produce to the consumer?"
> My reply is that if to better conditions for the farmer it is found necessary to raise the price of bread and meat, and the farmer receives the benefit, then the city wage earners are not only willing but anxious to support such legislation.
> We want the farmer of the West and the South to feel that employees of the manufacturing centers in the East are willing to make any reasonable sacrifice that will place the agricultural industry on a paying basis.[1]

The chief question that arises is not as to labor's attitude, but as to that of the agriculturists. How far do the farmers stand with labor? If the alliance of labor and agriculturists in certain states should succeed economically and politically, for example, how much of the benefit would the agriculturists claim for themselves and how much would they allow to labor?

The answer to this question depends first of all upon the relative voice of the radical small farmer and of the

[1] *Labor*, July 1, 1926.

conservative larger farmer in each locality in shaping the position of the agricultural community as a whole. Will the smaller farmer tend rather to co-operate with the large farmer, or will he find a closer affiliation with organized labor? The fate of the farmer-labor entente everywhere depends on the small farmer's answer to this question. For the farmers have a large majority over labor in every state where this alliance has been politically successful. The smaller farmers may come into power with the help of labor; when they get into power and attain some of their main objectives, they may yield to the temptation to co-operate with the larger farmers, and through them with certain of the industrial and financial elements.

In view of political results already achieved or in the process of achievement, it cannot be denied that organized labor's offer to co-operate with the farmers has brought very satisfactory results. But the opposition to organized labor among agriculturists is also very powerful. The Farmers' International Congress held in October, 1919, at Hagerstown, Maryland, put itself on record as opposed to all strikes and to the methods of organized labor, adopted a resolution against the "ever increasing wages" demanded, and stated that high wages were responsible as well as the profiteer for keeping up the cost of living. This Congress favored a Federal Board of Arbitration that would "give a square deal" to both capital and labor, it denounced the shorter workday, and concluded as follows:

We know that the forty-four hour week cannot feed the world, and we proclaim that it cannot clothe it. Those who advocate the short day in industry should not expect the farmer to work six hours before dinner and six hours after, with before-breakfast and after-supper chores thrown in.[1]

The farmers of the International Farm Congress in Atlantic City, in the same year, protested against the alleged policy of organized labor which urged greater production on the farms, while restricting the output of the factories.

The farmer delegates who sound this warning to labor [a resolution declared] know that the workmen in the factories, as a rule, are not trying to be efficient; that the output per man is greatly lessened, and that this policy is not only permitted, but encouraged by the labor organizations—even demanded, in effect, by some of them. . . . There is no moral, physiological, social, or business reason why all able-bodied men should not work a reasonable number of hours each day or week, and we hold that it is an economic necessity, becoming more pronounced each year, that they do so.[2]

A conference of the National Grange, the American Farm Bureau Federation, the Cotton States Board, and the Association of State Farmers Union presidents proclaimed that the railroad workers had no more right to strike than did the farmers, and that such a strike would starve the nation. These farm representatives presented to Congress a memorial which concluded with the following statement:

If the farmers who own and occupy the land have no such moral or legal right, then why should it be conceded by anyone that those who handle the farmers' products have a right to block the transportation or industrial facilities of the

[1] Declaration by Farmers' International Congress, October, 1919, Hagerstown, Maryland.

[2] Declaration by International Farm Congress held in Atlantic City in 1919.

country and thus jeopardise the food and clothing supply of the nation? [1]

T. C. Atkeson of the National Grange summed up the position of these powerful federations. "We decided," Mr. Atkeson said, "that the interests of the farmers and of organized labor were not identical; in fact, were diametrically opposed on some questions. The union man wants shorter hours and higher pay, which means higher prices to the consumer." [2]

The national agricultural conference called by President Harding in 1922 was dominated by similar sentiments. This was natural, as that body was a gathering not of elected delegates, but of personal appointees of the President, including very few representatives of the more liberal agricultural organizations and a considerable number of representatives of finance and industry only indirectly connected with agriculture. [3] Urging a *decrease* in railroad wages, the conference insisted "that the railroad corporations and railroad labor should share in the deflation in charges now affecting all industries."

The report of the committee supporting this resolution even assumed a position of hostility to organized labor in general and demanded a national decrease of wages in the name of the farmer.

What would the cost of production of farm products be if farm labor were allowed a wage commensurate to that received by the coal miner, the railroad worker, the brick mason, or the factory operator? Your committee has not the data upon which to base this calculation, but states without fear of contradiction that no price received, even at the

[1] February 7, 1921.
[2] Speech by T. C. Atkeson, representative of National Grange.
[3] New York *Times,* January 27.

peak of prices, will give the actual producer of farm products a wage comparable in any way with that normally received by all classes of union labor.[1]

Of course there is no ground for this last assertion. On the contrary, it may be doubted if, in the average year, the *annual* income even *of the average skilled laborer* (to say nothing of the unskilled and semi-skilled) will equal that of the *average farmer* if allowance be made for the farmer's house rent and produce consumed at home. But the main point is that, on the whole, the incomes of the average farmer and the average wage-earner are similar.

In reply to the anti-labor position of this conference, President Gompers, one of the two representatives of organized labor in the gathering, declared that if a resolution in this spirit was adopted, the conference must be regarded "as enemies to the working class of this country." But Gompers had very little support from the floor. It is true that Gifford Pinchot (now Governor of Pennsylvania) asked the conference not to "attempt to rise by dragging any others down" and that the representative of the Kansas Farmers' Union said: "Let us adjust the prices of farm products, and not throw anybody down. Instead of asking that credits be readjusted to lift these people, you are trying to pull labor down to their condition." [2]

But the conference carried out the main ideas recommended by its committee and passed the resolution.

"It would seem," observed President Gompers, "that if any class is to be deflated, labor already has been deflated. Between 4,000,000 and 5,000,000 are unemployed.

[1] New York *Times*, January 28, 1922.
[2] *Ibid.*, January 28, 1922.

Think of the waste! Millions of days of non-employment and non-production.

"If you in this conference declare that labor is to be deflated, how is it to be accomplished? By taking more reefs in the belt? How? Rentals charged now are beyond all reasonable consideration, and one-third of the laboring man's budget is his rent."[1]

Gompers pointed out that the conference was primarily an effort to separate labor and farm organizations:

Accepting the invitation to serve in the conference, the president of the American Federation of Labor shared the hope of the American people that it might be possible to bring about a more complete realization of the interests shared in common by the two great groups of producers in the United States and a clearer perception of the necessity for a greater bond of unity and a greater degree of co-operation.

It also was hoped that it might be possible to meet and overcome a great nation-wide propaganda designed by exploiters and profiteers to deceive both the workers and the farmers.

Every attack on the workers was greeted with an expression of approval which made it apparent that it would be practically impossible to prevent action by the conference reflecting the nation-wide propaganda of big business for an assault on the wages and the rights of the workers.[2]

Gompers had no difficulty in showing that the chief opposition to labor in this conference came not even from conservative agriculturists, but from the same elements that have steadily been attacking the progressive farmers' organizations.

[1] *Ibid.*
[2] *American Federationist,* March, 1922.

89

LABOR AND POLITICS

It is a matter of more than usual significance that the total negative note corresponds exactly with the number of railroad presidents, bankers, trust magnates, and big employers who were at the conference to help the poor farmer.[1]

The political tactics of labor's opponents were not new to President Gompers and the Federation. The main difficulty in maintaining the political entente of farm and labor organizations had always come from the machinations of partisan politicians and business magnates to keep them apart. As President Gompers had declared the year before:

Those who seek to exploit both the wage-worker of the city and the farmer naturally seek to make it appear that there are differences of principle in order to create suspicion and antagonism between the farmers and the city workers. In every case where this is done the point over which it is sought to make an issue is either a point of minor importance or a question of interpretation.

What the enemies of labor hope for and what the enemies of the farmer hope for is that labor and the farmers will disagree among themselves, and because of disagreement, weaken their struggle and make it ineffective.[2]

At the end of 1923, however, the Executive Council of the Federation felt itself able to report that "the efforts of certain interests to drive a wedge between labor and the farmers" had failed.

The Harding agricultural conference furnished conclusive evidence of the fact, to be seen from one end of the country to the other and every day, that the organized industrial capitalists and the conservative political elements at present in control of the national government

[1] *American Federationist*, March, 1921.
[2] Samuel Gompers in *American Federationist*, August, 1921.

are making desperate efforts to break up, or at least to prevent the further development of this farmer-labor rapprochement, and that these efforts have met with a certain limited measure of success. But organized labor and its progressive agricultural allies have had to fight this effort at disruption from the very beginning, and, on the whole, they have fought it successfully. Their more serious problem arises from the ultra-conservative position of certain important agricultural organizations already referred to. And these organizations are strongly represented in Congress.

The capitalistic large farmer is everywhere the great permanent check to full farmer-labor co-operation. There are also temporary and local obstacles in our agricultural sections that are peculiar to America and to the present period. American wage-earners mainly are of foreign extraction, while most of our farmers are of somewhat older American stock. As a result they tend to disagree on non-economic or moral issues. The tendency is for wage-earners to take a broad view of racial and moral questions and for farmers to take a more narrowly American view, for labor to be "wet" and farmers to be "dry."

At the present moment (1926) these non-economic issues seem to overshadow all others. But they had comparatively little importance a decade ago and they may soon diminish in importance any day until within another decade or less they may be reduced to their former comparative insignificance, while the economic problems remain. Capitalist politicians and periodicals, however, fully understand the utility of such issues in forcing the two great popular movements apart and are deliberately or instinctively doing everything they can to keep them alive.

Do organized labor and the progressive farm organizations understand this? Are they trying to compromise these issues so as to keep them in the background? And if they are, what are their prospects of success? The immediate future of the farmer-labor entente depends, more than it depends on anything else, on the farmers' and wage-earners' answers to such questions.

It may be answered at once that all militant progressives, whether urban or rural, are fully alive to this danger and have proved it by a consistent effort to subordinate these issues. All are agreed that such questions are of secondary importance when compared with the great economic questions. But it must be admitted that they have as yet made little headway in subordinating racial, religious, and moral issues in those districts where issues are paramount. Does not this situation, then, make the political outlook rather hopeless for the farmer-labor entente? No, because those districts where such issues are paramount are necessarily economically backward—and organized labor could have little to hope for in the way of economic co-operation from such districts in any event. Populism may have had a stronghold in some of them; but the new farmer-labor entente is along constructive lines, and has little in common with the primitive and economically reactionary doctrines of populism. Labor has as little to hope for from the most backward as it has from the largest and most prosperous and capitalistic of the agriculturists. While the labor-farmer entente is seriously checked, then, by the prominence of these non-economic issues in certain sections it is not crippled to the degree that might at first appear.

According to the view of American labor the farmer

or independent agricultural producer must always remain an essential and important part of the movement toward industrial democracy. The fact, made so much of by European labor unions and labor parties, that the farmer is an owner and small capitalist, while labor is not, that the farmer is in business and labor is not, that the farmer is often an employer—all seem to be secondary considerations, unless, indeed, the farmer is a capitalist and an employer on a comparatively large scale. These differences between the average agriculturist and the average wage-earner may and usually do result in putting them into separate social groups. But it is the American labor view that, after admitting all these differences, the *small* agriculturist has *far more* in common with the wage-earner than he has with the great financial and industrial interests, organized industry and organized business.

This position not only corresponds to the facts, but is clear cut and logical. It is somewhat less simple, perhaps, than the view of European socialism, which crudely divides society between capitalists and non-capitalists, employers and employees, and would consign the majority of American agriculturists to the capitalist camp. But American labor holds that a direct, logical, and unavoidable deduction from the principle of industrial democracy is that there must be no dividing lines between the masses of producers.

America is no longer a predominantly agricultural nation. The greatest strength of labor is precisely in those states where agriculture is of the least importance. Certainly not more than 20 per cent of the labor-unionists of the country are located in states where the radical agriculturists control or can hope to control. The labor-

93

farmer entente will doubtless continue throughout the more progressive and non-capitalistic agricultural sections. It may also continue to be effective in certain other states where the labor and agricultural forces are more equally balanced.

But one of the most important results of the farmer-labor entente, whether that entente develops or not, is that the political experience gained by the labor movement in co-operating with farmers can and doubtless will be applied to co-operation with urban middle-class elements which are also economically placed in a position resembling, as to income and in many other ways, the position of the wage-earner.

CHAPTER V

A NON-PARTISAN PROGRESSIVE
CONGRESS

*The Renomination of La Follette and other Progressive Senators
in 1922—The Conference for Progressive Political Action.*

THE first fair test of the "non-partisan" or bi-partisan
policy as applied to Congress was in the 1922 election.
In that year, for the first time, there was neither an
overshadowing Presidential election nor a third-party
movement to compete for the voters' attention. As the
Federation convention, held in June, pointed out, there
was "no independent political labor movement in the
field" to interfere with or minimize the political efforts
of unions.

Moreover, the entente with progressive agricultural
organizations was perfected not only in a few states, as
in 1920, but throughout the country, or, at least, in
every district where organized labor had indorsed progressive Democrats or Republicans for Congress. The
unions were able to report that "in every instance the
farmers were supporting or were willing to support the
same candidates as labor." [1]

How was this unity secured? It was not based on a
whole program worked out or put forward in common.

[1] "Non-partisan Successes" (American Federation of Labor pamphlet, 1922).

95

It is true that organized labor supported nearly all, if not all, the measures advocated by the progressive agricultural organizations—and *vice versa*. It is also true that several of the tests applied to Congressmen's records were to be found on both programs, such as opposition to the ship-subsidy and sales-tax bills. The Federation of Labor put in the foreground only a very few measures. Its campaign slogan was:

No judge-made laws.
No compulsory labor laws.
No sales tax.
No wage-earners or farmers to be enslaved (referring to the application of the anti-trust law against labor and farm organizations).
No subsidies for the privileged few.
No remission of fines for food profiteers.

Progressive agricultural organizations could find nothing to criticize and something to attract them in this negative and abbreviated program. But it can scarcely account for the large measure of labor-farmer harmony in the 1922 election.

Congress had been so reactionary that the Federation reported that "99 per cent of the work done by labor in Congress has been to defeat pernicious legislation." [1] "Compulsory labor, injunctions, the over-riding of law and Constitution, the (strengthening of the) Railroad Labor Board, the sales tax, the ship subsidy," were the things, Gompers declared after the balloting, that were "repudiated and condemned so forcefully and overwhelmingly in the 1922 election." [2] But these measures con-

[1] American Federation of Labor Convention, 1923.
[2] Samuel Gompers in International Labor News Service, November 11, 1922.

tain only a part, and a minor part, of the things the progressive farmers were fighting about.

The Conference for Progressive Political Action, which at one time embraced more than a third of the nation's labor-unionsts (see below), applied broader tests and put out a broader program, including several of the measures of chief interest to progressive farm organizations, such as the meat-packing bill, the strengthening of the Federal Trade Board, and government aid for farm exports. The former two measures had been officially indorsed also by the Federation and its representative had officially supported the third. But the Federation still held that only strictly labor questions should be emphasized in the election campaign and its political campaign committee reported that some confusion had been caused "by the distribution of legislative records of members of Congress that appeared to be sent out in the interest of organized labor" though these misunderstandings were soon eliminated.[1] This unquestionably referred to the Progressive Conference.

The danger of slumping into mere oppositionism—securing the irresponsible support of both big parties while they are in opposition and of neither while it is in power —is the chief reason why labor, as far as practicable, avoids indorsement of either party and has adopted an entirely different method (its so-called non-partisan policy) of political functioning. President Green pointed out to the writer several years ago that labor had found no great difficulty in making its oppositionism effective. Its political problem was not to negate, but to construct, and, for that purpose, to find a political *method* and *program*

[1] "Non-partisan Successes."

sufficiently broad to secure the lasting political co-operation of other social elements (farmers or urban middle
classes) without sacrificing labor principles and without
becoming entangled in party politics.

By 1922 the *method* of political co-operation had been
fully worked out—but not the *program*. The chief reason for the labor-agricultural unity at that time was not
so much what was common in their programs as the underlying fact, now more strongly realized than ever, that
organized labor and progressive farm organizations have
the same enemy, namely the organized or consolidated
business interests which accept the leadership of Big
Business. Both groups of organizations (labor and agricultural) found that the candidates indorsed by the Chambers of Commerce, for example, took their orders not
from progressive farmers or from organized labor, but
from the business interests.

The victories of organized labor and its allies in the
1922 election were far-reaching. These victories brought
into Congress such a powerful group of Democratic and
Republican progressives that it was able to organize the
House and often to control the Senate—though it had
to depend usually on the co-operation of the entire opposition—that is, of the conservative as well as the progressive wing of the Democratic party.

Twenty-three of the twenty-seven candidates for the
Senate indorsed by labor were elected, and one hundred
and seventy Representatives, also a dozen Governors, including such nationally known figures as the Republican
Gifford Pinchot, of Pennsylvania, and the Democrat Alfred E. Smith, of New York. In many instances, both in
the primaries and in the final election, candidates frankly

attributed their defeat to labor. A noted case was that of Philip Campbell of Kansas, chairman of the Rules Committee and one of the foremost Republican leaders in Congress.

Gompers's review of the results of the final election is interesting:

"There probably has never been an election in the United States [wrote Gompers] in which the result was more significant for principles and less significant for partisan politics. The repudiation of reactionary Republicans was no less striking than the sweeping success of progressive Republicans.

"Where the electors were more emphatic in retiring such Republicans as Mondell, Calder, Townsend, Kellogg, Sutherland, Frelinghuysen, and Poindexter, they were equally emphatic in electing such Republicans as Brookhart, Johnson, La Follette, and Frazier.

"Where the voters in Pennsylvania elected the progressive Gifford Pinchot as Governor on the Republican ticket, they elected the progressive Al Smith as Governor on the Democratic ticket in the State of New York. Where they elected the progressive J. J. Blaine as Governor on the Republican ticket in Wisconsin, they elected the progressive G. W. P. Hunt as Governor on the Democratic ticket in Arizona." [1]

The Congress elected in 1922 lived up fully to labor's expectations.[2] The voting records of the 170 Representatives (105 Democrats, 63 Republicans and two independents) who had received labor indorsement proved entirely satisfactory. The voting records of the twenty-

[1] International Labor News Service, November 11, 1922.
[2] Serving from March 4, 1922, to March 4, 1924.

three Senators labor had supported were also largely satisfactory—though with the notable exception that several of these voted against labor on the important measures restricting immigration and child labor. Nevertheless, this Senate was, on the whole, fully as progressive as the House.

The 1922 Congress justified labor's claim, made in the following year, that its non-partisan political policy had achieved signal successes ever since it was first inaugurated in 1906—"as far as Congressional elections are concerned." "In the ten Congresses from 1905 to 1925 labor secured the passage of 208 remedial laws. During the same period it has defeated hundreds of bills that if enacted into law would have subjected the wage-earners and the people generally to oppression." [1]

In the Congressional session from March 4, 1922, to March 4, 1924, all measures labeled as reactionary by the unions and their allies were defeated. The House rules were revolutionized under the leadership of La Follette and with Gompers's active support, the Mellon tax-reduction plan was defeated, and the soldiers' bonus was passed over President Coolidge's veto. The Barkley-Howell bill to repeal the semi-compulsory arbitration features of the Cummins-Esch Act, which regulates the railroads and railroad labor, and the bills to establish a governmental marketing corporation for agriculture failed to pass. But the new House rule, forced through by the progressives, giving a chance for 150 Representatives to force a vote on any bill, showed more than 170 votes in favor of these measures.

[1] "Legislative Achievements," American Federation of Labor pamphlet.

A NON-PARTISAN PROGRESSIVE CONGRESS

The achievements of this Congress were summed up succinctly by the Federation:

This Congress stopped the flood of immigration. It blocked the sales-tax gouge. It blocked the Mellon burdensome tax plan. It exposed the Veterans' Bureau graft. It forced (Attorney-General) Daugherty out. It drove (Secretary of the Interior) Fall into retirement. It gave the people the facts about the oil scandals.

Not one measure opposed by labor was enacted into law by the present Congress.

Among the most reactionary of these defeated proposals were the schemes of Secretary Mellon and President Coolidge and the consolidated interests to untax the rich and tax the poor.[1]

In addition the Federation listed seventeen statutes "of interest to labor" as *positive* achievements. Besides the immigration restriction bill, there was the Act against child labor, the increase of wages of postal employees, and the "adjusted compensation for veterans of the World War," the so-called soldiers' bonus—the last two measures enacted against the opposition of President Coolidge.

The La Follette nomination for President in 1924 had its origin in his overwhelming re-nomination for Senator in the Republican primaries of Wisconsin in 1922.

The sweep of La Follette's victory in 1922 opened the eyes of conservative editors, who saw that it was not a Wisconsin event, but a part of the new "progressivism" that had won Iowa, Nebraska, and other states. [2]

The new farmer-labor movement, whether for good or for ill, accepted him as its leader. In no less than a

[1] Report of Proceedings of 1924 convention.
[2] The Philadelphia *Public Ledger,* for example.

dozen states where this combination had been winning in the primaries the platform was the same.

The first plank, the repeal of the Cummins-Esch railroad law, which meant the abolition of the Railway Labor Board and of the dividend guaranty, appealed both to farmers and to labor. The plank calling for reorganization of the Federal Reserve Board was addressed primarily to the farmers, but democratic control of credit had been advocated by labor for years. The taxation planks, a profits tax, and increased income surtaxes and inheritance taxes, though addressed primarily to the farmer, were also labor planks. Finally, the demand for abolition of injunctions in labor disputes served to balance and round out the program.

Evidently this program was remote from state-socialism. But if it was mere "progressivism," then it was a more militant and radical brand of progressivism than that of Roosevelt or Wilson.

There was something else new about it. Organized labor was in "on the ground floor," a sort of junior partner, perhaps, but loyally accepted as essential to the success of the enterprise. And it was the first time that organized labor had found a means of adequately expressing itself under the American political system.

La Follette had been a leader in this movement from the beginning. He used the old party machinery, but for the purposes of his own state organization and not to serve the majority in control of the national party. Organized labor, acting through its non-partisan policy, was working on the same plan, but through both political parties.

The only outside political figure to address the American Federation of Labor convention in 1922 was La Follette. In the United States Senate La Follette had often stood alone for organized labor. In some forty test votes he only once had failed; for, as might have been expected, he voted against the labor clauses—as he voted against all other clauses—of the Versailles Treaty.

Senators Wheeler and Dill and Norris and Shipstead and Brookhart—to say nothing of other still newer Senators, may now approach La Follette's labor record. In 1922 it was unequaled.

Organized labor had had its political factions, but in 1922 they united on this political method and this program. Only in Nebraska, Minnesota, and New York was there any effort to set up a new party. The nomination of Howell by the Republicans in Nebraska, standing as he did for the repeal of the Cummins-Esch law, ended the third-party move in that State. In Minnesota alone did there remain a Farmer-Labor party—indorsed by labor after a vain effort to bring about a fusion of Democrats and the Non-Partisan League (see Chapter VI). In New York an American Labor Party promoted by a number of unions, but ignored by the State Federation of Labor, was still-born.

From 1922 to 1924 there appeared a new political movement, the Conference for Progressive Political Action, sometimes called the Cleveland Conference because it held its convention in that city. This was the national body which finally nominated Senator La Follette for President in July, 1924—though he drew his support in the main from entirely unrelated state political organizations resting on progressive agricultural groups, such as that of Wisconsin, and from the American Federation of Labor.

The Cleveland Conference was organized and controlled by a group representing a large part, though not the majority, of the American labor unions. It aimed to embrace also agricultural organizations, though only a few joined it (and they had comparatively little influence). Some of the organizers of the conference, which included socialist and radical organizations, hoped to see the movement result in a third party. This may also have been the ultimate hope of some of the labor-union leaders of the conference. But a third party was not its ostensible object and the labor leaders in it did not allow it to be turned into a third-party movement.

While Socialists, farmer-laborites, radical farm leaders and detached radical-liberals were numerous in the Executive Committee, the organization as a whole was consciously modeled after the British Labor Party and was based upon organized labor. It was organized in the first instance by certain labor unions, especially the machinists, the railroad brotherhoods and other unions of the railway shop groups. The Amalgamated Garment Workers, regarded as of Socialistic tendencies and outside of the Federation—was in it from the beginning and it had the support at one moment of the printers, the miners, the Ladies' Garment Workers, the Electrical Workers, and others of our largest unions. Its officers were labor-unionists and its constitution provided for absolute labor-union control—a control that could be counterbalanced by progressive farmer organizations only if these came into the movement in equal numbers with the labor-unionists, which they did not do. On the contrary the more progressive farm organizations showed the tendency more and more to give their support exclusively to progressive state organizations under their own control, such as those of Wisconsin, Minnesota, and North Dakota. In the first Cleveland Conference (1922) the labor-unionists represented (1,800,000) were allotted 188 votes, while the farm organizations, loosely estimated as having 900,000 members, were given 90 votes.

In the main it was a labor-union movement and the unions, in contrast to many state progressive movements, could hope to be a dominant political factor only in the industrial sections—from New England and New York to Missouri and Illinois. But in none of these states was progressivism strong enough to offer union labor any very material support. In a word, in every state where this particular radical-progressive organization (the Cleveland Conference) had any considerable strength it was in effect a labor and not a farmer-labor movement. It had no chance of capturing the Republican or Democratic party in any state. State labor parties—under that or some other name—were the only conceivable outcome.

This was precisely the socialist calculation. They joined the movement, as they openly said, in the hope that it would develop into a labor party—or a farmer-labor party dominated by labor.

The electoral tactics adopted by the organizations supporting the conference, namely the use of the old party primaries, and its friendliness to progressive Republicans and Democrats were policies at once American and democratic. But the clause of its constitution providing for control of the conference by labor unions—a result certainly *not* aimed at by some of its leading labor-union promoters—was a bodily importation of the undemocratic and un-American plan of organization of the British Labor Party—a plan which was not only to prove abortive under American conditions, but was bound to be extremely unpopular in this country and to react against the unions politically.

It is only in the light of this underlying fact of labor-union control that we can understand the final consent of the socialists and ultra-radicals in the conference—after a bitter struggle—temporarily to drop the proposal to form a third party and their willingness to accept a relatively moderate "program." Once this fact—complete control of the conference by a group of labor unions—is clearly grasped the whole movement becomes comprehensible. When the President of the Amalgamated Clothing Workers, Sidney Hillman, a Socialist and a member of the executive committee of the conference, explicitly and emphatically declared from the floor that it was "a *labor* conference," there was no evidence of disagreement.

Practically all the organizers of the conference were open admirers of the British Labor Party, and a large number openly desired to see a similar party, a farmer-labor party, at the earliest possible moment in this country. Many speeches lauded this British and socialist organization, while a number definitely proposed it as the model for this country. The British Labor party also took a large place in the printed propaganda of the movement. Relations could scarcely have been more intimate.

The British Labor party telegraphed to Cleveland that the way for American labor to assert its "political independence" was to form an American Labor party, while its official Press Service proudly predicted that "a permanent political organization along the lines of the British Labor party" would be the outcome! American democracy and labor—after a century of democratic experience—were to sit at England's and Europe's feet!

The German Socialists also hopefully predicted that the Cleveland convention meant "an American Labor party destined to play a part in the nation's affairs not unlike that now played by the German Socialist and British Labor parties" and that "the United States, England, and Germany, the world's leading industrial nations, would have three homogeneously organized and internationally affiliated parties in action."

This hope for an American Labor party affiliated to the Socialist International, was the hope of foreign-born Socialists and of European or Europeanized intellectuals influential in the conference. It was not the hope of La Follette or of those nearest him. If the La Follette movement should result in a new party, La Follette would see to it that the new party was based not upon a sectarian or labor or international organization like the British Labor party, but upon the democratic wide-open primary system of the United States. The difference is fundamental and irreconcilable.

La Follette, moreover, did not contemplate a third party. He knew that American institutions require two parties. He merely hoped that a new party might come to replace the Democratic party and that there might thus arise a new two-party realignment. As he said in his acceptance speech:

If the hour is at hand for the birth of a new political

party the American people next November will register their
will and their united purpose by a vote of such magnitude
that a new political party will be inevitable. If the people
in this campaign repudiate the Presidential candidates of the
Republican and Democratic parties—as in the providence of
God I trust and believe they will—we shall then witness the
birth of a new party.

But neither the American Federation of Labor, when
it later indorsed La Follette for President, nor even all
the unions in the Cleveland Conference, had any such
hopes. La Follette drew labor-union support not as
promising either a third party or a new second party—
but only as a protest against the domination of the two
old parties by their anti-progressive wings and as an effective means of aiding the election of progressive Republican and Democratic candidates for Congress and of
assuring similar candidatures in the future. La Follette,
they held, was nearer to these candidates than Davis or
Coolidge.

Senator Brookhart explained that the Progressive
Political Conference (the Cleveland Conference) had
been organized, according to its president, William H.
Johnston, chief of the Machinists' Union, "to head off
some radicals and Socialists in the labor movement in an
open conference, where the radicals would be many times
outnumbered and to lead the great, solid, and reliable
part of the labor unions to a sound American platform
in the old parties and in co-operation with the farmers."

Labor's political hopes and plans could not have been
better expressed. Certainly there was nothing Socialistic
about them. The presence of the Socialists, Morris Hillquit and Sidney Hillman, president of the Amalgamated

Clothing Workers, in the progressive conference did not lead the railway unions and brotherhoods to a radical position. Under labor union leadership the Cleveland Conference selected almost the same Congressional test votes as did the American Federation of Labor for candidates for re-election to the Senate and the House. With a few exceptions it supported the same candidates in the 1922 primaries and election—and they were well distributed between the two old parties, with only a handful of endorsements of independents.

CHAPTER VI

THE LA FOLLETTE CANDIDACY—
A LABOR-PROGRESSIVE EXPERIENCE

Labor Not Headed Toward a Third Party—Labor's Fifteen Points and What Happened to Them—The Socialist Supporters of La Follette Drive Away Labor Conservatives.

On August 2, 1924, the Executive Council of the American Federation of Labor, which included the present president of the Federation, William Green, as a member, unanimously indorsed Senators La Follette and Wheeler *as independent Republican and Democratic candidates* for President and Vice-President and declared their platform preferable to those of the Republican and Democratic parties. This action was given widely different interpretations at the time and has seldom been rightly interpreted.

La Follette's Labor Day message in 1922, significantly featured in the official organ of the American Federation of Labor, had been this: "The worker's weapon is the ballot. It is an effective and all-powerful weapon. Wielded with intelligence, it cannot fail to win."

Political action for labor, nation-wide and effective, this was what La Follette stood for. To the organized wage-earners of America the name of La Follette did not mean government ownership, the isolation of America in international affairs, or the condemnation of America's participation or of America's associates in the late war; and above all it did not mean a radical new party modeled on the British Labor party.

Nor was labor departing widely, if at all, from its traditional non-partisan policy.

Labor had entered into the 1924 Presidential campaign encouraged, early in the year, to the point of hoping for, if not expecting, a favorable hearing from at least one of the big parties. This expectation was apparently well founded in the case of the Democrats, since both the leading candidates for the Presidential nomination, Governor Smith of New York and Ex-Secretary of the Treasury McAdoo, had long records in the main acceptable to labor, and the preceding Democratic platforms of 1916 and 1920 had received a qualified labor indorsement.

The Federation, therefore, appeared hopefully at both Republican and Democratic conventions with a list of fifteen platforms planks and with a plea for the nomination of candidates friendly to labor. After a labor rebuff in the Republican convention at Cleveland in June, Gompers delivered a forty-minute plea in New York before the Democratic platform committee, presided over by William Jennings Bryan, which left no doubt whatever of labor's intentions if repudiated by that convention. "If we are disappointed here, as we were in Cleveland," said Gompers, "I leave it to your imagination where the masses of the people will go."

Immediately after the adoption of the unsatisfactory Democratic platform and the selection of the conservative Democratic candidate (Davis), the labor chiefs began to lay plans for the indorsement of La Follette, as an independent Republican candidate, running as such. Gompers's first precaution was to issue several public declarations reaffirming and restating the Federation's non-partisan political policy in order to make it clear that American labor at this time was not headed toward a Labor party on the British model, a Farmer-Labor party on the Minnesota plan, or any other form of third party.

The American Federation of Labor, it is true, had supported the formation of the state-wide Farmer-Labor party which sent Henrik Shipstead and Magnus Johnson to the United States Senate from Minnesota. But they did this only because they held that in Minnesota labor had been literally driven out of the Republican primaries. Senator Shipstead explained how it came about: "Last year [1922] a pre-primary convention law was passed by the Legislature of Minnesota. It was enacted for the purpose of keeping the old reactionaries in power by handicapping Progressive candidates who might file in the primaries. Therefore, this group of 281,000 voters, who so nobly withstood the poison-gas propaganda in the last campaign, nominated me as their candidate for the United States Senate on the Farmer-Labor ticket."

The Federation in its indorsement of La Follette not only definitely refused to approve of any new party idea, but left the door open to a future indorsement of Democratic or Republican Presidential candidates and platforms, if either of these parties reformed according to labor's requirements, though not otherwise. "We are judging on the basis of the conditions that exist," it declared, "and this judgment will be reversed only when the conditions upon which it is based are changed."

THE LA FOLLETTE CANDIDACY

Like La Follette, Gompers believed that a new party in this country, if it should materialize, would not be born in a day and that something like a political revolution would be required to bring it about. He was fully prepared to accept that revolution if it came. "If the time ever comes," he declared, "when neither of the now dominant parties responds to the will of the people, then the people will either rebuild one or both of them or abandon both of them in a great revolt and rebuilding."

But Gompers made no suggestion that this day was at hand. On the contrary, he made clear his belief that it was still far away. La Follette also had taken neither side of the question in his speech of acceptance on July 5th. He had merely expressed the hope that a new "aggressively progressive" party would result after the election as a consequence of the size of the vote he had obtained. But he clearly showed his belief later and before the election that the time for a new party was at hand. In this way organized labor was undoubtedly carried by La Follette somewhat nearer to supporting a new-party movement than it had bargained for.

La Follette, however, took all pains to assure labor that he recognized and valued its non-partisan policy and was not aiming to lead it where it did not want to go. Before his indorsement by labor he had already pledged himself not to endanger the election of progressive Republican and Democratic candidates for Congress or for state officers: "I would not accept a nomination or an election to the Presidency," he declared, "if doing so meant for Progressive Senators and Representatives and Progressive state governments the defeat which would inevitably result from the placing of complete third-party tickets in the field at the present time." [1]

In accepting the Federation's indorsement he again indicated that he was in full accord with its non-partisan policy, approving enthusiastically the Federation's statement that it was "not partisan to any political party or group," but only to "the principles of freedom, justice, and democracy," La Follette wired that it seemed to him that in this brief paragraph labor had "set forth a creed of citizenship which if accepted and acted upon by the great body of common citizens would rapidly make the government of our country what it was intended to be, the people's own instrument of service."

Nor did the Federation indorse the La Follette platform, but gave it merely a relative preference as "more clearly conforming to labor's proposals than any other platform"—a plain intimation that La Follette had failed to respond to some of labor's fifteen proposals presented by Gompers to all parties in June as representing labor's program for the campaign.

But this was not all. The Federation not only practically admitted that La Follette had failed it at certain points, but strongly and positively emphasized the fact that he had taken the opposite stand on a whole group of Federation policies, in fact on all those referring to foreign affairs. "On international issues," said the Federation, "the La Follette platform does not conform to labor's proposals."

And, finally, in full accord with its non-partisan policy, the Federation refused to discuss labor's attitude to the

[1] Speech of Acceptance.

114

La Follette platform and limited its discussion to a criticism of La Follette's attitude to labor's platform. It was unconcerned with party platform pronouncements except as bearing on its own campaign program or as opposing well-established labor principles.

But the Federation's attitude on the *entire* La Follette program, if not stated by the Federation, can be easily known. Points we do not find among the fifteen selected by Gompers and the Executive Council as crucial for the Presidential campaign of 1924 can be found in the action taken by the supreme body of the Federation (its convention) at its 1923 meeting.

In indorsing La Follette the Federation mentioned only six of its fifteen campaign points as having received his support—namely, its demand for "a remedy against injunctions"; for a guaranty of "the right to organize and to quit work collectively"; for "protection of the right of free speech," for "abolition of the Railroad Labor Board," for "ratification of the Child Labor Amendment," and for "a measure to annul the power of the Supreme Court to declare laws permanently unconstitutional," and two other labor-approved measures not included in the fifteen-point campaign program, namely, the direct election of the President and the election of federal judges. Nearly all these points, though of the first importance for labor, either had to do with political machinery or directly touch labor's organizations as such. Scarcely one of them has a general economic character.

Let us look now at the remainder of labor's fifteen points. Several of these were either of minor importance or had been accepted by one or both of the big parties. Labor's taxation plank, for example, while entirely in line with La Follette's, did not differ very materially from that of the Democrats. The two planks on military and international matters fall under the head of "international questions" already referred to.

There remain labor's demand for the modification of the Volstead Act in favor of 2.75 per cent beer and its demand for the repeal of anti-trust legislation. While La Follette in his letter of acceptance tried to revive interest in the Sherman Anti-Trust Act and in the first plank of his platform demanded that the power of government be used "to crush monopoly," the first plank in labor's platform urged that "industry and commerce be freed from legislative prohibitions that restrict development in conformity to economic requirements" and demanded "the repeal of anti-trust legislation and the enactment of legislation that will provide regulation in public interest and legalize economic organization as well as the constructive activities of trade associations."

This diametrical opposition on a fundamental economic issue helps to explain labor's partial and qualified indorsement of the La Follette platform.

Another broad economic issue held to be of the utmost importance by labor was mentioned neither in labor's fifteen campaign points nor in La Follette's platform, namely, immigration. The immigration law having been passed, immigration might have been held no longer an issue. But that law was menaced with vital modification from several directions. Moreover, it had been listed as labor's first point in a summary program under twelve heads published by the Federation's highest political committee as late as May, 1924, after the passing of the Immigration Act was assured. On this issue, as I have said, half of the Democratic and Republican Senators listed as progressives by La Follette and as friends by the A. F. of L. (though a very much smaller proportion of friendly Representatives) had voted to please their foreign born or foreign-minded constituents and against the labor unions.

So that if the La Follette movement was a third-party movement organized labor indorsed neither the third party nor its platform. Nevertheless, there was enough harmony between La Follette and labor to suggest the probability of a more thoroughgoing labor-progressive alignment on some future occasion. That harmony was based not so much upon the progressives' indorsement of the planks of most immediate interest to labor or upon a common program as upon the common fight of organized labor and of all other progressives against the economic interests that dominate the industry and the government of this country. In the words of La Follette, "the organized banking interests which own the railroads, control credit, and dominate the industrial life of the nation, control this government."

La Follette quoted Woodrow Wilson to the effect that "the trusts are our masters now" and that "we have come to be one of the worst ruled, one of the most completely controlled and dominated, governments in the civilized world." Dictatorship by plutocracy, La Follette declared, is "essentially undemocratic and un-American, destructive of private-initiative and individual liberty." He urged that to break the power of this system of predatory interests over the American people was the one paramount issue of the 1924 campaign.[1]

[1] Speech of Acceptance, July 5, 1924.

With this conclusion labor was in absolute agreement. Gompers declared that a vote for Coolidge or Davis was a vote to retain the incumbent administration, as both the tickets represented the same interests.[1] "The Republican party," he continued, "is owned and controlled by the reactionaries, by those who in order to give special privileges to the well-to-do, would place heavy burdens on those least able to bear them. The Democratic party is controlled by the same sinister influences."

The experiment of 1924 did not indicate that labor was moving toward a third party, but it did prove that there was common ground between labor and the other progressive elements throughout the nation. And the strength of these labor and progressive elements was expressed numerically not by that 18 per cent of the electorate that voted for La Follette, who suffered in popularity both because he seemed to be aiming at a radical third party and because of certain planks of his platform, but by that 40 per cent of the electorate that returned 186 progressive Republicans, Democrats, and Independents to the House of Representatives.

Labor was largely, though not wholly, united for La Follette. There were three important exceptions—the printing pressmen, the longshoremen, and the trainmen, one of the railroad brotherhoods (not belonging to the Federation). The New Jersey State Federation withdrew its support. Several important leaders, such as Lewis of the miners, and Hutchinson of the carpenters, were known not to favor La Follette. This was not a very large minority among organizations and leaders, but the elections indicated that perhaps almost as many union

[1] International Labor News Service, October 18, 1924.

members had voted for the Democratic candidate as had voted for La Follette—a not surprising result in view of the fact that the labor-union vote had long been predominantly Democratic.

Moreover, as the campaign progressed, it became increasingly evident not only that the labor and LaFollette forces were in some places divided, but that in others they were working against each other. This disharmony arose partly from the fact that Socialist and radical supporters in a number of states appeared to take charge, or at least to be extremely prominent, in the La Follette movement, thus driving the less radical progressives and labor-unionists either to vote the Republican or Democratic ticket or to vote for no Presidential candidate. This situation, as it developed in New York State, was given by James P. Holland, president of the New York State Federation of Labor, as the reason why the New York City Federation indorsed the Democratic candidate for President a few days before the election.

"I not only personally indorse the action of the [New York City] Council," Mr. Holland said, "but the same stand is taken with the representative labor leaders I conferred with in Buffalo, Albany, Rochester, and Utica. I fully agree with President Sullivan of the Central Trades and Labor Council that the Socialists have acted improperly during the present campaign. They have been endeavoring to make their support of La Follette an excuse for union men to vote for Norman Thomas, the Socialist candidate for Governor, after the unions had given their indorsement to Al Smith." [1]

In view of these local divisions and disharmonies labor and its progressive allies were not unduly disturbed by the

[1] Interview in New York *Times,* November 2, 1924.

relatively small vote given to La Follette—about one-sixth of the total. Reckoning by the ballots case for progressive Republicans, Democrats, and Independents for Congress, the size of the labor-progressive vote was more than twice as great. If this disharmony had been removed, as they held it might have been in a purely Congressional election, they were confident the labor-progressive vote would have been larger still.

CHAPTER VII

THE NON-PARTISAN POLICY MEETS A SEVERE TEST SUCCESSFULLY

Progressive Republicans and Progressive Democrats—The Labor Bloc in Congress—The Two Bi-partisan Blocs—Conservative and Progressive—Conflict Between the Executive and the Legislative at Washington.

JUST as the chief political aim of the labor movements of other countries is to secure a majority in their parliaments, so the chief political aim of American labor is, in co-operation with other progressive elements, to win a majority in Congress. Congress does not play the same predominant rôle in our political system as parliaments do in other countries. Still Congress is probably more important than the Executive—and its relative importance is bound to grow as democracy becomes more effectively organized and uses more and more effectively that branch of government over which it has the most direct and complete control and through which it has its most complete expression.

In the Presidential campaign of 1924 organized labor made a strenuous and successful effort to prevent the Congressional elections from being entirely overshadowed by the spectacular contest over the Presidency. Gompers and La Follette were prepared for a new party, but only as a possibility. What they had been aiming at for several years and were still working to promote in the 1924 election, was not a new party, but non-partisan Congressional government. La Follette had had fully as much to do as Gompers with the formation of the labor-progressive Republican-Democratic bloc in Congress. It is true that in his letter accepting the nomination for President La Follette said that he hoped for a realignment and the formation of "an aggressively progressive party" and that he was confident that the electors in November would give him a vote of such magnitude that a new party would be inevitable. But of what magnitude? La Follette gave an unambiguous answer: "If the people in this campaign repudiate the Presidential candidates of the Republican and Democratic parties, as in the providence of God I trust and believe they will, we shall then witness the birth of a new party."

La Follette was willing, then, to forsake non-partisan tactics, to subordinate the Congressional radical-progressive bloc, composed of Republicans and Democrats, and to indorse a new party, only in the contingency that he should be elected or come near to being elected President. He made repeated declarations at the time, as I have pointed out, that he would do nothing "to diminish the number of true Progressives nominally elected as Republicans and Democrats, serving the public in the House, the Senate, and many of the State governments."[1]

The first requirement for the election of progressive Republicans and Democrats is, of course, that they should not be opposed by independent progressive candidates. President William Green of the American Federation of Labor regards this danger to non-partisan Congressional

[1] Speech of Acceptance.

122

success as one of the very foremost grounds against any kind of an "independent" political movement. Referring to such friends of labor as Senator Wheeler and the late Senator La Follette and his son, the present Senator, Green asks, "Suppose these men who have been elected to the United States Senate and to the halls of Congress, who have fought labor's battles so well, had been candidates upon the independent political party's ticket? Would they now be either in the Senate of the United States or in the House of Representatives?" [1]

La Follette and the American Federation of Labor both realized that immediately after the 1924 election and for four years thereafter, unless La Follette should chance to win, the main political struggle would be for the control of Congress. Neither La Follette nor the Federation, therefore, intended to allow any possible new party movement to interfere with their efforts at the further building up of the Republican-Democratic radical-progressive bloc, unless to add a few third party men to it without changing its character, as had been done in the case of Senators Shipstead and Magnus Johnson of Minnesota.

Nor was there any major difference between the La Follette organization and the Federation as to which Congressional candidates should have labor-progressive support. The two organizations were entirely independent of one another in their Congressional efforts, but the Federation publicly claimed its leadership.

The Executive Council of the Federation declared:

In the campaign to elect men to Congress, regardless of their political group or party affiliation and deserving of labor's support, there must be unity of purpose and method;

[1] American Federation of Labor Convention, 1925.

123

therefore leadership must lie with the only organization having the right to speak for the entire labor movement. In this the American Federation of Labor yields to none, but will maintain steadfast its leadership, guidance, and direction.

To this declaration Vice-President Woll added the following highly significant explanation:

In the Congressional campaign, as has been clearly set forth in the report adopted, the American Federation of Labor, through its campaign committee, will assume leadership. It is now possible to state that there is no intention anywhere evident to question that leadership. It will be accepted throughout the labor movement, and we are confident that the qualifications of the American Federation of Labor to assume that leadership—which it has always assumed—will be thoroughly understood by all important factors in the campaign.

The reason for Woll's confidence that organized labor's leadership in the Congressional campaign would be recognized by all progressives was undoubtedly that an understanding to this effect—either specific or tacit—had been arrived at with La Follette and the chief organizations supporting him (though, of course, this would not hold the minor Socialist and radical groups which, while they supported La Follette, had their own legislative candidates).

There can be no question that the Conference for Progressive Political Action, which was supported by a large minority of the labor unions, was in complete accord with the Federation leadership. It had always shown a full appreciation of the importance of electing

[1] American Federation of Labor Statement of August 2, 1924.

Democratic and Republican progressives to Congress, even should these tactics exclude all hope of a third party.

William H. Johnston, president of the Machinists' Union, the chairman of the Cleveland Conference, fully appreciated non-partisan tactics. "We should remember," he said, "that the greatest political achievements in the history of our country have been brought about by non-partisan groups which have used political parties instead of permitting political parties to use them." This is precisely the American Federation of Labor idea.

If we organize a new party [Johnston continued] we must be prepared to dedicate all our energies to developing and strengthening that party. We must say to our friends in the old parties, men like La Follette and Brookhart and Frazier, who call themselves Republicans, and Huddleston, Wheeler, and Sweet, who call themselves Democrats: "We will not support you unless you come out of your old parties and join this new party which we have formed." Are we prepared to do that? I do not think so. That would be playing into the hands of the enemy, in my judgment. It requires no straining of the imagination to visualize the joys with which the members of the Old Guard in both parties would hail the announcement that the fighting progressives, led by La Follette and Huddleston, had been forced to abandon all efforts to control the primaries.[1]

This is precisely the position of the American Federation of Labor. Nor did the more "advanced" group of unions feel that a new party would necessarily prove more effective than the non-partisan policy, even if it were feasible. Answering one of the frequent assertions of British Laborite leaders that the American movement is politically a quarter or a half century behind the British

[1] *Current History*, October, 1924.

125

because of the absence of a Labor party in this country, *Labor,* the organ of the progressive railroad unions, declared that American labor with its non-partisan methods had progressed further than British labor with its Labor party and Labor Government: "Labor ventures the assertion that the American workers have as strong a grip on their Congress as the British workers have on their Parliament. The American workers have not organized a Labor party, because they have found they could secure better results by working through the American primary system—a system which is unknown in Great Britain. After all, results count, and, measured by results, the American workers can say with truth that they have achieved as much—politically and economically—as the workers of any other land. There is a new atmosphere in Washington, and it has been produced almost exclusively by the workers' vigorous non-partisan political action."[1]

The American labor movement is absolutely united, then, as to the practicability and the supreme importance of electing progressives to Congress regardless of their party affiliations. And in 1924 and 1925 several new steps were taken to make labor's effort in this field more effective. In the first place, the voting records of all Congressional candidates, instead of being sent privately to each Congressional district, were published nationally, "so that national attention may be centered on the Congressional contest as a whole." This nationalizing of the Congressional campaign was most necessary; indeed, it was the only means to secure wide publicity for the

[1] June 28, 1924.

whole campaign. Otherwise the metropolitan and large city press could notice only a few spectacular contests.

Next, better methods were devised to finance the campaign. According to the Federation constitution, all political funds have to be raised by voluntary contributions from the constituent unions. A fund of $23,000 was raised as against $4,000 expended in the 1922 campaign. This was still insufficient, in a vast country like the United States, even to pay printing bills, to say nothing of traveling expenses. It is a safe estimate that it was not 1 per cent of the sums directly or indirectly expended by labor's political opponents, such as the United States Chamber of Commerce and its local branches or the National Association of Manufacturers. But the sum raised indicates that from this date labor can and will seriously finance its political campaigns.

And, finally, labor has decided not only to nationalize, but to concentrate its efforts, not only to give general support to all the candidates it indorses, but to lend special assistance to those most in need of support.

"It will not be necessary," declared the 1925 convention, "to make any special effort in many Congressional districts. The returns show that a large majority of those districts that have sent to Washington men friendly to the labor and popular cause in the last two years are safe for democracy. Other rock-ribbed conservative districts show no signs of getting early political wisdom. There remain less than a hundred close districts to be held or captured—not more than a few in any one state— a task entirely within the range of practicable possibility for the national and local organizations of labor and its progressive allies."

LABOR AND POLITICS

American labor is hopeful as to its Congressional future. But it does not reckon without its host—and it is fully aware that the political activity of its opponents has kept pace with its own political activity. In fact, it attributes the measures of success secured by conservative and "reactionary" candidates in 1924 not only to divisions among progressives, but still more to the energy, the aggressiveness, the organization and the vast expenditures of the great business associations and combinations. So that labor's Congressional campaign has now taken on the character largely of a defensive and offensive against these organizations.

In the middle of the 1924 election, the Federation called attention to the fact that the great business interests had been carrying on a set campaign against Congress:

The reactionary interests are doing everything they can to belittle Congress. They do not like Congress—and they say they do not like it—because Congress is directly elected by the people. And since the direct election of Senators and the direct primaries Congress has come more and more to be truly representative of the people. General Dawes and other reactionaries have openly attacked Congress, direct primaries and the progressive group in Congress which passed so many progressive measures in the last session.[1]

This persistent and nation-wide attack on Congress, which still continues, has taken several forms. It began after the labor and progressive successes in the primaries of 1922 (and again in 1924) with assaults on the primary system—accompanied by animadversions on the direct election of senators. This attack still continues. The

[1] Campaign statement, October 12, 1924.

A SEVERE TEST IN THE 1924 ELECTION

Federation described this campaign in the following terms:

The assault on our democratic institutions has not only continued unabated since last year's Presidential election; it has been intensified and extended. The Executive Council refers to the nation-wide plot to weaken or abolish the primaries. All of the great reactionary newspapers and commercial organizations are enthusiastically and persistently at work in this campaign. It would carry the nation back a full quarter century to the narrow, corrupt, and inefficient partisan politics that governed the country before the days of Theodore Roosevelt, Woodrow Wilson, and Robert M. La Follette.[1]

The reactionary agitation at times reverted to criticism of the particular Congress then in session: "From the opening of the 1924 political campaign until its close a studied effort has been made to belittle and stigmatize the Sixty-eighth Congress, when as a matter of fact it has been the most progressive and responsive we have had in recent decades."[2]

There was nothing surprising or especially remarkable in the fact that conservatives disapproved of a progressive Congress. But no sooner had that Congress been organized than there was an entirely new cause for conservative alarm. For the Congress was organized and its rules were made by a non-partisan progressive and opposition "bloc." Here was a new and perhaps a permanent method of securing progressive legislation and of defeating anti-progressive legislation sought by business interests.

The next conservative onslaught began, then, early in 1924, when the Congress that had been elected in Novem-

[1] American Federation of Labor Convention, 1925.
[2] *Ibid.*, 1924.

129

ber, 1922, first showed its aggressive-progressive character. It was at this time that the conservative agitation
against "government by bloc" and "government by organized minorities" reached its first climax. (See Chapter
IX.)

The next phase of conservative counter-agitation was
the proposal that every President was entitled to a dependable or strictly partisan Congress, pledged and loyal to the
party platform and freed from other pledges and loyalties.
It was a plea for party and party government under the
safe leadership primarily of the President and secondarily
of party conventions. Even party caucuses of Congressmen were not to be trusted; the President was the autocrat nominated by the party convention and confirmed
as party autocrat by the election.

Behind this bold plan for simplifying the American
fòrm of government and substituting party rule, directed
by a single party leader, was organized business. The
Wall Street Journal, at the time of the Republican convention, declared that "Business" proposed "that the President shall govern the United States" and was "taking
steps to make its will effective." Certainly this was the
approximate purpose of the dominant business faction,
as the speech of Judge Gary, from which I shall quote,
demonstrates. Labor replied at once and at length:

Congress is to be subservient to the Chief Executive. It
is to be snatched out of the Constitution by political leger-
demain so that there will be only two effective branches of
government—the executive and judiciary.

If the present Chief Executive—Coolidge—had had a
"dependable" Congress there would have been no Teapot
Dome investigation. There would have been no adjusted

compensation for our boys who offered the supreme sacrifice in the great war.

The Constitution provides for three branches of government—the legislative, executive, and judicial. Should the political intriguers succeed in fooling the people so that they will vote for members of Congress who will blindly follow the dictates of the Chief Executive, then there will be only two effective branches of government—the executive and the judicial.

In the primaries of 1924, organized labor and its progressive allies were even more successful in nominating their candidates than they had been two years previously. Labor's review of the Senatorial situation gives a measure of that success:

Thirty-three members of the United States Senate sought renomination this year. Six of the most objectionable of the reactionaries have already been defeated in the primaries or conventions. Here is the list: Ball (R.), Delaware; Dial (D.), South Carolina; Elkins (R.), West Virginia; Mc-Cormick (R.), Illinois; Shields (D.), Tennessee, and Sterling (R.), South Dakota.

Every Senator supported by the workers in the primaries has been renominated. Those that had contests won by substantial majorities.[1]

When these primaries had demonstrated that, if the Congress to be elected in November would be "dependable" at all, it would not be very dependable, the conservative campaign passed into its latest and most violent and destructive phase, developing into a sweeping condemnation of Congress itself and a conscious effort to

[1] American Federation of Labor Convention, 1924.

discredit it and to strengthen the credit of the President and the Presidency for the contingency of a conflict between the executive and legislative branches.

The sneering libels on the last Congress because of its progressiveness [declared the Federation] have been replaced within the last year or two in a large part of the daily press by attacks against Congress generally and against Congressional government.

This newest reactionary campaign, unparalleled in its truculence and impudence, means nothing less than an effort insidiously to overthrow the American form of government and to replace it by a supreme executive. It is an attempt to set up in this country a system differing only in degree from the government of Mussolini, for which our standpatters cannot suppress their sympathy and admiration. With Congress subordinated there could be no democratic or representative government, only an autocracy, an oligarchy, a bureaucracy, or an unholy combination of these outworn forms of misgovernment.[1]

A newspaper as professedly "liberal" and important as the metropolitan organ of the opposition party referred to the Congress of the United States as "the most unpopular branch of the government" and attributed the small vote of the independent candidate for President in 1924 largely to his alleged advocacy of "unlimited Congressional supremacy"—an extraordinary conclusion in view of the *increase* in the number of progressive and bloc Congressmen and Senators in spite of the adverse conditions of that election.

The anti-Congressional crusade went so far that a conservative metropolitan newspaper protested that "Congress

[1] *Ibid.*, 1925.

has been painted in the undeserved colors of a political ogre." This conservative organ added that the propaganda had been so effective that "the ruling principle behind the popular attitude toward government" was that "there ought not to be any Congress." This had, indeed, become the attitude not of the people, but of high business circles and those fed upon their propaganda.

The Federation recognizes the enormous strength of this movement against progressive Congressional government. But it feels it has been steadily winning in the struggle:

Every decade and nearly every election [says the Federation] has shown a more progressive Congress—a Congress more truly representative of the people and of labor. The Congress elected last year to meet this December (1925) was no exception.

In spite of the overshadowing importance of the Presidential campaign nearly half of the present Senate and House were elected with the support of labor and of Republican, Democratic, and Independent Progressives, while scarcely a fourth were elected against the opposition of the popular forces.[1]

Having withstood the test of a long and highly organized attack by the consolidated business interests, under the unfavorable condition of a Presidential election—in which, moreover, the labor forces were divided—organized labor is confident of its political future.

Labor having succeeded in elections where Congress and Congress alone was the issue, the effort was made [by the anti-progressives] in this recent election to reconquer Con-

[1] Report of Proceedings of American Federation of Labor, 1925.

133

gress under the guise of a Presidential election declared to be the paramount issue. Our non-partisan political policy withstood the test and issued forth triumphant and with its forces intact. The opponents having played their strongest card and failed, the future belongs to labor and progress.[1]

A survey of the result of the Congressional election of 1924 showed considerable justification for labor's claim that it had "withstood the test and issued forth triumphant." The voting of that Congress when it met showed that labor had increased the members of its bloc in the House by nearly 10 per cent (from 170 to 186). This was accompanied by an increased influence within the Congressional delegation of one of the parties (the Democrats). In the House of Representatives elected in 1922, the labor bloc had been able to count on 105 out of the 205 Democratic members, or a bare majority of the Democratic delegation. In the House elected in 1924 labor counted among its tried and tested supporters 137 out of 183 Democrats, or fully three-fourths of the entire Democratic delegation.

On the other side, pro-labor progressives were severely reduced in the ranks of Republican Representatives. In the election of 1922 there had been 63 progressive pro-labor Republicans, or considerably more than one-fourth of all the Republicans in Congress. In the primaries and the election of 1924 these were reduced to 43, of whom 11 (10 La Follette Republicans from Wisconsin alone) were soon put out of the party, leaving only 32 among 240 regular Republican Congressmen.

[1] Convention of American Federation of Labor, 1924.

134

A SEVERE TEST IN THE 1924 ELECTION

These figures would seem to suggest a tendency which would bring about an ultimate (or approximate) realignment in Congress—the Republicans becoming conservatives, the Democrats progressives. But there are two large and obstinate facts working against this outcome. It may be doubted if the progressive Republicans expelled or reduced to discipline within the party organization in Congress can be kept permanently outside or permanently disciplined, while their numbers are likely to increase with succeeding elections. And it is also to be doubted (because of the peculiar situation in the South) if the proportion of conservative Democrats (one-fourth) can be further reduced—a proportion altogether too large to "discipline" on all occasions, and difficult to discipline effectively on any occasion unless through a Democratic President—and he would be likely to be as close to the conservative as to the progressive wing of the party.

As a matter of fact the Congressional session of 1926 showed that opportunist Democrats of the central faction of that party may at times gravitate even towards a conservative Republican President, in spite of previous coöperation with the progressive wings of both parties. Summing up this session, *Labor* said:

Assisted by the big-business Democrats of the South, the President had succeeded in effecting a coalition between the Democratic and Republican leaders.

This combination held its lines in both houses until the legislative program advanced by the great financial interests had been put across. This involved the passage of the Mellon tax plan. . . .

The Democratic-Republican combination in the House

continued to the end, at least so far as the leaders were concerned.

Garrett of Tennessee, Democratic floor leader, has been so friendly to the administration, that a prominent Republican recently boasted, "We have two Republican floor leaders in the House." [1]

[1] *Labor,* July 10, 1926.

CHAPTER VIII

THE NON-PARTISAN POLICY IN ITS LATER DEVELOPMENTS

The Old Slogan: "Reward Friends and Punish Enemies"—Project for Capturing Both Major Parties—Independent Candidatures Frowned Upon—The Prospects of a Realignment of the Two Parties—The Future of the Non-partisan Policy.

THE 1925 convention of the American Federation of Labor, held a full year after the La Follette experiment, and the first convention for forty-five years (with one exception) that was not presided over by Samuel Gompers, brought out a thorough discussion and review of the non-partisan political policy. The unanimous opinion was that that policy had proven itself more than ever sound in the 1924 election, but that there was need for further "enlargement and greater effectiveness." [1] This describes accurately the recent evolution of American labor's political policy.

The American labor movement has been built from the beginning on a non-party foundation. The constitution of the American Federation of Labor declares that "party politics, whether they be Democratic, Republican, Socialistic, Populistic, Prohibition, or any other, shall have no place in the functions of the American Federation of Labor." In forty-five years there has been no tendency

[1] Speech of Vice-President Matthew Woll in reporting to the convention on this subject.

137

to depart from this non-partisan principle. But the Federation's use of the term "non-partisan," while literally accurate, is the source of much of the public's failure to grasp an essentially simple policy. Repeatedly the Federation has explained that it is "partisan to men and to measures," partisan to candidates of parties, to principles and to planks of party platforms, but that it is "not partisan to parties."

Some of the earlier interpretations and applications of the policy, deriving from the days before 1910 when labor was still very weak politically, continued to be current even as late as the 1922 election. One of the earliest of labor's political hopes had been to send to Congress a small number of Representatives (Republicans, Democrats, or Independents) who should owe their election mainly to labor and to enlarge that group until it held "the balance of power." So we find surviving in 1922, alongside the broad political effort to unite labor, farmers, and other producers, the older and narrower tactics of concentrating on the endeavor to elect trade-unionists. The convention held in June, 1922, centered its attention largely on the prospect that "there are at least fifty Congressional districts in this country now represented by men who are not in accord with "our legislative program and who are generally hostile to our objectives, from which trade-unionists might be elected."

Labor now feels itself strong enough to subordinate these tactics, and it hopes, through an entente with other progressive elements, to secure, not an illusory balance of power, but a labor-and-progressive majority. For the balance-of-power idea often proves deceptive. It assumes that the little group holding the balance is situated *be-*

tween the two other groups and it assumes at the same time that these other groups are of approximately equal power—a conjuncture that seldom arises. From 1920 to 1922, for example, there existed a strictly labor group in the House composed of twenty-five to fifty Congressmen. It was able to prevent some hostile legislation, but it could achieve nothing of a positive character, either because the conservatives of both parties combined against it or because, even when its Congressional supporters were united with the entire opposition, they still did not amount to a majority. And the *maximum* obtainable strength of a purely trade-union group, even if we accept the above liberal estimate of its union proponents, would still be quite insufficient, under ordinary circumstances, to bring about any positive legislative results. The tactics followed from 1912 to 1920, and again by the labor-progressive bloc of 1922, achieved results by altogether different and broader methods. The reaffirmation of these tactics in 1924 and 1926 doubtless marks the final abandonment both of the effort to represent labor exclusively by "union-card" or strictly labor candidates, and of the hope to advance the labor cause materially in Congress through a mere balance of power.

A closely related political method is seen in the slogan of 1906, "reward friends and punish enemies," which was still largely employed in 1922 and, to a lesser degree, even in 1924. The slogan was useful, and perhaps sufficient, when first launched by a movement which represented a very small percentage of the electorate. But it was always crude and it finally lost much of its force when labor had evolved a definite test aside from vague "friendship." A candidate might be friendly, it was finally decided, but he was not friendly enough if his voting record was not right. He might be unfriendly in some ways, but if his voting record was up to the mark he had earned the right to support. In other words, when labor passed to *objective* tests applied by the Federation in Washington (not by local labor bodies in the local constituencies) and applied on a nation-wide scale, there was no further place for the old *subjective* standard.

The admonition to punish enemies became wholly obsolete when labor had evolved a method of nominating friends systematically and uniformly tested by their voting records in every district where there is any considerable labor vote (303 out of 435 in 1924). The defeat of enemies is now entirely subordinated to the election of candidates with satisfactory labor and progressive records. The defeating of enemies sounds vindictive and non-constructive, nor can it appeal very strongly to non-labor progressive voters. It was justified, however, when there were numerous districts where there was no progressive candidate and where labor was forced to support some more or less doubtful candidate against an "enemy."

One of the Federation's pamphlets issued during the 1920 campaign, entitled "Labor's Political Banner Unfurled," bears on the cover the device, "Stand faithfully by our friends and elect them. Oppose our enemies and defeat them; whether they be candidate for President, for Congress or other offices; whether Executive, Legislative or Judicial." [1] Yet the same pamphlet declares, on the first page, that "labor's partisanship in America has been to *principles*, not to *parties* or *men*." This is the later and more fundamental labor thought. It does not undertake

[1] From "Labor's Political Banner Unfurled," published 1920.

to judge candidates as men, or to classify them as friends or enemies—except as they are judged by the record of their votes on measures of interest to labor. The emphasis then passes wholly from their personalities to a limited number of definite acts.

There still survived in 1924 the old hope of the early capture of at least one of the great parties. This hope had its origin, of course, in the Roosevelt and Wilson experiences and it lasted on until the Democratic convention in June and July, 1924—when it was revived by the fact that the two chief candidates for the Presidential nomination were Governor Alfred E. Smith of New York and President Wilson's son-in-law and Secretary of the Treasury, William G. McAdoo. Both were reasonably satisfactory to labor, not because of their promises but because of their public records. It was hoped that if either of them should be nominated he might further liberalize the party—a beginning having been made under Wilson—until it might ultimately become thoroughly progressive.

Moreover, we must remember that labor had been immensely successful in 1922 in the primaries of both parties. So that we need not be too surprised to find the Federation convention held in June of that year resolving unanimously "to take a more active interest in the primaries—and, where there are no primaries, in the conventions—of both the old parties, and so getting control of the two old parties' machinery and ultimately controlling the machinery of our national government."

However, the idea of working for the capture of *both* parties—even when the real hope is only to capture one of them—squarely contradicts the tactics, successfully carried out by labor and the progressives in the agricultural states, of concentrating within the primaries of one only of the two parties in each state.

The hope of capturing either is now postponed, and for several reasons. The first is that the position taken by the Democratic party in 1924 removed it farther from labor than it had been for decades, both as to candidate and as to platform. The second is that the very nature of the Democratic party, as viewed by labor in 1924, precluded its early capture, since both parties were declared to be not only in the control of machine politicians, but "morally bankrupt" and "a menace and peril to our country and its institutions." [1]

But the chief reason why the hope of early capture of one of the two great parties has faded into the background—to be taken up again only at a later period if at all—was undoubtedly the relative success of the *non-partisan* progressive bloc in Congress in 1922-24 and the fact that it was returned in increased strength in 1924 (in spite of the unfavorable conditions of an overshadowing Presidential election).

A choice, it was realized, had to be made between building up a bi-partisan labor and progressive bloc in Congress and attempting to capture one of the two great parties. For the present, labor's choice has fallen upon the Congressional bloc.

Immediately after the Presidential election of 1924 there were further developments. The Federation finally came to the decision that in this election it had "deviated

[1] Declaration of August 2d, 1924, launching the pro-La Follette campaign.

somewhat" from the non-partisan policy.[1] In what did this deviation consist?

In the election of 1924 organized labor had protested that it was still non-partisan and was not indorsing a new party. But it did indorse La Follette and Wheeler, and these candidates publicly pledged themselves to inaugurate a new party if they secured a large enough vote. The Federation did not indorse the La Follette platform as a whole, but it declared that platform superior to the platforms of the two major parties and as therefore deserving of labor support, whereas until this 1924 campaign it had never gone farther than to indicate a preference between the platforms of the two major parties. In other words, it gave these elements of a third party exactly the same status as it had given the two major parties in previous elections. This was undoubtedly a departure and this is the deviation the Federation now pledges itself not to repeat.

But does this mean that the unions took no permanent step forward in 1924 and are now going back politically to the tactics they had followed before that year? Not at all. That election presented labor with a new problem arising from the fact that unsatisfactory Presidential candidates and platforms had been adopted for the first time by *both* the major parties. This problem absolutely compelled a new decision and a further development of political policy. Only three courses were open. Either one of the major party candidates and his platform had to be preferred *as the choice of two evils,* or labor had to remain wholly neutral as to Presidential candidates and platforms, or the independent candidate

[1] American Federation of Labor Convention, 1925.

143

and platform had to be preferred. Any one of these three courses would have been a new departure. The Federation now decides that the course actually taken, the qualified indorsement of La Follette and his platform, was a deviation. If the 1924 situation recurs, organized labor pledges itself, by implication, to take one of the other two courses as to the Presidency, indorsement of one of the major candidates or neutrality—ignoring independent Presidential candidates and their platforms.

"The American Federation of Labor," said the Executive Council, "has seen many independent or third-party movements come and go. Generally they exist for only one election. The launching of a third-party movement has proved wasted effort and injurious to the election of candidates with favorable records. The 1922 and 1924 campaigns definitely determined this fact."

The Federation of 1925 does not accuse the Federation of 1924 of having indorsed a third party. On the contrary, while the Federation admits that it "deviated somewhat," it gives strong reasons for the claim that, in the main, even in 1924, it had followed the non-partisan principle:

In the election of 1924 the A. F. of L. followed its traditional non-partisan political campaign procedure. This policy is persistently and often intentionally misstated. While it indorses no parties, it uses all. It indorses neither the two major parties nor any third party. It does indorse candidates of the two major parties and *occasionally* of third parties, or candidates running independently.

In the last election it indorsed 303 candidates of the House of Representatives, electing 186. Of those indorsed, 280 were Republicans and Democrats and 23 were Independents or representatives of minor parties. And labor emphasized the Congressional rather than the Presidential election. These figures give an accurate picture of labor's non-partisan policy and there is no excuse for further misrepresentation.[1]

In indorsing Senators La Follette and Wheeler for President and Vice-President, the Federation had not only pointed out that the former was running as "an Independent Republican" and the latter as "an Independent Democrat," but had added that this indorsement could not be construed as support of a third party or even of an independent party movement "except as such action accords with our non-partisan policy." Here, precisely, was the "deviation." A third-party movement was not indorsed, but it was encouraged by lifting it, for the first time, to the level of the two major parties—and thereafter treating it, as they had been treated, according to non-partisan tactics. But to treat a minor-party movement on the same basis as an existing major party was almost as helpful as an indorsement.

This is the justification for President Green's statement that labor in 1924 departed from its non-partisan program temporarily and committed itself "for the moment at least to an independent political policy." Green went on to show that the result has demonstrated the impracticability of the experiment:

The candidate [Green pointed out] was the strongest candidate that labor could have selected, a man with a record and a history, a great patriot, a man whose name was known in every hamlet, village, and home in America, a man with a brilliant record in the legislative bodies of our country.

Who could the independent political party have selected stronger and more influential than the late Senator Robert

[1] *Report of Federation of Labor*, p. 278.

145

La Follette? And yet the working people of America, even under our recommendation, would not go over into this independent political movement.[1]

Nor was the indorsement of the head of an independent movement for President the whole of the deviation. Not only does labor now see that a third-party movement was unintentionally encouraged in 1924, but it now admits that in that year it favored "every possible means of making it easier for independent candidates to be placed on tickets in the various states,"[2] and it regrets that action. Labor is still ready to favor independent candidates, but only on the twofold condition that their chances of election are excellent and that they do not stand in the way of a progressive Republican or Democrat with a favorable record. But in 1924, 180 of the 280 Republican and Democratic candidates indorsed for the House were elected, and only six of the twenty independent or third-party candidates, a sufficient demonstration that independent candidates had been indorsed without giving sufficient attention to their prospects.

All emphasis had been laid during this election upon the effort to secure satisfactory candidates in the primaries of the two major parties. But this effort had been weakened by the understanding, especially among the more radical unions, that in case of failure to nominate a desirable candidate in either of the major parties a third candidate could be indorsed—*almost regardless of his chances of election.* So we read in *Labor,* the organ of the Cleveland Conference (the Progressive Political Action):

The machine politician does not fear new parties. They

[1] American Federation of Labor Convention, 1925.
[2] Executive Council Report, 1925.

have seldom menaced his power. He has, however, received some body blows from the primary. Witness the triumph of La Follette's forces in Wisconsin, the many successes of the Nonpartisan League in North Dakota and other states, and the success of any number of progressive Congressmen.

With one-half the votes needed to elect an independent ticket, the Progressives can carry almost any party primary in any state.

It is because of these facts—so well known to the politicians and so little known to the people—that labor has been urging the workers everywhere to organize for active participation in the approaching primaries.

In Republican states fight in the Republican primaries. In Democratic states contest the Democratic primaries. In every state encourage the minority party to nominate its best men.

If you fail to name the right kind of candidate in the primaries you will be at liberty to throw your support to the minority party on election day or to organize an independent movement.[1]

The Illinois State Federation of Labor, under the presidency of John Walker of the Miners, which had been the most active labor organization in the endeavor to launch a labor party, reached the same conclusion.[2] In 1922 the

[1] *Labor*, April 1, 1922.

[2] The Illinois Federation, however, is now in the forefront in the successful application of the national Federation's non-partisan policies. In the 1926 primaries it supported the Republican candidate for the Senate who was nominated, Frank L. Smith, against the incumbent "Coolidge" candidate. The Illinois Federation claims, and is conceded by Smith, a large share of the credit for this result. Smith was supported largely because of his effective aid in getting an anti-injunction law on the Illinois statute-books and his rival was opposed as a complete "reactionary."

When United States Senator Caraway, a Democrat, accused the Illinois labor leaders of having been bought by the Republicans, President Walker pointed out that the Illinois Federation had endorsed fifty Republican and fifty-five Democratic candidates in these

Illinois Federation recommended that "no candidates should be put in the field by the workers themselves except where they have a reasonable assurance of electing such candidates or where there are no candidates on other tickets that can be depended upon to support labor's program." [1]

This position was indorsed by President Gompers in the name of the American Federation of Labor:

Under the action of the Executive Council, and in conformity with the A. F. of L. convention action, it is proposed to go into the primary elections everywhere to make certain that candidates favorable to the rights and interests of the workers are nominated. Labor will place such candidates in the field wherever necessary. [2]

If the Illinois Federation had used the word "and" instead of the word "or" its tactics would be those now decided upon; their resolution would then read "no candidates should be put into the field by the workers themselves except where they have a reasonable assurance of electing such candidates *and* where there are no candidates on other tickets that can be depended upon to support labor's program."

The labor attitude toward political parties was more clearly defined after the 1924 election. At the 1924 convention of the Federation, held immediately after the election, the Executive Council declared that the non-

primaries and said that he had neither received nor paid out a single penny ·in this or any other campaign.

The Illinois primaries of 1926 were no exception. In nearly every Western and Middle Western State organized labor, co-operating with organized agriculture (as in Illinois) could show similar victories.

[1] Illinois State Federation of Labor *Weekly News Letter*, February 18, 1922.

[2] *American Federationist*, March, 1922.

148

THE NON-PARTISAN POLICY

partisan tactics would "enable the wage-earners of our land to direct the political tendencies and activities of our nation, our states and municipalities, *without the necessity of concerning ourselves with the coming or going or realignment of any political party or group.*" [1]

The convention of that year did not take issue with this statement, but implied that it was only *one of two political possibilities,* the other being a party realignment: "No one will deny the inevitable change of political parties or groupings made imperative by the ever progressive enlightenment of the masses and changes in the social, economic, and industrial order of a people. There are noticeable at present throughout the world the manifestations of a change of political groupings representing on the one hand the desire to conserve the domination of material forces and wealth, property and property rights— and on the other, the hope and ambition to substitute the human aspirations and personal well-being of all our people as the controlling influence in our government affairs." [2]

This belief in the ultimate realignment of the two parties has now been the expressed position of the Federation for fifteen years. As early as 1911, during the heyday of Roosevelt-Wilson progressivism, the Federation had declared:

At length it has become evident to all open-minded men that important changes are pending in our methods of government, and especially with reference to the status of political parties. The spirit of revolt and change is abroad in the land, and the spirit of liberty which first inspired the revo-

[1] American Federation Proceedings, 1924.
[2] *Ibid.*

149

lutionary leaders in 1776 has again entered the hearts of the American people.[1]

While labor felt that American political evolution was moving steadily and even rapidly toward a progressive-conservative alignment, it did not at that time think that the realignment was yet at hand and held that it would be decidedly premature. Nor did the Federation believe that the genuinely progressive party, when it did appear, would necessarily be a labor party. "After the more complete organization of labor in the economic field," declared the convention of 1913, "there will be safer and greater opportunities for the creation and formation of a labor party, or a party pledged to the conservation of human right whatever the party's name might be."

President Green undoubtedly voiced the present view of the entire American movement when he expressed the opinion that such a party realignment is still not at hand.[2] "There may be a time," he says, "when we in America can organize an independent political party, when our nation becomes an industrial nation, as Great Britain now is. . . . We will have to change in America from an agricultural nation to a semi-industrial country before we can make a success along that line."

While the expression of the 1925 convention on this subject is more clear and concrete than that of 1913, the attitude toward the progressive party of the future remains substantially the same. The time, it is felt, has not arrived—though it is drawing nearer. What is new in American labor's political position is that there has developed, alongside of this established policy looking toward

[1] *American Federation of Labor Convention, 1911,* pp. 56-288.
[2] *American Federation of Labor Convention, 1925.*

the *ultimate* realignment of the two parties, another parallel policy, that of the non-partisan progressive bloc.

The bloc certainly need not interfere with a party realignment and evidently may even accelerate it. On the other hand, it may act as a partial substitute. Obviously such a vast change as a party realignment cannot take place within a few years. In the meanwhile the bloc system may be expected to continue, whether as an aid or as a rival to the approaching realignment. And when that realignment finally arrives, if it does arrive, the labor bloc and other economic blocs may continue to flourish in undiminished strength, though the progressive (as well as the conservative) bloc of blocs may have disappeared. (See the following chapter.)

But President Green, who has never been a believer in the present efficacy of an independent national political movement for American labor, does believe strongly in the efficacy of non-partisan action *under our present two-party alignment*—the two parties representing not progress and conservatism, but solely, or mainly, the "ins" and the "outs." This is the view of a very large part of American labor. *"With the constitutional instrumentalities at our command,"* Green says, "and with our *form of government,* the voters of America can make out of this government what they wish it to be." [1]

American labor's chief unsolved political problem just now (1926) seems to be the mode of co-operating politically with other progressive groups. Labor has already worked out means of co-operating with progressive farm organizations—in primaries, in elections, and in Congress. It has frequently voiced and demonstrated its willingness

[1] American Federation of Labor Convention, 1925.

to co-operate with other progressive groups, especially those of an economic character. The El Paso convention of the Federation, in 1924, called upon the Executive Council to "devise a plan to bring about the co-operation with the American Federation of Labor of other progressively minded groups composed of persons who were not by reason of their occupations or stations in life eligible to membership in the trade-union movement."

But the Executive Council in 1925 declared that Federation "should accept the support that is freely given of any group that has for its purpose the carrying out of the policy of the American Federation of Labor." Obviously this willingness to accept support without making concessions and without offering anything in return could serve as a basis neither for a progressive party nor for any other form of political co-operation with non-labor organizations or groups. The Council added that "in conducting all non-partisan political campaigns the American Federation of Labor will maintain control within itself of the decisions to be made and the procedure to be followed."

But this is a contradiction only on the surface. Labor stands for the fullest autonomy for all economic organizations. And it has co-operated with progressive farm organizations without fusion at any point. Each organization works out its own program and tactics and it is only then—before going into the primaries, the election, or a session of Congress—that an accord is reached. It is held far preferable that this accord should be somewhat loose and imperfect than that either organization should lose the liberty to evolve its political principles and tactics in freedom and independence. Labor's ideal of an economic democracy implies free and independent economic organizations in a position to co-operate as they please and to group and regroup themselves with other economic organizations according to "the question before the House." [1]

[1] One result is that the various popular blocs "overlap." Several estimates have been made of this overlapping in the last Congress. For example, there may be 200 Representatives pledged to organized labor and 200 pledged to organized agriculture, and the two groups may have no more than 150 Representatives in common. That would be enough to secure a large measure of harmony in the House, to control the House on many occasions and to warrant a flexible degree of co-operation in a very large number of Congressional districts. At the same time almost complete autonomy would be preserved for the labor and agricultural organizations.

For example, the voting in the House of Representatives on the Haugen bill in the 1926 Spring session was along sectional rather than progressive-conservative lines. The West voted for the bill, the East voted against it, and the South divided. A considerable majority of the 186 pro-labor Members voted for the bill, but a number of these abstained and others voted against it. In other words there was no complete unity between the labor and agricultural blocs —especially in view of the overlapping, the greater part of the pro-labor Representatives who voted for the bill being also members of the agricultural bloc.

But while organized labor did not, in this instance, bring organized agriculture a very large number of new votes, it undoubtedly gave the farmers valuable moral support and did its best to convert all the pro-labor Congressmen. Its partial failure can be attributed only to two factors, to its own incomplete political organization and to defects in the methods of farmer-labor political co-operation. As labor's political organization is improved and as the methods of farm-labor co-operation are bettered—a problem that is being worked at ceaselessly from both sides—the results in Congress may become more satisfactory.

CHAPTER IX

BLOC VS. PARTY GOVERNMENT

Labor Accepts and Defends the Two-party System as Moderated by the Bloc—Partisan Politics and Privilege—A Progressive Majority within the Opposition Party.

THE alternative to a party realignment—one party becoming progressive and the other conservative—which is now before American labor and its progressive allies is government by non-partisan Congressional bloc.

The American Congressional bloc, all allegations to the contrary notwithstanding, is altogether new and unparalleled in any country. The novelty consists in the fact that the American bloc is a group of legislators drawn from all parties and is directed against none, while the European blocs are composed of entire political parties and are directed against other political parties.

Conservatives have fully grasped the extraordinary and revolutionary significance of the new development. As a great newspaper of the Middle West has said:

This process cannot go on forever without destroying government by parties. . . . They will cease to mean anything if their candidates go into elections with involvements and commitments which have nothing to do with party principles or policies. . . . We shall have group denomination and not party control.[1]

[1] The Chicago *Tribune*.

154

BLOC VS. PARTY GOVERNMENT

Yes, we shall have government by bloc. But what is new about that in this country? The only novelty for the United States is this, that we shall have bi-partisan government by economic organizations of labor, agriculture and other popular producing groups, instead of the present bi-partisan government by business organizations.

President Coolidge and Vice-President Dawes denounce the bloc system as representing "organized minorities." General Dawes speaks of the cowardice of Congress before "the organized minorities of the soldier bloc, the farm bloc, the labor bloc, the maternity bloc, the good-roads bloc." [1] But the largest and most stable of these organized minorities, the farm organizations and organized labor, when acting together, represent a majority of the population. And rule by a majority composed of two or more organized minorities of this type—its composition changing from time to time, so as to bring into the government in the long run all the most important groups of producers—would provide the most solid possible foundation for efficient, representative, and progressive government.

The Congressional bloc is attacked by conservatives as an effort to destroy the two major parties, but in reality it stands for an adaptation of the two-party system to the needs of modern life and to the purposes of economic democracy. The tendency to handle leading political issues over the heads of the two parties by non-partisan or bloc voting leaves the parties, no longer pre-occupied and split by these issues, much freer than they were before to fulfill their primary function—administration. For under our political system, the two great parties are no

[1] Speech before National Budget Committee, 1922.

longer unofficial and extra-governmental as in other countries. They have become a semi-official part of the governmental structure, serving to secure an alternation in administration and a measure of popular control over the executive.

Because we elect our executives in this country, instead of having them elected by parliaments, our parties must, as a rule, obtain a majority (not a mere plurality) in order to win control of the executive. Because the parties must aim at a majority we have a two-party system—now greatly re-enforced by specific recognition in many of our laws. Because, as a rule, we have only two parties, each is made up of heterogeneous and conflicting elements and can with difficulty represent principles. Moreover, their function of electing to *executive* office gives them control of administrative appointments and favors, and these tend to hold the party together rather than any principle. Administration is their chief function and reason for existence. Each of these parties may come to make an admirable tool, because of the competition of the other party, for the promotion of administrative efficiency.

Under "bloc government" the old parties may be preserved as they are—one the Government and the other the Opposition, while such principles as they still represent remain altogether subsidiary to their overshadowing administrative function. This would leave nearly all but the most routine legislation under the protection of nonpartisan organizations such as those of labor and agriculture.

The great popular economic organizations, recognizing these facts, may be glad to preserve our two-party system, since it rids them of the burdens and dangers of office-seeking and partisan politics and leaves in the two parties a practical system of administration over which they can exercise their fair share of control. Since such economic organizations, in order to achieve their larger objectives, are forced to give some attention to political machinery, appointments to office and other dominating interests of partisan politics they may find two great *non-principled* parties (government and opposition) the most serviceable and least dangerous of political instruments for these purposes.

To Europeans and all others living under a parliamentary government this may appear to be rather a no-party than a two-party system—since with them political parties stand for principles, while with us the two parties have few, if any, principles, and none that are distinctive or fundamental or of the first importance. Such criticism is sound—from the European standpoint.

In Europe the "bloc" is a group of parties that builds a majority in parliament and forms or tries to form an administration or "government." In this country the bloc embraces no party, includes factions of both, and cannot form an administration. So that when leading conservative statesmen and editors assert that we are traveling toward the European bloc, it is clearly only to hide the truth and to cloak their opposition to a really effective, that is a non-partisan or bi-partisan, democracy.

Senator Fess says that if the bloc system is permitted as a principle, "popular government as we have always had it is at an end, and the bloc system of Europe is not only getting a hold here, but has become a permanent system." [1] Bi-partisan government "as we have had it" for the past

[1] New York *Times,* April 30, 1925.

generation—that is, by business blocs and business lobbies
—will, indeed, be at an end. The only remedy for the
popular bloc, as Senator Fess points out, is if the people
can be persuaded to return to partisan politics—leaving
the business interests to maintain an exclusive monopoly
of bi-partisan government—through their lobbies and
blocs. As he says, so long as the people "prefer the independent in politics and ignore party platforms and party
discipline, insurgency will grow."

Judge Elbert H. Gary, speaking for the United States
Steel Corporation and for our great corporate interests,
has even more explicitly laid down the people's duty to be
partisans:

There are political parties, well known, with formulated
platforms, discussed, considered, and then adopted. It is
the duty of the adherents of these parties respectively to vote
and act in accordance with these platforms except and unless
moral conscience prevents.[1]

Judge Gary says, further, that members of Congress
"have antagonized the President on questions settled or
voted upon by the large majority of voters." The voters,
according to this doctrine, decide all great national questions in voting for the President, for his party, and for his
platform. They decide nothing, apparently, when they
vote for Congressmen well known to be pledged to popular
measures by the great popular organizations of labor or
agriculture.

But the leading partisan of party government is no
longer Gary, or the spokesmen of organized business, or
statesmen like Root or Dawes, or the conservative Senators. With his inaugural message the leadership of the

[1] *Ibid.*, May 23, 1925.

movement passed to President Coolidge, when he proclaimed that loyalty to " the party majority in Congress"
is required by "common honesty and good faith with the
people who support a party at the polls." The progressive
Senator or Representative believes, on the contrary, that
his constituents voted for him and sent him to Congress
not to serve the party majority, but to serve them. The
President's conception of party government requires that
every important vote taken in Congress should follow
"the broad general lines of the party platform." Great
issues would be fought out exclusively in national party
conventions or secret caucuses; Congress would simply
register the will of the party majority. That was, indeed,
our form of government a quarter-century ago—before
Roosevelt and Wilson and before direct primaries and the
direct election of Senators were wrung from the business
interests by the people of the United States.

The president of the National Association of Manufacturers, John E. Edgerton, gave the Bankers Association a true statement of the cause of the "evil." "It all
goes back," as he said, "to those unhappy days of the
birth of the direct-primary law and the Amendment to
the Constitution to elect Senators by the direct vote of
the people." [1]

In language very slightly veiled President Coolidge con-
veys the same thought:

Direct primaries and direct elections bring to bear upon
the political fortunes of public officials the greatly disproportionate influence of organized minorities. Artificial propaganda, paid agitators, selfish interests, all impinge upon
members of legislative bodies to force them to represent

[1] Annual Conference of Bankers' Association, 1925.

special elements rather than the great body of their constituency.

When they are successful minority rule is established.[1]

The control of legislation by the co-operation of popular blocs representing in the aggregate the overwhelming majority of the population does not establish minority rule. On the contrary, it clearly disestablishes the minority rule of the "special elements" which have so long controlled Congress through the secret lobby and the use of the President's power to secure Opposition votes.

But it is hardly thinkable that the reactionaries will have their way in this matter, that the labor of a whole generation of intelligent, disinterested, and patriotic progressivism is going to be scrapped now to please the very party machines and big business interests against which it was originally directed.

As organized labor points out, "the people have been steadily turning away from partisanship and hide-bound partyism" and "the vote for progressive candidates who rise above party and have been true to the people has increased every election." [2] The Federation hardly goes too far when it claims that "partisanship governing legislation enacted by Congress has been shattered largely through the non-partisan political policy of the American Federation of Labor." But progressive farm organizations have been at least equally effective.

American labor does not believe there is the slightest chance that the nation will follow the advice of organized business and retrogress to partisan government—combined with government by a bi-partisan business bloc. It denies

[1] Address to William and Mary College, May 16, 1926.
[2] Convention of American Federation of Labor, 1925.

that blocs are destructive of parties, that they are foreign
or un-American, and that ours is a party form of government. Labor's official weekly news service says:

Those who condemn blocs and talk of "party government"
should read the history of the country.

A well-known lawyer and statesman (Elihu Root) recently pleaded for a return to the "good old days" when
party worship and party discipline were the joys of privilege.

Starting with the constitutional convention, blocs have
been the rule.

The claim that the government of the United States is a
"government by party" cannot be sustained by history.

Washington warned against the evils of partyism. Our
political and economic history is a record of blocs and party
formations, which are replaced by other blocs and other
parties.

To talk of the bloc system as of "foreign birth" is to
disregard the facts. The word is foreign, but the theory is
not.

This country was the first to establish a representative
form of government. From its inception voters have divided
into groups or blocs for economic reasons.

Experience has convinced the voters that the group system
is the best method to safeguard and advance their liberties.
They will undoubtedly stick to the policy regardless of the
fulminations of party bosses and statesmen.[1]

The leading metropolitan organ of the present administration rightly stated, in its final editorial before the Presidential election of 1924, that the paramount issue of that
election was government by bloc—that is, by popular bloc
(government by business bloc having been accepted without question):

[1] American Federation of Labor Weekly News Service, February 6, 1926.

LABOR AND POLITICS

The alternative, *Coolidge or Congress,* defines the whole issue before the voter [said this organ].

The whole Presidential campaign of 1924 has thus proved to be little more than an extension of that controversy between the President and the blocs of the Senate and the House which reduced the present Congress to a selfish group appeal.

Shall the national viewpoint of Calvin Coolidge prevail in Washington or shall the demagogy of Heflin and La Follette, *pandering to localities, groups and classes?* [1]

Here we arrive at the very bottom of the question. The view of the party machines and of the conservative interests is that differences between groups as well as differences of principle should be fought out first within parties, the party candidates then appearing before the electorate and in Congress, with a ready-made and finished program which supposedly excludes all local, group, and sectional interests and is based solely on the interest of *the nation.* The democratic view, on the contrary, is that there is no such thing as the interest of the nation apart from the interests of localities, groups, and classes, and that the place to bring about the necessary reciprocity and equilibrium is in the open, on the floors of Congress, and not secretly and deviously according to the practice of political parties, allowing the lobbies of business interests and secret caucuses complete control.[2]

[1] New York *Tribune,* November 3, 1924.

[2] Where there is a cross-division along both sectional and economic lines, organized labor and other national economic organizations believe the national economic alignment should take precedence. This may be seen from the following excerpt from a statement by Matthew Woll from which I have already quoted:

Great rejoicing was manifested in circles opposed to the farmer's best interests when the Haugen bill was defeated by a bi-partisan bloc of the East and South. President Coolidge's flirtations with the Bourbon South have produced their fruit—for the moment. But

BLOC VS. PARTY GOVERNMENT

Our constitutional system recognizes that for democracy to work effectively there must be decentralization. The decentralization we have had hitherto has been *geographical* and gives a voice to localities and to sections. What the popular blocs now do is to introduce decentralization and representation according to *occupations* and other natural and voluntary groupings. And these groups now act across party lines in Congress, exactly as sectional groups have always done and as business groups have always done.

For fully half a century all the leading business interests have lined up Congressmen to vote for them through a bi-partisan "lobby," the function of which was to form a secret bi-partisan business "bloc" among legislators. I need only mention a few of these interests, such as the railways, shipping, oil, meat-packers, sugar, lumber, water-power, protected manufacturers, for every reader to recall their well-known activities somewhat.

In the same way labor points to the inconsistency, if not the hypocrisy, of those conservatives who continually lecture the nation on the supreme value of party government, and yet continually rely upon bi-partisan action, even praising the conservatives of the Opposition for "rising above party." The Federation was particularly interested in the repeated bi-partisan votes that sustained President Coolidge in the Congress of 1926. "Citizens are continually lectured," remarked the Federation's Weekly

this desperate effort to divide the nation along sectional lines has been undertaken without reckoning ultimate consquences. The policy of divide and conquer may have gained for the day, but other days are to follow. The consumers and workers of the cities and the farmers of the country cannot longer be kept ignorant of their mutuality of interests. Big business is only hastening the day of a new regrouping of powerful economic, social and political forces.

News Service, "on the need for our party system and the indispensable part it plays in our form of government. This, however, is for public consumption—it is not practiced by its champions.

"Partisanship in this Congress—especially in the Senate—is unknown. In the House, Cannonism rules. In the Senate, party lines have been smashed on major issues, such as the tax bill, the world court, the leasing of Muscle Shoals (the hydro-electric plant), the proposed aluminum trust probe (directed against Secretary of the Treasury Mellon) and the Woodlock appointment (a conservative appointment to the Interstate Commerce Commission confirmed by the Senate through the extraordinary and sensational device of a secret ballot)."

"The party spirit and party discipline," the official labor service concludes, "have gone the way of the dodo and other extinct animals." [1]

Yet Judge Gary, like other leading spokesmen for the great corporations and organized business, continues boldly to assail the Congressmen of the popular blocs for having disregarded "their party platforms and even their professed party," and for having been antagonistic to the President. Fortunately, Judge Gary also discloses, in the same breath, the true nature of these Congressmen's offending, which has nothing whatever to do with parties. They have been inimical, it seems, to what Judge Gary calls "business." For, strange to say, our conservatives, from the President down, endeavor to concentrate public attention exclusively against the popular blocs and refuse to recognize the existence of the blocs repre-

[1] Weekly News Service of American Federation of Labor, April 3, 1926.

senting the great business interests. The business blocs, we are asked to believe, are doing "the nation's business" and what they do and ask for in government represents "the national interest." The President and the conservatives assail the popular blocs in Congress, on the other hand, as representing "organized minorities"—as if all the business interests were not organized minorities, and as if almost every citizen did not belong to one or more of them![1]

The American Federation of Labor calls attention to the fact that this question is wholly "a matter of terms." "When members of Congress ignore party lines and vote for a reduction of high income taxes and the inheritance tax, this group is called 'a coalition.'

"When other members of Congress ignore party lines to secure remedial legislation for wage workers and farmers, this group is referred to as 'a bloc'—a hateful thing of foreign importation that threatens our party system and even the fundamental principles of our government."[2]

But Judge Gary admits that the Congressmen of the popular blocs "have in part succeeded" and reveals the fear that, if "permitted," they will continue to succeed.[3] Elihu Root also feels that the future is dark for those who fear the coming of the bloc, by which he also means only the popular, open, and non-business bloc: "You see in our Congress," he says, "the beginning of government by blocs of men who have no use for parties ex-

[1] Interview in the *Saturday Evening Post*, February 6, 1926, by Isaac Marcosson.
[2] Weekly News Service of American Federation of Labor, February 6, 1926.
[3] New York *Times*, May 23, 1925.

cept to get elected, and when elected go their own ways
with no sense of (party) obligation." [1]

"Such a system was not contemplated by the framers of
the American Constitution," says Nicholas Longworth,
leader of the majority in the former House of Representatives and Speaker of the present House. "It simply won't
work here," Mr. Longworth added. But it has been
working here, in one form or another—for a good many
years. The sole reason why the popular Congressional
bloc is making such a disturbance among conservatives
is that it is working effectively and gives promise of
further development.

That the two leading popular "organized minorities,"
organized labor and organized agriculture, will continue
to function politically in a non-partisan or bi-partisan
manner in Congressional elections, seems a certainty.
That they will continue to be represented in Congress by
powerful non-partisan or bi-partisan blocs seems equally
certain.

The conservatives are concerned over all these various
minority blocs. But they are still more concerned over
the majority bloc of progressive Republican and Democratic congressmen that controlled the House and Senate
from March 4, 1923, to March 4, 1925—a bloc of blocs
composed of Congressmen pledged to labor, the farmers,
the war veterans, and other popular and progressive
causes.

The future prospects of this progressive bloc undoubtedly depend on continued co-operation between organized
labor and progressive agricultural associations. Certainly
that co-operation will last as long as farm organizations

[1] New York *Times,* May 15, 1925.

remain in the opposition and as long as they continue to meet the resistance of the administration. Even if the progressive bloc secures a lasting majority in Congress, and has to meet that most severe of all tests, success, it seems likely to hold together as long as it is opposed by an anti-bloc President.

The existence of a bi-partisan progressive bloc in Congress gives several possible political alignments; a clear bloc majority; a bloc-and-opposition majority; a one party anti-bloc majority; or a bi-partisan anti-bloc majority. A clear bloc majority has not yet developed. A bloc-and-opposition majority, on the other hand, existed for two years after December, 1923, and a bi-partisan anti-bloc majority also appeared during this and the following sessions.

It might seem that either the large progressive majority in the Democratic party would gradually make the whole party progressive or that the bi-partisan alignment in Congress of conservatives of both parties against progressives of both parties would lead to a new conservative and a new progressive party in place of the old. Either of these eventualities would put an end to the progressive bloc (though not to its constituent blocs). Both eventualities are prevented from developing by the solidarity between the progressives and conservatives of the South—united, at least outwardly, in one party by the race question. Other bonds such as the high tariff, hold the progressive and conservative Republicans together. But, above all, the entire machinery of elections, lgislation, and administration tends to perpetuate not only the two-party system but the two *existing* parties.

This rigid two-party system, however, does not prevent political forces from acting freely across party lines. It merely compels political evolution to find new channels—independently of parties which (necessarily, under our political system) have become rather official parts of the machinery of government than free and flexible organs of economic interests and public opinion.

Nor does the inevitable influence of conservative forces over the nomination and election of a President under our political system and under existing conditions prevent either the functioning of blocs in Congress or the development of a progressive bloc majority or even the formation of a bloc government. The nomination and election of an aggressive progressive President seems improbable. But it is not improbable that a president may be elected who would work with a majority composed of both wings of his own party acting together with bloc members of the opposite party. We may even envisage the early election of a President who would be progressive enough to consent that a Congress wholly controlled by a progressive bloc (without any conservative support) should be allowed to play that predominate rôle in government originally assigned to Congress under our institutions—a rôle actually played by the legislative branch in every other democratic nation.

[I have not discussed labor's advocacy of Presidential primaries, for two reasons—because the prospect for the early enactment of this reform seems not so bright as it was a few years ago and because it is very doubtful whether the enactment of this law would be sufficiently effective to assure the election of a militant progressive President. However, labor stands for "direct primaries for the nomination of all municipal, township, county, state, and federal offices"[1] and especially for "a Presidential primary law."[2]   And progressives are absolutely united in the belief that Presidential primaries would result in a more progressive type of President, though it is clear that primaries are more effective in their application to Congressmen.]

[1] American Federation of Labor Convention, 1907.
[2] *Ibid.,* 1914.

CHAPTER X

THE LABOR PROGRESSIVE PROGRAM: THE APPEAL TO THE CONSUMER

Liberalism and Progressivism—Are They in Conflict?—The Appeal to the Consumer—The Consumer's Chief Protection—Publicity—The Consolidated Profiteers Fight Publicity and Investigation—The Need for Some Measure of Governmental Control Over Necessities.

I

THE demands of American labor in the last decade constitute an American and a democratic program looking toward a gradual reconstruction of our economic society and its transformation into an industrial and social democracy.

American labor agreed with Woodrow Wilson when he said that "we are in a temper to reconstruct economic society, as we were once in a temper to reconstruct political society," and that "political society may itself undergo a radical modification in the process."

American labor shares its social and political program with the social progressives—that is, the militant and democratic progressives—of this country. The program aims to strengthen the great voluntary economic organizations of the people, such as those of labor and agriculture, attacks the power of the great corporations and of "organized business" and "organized industry" over our economic structure and our government, and works for measures of direct benefit to the masses.

The fundamental question has been raised whether American labor, in view of its belief in progress through voluntary organization, can consistently advocate any governmental program. Indeed, this question has been asked by the leading Democratic organ of the country.[1]

The New York *World* has contended that the struggle between Governor Smith and ex-Secretary McAdoo in the Democratic National Convention of 1924 illustrated the rivalry of two utterly opposed principles, which it calls "liberalism" and "progressivism." Its conclusion was that the Democratic party must choose between these two schools of politics and that it cannot stand for both. But are liberalism and progressivism necessarily opposed? The question is fateful for organized labor. If the answer is in the affirmative, labor is condemned to political impotence, torn between liberalism and progressivism within its ranks.

Here are the essential paragraphs of the editorial:[2]

Suppose we call the McAdoo-Bryan-La Follette point of view Progressive. What is this point of view? Roughly this: That those who are less well off shall obtain control of the government; that government shall be given more power; that this power shall be used to curb wealth and to regulate social evils. The essence of this progressivism is the unlimited right of the majority to rule, the extension of the power of government. Hence a leaning toward the nationalization of railways and other utilities. Hence the McNary-Haugen (farm-relief) bill. Progressivism of this sort replies to the old question, "Shall the people rule?" by

[1] The following pages are quoted, in part, from my article in the *American Federationist*, May, 1925.
[2] Published in November, 1924.

LABOR AND POLITICS

answering, "They shall rule all the time and as much as possible."

Now if this is to be called progressivism, then some other name belongs to those people who do not in the least like the kind of social order toward which these progressives are progressing. Take as the representatives of this feeling such men as Borah of Idaho, Smith of New York,[1] and Ritchie of Maryland. What is their point of view? Roughly this: That greater equality is to be obtained by reducing and repealing privileges now conferred by government on special interests; that greater liberty is to be obtained by contracting the federal power, by building up state and home rule as against federal power, and by seeking solutions of economic and moral questions *as far as practicable by voluntary co-operation, as little as possible by governmental order.*

If the La Follette-McAdoo-Bryan point of view is "progressive" then by every right of historical tradition this other point of view should be called "liberal."

These two points of view will contest for the leadership of the inevitable and the necessary opposition to conservatism.

American labor-unionism does not admit these alleged contradictions. Voluntary organization, it holds, can be made secure only by an increased popular control over government and an increased governmental control over industry. Big business can be kept from making the government its tool in industry and can be prevented from obtaining still more governmental privileges and from completing private industrial control over government— only by more efficient government control over industry. Above all, the danger of a State Socialistic Bureaucracy

[1] On the contrary, Governor Smith's position, as indicated by his quotations in the present volume as well as by his support of labor legislation, is decidedly progressive. Governor Ritchie, on the other hand, is typically anti-progressive.

THE LABOR PROGRESSIVE PROGRAM

entering into industry by means of despotic boards and commissions, and, at the cost of all voluntary organization, attempting to run it from within, can be forestalled only by the democratization and industrialization of these boards and by the effective government control of industry from without; the control of credit, of transportation, of incorporation; control of excessive profits through taxation; control of prices through publicity; legislative control over the exploitation and oppression of labor.

The anti-progressive brand of liberal, far removed from labor and every democratic movement, finds political democracy to be inconsistent with the liberal ideal of progress through voluntary organization. Either voluntary organization functions, they say, or political democracy functions! Both cannot function together! One of them must go! Let it be democracy! Using its championship of progress through voluntary organization as a pretext, the great organ of the tariff-reform bankers and exporters of Wall Street here makes an attack upon democracy that is especially damaging just because it is made in the name of a sound principle. With this sound trade-union principle of voluntary organization as its excuse, it frankly blurts out the hitherto somewhat veiled position of the reactionary wing of the Democratic party. It leaves no room for doubt. It advocates a Democratic party with the democracy left out; in so many words, it specifically throws over "the unlimited right of the majority to rule" which it rightly finds typified in the proposal of labor to check the powers of the Supreme Court and to use the powers of government to curb wealth and regulate social evils.

Especially obnoxious to the anti-progressive type of liberal, accurately and officially represented by the *World*, is the fact that, if progress through political democracy continues, it naturally and inevitably implies, as the *World* says, "that those who are less well-off shall obtain control of the government." Organized labor and organized democracy certainly do demand exactly that—or, at least, that "those who are less well-off" shall obtain a very much larger share, and the preponderating share, in control.

Progress by voluntary organization and progress by political democracy are regarded by labor not as two hostile or rival movements, but as interdependent parts of a single movement—*real or industrial democracy*. Organized labor in America has consistently supported both liberalism and progressivism. Conservatives disguised as liberals have had little success in their campaign to turn the labor of this country against progressivism. Nor have state socialists or radicals disguised as progressives succeeded in their efforts to get labor to abandon liberalism, or to substitute an all-powerful and supposedly benevolent government for the rights of individuals and of voluntary organizations. American labor has stood consistently for both of these absolutely essential principles of political progress and has steadily refused to be drawn into any sectarian movement that might split the forces of democracy.

II

The first progressive and labor aim, once the free functioning of the great voluntary organizations is assured, is

174

to secure control over the vast complex of corporations and allied business organizations that dominates the economic structure and directs the government.

And, finally, American labor and its progressive allies make direct appeal to the interest of the masses as consumers, as producers, and as citizens.[1]

Let us sketch, first, the appeal to the consumer. We find labor speaking more and more frequently in the name of the consumers—just as we find it speaking for ever larger and larger groups of producers, far beyond the union membership. "Organized labor being the only articulate portion of the great mass of workers who form the larger part of the population of the country" claims "a right to give voice to the grievances of the workers and to speak for them as consumers and as producers." [2]

During the era of high prices following the European war the progressive and labor campaign took the form largely of an attack against profiteering, high profits, and high prices—that is, it became in some measure a consumers' as well as a producers' movement.

The first of the series of anti-profiteering measures advocated by labor on behalf of the consumer were the federal licensing of corporations and publicity: "It is essential [the Federation declared] that legislation should provide for the federal licensing of all corporations organized for profit. Furthermore, federal supervision and control should include the increasing of capital stock and the incurring of bonded indebtedness with the provision

[1] The first two parts of this program have been treated in Volume II.
[2] American Federation, November, 1924.

LABOR AND POLITICS

that the books of all corporations shall be open at all times to federal examiners." [1]

This was followed, in the Bill of Grievances adopted by the officers of the railway brotherhoods and the unions of the Federation in December of the same year (1919), by a demand that all income-tax returns and dividend declarations should be made accessible "as a direct and truthful means of revealing excessive costs and profits."

No factor [the Federation continued] contributes more to our industrial unrest and instability than excessive costs of the necessaries of life. It is a demonstrated truth that the cost of living has advanced more rapidly than have wages. The claim that increasing wages make necessary increased prices is false.

Existing high and excessive prices are due to the present inflation of money and credits, to profiteering by those who manufacture, sell, and market products and to burdens levied by middlemen and speculators.

Three measures which had been advocated by organized labor and other progressive bodies were recommended by President Wilson for enactment. They were: the regulation of cold storage, legislation requiring commodities which are subject to profiteering and which enter interstate commerce to be marked with the price at which they left the manufacturer or producer, and federal licenses for corporations engaged in interstate commerce.[2]

The 1920 convention of the Federation developed a similar policy for the reduction of high prices consisting of six points. The four most important formulated as follows:

[1] American Federation of Labor Convention, 1919.
[2] Congressional Message of 1920.

176

THE LABOR PROGRESSIVE PROGRAM

1. Control of credit capital by those whose chief interest is the cumulation of profits results inevitably in the open door for profiteering. We repeat and emphasize the demand of organized labor that control of credit capital be taken from the hands of private financiers and placed in the hands of a public agency to be administered by voluntary and co-operative methods.

2. We demand that the government be authorized to buy standard commodities direct from producers and that these commodities be distributed through regular retail channels at a retail price to be fixed by the government. We demand that this power be made use of as a corrective for profiteering, and we call attention to the fact that the government has established a precedent for such action in its sales of surplus war supplies.

3. We urge that the U. S. Department of Labor compile and issue monthly statements of the cost of manufacture of those staples which form the basis of calculation in fixing the cost of living.

4. As a means of aiding these and other anti-profiteering measures the federal government should be authorized to establish permanent boards for the prompt investigation of profits and prices. All income and other tax returns should be available for inspection.[1]

Not only bankers and manufacturers, but middlemen, are held responsible for high prices. At its convention of 1920, labor protested against "the gross injustice practiced by those who contribute no useful service, but who stand between producer and consumer, grasping in avarice and pyramiding profit upon profit to a point that actually menaces the safety and welfare of our economic and social life." [2]

[1] Report of Executive Council of American Federation of Labor, 1920.
[2] *Ibid.*

177

This type of middleman has been accurately described by Secretary Hoover: "Certain speculative undertakings are necessary. For instance, our food is produced within a few weeks, and somebody must carry the risk in distribution during the entire year. The initiation of practically any tool of production or service is a speculation. On the other hand, the individual who injects himself into the normal flow of commodities between the legitimate distinct stages of distribution is poaching on the community and returning no service for the toll he takes. Where to draw the line between these extremes of rightful and vicious speculation is also difficult enough." [1]

It is against this parasite type of middleman that labor is moving, in alliance with progressive farm organizations, demanding not only effective public control of transportation and credit, but control of cold-storage plants and the meat-packing industry (the present Federal bill being by no means satisfactory), regulation of dealings in agricultural products, and governmental encouragement of co-operatively owned grain elevators and flour mills.

One of the most important of progressive policies is undoubtedly this governmental encouragement of agricultural co-operative organizations, through the extension of public credit. The successful application of such policies not only would improve the position of great masses of producers and consumers, but would tend to eliminate some of the most aggressive of our exploiting financial and industrial interests from government and the economic structure.

Even after the advent of the Harding administration the Federal Trade Commission, which had been largely

[1] December, 1919.

178

responsible for Wilson's three anti-profiteering policies, continued its advanced and constructive recommendations. Among the policies it recommended, in thorough accord with organized labor, was the making of an effort toward the reduction of retail prices. "The first object should be to increase rather than lessen the purchasing power of the ordinary consumer," it declared, and "there should be all possible legislative encouragement of co-operative associations of consumers and of agricultural producers." The commission also asked for authority "to continue its efforts to obtain and publish information respecting the ownership, production, distribution, cost, sales, and profits in the basic industries more directly affecting the necessities of life—shelter, clothing, food, and fuel—for the information of Congress and the promotion of the public welfare." [1]

The Federation fully indorsed all these proposals. The law enacted at the recommendation of the commission for the meat-packing industry in 1921 imposed a publicity policy—to a limited degree. Though it gives no power to the commission itself, it authorizes the Secretary of Agriculture to require from the packers "such accounts, records, memoranda as will fully and correctly disclose all transactions in their business, including the ownership of such business by stockholding or otherwise." But this was the sole remedy against profiteering accredited to the anti-progressive Congress of that year. The rest of the commission's as well as President Wilson's recommendations were ignored.

The Federation Convention of 1921 also indorsed the report of the Commission recommending "the early

[1] Federal Trade Commission, April 16, 1921.

179

acquisition by the railroads (then governmentally operated) of the principal and necessary stockyards and of all refrigerator cars and special-equipment cars used for transportation of meat and meat products and perishable food products, and further providing for governmental information and non-financial assistance to co-operative, municipal, and governmental, slaughter-houses, packing plants, and warehouses."

As additional means for keeping down the high cost of food the Federation's reconstruction program (1919) had urged the following land policies:

The private ownership of large tracts of usable land is not conducive to the best interests of a democratic people.

A graduated tax upon all usable lands above the acreage which is cultivated by the owner.

Government experimental farms, measures for stock-raising instruction.

The irrigation of arid lands and reclamation of swamps and cut-over lands upon a larger scale under direction of the federal government.

That municipalities and states should be empowered to acquire lands for cultivation.[1]

III

Let me sum up the remedies offered by the labor progressives to the consumer. The first and most important is publicity. No uninformed procedure is contemplated. It is the profiteers who fear investigation and fight publicity. For example, leading coal interests secured an

[1] From *Reconstruction Program*, June, 1919.

injunction against the Federal Trade Commission forbidding the investigation of profits in their industry—an extraordinary proceeding in view of the fact that the law passed by Congress gave the Commission full power, and in view of the demand of the country to know the exact financial situation in the industry. The full report of the Federal Coal Commission was first allowed to reach the public only by the private efforts of its secretary, nearly two years after its completion—and all its recommendations for publicity were ignored.

Four out of the five publicity proposals above mentioned as advocated by labor were favored by President Wilson, by Congress, or by the Federal Trade Commission. The fifth, providing for monthly governmental statements of the costs of production of staple articles of general consumption, was no less rational, practicable, and important.

Labor's interest in information about profits is not theoretical; it is based upon the necessity of having such information as a correct basis for the determination of wages. No approximately reasonable wage settlement can be made unless the negotiators have an accurate idea of the profits being made in the industry and in the nation. That such information and such forms of publicity are practicable is indicated by the successful taxation of excess profits by the American and other governments during the war.

The natural demand of labor for publicity and the grounds of employers for opposing publicity were thoroughly exposed during the Anthracite Coal Strike of 1925-26. President Lewis pointed out that this opposition was one of the miners' chief grounds for refusing arbitration by uninformed outsiders.[1]

Ellis Searles, editor of the United Mine Workers' official journal, pointed out the reasons why the employers opposed publicity. He called attention to the miners' claim that an investigation of the operators' books would show an over-capitalization upon which they pay fixed charges; excessive royalties which add to the cost of coal to the consumer; many cases of wasteful methods of mining; gross inefficiency in operation, extravagant mismanagement and high profits.

"We charge," said Mr. Searles, "that these books would show that the operators can pay an increase to the mine workers without increasing the cost of coal to the consumer. We say, too, that these companies refuse to show their books because they do not want these facts known to the public." [2]

[1] "It would be impossible to have a fair arbitration in the anthracite industry, even if the mine workers agreed. The books and records, all the facts of the industry, are the exclusive possession of coal companies. The miners have none of these. Every fact in regard to investment, capitalization, production costs. royalties, salaries of officers, selling prices, dividends, profits, efficiency or inefficiency of operation and management, and ability to pay a living wage, is hidden in the books of these companies. What chance would the miners have under such circumstances?

"The miners were compelled by the President of the United States to arbitrate with these same anthracite companies in 1920. The miners demanded that the companies permit a full examination of their books. The companies fought for weeks against doing so, and they finally succeeded in keeping their books tightly closed so that the facts could not be known. These are the same companies who demanded in the strike just ended that the miners again arbitrate with them. Is it any wonder that the miners refuse to be burned twice by the same fire?"—(American Federation of Labor Weekly News Service, February 20, 1926.)

[2] American Federation of Labor Weekly News Service, February 6, 1926.

These identical charges were made by the United States Coal Commission of 1923.

Already publicity measures have proved that the high profits prevailing in every direction cannot stand the light of day and that many may not be able to survive it— even were no further remedial measures undertaken. But there are several tried and tested ways of controlling excessive profits, once their existence is established, and this fact constitutes another powerful reason why the profiteers propose to fight remedial measures to a finish at their first stage—publicity.

This defensive campaign has been called a fight for "the private ownership of public facts." Once the right of the public "to public ownership of the essential facts of business and industry" has been established—and it is being established—private ownership and operation in the field of production will no longer be a menace to the public welfare. Private initiative and responsibility will have been preserved, but public control—in the measure needful—will have become a certainty.

The fight of the Coolidge administration against income-tax publicity and against the publicity of the extortionate business practices exposed by the Federal Trade Commission shows that the powers that be recognize that there is nothing more fundamental and vital to capitalist government than to keep the public ignorant of the facts.

As opposed to this policy of fact suppression the labor-progressives are agreed that the first function of all governmental economic boards and commissions—whether they are dealing with tariffs, taxes, railways, coal, or trade practices—is publicity. Organized labor expressed its confidence in "the exhaustive expert investigations and constructive work"[1] of the Federal Trade Commission soon after as it was established and urged that existing vacancies be filled by men of the type then serving.[2] It was primarily a fact-finding body at that time and was so administered, labor declared, as to be "one of the most valuable activities under government auspices." When the board, gradually filled by men of the opposite type, began to withhold facts of interest to the public and was at the same time given by Congress certain semi-judicial functions and, by interpretation of these functions, began "passing judgment on labor contracts," the Federation reversed its previous verdict and found that the Commission was "venturing into a field never intended for it."[3] This is typical of the labor attitude to all such boards and commissions. As *fact-finding* bodies they are invaluable, as intermeddling *semi-judicial* bodies they are obnoxious and dangerous, while their functions as *regulative bodies* are, as a rule, not yet effectively developed beyond these stages. (See Volume II, Chapters VI-X.)

Publicity is the first consideration not only for employees and consumers, but also for small investors. The joint demand of all three groups may soon become irresistible. Discussing the inability of the scattered small owners to control our large corporations, Prof. W. Z. Ripley says:

One remedy stands forth pre-eminently. Publicity of accounts and their standardization are likely to be most serviceable as a check-up on otherwise unrestrained control of intermediaries (such as bankers and voting and management

[1] Convention of American Federation of Labor, 1920.
[2] *Ibid.,* 1919.
[3] American Federation of Labor Convention, 1923.

trusts). These millions of investors and the public, even if they have so confidingly given their possessions over into the care of others, have a right to full and complete, unmitigated information. There lies an appropriate function for a rejuvenated and enlarged federal commission, to discharge an obligation of the federal government to a great and in many respects a helpless body of our citizens.

How far can such standardized public accounting be applied? It has been applied successfully to railroads and public utilities. Professor Ripley points out that it cannot be so successfully applied to all forms of private business. While this is true, it does not touch the main question, which is to apply the measure not to all forms of private business, but to the largest and most highly organized forms of business—those which show important elements of monopoly. The high degree of organization of such business would beyond question, permit a considerable degree of standardization and publicity.

There are other measures for controlling high prices, besides publicity. The federal licensing of corporations to protect employee, investor, small taxpayer, and consumer, has already been referred to. For the direct control of distribution we have the proposal to extend public credit to co-operatives and to regulate commodity speculation and marketing.

Governmental encouragement of co-operation, both among small producers and among consumers, can take too many forms for a brief summary. The United States Department of Agriculture is already well advanced in this work. Increased governmental appropriations, not for subsidies, but for investigation, and promotion, and for improvement of credit facilities, could accelerate it indefinitely.

There is the proposal—widely favored in England even outside the Labor Party—for government purchase and sale of leading staple commodities, as widely practiced during the war. Where undue speculation is proceeding the government may buy an entire crop. The proposition to buy the Cuban sugar crop was put before the American government by leading experts during the war, and would have saved the American people hundreds of millions of dollars. The same principle was indorsed by the Congressional progressive group on November 30, 1922, in a demand for the "government control of necessities of life when necessary to prevent profiteering in coal, oil, sugar, and other necessities."

And finally, we have the possibility of using the governmental power over credit to control both excessively high prices and all other anti-social practices disapproved by the public. The proposed public control of credit is in the interest of the masses, both of consumers and of producers. The Federation demands "the organization and use of credit to serve production needs and not to increase the incomes and holdings of financiers." "Control over credit capital," it continues, "should be taken from private financiers and should be vested in a public agency, able to administer this power as a public trust in the interests of all the people." [1]

In the labor and progressive view the control over American industry and business is largely (though, of course, not wholly) centered in finance. "The public

[1] "Bill of Grievances," American Federation of Labor and Railroad Brotherhoods, December 13, 1919.

must concern itself to-day with the control of money,"
wrote President Gompers, "only because money is an
instrument through which an improper power is wielded."[1]
High finance, he said, must be deprived of its power over
production, and "its roots must be dug out of our industrial fabric."[2]

Labor's "Bill of Grievances" was equally positive:

Credit is the life blood of modern business. At present,
under the control of private financiers, it is administered
primarily to serve not the needs of production, but the desire
of financial agencies to levy a toll upon community activity
as high as "the traffic will bear."

Credit is inherently social. It should be accorded in proportion to confidence in production possibilities. Credit as
now administered does not serve industry, but burdens it.
It increases unearned income at the expense of earned income. It is the center of the malevolent forces that corrupt
the spirit and purpose of industry.[3]

An illustration of the possibility of the constructive
use of government credits for an object of equally great
importance to consumers and to a large class of producers,
was labor's proposed governmental housing policy:

The government should inaugurate a plan to build model
homes and establish a system of credits whereby the workers
may borrow money at a low rate of interest and under favorable terms to build their own homes. Credit should also
be extended to voluntary non-profit-making housing and
joint tenancy associations. States and municipalities should
be freed from the restrictions preventing their undertaking
proper housing projects and should be permitted to engage
in other necessary enterprises relating thereto.[4]

[1] New York *Times,* July 23, 1924.
[2] Articles for Wheeler Syndicate, September, 1923.
[3] December 13, 1919.
[4] American Federation of Labor Convention, 1919.

In accordance with this policy, bills were proposed in Congress providing for the establishment of a bureau in the Department of Commerce to be known as the Building Construction and Housing Bureau, and for the use of money deposited in the postal savings banks in the building of homes. Both bills were pigeonholed. Labor later adopted the proposition advocated by many housing associations of a federal home loan bank.

The most important proposals for the use of public credit for the housing of the masses yet put forward in this country were contained in the 1926 message of Governor Alfred E. Smith of New York. Governor Smith recommended that either municipalities be authorized to issue bonds the proceeds of which should be loaned to limited-dividend building associations or that a state housing bank should offer home-builders the same credit facilities now given the farmers by the federal land banks.

A state housing board would pass upon the new projects and they would be economically financed by the state housing bank through the privilege granted it of condemning and purchasing land by the power of eminent domain. The actual construction would be carried on by a new limited-dividend and specially regulated private companies to which the bank would resell the land at cost. In addition these companies or the bank would have the privilege of issuing tax-exempt bonds.

In defense of this plan Governor Smith said:

Let us make no mistake; housing is charged with a public use even more vitally than coal or electricity, or traction or transportation. It is one of the three necessities of civilized existence—food, clothing, and shelter. As a fact, half of the indispensable equipment of the modern home is supplied by the city. The municipality supplies the water supply, disposes of sewage, acquires or sets aside land for parks, recreational facilities, streets, and roads. Shelter is more important than a public utility; it is a public necessity.[1]

The proposed state housing bank was enthusiastically supported by organized labor and as bitterly opposed by the leading real estate, financial, and business interests.

[1] New York *Times,* February 28, 1926.

CHAPTER XI

THE LABOR PROGRESSIVE PROGRAM: THE APPEALS TO THE PRODUCER AND TO THE CITIZEN

Conservation of National Resources—The Farmer-Labor Platform—Reforms That Benefit All Citizens—Democratic Taxation: for Graduated Income and Inheritance Taxes—For Federal Subsidies to States for Social Purposes.

LABOR'S policies looking toward direct government control of credit have been mentioned. In addition, labor advocates a whole series of large-scale government credit measures, as remedies for unemployment. Such measures aim to benefit the citizen as a producer rather than as a consumer.

"Upon the shoulders of those who control legislation," the Federation declared in 1922, "must rest the responsibility for the present unemployment." [1] Labor complained that the ultra-conservative Congress of that year refused to enact any measure for relief, paying no attention even to the recommendations of President Harding's Unemployment Conference, and that it gave no heed whatever "to the specific recommendations of labor for dealing with a problem which meant life itself to so many of our people."

Labor's recommendations, aside from an appeal for

[1] Circular of American Federation of Labor National Non-partisan Campaign Committee, May 1, 1922.

more system and better organization in private industry, were based on a program of government expenditures for public works. These expenditures, being in the nature of investments to build up new capital for the nation, would be paid for not by new taxes, but by new extensions of government credit or loans—and by taxes only to cover the interest on these loans when not immediately and directly productive. Labor recognizes that "public works and productive investments should be an integral part of a definite national program for conservation and development, and not primarily expedients to relieve unemployment." Extension of credit for investment projects of such a character, labor feels, will be based upon absolutely sound security.

The chief fields for the extension of credit for public works, according to labor's program, are:

1. *Reclamation.*—Development and extension of the reclamation of arid, swamp, and overflow lands.

2. *Water power development.*—Development of such part of the undeveloped water power in this country as would find an immediate market, this development to include the powers at Muscle Shoals on the Tennessee and others in the Appalachians, the Rocky Mountains, and the Pacific Coast Ranges.

3. *Inland waterways (canals, rivers, harbors).*—Development of the Mississippi River and its tributaries for domestic supply, navigation, irrigation, water power. Development of inland and coastwise canal systems along the Atlantic and Gulf states, thus affording cheap transportation of bulky freight and giving protected passage to our coastwise shipping. Further development of rivers and harbors of this country in accordance with the foregoing and with the report of the chief engineers.

4. *Public highways (roads).*—The principle of the public

roads bill enacted by Congress several years ago and now re-enacted by the recent Congress appropriating $75,000,000 and calling for a like expenditure by the States is sound.

5. *Forestry.*—Development in the national forests of roads, trails, telephone lines, fire towers and other permanent equipment for preventing and putting out devastating fires in accord with the principles laid down by the U. S. forestry service. There are more than 150,000,000 acres of national forests. Reclamation of more than 80,000,000 acres of man-made desert once rich forest land. Forest devastation is adding to this desert yearly some 3,000,000 acres— an area as large as the State of Connecticut.

6. *Housing.*—The A. F. of L. went on record in 1919 as demanding the use of the credit of the federal government for housing purposes. This can be done through a federal home loan bank similar to the farm loan bank.[1]

That is the national program. An earlier convention of the Federation emphasized, in addition to these national measures, municipal and state undertakings, such as public buildings and schools.[2] In view of the scandalous shortage of public-school facilities in so many of our large cities, this policy, involving huge sums, is of the first importance.

All of these projects, as remedies for unemployment, should be accelerated in periods when employment grows slack and postponed in periods of exceptional prosperity. President Harding's Unemployment Conference, organized under the presidency of Secretary of Commerce Hoover, recognized the high value of the principle of expending public works in times of industrial depression, and Senator Kenyon introduced a bill providing for the long-range planning of public works. But long-range

[1] American Federation of Labor Convention, 1922.
[2] *Ibid.,* 1908.

planning requires liberal Congressional appropriations of government credit, and the whole reform becomes of real importance only if the expansion of public works is on a very considerable scale.

For such expansion there is no favorable sentiment in the present national administration or among the dominant capitalist elements of either party. On the contrary, President Coolidge and the capitalists are opposed to it. The reasons for this opposition are obvious. The people are the chief beneficiaries of every project above listed, and capital gets only a secondary benefit. Second, while the nation as a whole, including capitalists, would gain enormously by keeping the wheels of industry going, the interest on some of these public investments would be paid—at least for a time—by taxes levied largely on the wealthy and on large corporations. Third, many government credit operations deprive private bankers of profits they would otherwise make, and all of them draw for public purposes upon capital and labor that might otherwise have been used for private purposes. From even the soundest of public investments the public benefits primarily, and capital only indirectly. With private investments the situation is reversed.

Labor's appeal to consumers has been summarized; no part of it is directed against the farmers, our largest group of producers, and nearly all of it appeals to them as strongly as it does to labor. Indeed, many of the measures mentioned came from agricultural progressives in the first instance. Among these agricultural producers' policies favored by labor have been the proposed control of the Packing Trust and support of the Federal Trade

Commission in its warfare, while it was in progressive hands, against industrial combinations among the makers of farm machinery, fertilizers, and other things required by the farmer in his business.

Labor stands with the farmers also for governmental supervision or control of all monopolistic corporations and of credit (see Volume II, Chapters VI to X).

On more altruistic grounds, or in exchange for the farmers' support of labor measures, organized labor, as I have shown, has favored government aid for farm exports and the other chief measures demanded by the agricultural masses.

With a social program directed against the farmer's chief political enemies and in favor of most of the things he demands, either as producer or as consumer, organized labor seems to be justifying its electoral slogan: "Whatever injures labor injures the farmer. Whatever benefits labor benefits the farmer. Whatever is the interest of labor and the farmer is the best interest of all the people except the privileged few." [1]

Labor has not developed a program directed to specified groups of producers other than these measures and policies shared with organized agriculture. But labor's principles with regard to industry and the economic structure as a whole, as discussed in Volume II, are addressed to producers generally.

II

There remains a third group of social reforms put forward by labor and its progressive allies—reforms that

[1] American Federation of Labor National Non-partisan Campaign Committee, August 26, 1922.

benefit not producers or consumers as such, but all citizens (with the possible exception of the privileged few). These are the measures by which concentrated wealth and great fortunes are taxed for the benefit of the nation or the masses of its citizenship. Whether the proceeds of these special taxes (or special tax rates) are used, (1) to increase the wealth of the *government* by reducing the national debt, or (2) to increase the wealth of *the nation as a whole* by being expended productively by the government, or (3) to raise the standard of living and productive efficiency of the people by more liberal expenditures on education and health, the nation gains and everybody in it gains, except, possibly, the privileged few.

Even the wealthy few lose nothing if, as seems probable, they have more than is good for their own welfare. Certainly a large part of them do have more than is good for the public welfare and certainly the influence of their surplus wealth, both on private and on public life, is evil. Though a small minority of the wealthy may be giving the public a return for their wealth which is comparable to the amount they take from the national income, still the principle of benevolent economic despotism, as practiced by this minority, is utterly antagonistic to the welfare and—if on a sufficiently large scale—even to the existence of any democratic society. Any good there may be in great fortunes is altogether outweighed by the public uses to which the nation could put this wealth. Even if all the rich were benevolent philanthropists, this would still hold true. But among multi-millionaires those whose expenditures are predominantly philanthropic are few and those whose limited philanthropies are over-balanced by vast private expenditures are many. And among mere millionaires and those of millionaire or semi-millionaire incomes the proportion of efficient philanthropists is even less, and this is the important fact since the total wealth of this group wholly overshadows the total wealth of the multi-millionaires.

Theodore Roosevelt recognized this situation when he said, half a generation ago, that no man ought to be allowed to inherit more than a million dollars, and the State of Oklahoma, taking him at his word, passed an inheritance tax to that effect, taking a very large part also of semi-millionaire legacies.

Writing against revolutionary Socialism and the panacea of government ownership in 1919, Herbert Hoover said: "Bankruptcy of the Socialist idea does not relieve us from the necessity of finding a solution to the primary question in the better division of the products of industry and the steady development of higher productivity." Continuing the thought in his booklet, *American Individualism,* in the following year, he wrote: "We have learned that the impulse to production can only be maintained at a high pitch if there is a fair division of the product. We have also learned that fair division can only be obtained by certain restrictions on the strong and the dominant." This argument for the special taxation of wealth is vital. Conservatives lay great weight on the point that every interference with the present system of production threatens productivity. Hoover, on the contrary, points out that productivity rises with every betterment in the distribution of wealth.

On another occasion Hoover went into more detail:

The present inheritance, income, and excess profits taxes tend to a better distribution of wealth. It has been proposed to extend these taxes in larger fortunes beyond their mere purposes of revenue, to accomplish better distribution and better equality of opportunity, thereby recovering to the community extravagant gains. The inheritance tax is theoretically a direct transfer of capital to income in the hands of the state, and thus might be criticized as stifling the increase of capital. Practically this would be answered if the state applied such receipts to the extinction of national debt or to the reproductive expenditure in the improvement of the national properties in rivers, lands, and so on. *Such a curative of unfair distribution of wealth is no violation of the social principles stated above.*

The social principles referred to are those of "American individualism" as Hoover conceives it. Yet within five years we have Hoover's immediate chief, President Coolidge, denouncing these same principles of Roosevelt, Wilson, and Hoover—and of nearly every modern government, for the last quarter century—as "Socialism." No better measure could be had of the aggressive reaction against democracy and toward capitalism that is for the moment in control of this country.

"I do not believe that the government," said President Coolidge, "should seek social legislation in the guise of taxation. If we are to adopt Socialism it should be presented to the people of this country as Socialism and not under the guise of a law to collect revenue." [1]

President Coolidge did not stop even with this extraordinary statement. He went on to defend swollen fortunes as a blessing and said that he did not feel "that large fortunes properly managed are necessarily a menace to our institutions," but that "they have been and can be of great value for our development." On another occasion

[1] February 18, 1925.

Mr. Coolidge spoke of our great fortunes as the foundation of all our art, science, and learning:

We justify the greater and greater accumulations of capital [said Mr. Coolidge] because we believe that therefrom flows the support of all science, art, learning and the charities which minister to the humanities of life, all carrying their beneficent effects to the people as a whole.[1]

The President has argued that inheritance taxes mean the using up of capital for current expenses, calmly inviting the public to forget the simple fact, well known to him and pointed out by his own Secretary of Commerce, that very many governmental expenditures mean not current expenses, but capital investments. For example, it is estimated that the United States is now expending $1,000,000,000 a year on highways—against $50,000,000 three decades ago. This is mainly capital investment— and is so widely recognized as such that roads are often paid for by the issuance of bonds. This, the nation's, capital will soon overshadow the amount privately invested in the roadbeds of our railroads. And the federal subsidy for roads is by far the most important of these federal subsidies of states that Coolidge wants abolished as being socialistic and as interfering with state rights— though, strange to say, he parades "the work for good roads" as one of the first of the federal government's achievements.[2]

President Coolidge and the financial magnate who serves him as Secretary of the Treasury usually put their argument for the abolition of federal inheritance taxes on the ground that they should be levied by the states—a

[1] Address to the Alumni of Amherst College.
[2] Message of December 8, 1925.

position that in view of their attack on the very principle of the tax itself (whether state or federal) can be explained only as an indirect way of getting it altogether abolished—which is what Mellon avowedly desires. For, it is pointed out, those men of wealth who do not already have homes in several states can choose for their legal residence a state like Florida, where the constitution forbids inheritance taxes.

Coolidge and Mellon assert, against the experience of America and of every nation, that *all* taxes are paid by the masses. On this point Coolidge says: "No matter what anyone may say about making the rich and the corporations pay the taxes, in the end they come out of the people who toil. It is your fellow workers who are ordered to work for the government every time an appropriation bill is passed." [1] These are almost the words of the "Platform of American Industry" of the National Association of Manufacturers: "The taxation and dissipation of the sources of wealth inevitably affect the whole population. The burden is ultimately carried by all in the form of increased cost of living."

Progressives are as anxious as conservatives that national wealth should not be wasted. They hold that it is never more wasted than when left in the hands of the rich. They do not deny that the rich and the corporations endeavor to shift as much as possible of the burden of taxation to the public by increasing prices and rents, and that they succeed in part. But they succeed only in part, and the burden of evidence of economists is that it is not a very large part. Mr. Coolidge himself admits that the wealthy pay when he defends the untaxing of the

[1] Labor Day speech, 1924.

rich on the ground that they should be left their fortunes, implying that taxes might take them away.

Secretary Mellon would go so far as altogether to abolish all direct taxes in favor of indirect taxes. He has frankly stated that his "ideal system of taxation" would be "to do away with all other taxes and make an equitable tax on all turnovers—all sales of real estate, goods, wares, and merchandise." [1] However, all progressive reforms in all civilized countries for half a century and more have aimed to diminish indirect taxes because they are paid by the masses chiefly and have increased direct taxes because they are paid chiefly by the wealthy and well-to-do. The Mellon tax philosophy would attempt to reverse the direction of social progress.

On the subject of taxation the 1921 convention of American Federation of Labor declared:

There can be little doubt that the outcry in interested quarters against the excess profits tax is primarily caused by the salutary fact that that tax is one of the few that cannot easily be shifted to the consumer, while the turnover sales tax is an amazingly brazen attempt to pile up on the consuming masses a share of the burden of taxation greatly disproportionate to their ability to pay.

The same reasoning would, of course, apply in favor of all other direct taxes, such as those on incomes and inheritances, and against all indirect taxes.

The multi-millionaire, Senator Couzens of Michigan, who indorses the Coolidge-Mellon principle of untaxing the rich, is yet frank and accurate in giving his reasons. He says that the 1926 reduction in the surtax on larger incomes means a reduction not to the entire nation, as

[1] Testimony before U. S. Senate Finance Committee, September 8, 1921.

they say it does, but to 594,00 persons. He would not deny that the tax reduction for the majority of these (those with the smaller incomes) is slight. While the taxes of the remainder of the larger taxpayers, numbering perhaps 200,000 of our richest citizens, is lightened considerably, it has been pointed out that nobody but them and their direct dependents receive any benefit whatever from this reduction. The other 40,000,000 breadwinners, until now the co-heirs to the benefits of the expenditure of the proceeds of these taxes, simply have had a further $200,000,000 a year taken away from them and added to thousands of fortunes and incomes already swollen beyond anything known in the history of mankind.

Nothing could be more instructive of the social struggle between the concentrated wealth of this country—divided among 200,000 or 300,000 persons, or with all their direct dependents hardly a million individuals—against the rest of the 40,000,000 breadwinners!

Against this uttermost reaction labor favors "sharply graduated income and inheritance taxes" levied at Washington.

Taxation [says the American Federation of Labor] should rest as lightly as possible upon constructive enterprise. Taxation should provide for full contribution from wealth by a tax upon profits which will not discourage industrial or commercial enterprise. There should be provided a progressive increase in taxes upon incomes, inheritances, and upon land values of such a nature as to render it unprofitable to hold land without putting it to use, to afford a transition to greater economic equality, and to supply means of liquidating the national indebtedness growing out of the war.[1]

[1] "Reconstruction Program," 1919.

201

It is the definite purpose of this taxation policy, first, to produce greater economic equality between citizens, and, second, to lessen the debt of the nation to private individuals, and this without putting any undue burden on active capital.

The labor and progressive campaign for democratic taxation received a temporary setback in 1926. Congress adopted the Mellon tax-reduction plan, but only by means of a bi-partisan vote. The progressive Republican vote against it was so considerable that had the same Democrats continued to oppose it as in 1924, it would again have been defeated. Those who voted for the Mellon plan in 1926 did not, however, swing the Democratic party with them and the progressive taxation policy has every prospect for a majority in succeeding Congresses. In 1924 the Democratic party, at its quadrennial convention had denounced the Mellon plan as "a device to relieve multi-millionaires" and pledged itself to accept "the issue of taxation tendered by President Coolidge." That remains the official position of the party as a whole—and the sincere position of its progressive majority.

But labor and the general public demand increased expenditure, above all, for public improvements and for public education and health—and this means not decreased but increased taxes. Wealthy taxpayers and well-to-do capitalists may oppose all new governmental activities because all (or nearly all) require an increase of taxation. But this is precisely the reverse of the state of mind of labor and the huge majority of the electorate. Governor Smith of New York expressed the labor and progressive standpoint when he said:

THE LABOR PROGRESSIVE PROGRAM

You have either got to cut down the activity of the State, and decide it will embark on no new activites, or be prepared to see a rising cost of government, year in and year out.

Now I dispute the oft-made statement that people resent increase in taxation. I do not believe that is true. I think resentment against the government comes from knowledge of wasted money, not money that is properly and judiciously spent.[1]

Governor Smith favors keeping taxation to the minimum consonant with desirable new activities and the resultant unavoidable rising costs of government. But to accomplish this he would cut down "the waste of government" and not cut down its beneficent functions. This is the labor and progressive standpoint.[2]

III

An infinite variety of social uses have been proposed for the surplus wealth retaken by society from the wealthy individual and the great corporation. One use, beneficial to the government and therefore to every citizen in proportion as he secures benefits from the government and also in proportion as he pays taxes, is the repayment of the national debt. The National Catholic Welfare Council points out that "our immense war debt constitutes a particular reason why incomes and excess profits should continue to be heavily taxed. In this way two important ends will be attained: the poor will be relieved of injurious tax burdens, and the small class of specially privileged capitalists will be compelled to return a part of their unearned gains to society."

[1] New York *Times*, February 3, 1926.
[2] Message to New York State Legislature at its opening session in 1926.

It was in accordance with this principle that the Federation demanded "a rapidly progressive tax upon large estates" and "that the highest (graduated) rate of taxation levied during the war upon incomes and excess profits be retained until the full money cost of the war is paid." [1]

But while this debt-payment policy would benefit the entire nation, it would chiefly benefit the middle group of taxpayers, and is therefore not insisted upon by progressives to the prejudice of other forms of government expenditure.

A second form of national expenditure advocated by progressives is the investment of government wealth to increase the nation's capital. This is typified in the federal good-roads bill, enacted in 1916. The entire nation benefits, and especially those capitalists who are now so largely owners of commercial trucks. But the conservatives revolt even against such federal expenditure, since it is paid for partly by taxing the rich. They want the roads to be financed by the states where the small owners of automobiles, numbering so many millions of persons of modest means, pay most of the tax. This federal roads subsidy, which already takes $75,000,000 a year from the federal treasury, is particularly hated by conservatives because, more than any other, it suggests the possibility of the further expenditure of large sums—obtained in considerable part from great fortunes—for the benefit of the nation.

A third group of national governmental expenditures directly for the benefit of the masses, and only very indirectly for the benefit of the capitalists, is typified by the federal subsidies to the states for educational purposes,

[1] American Federation of Labor Convention, 1921.

now totaling only $11,000,000 a year, but to rise somewhat higher within the next few years. It is these outlays that most infuriate the wealthy conservatives and their political spokesmen. Wealth taken from the wealthy and expended on the masses! Yet this is precisely the type of government expenditure that appeals most strongly of all to labor—and to every true democrat and genuine progressive. That eminent and conservative educational authority, Charles W. Eliot, calculated that America ought to spend several billions more on her public schools (several times the present amount), a truism to any thoughtful and truly patriotic American.[1]

Emerson called public education "the most radical of revolutions"—this, namely, that the poor man, whom the law does not allow to take an ear of corn when starving nor a pair of shoes for his freezing feet, is allowed to put his hands in the pockets of the rich and say: "You shall educate me, not as you will, but as I will; not alone in the elements, but by further provision, in the languages, in the sciences, in the useful arts, and in the elegant arts."[2]

The revolution Emerson speaks of is far from complete. But it is proceeding steadily to-day, and public schools, as he describes them, mean that the state is gradually undertaking to do everything that can be done through schools toward establishing economic and social democracy. In other words, the nation is using the schools to give the maximum development to the nation's children regardless of their parents' incomes. And it is

[1] "More Money for the Public Schools."
[2] Essay on Education.

just because the schools mean all this that there is such a continuous and aggressive campaign on the part of large taxpayers who do not send their children to public schools against rising public expenditures for education.

Public education expenditures are not yet nearly enough to provide for the education described by Emerson— though his is the accepted American standard. The classes would have to be half the size they are, the miserable teachers' salaries would have to be increased 50 per cent and all other expenditures augmented in proportion, or more than proportionately, for the secondary schools and all the newer branches of education.

Public-school expenditures have been rising but only with the cost of living and not in proportion to our increasing wealth. They do not yet reach the total of our tobacco bill, and take little more than we pay for confectionery and sweet drinks. They do not absorb 2 per cent of our national income. Yet if we had retained our federal taxation of large incomes and inheritances and excess profits as they were in 1920, as was advocated by labor, we could easily provide the billion or more necessary to double our national education fund, without drawing heavily upon the resources of the poorer states that are most in need of educational and other subsidies.

A glance at the public-school program of the American Federation of Labor will show that it would require several times our present public-school expenditures and would have to be supported by liberal federal subsidies. The key-note to the Federation's public education policy is contained in its demand for "the liberal, ungrudging reorganization and increase of school revenues as the only means of maintaining and developing the efficiency of our public schools"[1]

The Federation points out specifically just where vast increases in school expenditure are required:

(1) School building programs must put an end to the half-time evil and congestion. "The public school must be maintained as a civic model, not permitted to become a symbol of degradation."

(2) There must be a drastic reduction in the size of classes; in other words, a very large increase in the number of teachers.

(3) There must be "a thorough-going revision upward of the salary schedule of teachers in public schools, normal schools, and universities."

(4) There should be a minimum school-leaving age of sixteen and liberal provision for older pupils in continuation schools.

(5) Free text-books.

(6) Complete systems of modern physical education under specially trained instructors.

(7) Ample playground facilities.

(8) Medical and dental inspection.

This program does not even touch upon the arts, music, manual training, modern languages, and the so-called "frills" of the public schools (which labor also favors, though it does not wish to over-emphasize them). It does not deal with the special expenditure necessary to give the wage-earners' children a really effective opportunity for higher and technical education. But the above points are those stressed by labor, and they are enough to show the vastly increased expenditures it believes are de-

[1] American Federation of Labor Convention, 1919.

manded if our schools are to be a real and an adequate expression of democracy.

The Federation demands for the wage-earners' children "opportunity for the fullest possible development." But it recognizes that some states have not even approached, and because of their poverty will not approach, the fulfillment of such a program. And therefore it favors, in addition to liberal local expenditures, liberal state expenditures and liberal federal subsidies: "The government should exercise advisory *supervision* over public education, and where necessary maintain adequate public education through *subsidies* without giving to the government power to hamper or interfere with the free development of public education by the several states." [1]

The Federation, true to its own foundation principle and to American democracy, stipulates that "local autonomy" must be safeguarded. But it will not allow this principle to be used either by the wealthy taxpayer or the partisan of private schools, lay or religious, against the public schools. It is pledged to federal subsidies for technical and agricultural education, for physical education, for the extension of education among the adult population, for Americanization, for the removal of illiteracy, and for physical education.

As much money could be as well invested in the nation's children for health as for education, every dollar wisely invested in each case being destined to return to the community in the increased economic efficiency of its citizens, to say nothing of the gain in national happiness.

The objections offered to the present small but

[1] American Federation of Labor Convention, 1919.

promising beginnings of these two types of federal expenditure by Republican and Democratic anti-progressives are astounding. The President says that to subsidize the states, so that the poorer states receive many times what they pay in income and profit taxes while richer states get only a small fraction of what they pay, means that "we impose unfairly on the strength of the strong and we encourage the weak to indulge their weakness." This argument, labor-progressives have pointed out, if applied to the individual, would forbid all taxation from which the wealthy citizen did not receive as much as he paid. In other words, it would end all taxation of the rich except that approved by the rich!

Labor progressives point out that no such anarchistic or anti-governmental doctrine has been put forth in high places in this country for nearly a generation, and that no modern nation has been so anti-democratic as to attempt to put any such doctrine into practice. A large part of all taxation takes from those who have in order to give to those who need. And this especially is true as between geographical districts. If, for example, all money taken from the nation's financial center, New York City, should be returned to New York City—and similarly with other wealthy centers—and if no needy section anywhere received money from outside, this would mean that the national government could take no step to promote any costly national development except within our richest sections.

If, in these national subsidies to states, money is taken from one state and given to another, says the Democratic Governor of Maryland, "all idea of state initiative and accomplishment might as well be abandoned." On the contrary, in the progressive and labor view, this policy marks the very beginning of all great governmental initiative and accomplishment for a large majority of the states and for a large majority of the population. And as these national expenditures come more and more to take the most social of all forms of governmental expenditures—exemplified by subsidies for education—the proportion of the population that receives more than it pays will rapidly increase. Nor do the wage-earners and the masses of the Northeast grudge the taking of this money from the wealthy residents of their section—money drawn from the entire nation—and its use for the development of the nation.[1]

[1] The anti-progressive argument that federal expenditures distributed among the states according to population or need are an injustice to those states that pay most of the taxes is, often, not to be taken seriously. For this argument is very commonly accompanied by an attack on these same governmental expenditures even if financed by the states themselves! This is frequently the case with the statements of President Coolidge and Secretaries Mellon and Hoover, the chief conservative spokesmen on these questions. Their main position is, briefly, that "the people" ought to do almost everything for themselves without utilizing their government—a principle that applies equally against the states and the national government.

A typical presentation, with a somewhat more frank and rounded expression of this *laissez-faire* or anti-governmentalist position than usual, is that of United States Senator Wadsworth of New York. Senator Wadsworth bluntly disapproves of all the great progressive federal legislation of the last fifteen years, beginning with the amendment to the Constitution permitting the present federal income tax. The federal government has been guilty of the offense of undertaking "a large number of new and important functions," says the Senator. In other words, *governmental* functions should not be extended! The federal subsidies to states for good roads and education he regards as only a part, and apparently a minor part, of the offending. Other governmental functions he objects to could not have been undertaken by the states, at least in any large measure or with any high degree of efficiency. The Federal Trade Commission is condemned as inquisitorial; the Tariff Commission, the Farm Loan Board, the Shipping Board, the Emergency Fleet Corporation, the laws to regulate the meat packing industry, are all held up as horrible examples—(*The Nation's Business*, March, 1926, and the New York *Times*, April 11, 1926.)

This is undoubtedly the position of "business" generally and of all anti-progressive political factions. Their use of the states' rights argument is obviously an afterthought.

CHAPTER XII

RISING WAGES AS PART OF A SOCIAL PROGRAM

Labor Rejects Fixed Wage Status—Labor Insists upon a Fair Division of the Product for All Producers—The Revolutionary Effects of Immigration Restriction—The New Wage Policy

"THE very essence of great production," says Herbert Hoover, "is high wages and low prices." [1]

Business is beginning to recognize that a major problem before the nation is to distribute wealth "so that it will not concentrate into the hands of a few," since such wealth concentration would destroy "the broad purchasing market necessary to absorb our production." [2] Capital is finding out that the most pressing need of American commerce and business is "to increase the purchasing power of the people." [3]

President Gompers once calculated, at a time when official statistics showed that there were five and a half million unemployed in this country, that this unemployment had subtracted from the purchasing power in our home market "an amount equal to the wages lost, or $27,500,000 per day." In the same way a 20-per-cent decrease in wage rates would mean additional daily loss

[1] Speech before the United States Chamber of Commerce, May 12, 1926.

[2] Speech before Washington City Club, December 19. 1923, by Julius H. Barnes, president United States Chamber of Commerce.

[3] Former Secretary of State Charles Evans Hughes.

of $10,000,000 a day in purchasing power—and the decrease in wage rates during the period of which Gompers was speaking (1921-22) was, in fact, at least a large fraction of 20 per cent.

High wages, labor holds, are the basis not only of maximum consumption and of maximum production, that is, of economic progress and development; they are the basis, too, of the highest citizenship. The working people, in improving the conditions under which they live, are "making more valuable to the country their services and their citizenship." [1]

President Harding declared that the wage-earner must be placed in an economically sound position: "His lowest wage must be enough for comfort, enough to make his house a home, enough to insure that the struggle for existence shall not crowd out the things really worth living for. There must be provision for education, for recreation, and a margin for savings. There must be such freedom of action as will insure full play to the individual's abilities."

This is about as high a *concrete* standard as any of those set by organized labor. Some of the union leaders have suggested that President Harding did not fully realize what this standard would mean when translated into dollars and cents. It would mean that a very large share of the product of industry, much higher than at present, would go to labor. But, after all, it is a fixed standard—and fixed rather according to the supposed needs of the wage-earner than according to what the country can afford.

[1] Reply to the questionnaire of the National Republican Advisory Committee, 1920.

Labor's objection to the fixing of wages (for any but the least skilled) even according to a comparatively liberal standard, is that it provides a *status* for the worker, like the social systems of the eighteenth and earlier centuries, instead of maintaining for him an unlimited opportunity for advancement.

The Federation, therefore, has definitely rejected "the living wage":

The American trade-union movement believes that the lives of the working people should be made better with each passing day and year. The practice of fixing wages solely on a basis of the cost of living is a violation of the whole philosophy of progress and civilization and, furthermore, is a violation of sound economic theory and is utterly without logic or scientific support of any kind. What we find as a result of this practice, so far as it has gone, is that there is a constant tendency under it to classify human beings and to standardize classes, each class having a presumptive right to a given quantity of various commodities.[1]

In the great Anthracite Coal Strike of 1925 and 1926 the Miners' unwillingness to accept a specially fixed status as wage-earners was one of the chief reasons why they refused outside arbitration of wages:

Arbitration of wages, said President John L. Lewis, means arbitration of the right to earn a living. It means that a third person—an outsider—decides whether the worker and his family may live on a $1,000 level or a $2,000 level, because the outsider determines how much money the man may earn a year. No fair-minded person can defend such an unsound idea. Such a plan would give the outsider power to determine how much money the man might have to spend

[1] American Federation of Labor Convention, 1921.

for food, clothing, shelter, fuel, and the comforts of home for his family and for the education of his children.[1]

Labor sees no necessary limit to a steadily advancing wage standard except that it must have a reasonable relation to the total product of American industry. Each industry must pay wages proportionate to the advancing national productivity or it is not fit for America. Even if an establishment, or a corporation, or a whole industry cannot pay what labor asks, labor does not accept this as necessarily conclusive. Labor's contention in such a case is that the industry should either be organized in a way to pay wages proportionate to those of other industries or that it should cease to exist, leaving other industries free to absorb the labor and capital now going into it.

Labor applies the same reasoning to inefficient establishments or corporations. Wages for an industry must not be fixed low enough to enable inefficient undertakings to operate. On the contrary, the industry, the consumer, and the nation are benefited when a reasonable wage settlement forces them out of business. Otherwise labor, the consumer, and the nation *pay for their inefficiency.* As President Lewis said of some of the propositions presented by the mine owners in the strike of 1925-1926:

They then presented to the mine workers their proposals that the mine workers, in effect, be penalized for every subnormal physical condition appertaining to the anthracite collieries, for every inefficiency of management, for every inefficiency of their sales organization or for every defect of their financial arrangements, and to secure such a contract

[1] American Federation of Labor Weekly News Service, February 20, 1926.

they camouflaged their demands with a request that the mine workers agree to arbitrate their wage.[1]

By refusing arbitration based on what such mine owners might be able to pay the organized miners gave a powerful impulse to more efficient production—jeopardizing the existence of the less efficient establishments.

In 1920 the Federation demanded, instead of a living wage, the *improvement* of the existing *American standard*. The American standard was defined as *"a standard of living fitting to our time and our country"*—a loose formulation, but scientific in recognizing time and place as essential factors. A further demand was made that the industrial system must be brought to a point where it offers to the workers *"a constantly increasing* measure of life and a constantly increasing margin of safety."[2]

In view of these formulations it may be asked, "If labor is constantly raising its standard, has it any standard at all?" Perhaps not; there is always a minimum but never a maximum.

President Lewis pointed out in a hearing of the U. S. House of Representatives that *"the actual productive capacity of the United States* is amply sufficient to insure every worker a wage upon which he can subsist and maintain a family in health and modest comfort,"[3] giving the authority of the National Bureau of Economic Research and the U. S. Bureau of Labor for the statement that in 1922 there was in the United States an

[1] Reply to questionnaire of National Republican Advisory Committee, 1920.
[2] Reply to questionnaire of National Republican Advisory Committee, 1920.
[3] *United Mine Worker*, March 1, 1926.

average per capita income of $700 and a family income of $3,500 a year and that in view of these figures "it is clear that the national income would easily permit a fair living wage to the humblest worker, *without infringing upon the justly higher claims of skill, training, managerial ability,* or (upon) capital investment. There is ample for all." (N. B. The living wage is applied to the humblest only.)

American labor, in spite of the continued use even by some unions of the misleading term, "living wage," is not only ceasing to base its demands on any concrete and static standard, but is demanding what it regards as a reasonable share of the annual product of the nation's industry, though without denying "the justly higher claims of skill, training, managerial ability, or invested capital."

American labor, in other words, wants to see all the other essential factors in industry liberally paid. Nor does it suggest holding any of them down to the level even of its relatively high American standard of wages. The American wage-earners are neither "levelers" nor communists.

The wage principles of American labor are certainly advanced, but they are not revolutionary. Labor does not aim at destroying any other group of actual producers, nor does it object to their relatively higher incomes or to reasonable profits. It aims only at non-producers, parasites, and speculators, and at excessive and unearned profits.

The figures quoted by President Lewis show that labor recognizes that the total annual product of the nation is so limited that, even if it were divided equitably it would not furnish very satisfactory incomes to the masses. Even the radicals are coming to recognize that the possibility of increasing wages through a more equitable distribution is limited and that any great increase—such, for example, as an all-round raise of 100 per cent perhaps or even 50 per cent—would be practicable only with a greatly increased efficiency of industry. With the present annual production of the nation giving an average family income of $3,500, an income of $2,000 or $2,500 a year may be a practicable goal for a considerable number of wage-earners, but anything beyond that, labor understands, would have to be limited to the most skilled.

Therefore, an increased national product, greater productivity on the part of labor, and an "efficiency wage"—that is, such a wage as will produce the maximum productivity—these are fundamental aims of the American labor movement. The railway unions, in presenting their case for higher wages to the Railroad Board in 1922, asked for a wage "productive of genuine industrial economy and efficiency." Their theorist, the late Glenn E. Plumb, formulated the principle as follows: "At some point to be determined only by those who have the required intimate knowledge of the industry is found a rate of pay which induces the highest degree of efficiency. Beyond this rate of pay wages ordinarily should not rise unless accompanied by a corresponding rise in efficiency. Below this point wages should not fall." [1]

But the efficiency wage is psychological and cannot be measured in concrete terms. The wage-earner must not only have all of his fundamental physical needs provided for so that he can keep in good health and con-

[1] *Labor*, February 4, 1922.

dition, he must *think and feel* that he is being justly treated. If he believes he is being wronged his morale will be lowered and his efficiency damaged.

> I do not mean [says Jewell] that the employees will consciously slacken on the job. I am simply pointing to the well-recognized fact that wages below a certain just and reasonable level, *wages which do not satisfy normal desires,* destroy the sense of co-operation between employees and management, and actually prevent a man from giving the highest efficiency of which he would be capable under just conditions.
>
> The decision of the Railroad Labor Board creates rates of pay which do not measure up to a minimum *efficiency* wage. Management gets just what it pays for. If it pays a man the least it can get away with, the man gives the least he can get away with.[1] (My italics.)

Now, one of the chief factors which the wage-earner feels should be considered in fixing a just wage is the profits being made in the industry. As the minority of the Railroad Labor Board remarks, "the increasing antithesis between profits and just wages will result in lowered morale." The Board referred to the fact that earnings and dividends were rising at a time when wages were being reduced.

Labor has its eye fixed not only on its own needs, but on the progress of industry and the increasing wealth of the country, and it works contentedly and efficiently in proportion as its wages draw near to its aspirations— based on what it believes it *can* be paid. So that the

[1] Statement by Bert M. Jewell, president of the Railroad Department of the American Federation of Labor.—New York *Times*, June 6, 1922.

efficiency of labor and the productivity of the nation depend not upon any fixed minimum wage standard—no matter how high—but upon a fair division of the product.

"We have learned that the impulse to production can only be maintained at a high pitch if there is a fair division of the product," as Herbert Hoover has pointed out.[1]

Among the official conclusions of the United States Industrial Relations Commission in 1915 we find a statement that puts the labor view of the wage question in a nutshell. "The crux of the question is: Have the workers received a fair share of the enormous *increase* in wealth which has taken place in this country, during the period, as a result of their labors? The answer is emphatically, No!"

Has there been "a fairer division of the product?" On the contrary, what has been happening to wages in America has been a movement in the opposite direction. Instead of a fairer distribution of the product, the tendency has been markedly retrogressive; *labor* (with the possible exception of a very few years) *has been getting a smaller and smaller proportion of the product year by year.*

Dr. Wilfrid I. King, a statistical authority, has estimated that the real wages of our factory workers per year fell from $635 in 1889 to $568 in 1914—that is, $77, or more than 12 per cent in this twenty-five year period. During this period the production of the country per capita had risen 36 per cent and the per capita pro-

[1] *American Individualism*, p. 11.

duction of manufacturing industry at a slightly higher rate.[1]

Real wages recovered somewhat after the war and reached a point in 1919 scarcely exceeded again even to-day. Yet in 1919 the *real* wages of factory workers were only $625—that is, $10, or 2 per cent, less than thirty years before—and far below even a "living wage." [2]

The war caused a fall in real income per capita for the nation as a whole and there was at the same time a certain increase in real wages. That is, during the war and for a short while afterward labor *increased its proportion of the national income.*

But this improvement was a result of a temporary cause —the war—and by no means counterbalanced the retrogressive tendency of the previous quarter century.

This temporarily beneficial effect of the war was soon checked, so that, by 1923, the proportion of the product received by labor had scarcely risen at all even during the exceptionally favorable decade 1913-23. Herbert Hoover calculated that the average product per capita for the nation as a whole (measured in real and not in mere money values) rose between 10 and 15 per cent from

[1] Wesley C. Mitchell, New York *Evening Post,* June 7, 1922.

[2] Mr. Edgar Palmer of the University of Wisconsin has furnished me with additional figures, covering manufacturing industry, from King, Douglas, Knaut, Hansen, and the Federal Census. They give a result very similar to the figures above quoted, indicating a slight fall in real wages from 1890 to 1914 (7 per cent, instead of 12 per cent, as above). Palmer's figures show, further, the same practical stagnation in real wages from 1890 to 1919 (plus 3 per cent instead of minus 2 per cent, as in my figures). During this latter period per capita production, Palmer points out, had increased 80 per cent! These figures show that, from 1890 to 1923, real wages had increased 23 per cent, while per capita production had almost doubled—increasing by 95 per cent.

1913 to 1923.[1] (In manufacturing industry, the increase was 28 per cent. See below.) Real wages rose 17½ per cent during that period.[2]

Hoover pointed out that the rise in national productivity had been due largely to wage-earners: "It is a monument to the directing brains of commerce and industry and the development in intelligence and skill of the American workingman."

There is no doubt as to the rapidity of our economic progress, or that it is partly due to labor, or that labor, and especially organized labor, is at last receiving a certain share in our new wealth. Labor as a whole had not been receiving any share in this increment of our prosperity until about 1913. The present change for the better is no doubt due mainly, not to the effect of the European war, which was temporary, but to our immigration exclusion policy, which was brought about largely (though not wholly) by the political activity of organized labor.

The restriction of immigration is regarded by American labor as its greatest political and legislative achievement. Senator Lodge was undoubtedly right when he described it as a revolution in the American social system. Immigration restriction has two effects on the economic position of labor, both of the first magnitude. It raises the value of labor compared with other occupations, enabling it to keep its proportion of our rising national income to-day, and possibly, to increase its proportion to-morrow. But the restriction of immigration has a second

[1] Speech before New York Chamber of Commerce, May 8, 1923.
[2] New York *Times*, July 14, 1925.

effect; it diminishes the proportionate number of wage-earners in comparison with other occupations. This tends to augment the overcrowding in these occupations and to lessen the opportunity for wage-earners and their children to rise into them.

This is a revolution, indeed. For why is it that American labor—if it was going backward in real wages for a quarter of a century before the war while the rest of the nation was going forward in real income—did not develop a movement of bitter and radical discontent, such as we see in so many European countries? There is only one possible answer. While the economic status of many wage-earning occupations was going backward if not positively, *at least, when compared with other occupations,* the relative position of the *individuals* filling these occupations—and of their children—was being raised. Because of the flood of new immigrants nearly every wage-earning employment was being refilled every generation by newcomers from Europe, while the older employees (or their children) secured better jobs. Immigrants who had been getting from 50 cents to a dollar a day in *real* (not money) wages in Europe received two dollars immediately upon arrival in this country and considerably more (for increased skill) after they had been here a few years. Often by a change of employment they further improved their wage, while their children almost invariably advanced to still better paid employments.

While nearly every wage-earning employment except those best organized went backward when compared with other employments, nearly every wage-earning employee advanced. At every step this advance of the individual wage-earner was due to immigration, and not to any improvement whatever in the relative position of the wage-earning employments.

But now that immigration is practically suspended, the individual wage-earning employee will be able to advance himself, as a rule, only by the advance of his employment —a method of advance facilitated, however, by this same restriction of immigration. This means, of course, a wholly new outlook and new mentality for American labor. *And the fact that wage-earners must now elevate themselves, mainly, as a group and not as individuals, gives a wholly new importance to the labor unions which are organizing that group.*

Labor is now beginning to receive a slightly increased proportion of our new wealth, then, not through the natural working of our economic system, but because of its own organization and the political power which (with the aid of certain other groups) brought about and maintains the restriction of immigration.

But just what share is labor receiving? And what share does labor demand?

At its annual convention at Atlantic City in 1925, the American Federation of Labor launched "a new wage policy."[1] The novelty of this policy consisted in changing the emphasis finally and wholly from what labor needs, to what labor believes industry and society ought to pay and can pay—with advantage to the nation as a whole.

"Social inequality, industrial instability, and injustice must increase," declared the Federation, "unless the

[1] Introduced by John Frey, President of the Ohio State Federation of Labor.

224

workers' real wages, the purchasing power of their wages, is advanced in proportion to man's increasing power of production."

This new wage policy was widely misunderstood or wilfully misinterpreted in the public press. But it was hailed as profoundly constructive by many business leaders. Herbert Hoover seized upon this new policy to illustrate the contrast between American labor and European labor (though it must be pointed out that the most recent tendency of continental labor developed since the World War, coincides with that of American labor). On this point Hoover said:

Our original trade unions sprang from the Old World labor movement and naturally adopted its conceptions. But the demonstration of the enormous distance which our organized labor has traveled from the tenets of the old world needs no further proof than the new vision of wage crystallized by the American Federation of Labor at its last annual meeting.

The background of those proposals is an urge for improved methods, elimination of waste, increase of production, and participation by labor in the resulting gains.[1]

This wage policy is based on a proposition that is almost a truism. Nobody in a political democracy like ours stands openly for an increase of social inequality, and it is also clear that this can be prevented only by increasing of wages in proportion to man's increasing power of production. But the logic and implications of this proposition go farther—*for democratic progress demands not only that social inequality and industrial injustice should not increase, but that they should be diminished.* So that all

[1] Speech before United States Chamber of Commerce, May 12, 1926.

true democrats and progressives, as well as labor-unionists, stand for wage increases not only in proportion to man's increasing power of production, but at a greater ratio. If wages are raised only in proportion to economic progress, we should be insured, it is true, against reaction and retrogression; but the present division of the product would be maintained and existing inequalities would be continued.

Interviewed a few days after the passing of this resolution, the president of the Federation, William Green, said: "We ought to know, and the public ought to know, how much the per capita output of the workers in the nation as a whole and in each of the leading industries has increased."[1] This suggests two nearly related wage standards, measured by the per capita increase of real output, first, for the nation as a whole or the average citizen, or second, for industry.

The figures already quoted indicated that, during a period when the average real income per capita *in the nation as a whole* was increasing (from 1913 to 1923), as Hoover says, between 10 and 15 per cent, the real output per capita in *manufacturing industry* was increasing 28 per cent. Since real wages increased $17\frac{1}{2}$ per cent, we see that wages are already rising "in proportion to man's increasing productivity" in this country, though not in proportion to "the increasing productivity of the industrial worker."[2]

---

[1] New York *Times,* October 18, 1925.

[2] The Federal Reserve Board reports a 30-per-cent increased production in American factories in 1925, as compared with 1919. Despite the increase of nearly a third in output, the board reports that there are fewer workers employed and that those at work are paid but 7 per cent more in real wages than in 1919.

RISING WAGES AS PART OF A SOCIAL PROGRAM

President Green's statement and the Federation's position as a whole show that this higher standard—which is measured by the increasing productivity of the industrial worker—is labor's real standard. It would lead to a wage advance more than proportionate to "man's increasing power of production," and so to a more and more equitable distribution of the product and to greater social justice and equality.

The conclusions to be drawn from the fact that labor has set up this higher standard as its goal, but has attained only the former (and lower) standard are far-reaching. For what will happen if labor continues to improve its position merely in proportion to man's increasing power of production while securing a constantly smaller part of the product of *manufacturing industry*? Wages would be increased, like the average incomes of all other social groups, at the rate of 1 to 1½ per cent a year or 10 to 15 per cent a decade. Besides accomplishing nothing toward a better distribution of wealth and the correction of existing social inequality and industrial injustice, this rate of improvement could not satisfy the rising concrete standard of the industrial wage-earner—in view of the far more rapid increase of his product and the far more rapid improvement in the income of other factors in *industry*.

Those who own and control industry, and the higher salaried and professional employees closely associated with

---

The Indices of Production of Stewart (*American Economic Review,* Vol. XI. p. 68) and of Day (*Review of Economic Statistics,* Vol. VII. p. 208) indicate an increased per capita factory production of 80 per cent from 1890 to 1919, during which period real wages (see above) increased 3 per cent.

So while the per capita factory product rose from 100 to 236, real factory wages during the same period (1890-1925) rose only from 100 to 110.

them, are receiving the lion's share of the per capita rise
in the national income. That share is considerably greater
than the 28 per cent increase per decade in the productivity
of industry as a whole, since labor is taking out of this
only a 17½-per-cent increase.

But the rest of the community outside of industry, such
as the minor salaried and professional classes and the
producers with the smaller incomes, fail to get a share
proportionate either to the very rapidly increasing
product of *industry,* or to the less rapidly increasing
product of the *nation as a whole.* For if labor receives
approximately its proportionate share of the increase of
the national income (or slightly more than that) and the
industrialists and other factors of industry receive a great
deal more than that share, the remainder of the community are getting little or nothing of our new wealth.

The National Catholic Welfare Council points out that
neither wage-earners, salaried workers, nor farmers have,
of late years, increased their incomes anything like proportionately to the great increase in production. In other
words, they are all "falling behind." "The largest sections of the people that are falling short are the wage-
earners, the lesser salaried workers, and the farmers. Of
these three, the farmers and the lesser salaried workers
are falling farthest behind." [1]

Organized labor has repeatedly and officially taken
cognizance of the farmers' economic troubles. For example, President Green of the American Federation of
Labor pointed out that "the loss in the value of capital
invested in American agriculture since 1920 has been

[1] American Federation of Labor Weekly News Service, February 6,
1926.

$20,000,000,000; the total for 1920 was $79,000,000,000 and for 1925 $59,000,000,000." [1] As it has been argued that this loss was due to the fact that agriculture was overcapitalized in 1920, other figures tell the story more incontrovertibly. Secretary of Agriculture Jardine, in his report to the President on December 8, 1925, shows that the purchasing power of farm products in that year was only 87 per cent of their pre-war purchasing power. The loss from 1920 to 1925 was even more rapid, especially in certain sections. Yet during both these periods there had been a rapid increase in national production and a still more rapid rise in the product of manufacturing industry.

Labor, then, is falling farther and farther behind the industrialists and their associates, but is gaining in relation to other social classes. If this tendency were continued indefinitely, it would *ultimately* bring about the division of society into three separate groups with more or less separate interests, labor being the middle group. But this conclusion has no validity. For labor started as the lowest group, and the tendency to gain on the minor salaried and professional classes and the small producers has been going on only a short time, scarcely longer than a decade.

On the whole the wage-earners have not yet overtaken the middle classes in income, economic position, or opportunity. So that the *present* tendency is for labor to draw closer to the other numerically important social groups and not farther away. Labor could continue its present rate of advance relatively to these classes for a good many years before overtaking or drawing away

[1] *American Federationist,* February, 1926.

from them. (And before the wage-earners' rate of progress had surpassed their rate of progress the competition of the children of these classes for wage-earners' positions would become effective.) *What is happening is a tendency of labor not to rise above these other social groups, but to attain their economic level and so to bring about a solidarity of interest with these groups, and a division of society not into three but into two parts.*

So that labor's demand for wage increases and improvement *in proportion to the increasing production of industry* is not directed against those other social groups which, if they are advancing at all, are advancing less rapidly than labor. Labor wishes to improve its present position mainly in relation to the owners and managers of industry, and their associates and dependents. It expects all the other popular social groups also to improve their position relatively to the owners and managers of industry.

Nor does labor aim to secure any advance at the expense of the great body of consumers. Labor believes that the benefit of increasing productivity, of better co-operation with employers and of improved technical processes belongs largely to society and in large part should go to consumers—through lower prices. The unions say they are the only agency through which the wage-earners may offer to industry "co-operation in the improvement of industrial processes and the expansion of productive energy *with that improvement of the product and lowering of prices justly demanded by the public.*"[1] (See Chapter X.)

American labor's demand for a more equitable distri-

[1] American Federation of Labor Conference, February 21, 1921.

bution of the product represents the standpoint of *all producers with low incomes,* and labor so understands it. Labor's wage policy thus tends not only to bring it closer in income to the other great groups of the population, but it tends also to give all these groups similar social aims. For, if the annual increase in the income of the nation is not at present going mainly to the producing and consuming masses, this means that the greater part of the benefits of civilization and progress are being absorbed by privileged classes, which, even if they count millions of members, constitute but a small minority of the nation. If the standard of living of the masses is not being raised just as fast as the growing efficiency and productivity of the nation permit, the maximum attainable development of the abilities and character and efficiency of the nation are being sacrificed.

"If we would build up character and abilities and standards of living in our people, we must have regard to their leisure for citizenship, for recreation, for family life," says Herbert Hoover. "These considerations, together with protection against strain, must be the fundamentals of determination of hours of labor. (This would, of course, apply equally to wages). *These factors being first protected, the maximum production of the country should become the dominating purpose."* But these factors are the foundation of national efficiency and maximum production—as well as individual development.

It might be answered that a limited sacrifice of the development of the average man would seem to be socially justifiable if it is made in order to secure for society the maximum development of the more capable. But exceptional character and capabilities are not limited

231

to any group. They are found among the families of all groups and any failure to do all that is possible for the families of the people would result in the crushing or crippling of a very large part of the exceptional capacity and native genius of the nation.

Labor cannot be expected to work at its highest efficiency so long as it feels that its wages are being held down and its opportunities for development limited because of the excessive profits and the costly management of those who conduct industry solely for profit (instead of the highest efficiency).[1] Moreover, labor feels that even a so-called efficiency wage cannot produce maximum labor efficiency unless wage-earners at the same time have a reasonable voice in the conduct of industry so that they can co-operate effectively to increase the product.

As the national officers of the American Federation of Labor unions and the railroad brotherhoods have declared:

Creative power lies dormant where autocratic management prevails. No employer has a vested right to the good will of his employees. That must be earned, as between men. It can be earned only when management deals with workers as human beings and not as machines. *There cannot be a full release of productive energy under an autocratic control of industry.* There must be a spirit of co-operation and mutuality between employers and workers. We submit that production can be enhanced through the co-operation of management with the trade-union agencies which make for order, discipline, and productivity.[2] (My italics.)

[1] See Note, p. 233.
[2] Manifesto of December 13, 1919.

RISING WAGES AS PART OF A SOCIAL PROGRAM

The Federation has suggested the first step by which a large part of labor could be gradually and scientifically put upon an efficiency wage, namely, "the availability of production and cost and expenditure records so that both management and workers shall have an opportunity to know what is accomplished in the establishment in which they are producing."

But that is only the first step. To bring labor to the maximum efficiency and industry to the maximum productivity, the American labor movement believes, requires new organization and policies in the administration of industry and a new economic program in government.[1]

[1] These questions are dealt with in Volume II.

NOTE—Labor does not expect any early or large increase in wages without the cutting down of excessive profits (see Volume II, Chapter V). This is why it differs even from enlightened employers. For example, Owen D. Young, Chairman of the Board of Directors of the General Electric Company, favors a "cultural wage, that which will enable the men to develop to such a point that they may take advantage of all the great opportunities which are offered to the citizens of the United States." "When that time comes," he continues, "then all men will be free and equal. The great objective of a free government and of a high industrial order is to establish equal opportunity for all men." But in the same breath Mr. Young puts forth a sweeping defense of profits entirely out of line with the position of labor, which sees little prospect of equal opportunity or a cultural wage as long as "profiteering" continues unchecked. (Address before Industrial Conference Board—May, 1926.)

233

Volume II

LABOR AND GOVERNMENT

INTRODUCTORY

ADDRESSING the Eighth International Conference of
the International Labor Office, Director Albert Thomas
said that "too many Europeans still live with the idea that
Europe is the undisputed center of the world and are un-
aware of the tremendous significance of the rise of economic America," and raised the question whether America
is not working out "a new philosophy of industrial relations."

The eminent position of Thomas as a political labor
leader and Socialist, as well as Director of the International Labor Office, might suggest that the standpoint expressed has become world-wide and is as widely accepted
in labor circles.

However, this standpoint, as applied to American labor,
is not accepted by some branches of the labor movement.
British labor and Labor Party leaders almost uniformly
declare American labor to be 25 or 50 or 75 years behind
British labor and statements to that effect have been frequently made by British Labor Party leaders visiting this
country. Arthur Greenwood, for example, has said that
"as regards the organization of industrial relationships,
the United States is already about three-quarters of a
century behind Great Britain."

The present book is not addressed primarily to British
or European labor, so that European views of the American labor movement, whether favorable or unfavorable,

3

might seem to be of secondary importance. But, unfortunately, these views not only flourish in this country but often prevail over all others, both among our Europeanized intellectuals and liberals unfamiliar with the practical conditions of this country and among wage-earners who have not yet become Americanized. Where both of these elements are exceptionally strong, as in New York, the European view of America frequently predominates; and, in the case of New York it is especially injurious, as it tends to permeate the press, periodicals, books, and colleges of the entire country.

The late President Gompers and the American Federation of Labor dealt frequently with this strange but exceedingly serious obstacle to American understanding of the American labor movement—and President Green has the same situation in view when he points out that the labor organizations of our country "have steadily refused to embrace any imported philosophy, no matter how it may be disguised or how seductive it may appear." American labor, he adds, is "sound, constructive, practical and rational," but at the same time it has been forced to become militant "because of the opposition which has come to labor at every turn of the road."

No better characterization of American labor policy could be desired—and it challenges squarely the European Socialist view still so widely prevalent, even in conservative quarters of this country.

Only a small part of the writing concerning American labor and almost none of the books or articles that touch upon American labor's political and governmental policies, have been altogether free from these European preconceptions. Therefore, the picture of American labor policy

4

drawn in the present volumes flatly contradicts that which
has come to predominate in our literature and even in our
academic writings under the influence of European, and,
especially of British, ideas and standards.

If the reader will weigh the evidence presented in the
present volume, he will see that American labor has
evolved for itself, in equal independence from American
Capitalism and European Socialism, both a definite and
distinctive goal of economic democracy and original tactics and policies for reaching that goal. But he must free
himself from European preconceptions. And he must also
remember that the position of the American movement is
less definitely formulated, both because American labor
is opposed to excessive and premature formulation and because the movement is somewhat younger in this country
and its policies on some questions are only in the process
of taking shape. This is especially true of the overshadowing question of "the government of industry"
dealt with in the present volume. But that fact furnishes
no valid excuse for the uninformed European view that
American labor has no policy on these underlying issues.
The truth is only that this policy is still in the process of
evolution out of the growing experience of the movement
—instead of having been handed down from the closet of
some intellectual outsider as has so often happened with
the labor movements of Europe.

II

It was only after "American Labor and American
Democracy" was written as a single book that it was decided that it might be practicable and desirable sooner or
later to issue it as two more or less separate volumes.

INTRODUCTORY

This made necessary the selection of two volume titles. The titles finally chosen, Labor and Politics, and Labor and Government are approximately accurate. The titles sufficiently indicate two closely related subjects—or two phases of the same subject. But the three concluding chapters of the first volume, dealing with the labor and progressive program, might almost as well have been made a part of the second volume. Also the concluding chapter of the first volume, Rising Wages as Part of a Social Program, and the initial chapter of the second volume, Is American Labor becoming Capitalistic, may both appear to be somewhat detached from the subjects announced in the volume titles, since they deal with economic rather than politico-economic questions. But their relation to the title of the book as a whole, American Labor and American Democracy, is evident.

Logically the second volume should precede the first, and the volumes were, as a matter of fact, written in that order. The American labor movement always has been and doubtless will remain, fundamentally economic in character, and the second volume more evidently acknowledging that fact, might almost as well have been entitled, Labor, Industry and Government. It deals with organized labor's main and ultimate economic-political problem, the government of industry. However, labor's position on this great question is still in the process of evolution and cannot be so surely or completely formulated as its policies on other economic and political questions. Moreover these latter policies, along with new political methods and tactics, have been crystallizing for a considerably longer period.

In other words the matters dealt with under the title

INTRODUCTORY

Labor and Politics were, as a matter of fact, *historically* prior. But they also come first *psychologically*. It was the simple and natural order for labor to work out, first, a political method which did not endanger its economic character or independence, then politico-economic policies which could be executed by this method, and finally a politico-economic goal which it might hope to reach gradually after some of these policies had become effective and after the accumulated experience and power gained in the application of the new political method had convinced it that it could safely and wisely invest a part of its time and energies in larger and somewhat more distant objectives. This was the historic and psychological order for labor, and it is the natural and psychological order for the average reader. If it seems to put the political before the economic, this is done only on these practical and historical grounds—and not as any indication that in labor's thinking the political precedes the economic. That the reverse is true the text amply demonstrates.

7

LABOR AND GOVERNMENT

CHAPTER I

IS AMERICAN LABOR BECOMING CAPITALISTIC?

Labor Banking and Labor Insurance—"Employee Ownership" as Labor Sees It—Labor Capitalism an Illusion—Profit-sharing, Real and Nominal.

Is American labor passing over to capitalism? Labor banks, labor insurance companies, "union-management co-operation," "employee ownership," and "employee representation" might seem to point that way.

These new developments, it is widely asserted, mean the end of the labor movement as we have known it. Henceforth, we are told, organized labor, absorbed by its new capitalistic experiments and circumscribed by the new benevolent and "democratic" institutions organized by employers, is bound to apply its economic and political power less and less against capitalists and capitalism. This interpretation has been made so often and in such high places that it must be disposed of before we can get a clear conception of the foundations of American labor policy.

Whatever may be the ultimate answer of history to this question, American labor itself certainly does not believe it is "passing over to capitalism." Even if the labor banks, for example, should meet no obstacles, and if they should reach their maximum conceivable development with several billions of dollars in deposits, labor realizes that they would still control only a very minor proportion of the industrial capital of the country. And even if wage-earners should vastly increase their ownership of corporation stock, labor realizes that they will seldom if ever be more than minority shareholders.

Peter J. Brady, president of the Federation Bank of New York, one of the largest of the labor banks, gives us a picture of the probable outcome as labor sees it. The labor banks, like the new labor insurance companies, were formed, not to make capitalists of laborers, but, on the contrary, to strengthen labor organizations in their struggle against capitalist domination. "Bankers with false notions of their duty," says Mr. Brady, "were using the money of the members of the unions to dictate the relation that should exist between employers and their employees." The labor banks were formed "to remedy this condition." This is the official Federation view. The first labor bank was organized by the Machinists at Washington in 1919, mainly to strengthen the unions in their wage-struggle—and that remains to-day a primary object of every labor-union bank.

The American Federation of Labor, in its 1922 convention, discussed the hostile attitude of banks to organized labor at length and arrived at the following clear-cut conclusions:

Bankers, generally speaking, have been opposed to the trade-union movement. Unquestionably, too, the hostile attitude of manufacturers' associations, merchants' organizations, and trade associations has largely influenced the policy of banks in their dealing with firms that express a sympathetic and encouraging attitude toward trade unions. Investigation has disclosed the fact that in a number of cities banking institutions have used their banking facilities to compel employers to assume an attitude toward trade unions which would weaken if not destroy the organizations of the wage-earners. In some instances this control over banking facilities has been used to enforce a reduction of wages; in other cases to further the so-called "open-shop" or "American plan" idea, while in other cases both these repressive objectives were the ends sought.

Thus employers have been threatened not alone with curtailment of trade facilities, but obstacles have been placed in their way in securing proper credit with which to purchase the necessary raw material. Likewise, threats have been made to call in loans or to deny further loans or to "freeze" credits *unless industrial relations, policies, and employment conditions prescribed by these associations of manufacturers or merchants are complied with.* [1] (My italics.)

Labor banks were originated as a means of defense against non-labor banks. "Labor banking institutions," said the Federation convention of the following year, "cannot possibly operate as a remedy for economic injustice and industrial unrighteousness. That they can be made helpful supplemental agencies to the trade-union movement cannot be successfully controverted."

The labor unions entered into banking not to form a new branch of capitalist finance or to join hands with capital, but "by pooling their funds and savings to attract to themselves the additional earning power of their money and to balance the credit power now exercised by employing interests." [2]

[1] American Federation Convention, 1922.

[2] At the time of writing union labor banks in this country were estimated to number forty, with resources of $200,000,000.

In a summary of the labor banking movement in the United States published a year previously (1925), it was shown that in nearly every large city a labor bank had been organized or was being organized. The largest and second oldest, the Locomotive Engineers' bank in Cleveland (founded in 1920) had already accumulated resources of

13

LABOR AND GOVERNMENT

In deciding to go into the life-insurance business in 1924 the American Federation of Labor explained that it was governed by the same motive: "The financial ramifications of the insurance combination are unlimited and inconceivable," it declared. "Insurance constitutes one of the most powerful single units in the financial oligarchy in our land. Its ramifications extend to all parts of the civilized world. It is alleged that the tremendous resources at the disposal of the insurance combine have been and are used in the attempt to crush organized labor."

It was on these and similar grounds that the Federation decided to enter into the insurance field and recommended the establishment of a "joint insurance enterprise, owned and controlled by organized labor." That enterprise has now been launched, and the Union Labor Life Insurance Company has been incorporated. This step was not taken hastily, but was the outcome of two years of investigation by Vice-President Matthew Woll and George Perkins, president of the Cigarmakers. The new insurance company is owned by trade-unionists and trade unions and officered by trade-union officials.[1] Its profits are to be

---

$25,000,000. The second largest, the Federation Bank of New York, had $8,000,000 of resources within the first year of its operations, and the Locomotive Engineers' Bank of New York had brought together $7,000,000 within the same period.

[1] The unions represented by leading officials upon the directorate already include the Photo-engravers', Cigarmakers', Federal Employees', Post Office Clerks', Maintenance-of-way Employees', Plumbers', Switchmen's, Typographers', Printing Pressmen's, Railway Carmen's, Machinists', Bakers', Musicians', and Ladies Garment Workers'.

The first labor union insurance company was organized by the electrical workers, as the result of six years of study, in 1922. The Union Co-operative Life Insurance Association, with a capital and reserve of two hundred thousand dollars, was chartered under the laws enacted by Congress of the United States for the government

shared by stockholders and policy-holders. It builds first of all on the fact that many unions are already doing an insurance business on a moderate scale and that the new labor company will be favored above other so-called "industrial" companies by millions of labor-unionists and their labor sympathizers. But its primary aim is to compete with "group insurance" of employees by employers by offering insurance through the trade unions.

The Federation lists "insurance provided by employers" as among the newer devices fostered on a wide scale "to prevent the organization of the workers into trade unions" —other methods being all so-called "employee ownership" and "employee representation" plans that emanate from sources other than the workers themselves. Both employers' insurance of employees and employers' plans for employee stock ownership, organized labor believes, were instituted primarily "to weaken the ties binding wage-earners to trade unions." (See Note at end of Chapter.)

Many capitalists and capitalist organs have thought that labor banks would tend, in a sense, to turn laborers into

of the District of Columbia, with its home office in Washington, D. C. The entire capital and reserve was subscribed exclusively by electrical workers.

Among the most important conclusions of the union's commission which recommended this action were the following:

"That insurance companies on account of their enormous investments were a very potent factor in industry and influential in determining the industrial relationship attitude of many corporations and employers openly hostile to labor, and that insurance companies were rapidly approaching the point where they should practically control the industrial and commercial life of the nation.

"That corporations and employers are rapidly adopting the practice of insuring employees under what is known as the Group Term Plan, this practice having been adopted partially if not entirely for the purpose of shackling workers to their jobs under the guise of philanthropic interest." (See *American Federationist*, May, 1926.)

capitalists, that is, would give them the capitalist point of view and direct their minds away from the struggle to improve wages by organization and collective bargaining. Labor banks were instituted, as I have already shown, to strengthen labor's hands in collective bargaining with capital. And, far from converting labor to the capitalist-banker's viewpoint, the labor banks have re-enforced labor's long-standing demand for public control of capitalist banks. The union position has long been that "credit as now administered too often serves to increase unearned incomes at the expense of earned incomes and constitutes a burden upon essential and necessary industry"; that credit, being in the control of private financiers, is used "to increase their holdings and incomes" and "to levy a toll upon the community as high as the traffic will bear."

"It is not anticipated that labor banks can or will correct this evil," and it is held that this can be accomplished "only through a properly constituted and efficiently managed public agency." The unions have not yet devised any specific measure for such banking control, but they favor *"a public agency administered by voluntary and cooperative methods";* and they are evidently working toward some modification in the statutes or in the administration of the Federal Reserve Board:

We have pointed out the *ideal of credit administration through a public agency.* We feel constrained to point out that no appreciable progress toward that end has been recorded. Through the growing number of labor banks some progress toward the ideal may be made. Most progress consists of a compromise between conditions and the ideal. As banks, we look upon these institutions as helpful, even though they constitute no remedy. They may force remedies for some of the more glaringly inexcusable exploita-

tions of the banking and financial world. If there is hope
to be seen in the development of labor banking institutions
we feel that it must be through the development of a great
agency for the constructive administration of credit. (My
italics.)

According to the expectations of organized labor, labor
banks will use their experience and knowledge not only to
strengthen the labor organizations in the wage struggle,
but to bring about public control over the most formidable
and determined of labor's opponents—finance.

Undoubtedly labor banks are bringing organized labor
and financiers and owners of industry closer together.
Already labor-bank depositors are seeking their bank's advice as to investment and prominent labor bank officials
and union leaders are being made directors of other banks.
Mr. Brady believes that the workers who are invited to
invest in the shares of their employer's corporations will
put their proxies and votes in the hands of labor banks
to represent them at stockholders meetings. He thinks
they will secure representation in these corporations by
having labor bankers made directors. This he believes
will mark the beginning of a new era and that "eventually
American workers will share in the management of industry in this feasible way." [1]

That is, under this new dispensation, the workers will
endeavor to share in the management *not as small individual capitalists, powerless and nondescript, but as organized wage-earners.* There is all the difference in the
world. True, organized wage-earners are in some measure becoming capitalists, as alleged, and in so far they
are drawing closer to other capitalists. But they expect

[1] *American Federationist,* September, 1925.

to use their capital and their newly gained knowledge of other capitalists in order to bring those other capitalists to concede to wage-earners as wage-earners a large share of the product and a larger voice in the control of industry.

Labor regards the labor banks as a mobilization of the capital of wage-earners—a mobilization of capital corresponding to the mobilization of labor in the unions. The unions control both—and they are no more ready to allow their money to be used for purely capitalist objects than they would be to allow their mobilization of the labor supply to be used for such purposes.

But we are told that the new capitalism is making a capitalist of the wage-earner in another way—through the diffusion of corporation shares among employees. It is largely due to this influence, an editorial of a leading conservative newspaper alleges, "that the American Federation of Labor is staunchly capitalistic."[1] Yet this organ admits that the diffusion of share ownership usually means "a measure of banker's control" and leaves the corporation an "autocracy" as before. How labor's position as wage-earner and petty stockholder under such a corporation could make it "capitalistic" minded this great newspaper does not explain.

The most extraordinary claims, however, are being made for this stock-distribution movement by the most eminent leaders of opinion—beginning with the President, who concludes that it proves that "the people of this country own this country." These statements would be justified only if the word "own" did not imply control. (But

[1] The New York *Times*.

it does imply control and any other use of the word is a deception.) The people of this country do nominally "own" a very large part of the country—but in the case of the corporations they do not control.

A former Secretary of the Treasury goes so far as to say that this movement is in its infancy, that "there is no limit to its development," that it is the fundamental solution of the problem of capital and labor, and that "labor is more and more realizing that the ideal and sensible thing to do is for every laborer to become a capitalist, a small one if necessary, a big one if he has the requisite character, industry, and will power."

Professor Thomas N. Carver, of Harvard University, has been the chief academic prophet of the new dispensation. He believes this is the coming revolution in America and that it means the real democratization of industry. He believes that the "ownership of the factories and the plants by the workers themselves is coming more rapidly in this country than it can possibly come in any other," and that "where the workers in an industry actually own it or own a considerable share in it they automatically acquire a place in its councils" and that "the participation of labor in management does not then have to be artificially promoted."

Professor William Z. Ripley, also of Harvard University, has shown, on the contrary, that the spread of employees' and consumers' ownership, accompanied by the fact that a very large part of these shares have been deliberately deprived of the right to vote, has led to "irresponsible control of the corporations by intermediaries, most commonly bankers, so-called." "The wider the diffusion of ownership," he points out, "the more readily does effective control run to the intermediaries, promoters, bankers, management companies . . . holding companies, voting trusts, and investment trusts." All these, says Ripley, "set off ownership from responsibility in management," and, as he points out, "uncontrolled power is always certain to entail abuse":

All kinds of private business are being bought up by banking houses, and new corporations are being substituted for the old in order that the purchase price (and more) may be recovered by sale of shares to the general public. But the significant change is that the new stock thus sold is entirely bereft of any voting power.

Every kind of business is being swept into this maelstrom. All of our public utilities, except railroads, chain and department stores, foodstuffs, washing machine, refrigerators, confectionery, make-believe silk stockings, toilet and beauty preparations, our daily bread, our cake, even our home-made pies!

There is no concealment about it. Practically every prospectus concludes by a statement that the business will continue to be managed by those who have brought it to its present high pitch of profitableness.

How can there be other than a whirlwind of abuse of power under such conditions?[1]

Professor Ripley proceeded to show that "the second financial fashion, the wide distribution of stock among employees and consumers and the public" tends to reinforce this divorcing of ownership and control. This conclusion scarcely needs corroboration. But H. T. Warshow of the National Lead Company, who has made a careful study of the whole movement, points out that "it has strengthened the controlling interests." "One of the

[1] Address before American Academy of Political Science, December, 1925.

results," he says, "of this great diffusion of stockholding is the possibility of controlling a large corporation through a comparatively small portion of the total stock of the corporation concentrated in the hands of a single individual group."

The momentous import of this divorce of ownership and control can scarcely be overstated, and, far from showing any tendency toward the democratization of capitalism, it immensely strengthens labor's case both as to the inordinate profits and as to the autocracy of our present industrial system. The corporations of the United States are valued in the Federal tax returns at $70,000,-000,000 and represent the dominant factor of our whole economic structure. As Professor Ripley says, when owners no longer control what they own "the successful functioning of our capitalist system is placed in doubt" and "the whole theory of business profits goes by the boards"; based as it is on supposed control by owners, the relation between capital and labor is revolutionized and a social and political issue of the first order looms before us.[1]

Our federal Secretary of Commerce, Herbert Hoover, presents the situation with a different interpretation altogether, contending that, through the diffusion of stock ownership, control is passing into the hands not of bankers and other intermediaries, but of the immediate management. But such control by management, however benevolent or even beneficent, is just as autocratic and irresponsible toward employees, owners, and the public as control by the banks and holding companies. Hoover says that "the ownership of utilities and large manufac-

[1] *Atlantic Monthly*, January, 1926.

21

ture has to a large degree been divorced from management . . . and is rapidly being diffused over millions of individuals, none able to dictate to management," and that the new power left in the hands of the management is tending to give it "a new vision of relationships" in which capital is being relegated to a subordinate rôle. With increasing security, he says, capital comes cheaper and management is bound to assign to capital an ever smaller share of the surplus product of industry and to devote a larger share of that surplus to the consumer in order to attract business and to labor in order to secure service and contentment. Capital, he contends, will receive consideration "only to the extent that it shall be commanded on the best possible terms for the expansion and conduct of the industry."

Such an enlightened managerial control as Hoover predicts, would doubtless give better treatment to labor than it now receives. But the world has yet to see any autocracy, whether of bankers or of management, which does not give a high consideration, if not the highest consideration, to its own interests and connections. And, moreover, while there has been a divorce between management and ownership, there are few if any signs of divorce between management and finance (see Chapters III to VI).

Hoover emphasizes the point that the professional managers have "but little participation in ownership" and that, therefore, they do not feel "so dominant a pressure for profits to owners" and so tend toward granting "a larger dividend to workers and customers." This calculation, while partially justified, does not take into account the managers' interest in very high salaries and their possible relations both with financing corporations and with those corporations from which their own organizations buy and to which they sell. High salaries Hoover speaks of as if they were granted exclusively for "skill and experience"—with no reference to the fact that managers, according to his own theory, are increasingly in a position to fix their own salaries and those of their associates. The money-making, legitimate and illegitimate, of managers through their relations with subsidiary business connections, real-estate transactions, and stock speculation or investment, needs scarcely be dwelt upon.

Professor Carver contends that the new developments are causing a gradual and peaceful revolution toward a *democratic capitalism.* Together with our relatively high wages and the capitalization of savings through savings banks, he says they are bringing about the gradual disappearance of a distinctively laboring class and that at the same time the capitalist class is gradually being eliminated through reduced rates of profits and interest. The ultimate outcome, he believes, will be a democratic social system based on "occupational equality"—a system under which there will be little disparity between occupations and incomes and the laborer's child will enjoy the same opportunities as the rich man's.

American labor does not agree that there is a leveling up of the wage-earners relatively to other occupations *except through the result of labor organization and collective action,* economic and political, or that wages are likely to be raised sufficiently to work toward "occupational equality" and "the gradual disappearance of a distinctively laboring class" except in proportion as the labor

¹ Speech before United States Chamber of Commerce, May 12, 1926.

movement functions effectively on the economic and political fields. Labor values the new developments of the so-called "labor-capitalism" chiefly just because they give it *a new knowledge and understanding of capital that will strengthen labor as an organized power.*

Nor does labor see any signs of the elimination of the capitalists either through such "reduced rates of profits and interest" as is now taking place or through "the new vision of management."

As an outcome of these new developments there is undoubtedly a tendency toward "occupational equality" of labor with certain social groups—but labor has never believed that they tend to produce any equality with the controlling capitalists. Labor banks and insurance companies, labor colleges and high wages, are doing much to put labor on a level, economically and politically, with the great mass of small producers and salaried and professional groups. The new developments also give labor common ground with the small shareholder and investor and the great body of consumers. They point toward economic democracy through the obliteration not of the broad lines that separate the controlling capitalists from all other social groups, but of the lesser lines between these other groups. (See Volume I, Chapter XII.)

Instead of bringing small investors, consumers, and employees into a partnership with capital, labor points out that the diffusion of stock ownership and related movements unite all these elements in resistance and opposition to the capitalist groups that are hoping by these means to strengthen their control.

The National Catholic Welfare Association has pointed out that the employee-consumer ownership plan may be sound financially and highly beneficial both to the corporation and to the small investors, but has been promoted not to give employers and consumers or other small investors any real voice, but to acquire "new friends against rate cuts, wage demands, and government ownership." "The management is able to avoid responsibility by asserting that employee-owners demand that rates be kept up and consumer-owners that wages be kept down. The only real hope in the movement is that it may get beyond control through a union of consumers and employees."

Organized labor is not tempted from its course by these new corporation policies, no matter how sincere they may be nor how carefully worked out by employers and their experts nor how beneficial in some ways. Profit sharing —of which employee ownership is a form—is regarded by organized labor, along with the institution of shop and industrial councils, so-called "industrial democracies" or "industrial republics" and other forms of employee representation organized by employers, either as a method of abolishing labor unions or as "one of the methods by which employers may bind their employees closer to them." [1]

Boris Emmett, in a study of American profit-sharing based on all obtainable documents, reached the same conclusions as organized labor.[2] He drew his conclusions in part from personal investigation, in part from a publication of the United States Bureau of Labor statistics which was the result of a study of all profit-sharing plants known to be in existence in the United States

[1] *American Federationist*, May, 1916.
[2] *Journal of Political Economy*, vol. xxvi, pp. 1019-1035.

(some sixty). That the object of these plans was mainly to bind the employee to the particular employer is indicated by the fact that in all the plants except one, discharge and leaving employment act automatically to terminate the employee's rights. "In all of the plans except one, discharge and leaving employment act automatically as causes for forfeiting the share of profits for the current year." [1]

The favorite plan of profit-sharing, as I have said, has become "employee ownership." The best known of these plans is that of the United States Steel Corporation. Dr. Gulick, of Columbia University, says that this stock-subscription plan, like the corporations housing and pension schemes, is "available for fighting unions and for limiting independence and initiative." [2]

President Gompers very plausibly denied the term

---

[1] Boris Emmett in *Trade Unionism and Labor Problems,* p. 252.

Emmett summed up these schemes as follows:

"The profit-sharing field is rather unique in the sense that under its arrangements additional duties carry with them no new rights. Under most of such schemes the employees are constantly reminded of the fact that they are no longer mere employees, that they are partners in the business and are therefore expected to conduct themselves as such—to avoid any moves or acts, such as requests for better conditions and higher wages, that will inconvenience the business. These new duties, however, involve no established rights to benefits, for each of the schemes specifically reserves to the employer the right (1) to determine which of the employed shall participate and under what conditions they may do so, (2) to hire and fire at pleasure, and (3) to discontinue or modify the entire arrangement without notice or consent of the employees. Legally shares in profits thus become mere gratuities, which the employer may or may not dispense.

"In fact, no profit-sharing firm is known to have in operation any system of collective bargaining or of definitely established friendly relations with trade unions." *Op. cit.,* pp. 255-260.

[2] "Labor policy of the U. S. Steel Corporation," by Dr. Charles A. Gulick, Jr.

profit-sharing to this plan, in view of the very small part of the profits the corporation had turned over to labor. "The autocratic steel industry," he said, "has inflicted upon the workers in that industry what it is pleased to call a profit-sharing system. It is ludicrous to say that the steel trust has shared any of its profits with its workers, and it is also untrue. The steel trust merely pays to the workers, under the guise of profits, a portion of the money which it sets aside for wages and which acts as a substitute for wages." [1]

It is absurd to say that because a stockholder who happens at the same time to be a wage-earner still retains his vote as a stockholder that labor when given stock is given "a voice in the management." Yet that is precisely the ground taken by Judge E. H. Gary, who is not only president of the Steel Corporation, but one of the leading spokesmen of organized business in this country.

Judge Gary says that employers in America believe that the employee "should be considered an associate and not an inferior, that so far as practicable he should be given an opportunity to purchase an interest in the business he is connected with, having the same rights, advantages, and responsibilities, and standing on the same basis as all other stockholders, also that he should be subjected to the same restrictions concerning behavior, attitude, and accountability to the laws that relate to the employer."

We do not believe that he should be entitled to a voice in the management of the employer's property or business unless he has a pecuniary interest and corresponding responsibility.[2]

[1] Wheeler Syndicate, September 5, 1922.
[2] Speech in New York City, May 21, 1926.

In other words, Judge Gary and the numerous and powerful employers for whom he speaks do not propose to give labor any voice in industry unless they are compelled to do so. They will allow the wage-earner a voice exclusively as a stockholder, and in no measure whatever as a wage-earner. Moreover, they know that the small and isolated stockholder has no real "voice in the management."

The new schemes for encouraging stock-ownership by employees may be enlightened, intelligent, and beneficial from several standpoints, but labor regards it as a plain if not a willful misstatement to say that they give labor "a voice in the management."

The employee ownership panacea presents itself in exactly the same light to William Green, the present president of the Federation. "Many wage-earners have had dreams of ownership in industry," says President Green, "but even so, we all know that *whatever the ownership, private, governmental, or employee,* the vital problem for us is the terms and relations we have with management. To deal with this problem, labor must always have its voluntary organizations directed and managed by itself." [1]

There is no other conceivable way by which labor can secure a voice in the management.

[1] *American Federationist,* April, 1925.

Note—Employers' group insurance of employees increased from $13,000,000 in 1912 to $3,264,000,000 in 1924! Stock ownership by employees is now estimated at a total of $5,000,000,000. (Abraham Epstein in *Current History,* July, 1926.) Yet such huge sums of capital are but very small fractions of the capitalized value of America's wage bill, or of the total industrial and financial capital of the country.

CHAPTER II

LABOR CO-OPERATES WITH CAPITAL, BUT REFUSES COMBINATION

"Employee Representation" and Company Unions—Union-Management Co-operation—The Baltimore and Ohio Plan.

"EMPLOYEE REPRESENTATION," "shop unions," and the varied plans of labor organization under employers' direction which go by the name of "industrial democracy" and "plant councils" are alike in this—that in putting an end to the labor problem they would, if sufficiently successful, put an end to the labor movement.

There are now thousands of "company unions" in existence where there were hundreds before the war. "Employee representation" has spread so rapidly of late—together with group insurance of employees by employers and a more scientific management and better treatment of the labor force—that a large part of the public has concluded that these new employers' policies have marked out the final limit to the labor movement, and that the labor unions are destined to play a steadily less and less important part in society.

"Organized labor's danger," says a leading newspaper, "is in its own success. It has taught, not altruism, but enlightened selfishness to many employers, and several of the largest industries are not unionized *because they grant collective bargaining, high wages, and an elaborate system of benefits to their employees.* But sincere union leaders, men who are not merely ambitious for their own power and profit, will contemplate such competition with satisfaction rather than regret. *And unionism, though it will not have in the future as important industrial and social functions as in the past,* has still a wide field of service and a powerful influence." [1] (My italics.)

Let us see what organized labor thinks about this. When employers say they accept "the principle of collective bargaining" but refuse to concede to labor the free right "to choose its own representatives," they expose the foundation of their so-called employee representation. American employers as a whole "accepted" collective bargaining after President Wilson's First Industrial Conference in 1919. Yet the right of labor in each plant to elect representatives of its own choosing was denied by the employers' delegation at this conference—though it had been granted two years previously (during the war) to millions of wage-earners by the United States government acting through the War Labor Board. The government recognized and affirmed "the right of the workers to bargain collectively through chosen representatives." The right was widely defended also by the press, by educational authorities, and by church organizations, as well as a few important bodies of employers, such as the New York City Merchants Association and the New Jersey Chamber of Commerce. It was also definitely recognized by the United States Railway Labor Board in its decision in April, 1921, in the following very explicit language:

[1] Chicago *Tribune,* October 7, 1925.

LABOR CO-OPERATES WITH CAPITAL

The right of railway employees to organize for lawful objects shall not be denied, interfered with, or obstructed.

The right of such lawful organization to act toward lawful objects *through representatives of its own choice,* whether employees of a particular carrier or otherwise, shall be agreed to by management.

The majority of any craft or class of employees shall have the right to determine what organization shall represent members of such craft or class. Such organization shall have the right to make an agreement which shall apply to all employees in such craft or class. No such agreement shall infringe, however, upon the right of employees not members of the organization representing the majority to present grievances either in person or by representatives of their own choice. [1]

The board buttressed its decision by a body of rules securing the position of the unionists and protecting the employer. The rule against discrimination is typical:

No discrimination shall be practiced by management as between members and non-members of organizations, or as between members of different organizations, nor shall members of organizations discriminate against non-members or use other methods than lawful persuasion to secure their membership.[2]

This decision was so wholly in accord with the labor view that the Executive Council of the Railway Department of the American Federation of Labor, representing half a million organized workers, indorsed it without qualification:

This decision of the Labor Board will not only have a very strong and beneficial effect upon the transportation industry, but it will mark the real beginning of industrial law, so to

[1] From the *National Labor Digest,* May, 1921.
[2] *Ibid.*

speak, and of a code of principles which will be used as a basis of procedure in all our basic industries.

It is the most courageous and forward-looking decision that we have so far had in this country from a government tribunal in the development of a correct basis for industrial relations and conditions.[1]

Moreover, President Wilson's Second Industrial Conference, which met in January, 1920, definitely endorsed the right of "unrestricted selection of representatives by employees," recommending provisions for fair elections in order that the majority of the employees might be represented.

President Wilson's Second Industrial Conference, it may be admitted, undertook a very serious study of the labor problem. Labor protested against its personnel, which included only one wage-earner, the chairman, Secretary of Labor, William B. Wilson, while it embraced a number of employers and persons closely associated with employers. Nevertheless, the membership was composed of persons of exceptional information and capacity. If it represented the employing class, it represented the more progressive wing. Herbert Hoover, while himself a life-long associate of big business, brought to it, besides his unquestioned humanitarianism, the scientific engineering spirit.

The sharp contrast between the findings of this liberal though capitalistic commission and the position of organized labor may be seen in the basic demand of the commission for *"the organization of the relationship between employer and employee."* This is undoubtedly an accurate definition of the underlying aim of all reforming

---

[1] From the *National Labor Digest*, May, 1921.

employers—as well as many other non-labor reformers. Labor, on the contrary, desires first of all *the organization of labor.* It is willing and eager that the other social groups and interests should be organized, and it believes all groups should *then* be brought together (see Chapters III to VI). This labor view, indeed, is very close to a view put forward by Mr. Hoover himself when he advocates the organization and co-operation of all industrial and commercial interests and groups, including labor.

The Second Industrial Conference, however, indorsed the very opposite principle to voluntary co-operation, namely "employee representation," under the name of representative government in industry, shop committees or works councils.

It is not to be wondered at, therefore, that organized labor rejected the findings of this industrial commission, without referring to its important beginnings of broad, constructive thinking on the labor problem. President Gompers presented labor's verdict:

In industries where the employees are not organized, no machinery of any kind, whether supervised by governmental agencies or otherwise, can produce industrial justice. Organization of the workers is the fact upon which must be predicated the existence of any machinery for the settlement of disputes or the extension of the principles of democracy in industry. Unavoidably organization of independent shop units of employees is a menace to the workers, for the reason that it organizes them away from each other and puts them in a position where shop may be played against shop.[1]

The issue is here clearly defined. Organized labor believes that the shop organization of labor should be a part

[1] Samuel Gompers in press of March 19, 1920.

of the labor organization of the entire industry, which, in turn, should be a part of the labor movement as a whole. The employers, on the contrary, regard the shop organization as a part of the organization of the establishment and of the corporation or industrial unit. With hardly an exception, employers are unwilling to give their "employee organization" the right to function as a part of the labor-union movement. In explanation of the labor standpoint Gompers continued:

There can be no objection to the closest relations of co-operative nature between employee and employer in the shop, but these relations must never take on such a form as to separate the workers in that shop from the rest of their fellow workers in the industry.

Furthermore, trade-union organization includes organization within the shop and offers the fullest opportunity for co-operative relations between the workers in the shop and the employer. There is no limit to which good relations between employees and employers may be developed through the agencies provided by the trade-union movement.[1]

The very essence of the so-called "employee representation" is that the employees of one concern shall not act in unison with the employees of any other concern—in a word, that employees shall not be free to have "representatives of their own choosing"—which is precisely the *sine qua non* of organized labor. The plan as stated by the Pennsylvania Railroad is as follows:

The management deals collectively with the men through employee representatives.

Any employee can belong to any union he desires. No employee is disqualified to vote, to be nominated, or to be

[1] Samuel Gompers in press of March 19, 1920.

34

elected because he happens to be a member or officer of any organization.

The management simply insists upon dealing with the employees themselves through employee representatives *and not with representatives of absentee organizations to which they may belong.*[1] (My italics.)

The employer, by this device, not only deals with a smaller instead of a larger organization, but he deals with wage-earners instead of wage-earner experts; he deals with those under his power, and he treats with a body that, as a body, knows nothing of alternative employment in other concerns and is unfamiliar with the conditions of the entire industry and the labor market as a whole.

Naturally the employer would prefer to deal directly and solely with his own employees without any such formidable body as a labor union or the labor movement behind them. But the balance would not be equal. The manufacturer has with him not only all the manufacturers involved in the Manufacturers' Association, but the Chambers of Commerce and capitalistic and financial interests generally.

The most famous of the employee representation plans, the Industrial Republic, organized in the Colorado Fuel and Iron Company by John D. Rockefeller, Jr., Mackenzie King, now Premier of Canada, and others, has recently been the subject of a thoroughly scientific report. Here are some of its most important conclusions:

The company and employees must be equally represented when action on a dispute of this kind (relating to wages and conditions of employment) is taken, and the decision of the majority is binding. These provisions, however, all relate

[1] "Employee Representation of the Pennsylvania Railroad."—Leaflet issued by the railroad.

to the settlement of grievances. They do not insure a share in determining conditions before grievances occur, and hence, perchance, preventing them. *Nor do they insure any share in determining standards for the industry as a whole.*

Basic wage rates have not been within the scope of negotiations through the plan. Competitors' rates are accepted by the company as its own, and nowhere is the "competitor" defined.

The employees' representatives are ill prepared to be advocates for the miners, as was pointed out by a number of men. They explained that they had to work hard in the mines; many of them were uneducated; they had no time to read. What match were they for the educated, experienced executives of the company before whom they must advocate the interests of the men?[1] (My italics.)

Employees' representatives chosen in this way are not only ill prepared; they are subject to discrimination and discharge.

William Green, president of the American Federation of Labor, points out that the job of representing a group and of promoting their interests is in a very real sense a technical calling requiring special experience, education, and character. It is for this reason, and because any employee representative who showed independence would be subject to discrimination or dismissal, that organized labor not only refuses to accept the "company union," but opposes it. President Green says of the report just quoted:

It shows that the employee representation plan has not taken root in the industrial life of the Colorado Fuel and Iron Company and become a real economic agency; the men do not voluntarily take part in the election of their "representa-

[1] *Employees Representation in Coal Mines,* by Ben M. Selekman and Mary Van Kleeck, in the Industrial Relations Series of the Russell Sage Foundation.

tives"; few difficulties are referred to the council for adjustment; men do not expect or get from their "representatives" maintenance of rights or increasing benefits; not even wages or hours are determined by these agents.

It isn't their organization but the instrumentality of the company with which it originated and which in reality controls it. It gives the workers no guaranty of stability of employment if they manifest any initiative for self-interest or on behalf of their group even as prescribed by the company.[1]

In fact, there remains no doubt as to the underlying motive of the overwhelming majority of the company unions, employee representation plans, and shop committees. As we read in the American Federation of Labor Weekly News Service:

The National Industrial Conference Board is investigating the company "union."

The board is composed of a score of manufacturers' organizations, including the most anti-union in the country.

In its questionnaire the board says:

"We want in particular to know to what extent in your experience works councils and similar forms of employee representation have been introduced or managed as a device for offering trade-unionism in the plant?"

This, in a few words, is the reason for the company "union."

Can it offset trade-unionism? is the question these employers would like answered.

This is the first time opponents of organized labor have frankly told why they favor the company "union."

This, in itself is a gain. The issue is clarified by the admission of union foes.[2]

President Green argues for the maximum of co-

[1] *American Federationist*, March, 1925.
[2] April 17, 1926.

operation of the unions with employers and agrees that this requires shop organization. But he says that only those shop committees formed under labor-union direction can satisfy labor and give the maximum of co-operation and he refers to the Baltimore and Ohio Railroad and the shipbuilding plants for example (see below).

Employee ownership and employee representation may, in this form, constitute the first step in constructive progress. But they are being promoted both by employers and by certain social reformers as something altogether beyond that, namely as a panacea for social conflict and as a substitute for voluntary labor organization. The Pennsylvania Railroad triumphantly quotes in defense of its plan the following paragraphs from a Pastoral Letter of the American Catholic Hierarchy:

While the labor union or trade union has been, and still is, necessary in the struggle of the workers for fair wages and fair conditions of employment, we have to recognize that its history, methods, and objects have made it essentially a militant organization.

The time seems now to have arrived when it should be, not supplanted, but supplemented by associations or conferences, composed jointly of employers and employees, which will *place emphasis upon the common interests rather than the divergent aims of the two parties, upon co-operation rather than conflict.*

In a word, industry would be carried on as a co-operative enterprise for the common good, and not as a contest between two parties for a restricted product.[1]

There is here an incomplete description both of organized labor and of "employee representation." *Organized labor does not deny or undervalue common interests*

[1] From Pastoral Letter of the American Catholic Hierarchy.

merely because it recognizes divergent interests. Nor does co-operation between employers and employees *necessarily* mean co-operation for the common good. On the contrary, it has sometimes meant collusion against the common good, and the consumer has no protection comparable with what he has when the owner and the worker are not combined.

The more carefully these employers' plans for employees are examined the more certain it will become that, if successful, they are likely to be paid for in large part by the consumer and the public. When they do make a bid for the support of the public as well as the employee, it is the public as an investor and not the public as a consumer. For example, there is no industry in which more consumers are more deeply interested than the coal industry. It was the coal consumers who chiefly caused the appointment of the United States Coal Commission, whose final report favoring the consumer was not published until two years after its preliminary report, because of employers' opposition. Some of the more advanced employers in this industry try to co-operate with employees and to interest the public as investors in the coal business—but without a word as to the consumer. If we did not note that the consumer is omitted from the reckoning. the following employers' proposal might seem almost like a panacea: "Is it not time for us to decide whether the opinion that any business should be owned and operated entirely in the interest of those financially concerned should give way to the position that, in order to be entirely successful and avoid all disputes and lack of co-operation. a business of whatever size and kind must be considered as a combination between those financially interested i. e., productive labor and the management that directs the disposal of capital invested, the labor used on production, and the sales of the product?"[1]

If organized labor were converted to this doctrine and if it were put into effect, the result might or might not develop ultimately into a form of social progress. But certainly it would not be progress along the democratic road American labor is now traveling. It would amount either to a reversion to capital-and-labor combinations against the community which were far more prevalent a generation ago than they are today, or to an advance not toward industrial democracy, but toward a capitalistic form of syndicalism or guild socialism.

The development of the American labor movement is away from any thought of combination with employers against the consuming public toward an appeal to the public to join labor in reducing profits within reasonable limits—in order that wages may be raised and prices lowered. American labor is moving away also from employee representation under the ægis of the employer toward occupational or economic representation for labor and for every producing group with the support and approval of the state that is, the industrialized and democratized state, that is now coming into being (see Chapters III to VI).

The official organ of the American Federation of Labor for January, 1921, reprinted—evidently with approval—an address of Herbert Hoover's in which he had declared:

There has been a great increase in shop committees as a

[1] From *The Coal Industry, Labor and the Public*, p. 125.

LABOR CO-OPERATES WITH CAPITAL

method of organization. Where they have been elected
by free and secret ballot among the workers, where they are
dominated by genuine desire on both sides for mutual co-
operation in the shop they have resulted in good.

Organized labor has opposed some forms of these committees because of the fear that they may break down trade
organization covering the area of many different shops.

There would be little outcry (from employers) against
the closed (union) shop if it were closed in order to secure
unity of purpose in constructive increase of production by
offering to the employer the full value of the worker's mind
and effort as well as his hands.[1]

In advocating the *union* shop committee under these
conditions Secretary Hoover took a position almost identical with that of organized labor.

I quote Secretary Hoover not merely as representing
an influential and a comparatively advanced employer's
view, but as indicating the conclusions inevitably reached
by the well-informed expert. He proceeded to out-
line the constructive policy that has since been partly
carried into effect by the Baltimore and Ohio Railroad:

The solution of the industrial problem is not solely the
prevention of conflict and its losses by finding methods of
just determination of wage and hours. Not only must solution of these things be found, but, if we are to secure increased production and increased standard of living we must
awaken interest in creation, in craftsmanship, and contribution of its intelligence to management. We must surround
employment with assurance of just division of production.
We must enlist the interest and confidence of the employees
in the business and in business processes.[2]

The Baltimore and Ohio Railroad, under its liberal

[1] Speech of March 24, 1920.
[2] Secretary Hoover in speech of March 24, 1920.

41

and farsighted president, Daniel Willard, has developed
a labor policy in sharpest contrast to that of the Pennsylvania Railroad. It has favored the organization of
shop committees—under the railroad shop unions, and
has evolved, together with the unions, an entirely new
plan of union-management co-operation corresponding
largely to the principles laid down by Hoover. Adopted
by several other railroads before it was two years old,
and indorsed by all the labor unions, radical and conservative alike, this experiment has now become the classi-
cal illustration of the possibilities of shop committees and
genuine "employee representation" *under the labor unions.*
The labor-union inception of this plan is best described
in the words of President Willard himself:

Some weeks before the railroad strike of 1922, Mr. W. H.
Johnston, president of the Machinists Union, and Mr. O. S.
Beyer, Jr., an engineer of high reputation and broad experience, called at my office in Baltimore and said that they
would be glad to co-operate with the officers of the company
in an attempt to develop a plan under which the workmen in
the shops might co-operate in greater degree toward improving the efficiency of the operations. Such a suggestion coming from such a source was most unusual; in fact, was
unique in my experience. However, the suggestion was
accepted in good faith and a plan had been worked out to
put it into effect some weeks before the beginning of the
strike of the shopcrafts in 1922. After the strike had been
settled and things had begun to move again in a more normal
manner, discussion of the subject of co-operation was renewed and arrangements were made to give the plan a trial
at our Glenwood shops located near Pittsburgh.

I wish to make acknowledgment of the effective co-operation which we received from the very first from the men
chosen to represent our employees, as well as from the

grand officers of the respective unions. Before a very long time had elapsed we could see that we were also beginning to get the earnest co-operation of the men themselves. After the experiment had been running a year it was decided that there was at least enough merit in the plan to justify its extension to the principal shops all over the Baltimore and Ohio system.

An arrangement was signed on February 25, 1924, and by the time it had been in effect only eight months President Willard reported that 657 shop meetings had been held, that more than 5,000 suggestions had been made to the company—and that more than two-thirds of them had been accepted—the reason for the high proportion being that the men were advised at every point by their own engineers serving under Mr. Beyer.

At each locality where there are Baltimore and Ohio shops the local chairman of the shop committee of each local union meets with representatives of the management every two weeks. Every three months (more often when necessary) the "general system chairmen" of the various unions meet with the general mechanical officials of the railroad at Baltimore. And finally we have "employee representation" of all the shop employees of the Baltimore and Ohio System in the annual or bi-annual convention of the Federation of the union employees in all mechanical branches.

The president of the Railroad Department of the American Federation of Labor, Mr. Bert M. Jewell, has summed up the foundations of the plan in four points:

First: That management must grant and agree to full and cordial recognition of the *bona fide* trade union.

Second: That management extend to these *bona fide* trade unions and their representatives constructive, as well as protective duties and responsibilities in the operation of the railroad.

Third: That management and these trade unions upon this basis and in this spirit, agree to co-operate.

Fourth: That management agree to share fairly with these workers, and to negotiate same through these trade unions, the results of their joint efforts.[1]

Mr. Jewell points out that both sides have gained and that neither has lost anything under this arrangement:

These co-operative committee meetings do not have authority to decide questions. Management representatives retain the authority and responsibility of operating the railroad.

The employees have not surrendered any of their rights, authority, or power—they have strengthened the hold on that which they had attained; they have enhanced their opportunity and increased their power to *more fully protect their original investment* (*i.e.,* their labor) and secure a more adequate return thereon. The management has not surrendered any of its rights, authority, or power.[2]

The engineer largely responsible for the plan, Mr. O. S. Beyer, gives us a glimpse into the importance and the wide variety of the subjects discussed in these co-operative meetings when he classifies them under the following illuminating heads: "Job analysis and standardization. Better tools and equipment. Proper storage, care, and delivery of material. Economical use of supplies and material. Proper balancing of forces and work in shops. Co-ordinating and schedule of work through shops. Improving quality of work. Conditions of shops and shop grounds, especially in respect to heating, lighting, ventilation, safety, etc. Securing new business for

[1] *American Federationist,* June, 1925.
[2] *Ibid.*

LABOR CO-OPERATES WITH CAPITAL

the railroad.   Securing new work for the shops.   Stabilization of employment." [1]

Leaving *financial control and management* to be checked and supervised by some "public agency," this Baltimore and Ohio plan opens the way to the natural evolution of union co-operation with *production management,* in a field—the shop itself—where there is little temptation for, or possibility of, combination of capital and labor against the public.   Its popularity with all unions and its indorsement by the 1925 convention of the American Federation of Labor demonstrate once more that it is a fundamental purpose of labor organizations to promote co-operation with management—and, especially through union shop committees and genuine voluntary employee representation.

American labor has shown its readiness to co-operate with employers frequently in the past.[2]   Labor's enthu-

---

[1] *American Federationist,* August, 1925.

[2] I have concentrated attention on the Baltimore and Ohio plan partly because of the need to economize space, partly because it is the most important, recent, and significant of organized labor's experiences in co-operation with management.   But it is in no sense isolated as a demonstration of organized labor's willingness and ability to co-operate or of its use of its own experts to make co-operation efficient. Nearly all the so-called wage agreements, such as those with the Typothetæ and with the newspaper publishers, have contained numerous clauses providing for co-operation, and these agreements have been in practical working effect for decades.   But the place to describe them would be in a history of collective bargaining.

One further illustration may be mentioned as showing that the tendency of labor to employ experts to aid the industry is not limited to the Baltimore and Ohio experiment.   The Printing Pressmen, under the presidency of George L. Berry, have established an Emergency and Production Department which provides a service to the newspaper industry of America at the expense of the union.   This department, which is connected with the union's technical school, maintains a staff of expert engineers familiar with newspaper production and an office for giving information and advice to those engaged

45

siasm for this more scientific and thorough plan of co-operation adopted by the Baltimore and Ohio Railroad does not mean, any more than those previous experiments in co-operation, that the unions are ready to dissolve and abandon their function of bargaining with employers, or that labor has lost its identity in a partnership with capital, or that labor has become capitalistic—at least not in the usual sense of that word.

Like the other new developments, such as labor insurance, labor banks, and "employee ownership," labor-management co-operation brings labor *closer* to capital and to industry. But that does not necessarily mean that labor organization is being *absorbed* by capital, even to the smallest degree. The unions believe, on the contrary, that closer co-ordination makes labor organization at once more efficient and more powerful, more valuable to the industry *and more useful and necessary to the wage-earners—and not merely as small capitalist owners.* If organized labor is "passing over to capitalism" it is passing over not to the present oligarchic capitalism, but to a capitalism so thoroughly democratized that it will doubtless bear some other name.

Organized labor does not believe that either the conclusive demonstrations it has given of the sincerity of

in the newspaper industry. Six hundred daily newspapers are examined and their defects are "noted and filed for monthly references." These are sent to the newspapers accompanied by a proposed remedy. "If in the course of sixty to ninety days the remedy is not applied, then one of the engineers of this department is sent to the city and into the pressroom of the newspaper in question and the remedy is applied."

The department is now frequently called upon by newspaper publishers "to pass upon the subject of machinery and processes, to lay out pressrooms, to pass upon architects' plans."—(*American Federationist,* February, 1926.)

LABOR CO-OPERATES WITH CAPITAL

its plea for good will, co-operation, and greater efficiency in industry or the proofs it has offered of its capacity to put co-operation into practical effect will overcome employers' resistance to labor organization and its implications. Too many employers and corporations (nearly all) are receiving a large part of their incomes from unearned and excess profits—as distinct from their services to industry. Labor believes that the element that leads the resistance to its demands, both for a progressively higher share in the product and for a progressively larger share in the control of industry, is these "profiteers," and that there is little prospect that they will yield anything either of their illegitimate profits or their arbitrary power —except under economic or social compulsion:

The trade union movement [labor claims] seeks the highest possible development of our industrial life. What is necessary to understand is that the highest aggregate productiveness is dependent upon the full release of a good will and initiative by removal of repression and arbitrary control in industry. This is the function of management, with the co-operation of the workers in their organized capacity. *The chief obstacle is found in financial forces which control industry from the primary point of view of speculation and dividends.*[1]

[1] Samuel Gompers in Wheeler Syndicate, September 3, 1922.

CHAPTER III

LABOR CHALLENGES THE DOMINATION OF CAPITALISM

Does American Labor Accept the Capitalist System?—Financial Domination Injurious to Production.—Industrial Democracy Through Evolution—A Step at a Time.

AMERICAN labor recognizes the tendency toward capitalism in this country. It does not believe that we are living under a "capitalist system of society," as Socialists contend. But it sees the capitalists highly organized, dominant in industry, and often dominant in government—and it regards organized labor as the chief of the democratic forces preventing the full establishment of capitalism.

The last speech made by the late Samuel Gompers to the American Federation of Labor was devoted in part to a solemn and final restatement of the labor view of capitalism: "To-day," said Gompers, "in our country, and in the other democratic countries, there is, to a larger or smaller degree, an autocracy of what has come to be known as *capitalism;* in other words, *the dictatorship of wealth, of employers, of profiteers, of the possessors of material things.* The only influence of power which challenges this employer's autocracy and dictatorship, is the American labor movement of our country, and all other democratic industrial countries."[1] (My italics.)

[1] American Federation of Labor Convention, 1924.

LABOR CHALLENGES CAPITALISM

This statement was typical of Gompers; it is conscientious and forceful. He did not say that we are living under an autocracy of capitalism; he said America is a democratic country within which there has developed an autocracy of capitalism. It is still a democratic country and capitalism is challenged more or less effectively by organized labor, and other democratic forces. And he was international-minded; he saw that the situation is similar in other democratic countries.

The menace of capitalism in America has been fully recognized outside of labor's ranks. Herbert Hoover has spoken of the need for remedying the social and economic ills that arise from "the aggregation of great wealth with the power for economic domination" and of the importance of avoiding capitalism as well as Socialism.[1] Woodrow Wilson, in the last article he wrote, said that it was "against capitalism under one name or another that the discontented classes everywhere draw their indictment," and that the question had arisen whether "the system we call capitalism is indispensable to modern civilization."[2]

American labor aims to check the development of capitalism and to further the development of industrial democracy. But it does not aim to abolish capitalists or privately owned capital. On the contrary, it recognizes the value of the constructive type of capitalist to-day, and, when the menace of capitalism shall have passed, it believes that "captains of industry," having ceased to be industrial generalissimos and financial dictators, will function far more effectively than they do to-day.

As a consequence of the balanced position of American

[1] Speech of November 19, 1919.
[2] *Atlantic Monthly*, August, 1923.

49

labor on this question many extremists, both radical and conservative, have concluded that our labor movement does not oppose capitalism at all—and there are undoubtedly certain points in labor's position which, hastily analyzed, might seem to support that conclusion. We read in the official organ of the American Federation of Labor, for example, that it stands "squarely for the defense and maintenance of the existing order and for its development and improvement."[1] We might conclude that the Federation stands for the "capitalist system" if we did not know that American labor regards the existing order as being fundamentally democratic and only incidentally and partially capitalistic.

Then we find it stated in a book published under the direct auspices of the Federation that, after the war "Mr. Gompers and the Federation adhered without faltering to their established policy of accepting the capitalist system and bargaining with it."[2] But the truth is that the Federation does not bargain with the "capitalist system." It bargains with capitalists—and it denies that we are living under a capitalist system. It calls the social system or the lack of system, under which we live, a democracy; it believes that we live under a democratic form of government. It recognizes, at the same time, the tendency toward capitalist rule or capitalism, toward a capitalist system; the American Federation of Labor does not bargain with such capitalism but fights it without compromise.

The strongest evidence that might be interpreted as showing that American labor accepts the capitalist system

[1] *American Federationist*, June, 1923.
[2] *A Short History of the American Labor Movement,* by Mary Beard, p. 177. Published by the Workers' Education Bureau.

and does not fight against it is drawn from the Portland convention manifesto of 1923 and from certain contemporaneous statements of Gompers in his speeches, articles, and autobiography. However, this evidence could never have been honestly interpreted as accepting the present capitalist control of industry—except if that control is revolutionized by giving a voice to all the essential factors of our economic structure. Or, as Gompers phrased it in his autobiography: "The organization of management, finance, and producing workmen is the way to develop discipline and information within those groups. The next step, to my mind, is co-operation of all the groups with the pooling of information to determine control of the industry. The industry would thus become self-regulated and disciplined, while checks interposed by organized consumers would deter non-social tendencies." [1]

But is the Federation willing to accept the capitalist system even in this form—according to which a voice is given to each essential economic factor? No. For not only is the democratic political structure still regarded as the final arbiter in industry (though it is not to intervene in internal matters), but still another condition precedent to the acceptance even of such a revolutionized capitalism is that the active *management* of industry, in co-operation with organized labor and other voluntary economic organizations, shall oust the *financial* control!

"I am confident, and all labor is confident," wrote Gompers, "that when management with the help of labor succeeds in releasing itself from the short-sighted, selfish, and unintelligent control of what we may well call financial oligarchy, most of the present restrictions of output

[1] *Seventy Years of Life and Labor*, Volume II, p. 22.

will disappear and most of the disputes between employers and workers will be avoided.

"Future welfare demands co-operation between management, labor, and engineers for the release of all industry from a senseless, wasteful, unsocial, and brutalizing control of powerful high finance." [1]

It was held by the Portland convention that the operation of industry by finance and primarily for profits was injurious to the industry as a whole, *including the active management and even such owners as put the welfare of the industry above profits:*

Too frequently the group that controls investment or credit controls the policies of industry. When this occurs, industry finds itself guided by the desires of those who seek returns on investment, with little or no regard for any other factor. Modern industry, as we have repeatedly declared and as is conceded by all who understand, functions largely with the assistance of credit. But credit, which is the life blood of productive industry, is continuously purloined for purely exploiting, profiteering, speculative, and wasteful purposes. It is not infrequently employed for the purpose of withholding commodities from their proper channels in order that inordinate and criminal manipulation and profiteering may take place. *Every perversion of the proper functions of industry eventually strikes back at industry and leaves its damaging mark.*[2] (My italics.)

The supposition was that industry, once all its essential factors are organized, will purge itself, without political aid, of the dominance of profits and finance:

Industry, as it becomes more intelligently and thoroughly organized and co-ordinated, as co-operative relations are

[1] Wheeler Newspaper Syndicate, September 17, 1923.
[2] American Federation of Labor Convention, 1923.

extended, will in self-defense purge itself of the wrongful, wasteful, uneconomical, anti-social, and criminal misuse of credit power. Credit power is one of the most vital powers in the modern world and it arises out of the very existence of the people themselves, being but a token, or guaranty of their ability to use and consume. This power, which rises out of the people, out of the fact that they live and must use commodities, must be stripped of its abuses and administered in accordance with the demands of a normal, rational industrial life in the interests of service and production and not solely or mainly in the interests of profits and perversions of our industrial system.[1] (My italics.)

This hope to secure a divorcement between industry and finance had been definitely formulated by the 1922 convention of the Federation, though at that time the Executive Council frankly confessed that they had found no practical program that gave any promise of accomplishing it:

An effort should be made to secure a complete divorcement between related financial and industrial and commercial enterprises. We are not prepared at this time to submit a definite program because of the complexity of the problem involved, but the E. C. is authorized to give this subject further consideration and attention and to take such action as may be helpful in having this financial strangle hold removed from the throat of our industrial and commercial life.[2]

The idea of this divorcement is not confined to labor. It is in the mind of Herbert Hoover (see Chapter I) and, in view of his cordial relations at that time with organized labor, there can be little doubt that Hoover's view had a certain influence over the Federation. Hoover, as I have said, pointed out that "ownership of industry has been

[1] American Federation of Labor Convention, 1923.
[2] Convention of American Federation of Labor, 1922.

53

largely divorced from management," that management is becoming more and more dominant, that capital is coming to be less and less regarded, and that management, freed more and more from the control of owners, would give consideration mainly to consumers and employees. This was precisely the hope that underlay the Portland manifesto. See Note, p. 49.

But, though labor may hope for the ultimate divorcement of finance and management, labor is by no means disposed to trust in that eventuality. Much as labor would desire to see the separation take place, it has shown little faith that the divorcement is actually occurring. On the contrary, labor finds that management often has an influence over finance quite as anti-social and profiteering in its tendency as the influence of finance over management (see Chapter IV). This was clearly restated by the 1922 convention:

The initiative and source of influence over the use of deposits and funds in banks and the use of banking facilities in fighting organized labor do not always rest with the banks. Indeed, the banks are as much subject to the influence of manufacturers, merchants, and trade associations as the individual merchant and manufacturer are subject to the bank's influence and control. Investigation has demonstrated that in a number of cities chambers of commerce, manufacturers' associations, so-called citizens' committees, and other varying forms of associations, dominated by business men, have exercised their collective influence and association with banking institutions to compel employers, who desired to deal fairly with the trade unions, to alter their course and to assume a hostile attitude toward the organizations of the wage-earners.[1]

[1] Convention of 1922. See also Chapter I.

LABOR CHALLENGES CAPITALISM

Indeed, the literature of American labor will show that organizations of employers and business men are even more often regarded as being the leaders against the social program of labor—and the consumers' program indorsed by labor—than is finance. With this fact in view the Portland bid for the co-operation of management and enlightened employers against financial control and against the operation of industry primarily for profits becomes a somewhat empty gesture as far as practical results are concerned, though it remains significant as showing labor's willingness to co-operate with private management freed from financial control.

The very next convention, held at El Paso in 1924, showed that the hope to align management against finance and forward-looking employers against the operation of industry fundamentally for profits must be abandoned, at least temporarily:

The pronouncement of last year's convention, pointing out that industrial democracy must evolve mainly through industry itself and not through government, presupposed the co-operation at least of the bulk of organized employers. So long as that co-operation is not forthcoming in sufficient volume—and it has not been forthcoming—the evolution toward industrial democracy must give place temporarily to a wasteful economic and political struggle.

Labor's constructive policies outlined in last year's convention eloquently set forth hope for industrial democracy to be attained in co-operation with every useful element in industry, including forward-looking employers, can be understood only in connection with labor's utter, inevitable, and irreconcilable opposition to the conduct of industry exclusively or fundamentally for profit. Industrial democracy must be as clearly defined by what it moves away from as by what it moves toward.

LABOR AND GOVERNMENT

The hope that existing managements can be separated
from finance and excessive profits and salaries may, or
may not, prove illusory. But the fact that labor had that
hope shows that it has never for one moment aimed at
compromise with capitalism in industry, and that at Portland labor was led to believe it had found a relatively
short and direct way to abolish capitalism in industry.
Warfare against the control of industry by finance and
against the operation of industry primarily for profits is a
fundamental and permanent feature of labor's policy,
while the hope that the co-operation of management can
be secured *for the purposes of this warfare* was certainly
incidental and is perhaps temporary.

There is found in the Portland manifesto itself a basic
attack on capitalism—unrestricted profiteering—in industry. "The industrial destinies of the country have thus
far been finally in the hands of one group in the nation's
industrial organization," says the manifesto. Labor's one
great aim, it continues, is to restore the balance and put an
end to the operation of industry for the dominant purpose
of private profit:

The operation of industry for the dominant purpose of
producing private profit has led to a multitude of abuses.
It has produced all of the evils of autocracy because it is
autocratic. Every factor that enters into the sustenance
or operation of industry must be safeguarded and its just
reward assured, but there must be an end to final control
by any single factor. We have had and must continue to
have, until democracy finds its way into industry, abuses for
which all producers and all consumers have had to pay
through profiteering and privation.[1] (My italics.)

If managements will not or cannot co-operate to purge

[1] American Federation of Labor Convention, 1923.

56

industry of the domination of profits and finance, organized labor and other popular economic organizations have no recourse but to move to bring about this purging through the use not only of their purely economic powers but of the powers of government. And even in the midst of the birth-pangs of the Portland idea this was never forgotten. At that time President Gompers appealed to legislators "to curb the piracy, the profiteering, and the ruthlessness of great financial powers seeking to impose their will upon the world of industry." [1] Gompers fully recognized the need for Congress not only to protect against the industrial combinations, but to supervise them.

"Modern industry," he pointed out, "must have supervision and there must be a guardianship for the people in general against attempted predatory conduct on the part of any compact, powerful single group." [2]

[1] For Wheeler Newspaper Syndicate, September 17, 1923.
[2] *American Federationist*, May, 1923.

NOTE—Hoover is by no means alone in preaching "the new theory of management." According to Owen D. Young, Chairman of the Board of Directors of the General Electric Company, now that stockholders have ceased to be real owners and have become mere investors "interested in the balance sheet and their dividends but not in the business" and ever ready to sell their stock, both managers and workers have ceased to be mere employees. "The managers of great concerns are no longer the paid attorneys of the capitalists to depress wages and boost the market in order that profits may be high. They are, instead, trustees of an institution, the object of which is to bring labor and capital into partnership for economical production on a vast scale." These trustees must "command" the market and cheap capital. Otherwise, apparently, they are enlightened despots. (*Saturday Evening Post*, August 14, 1926.)

CHAPTER IV

THE SOCIAL STRUGGLE

American Labor Opposed to the Class-struggle Doctrine.—American Labor Takes Its Stand with All Who Perform Useful Social Functions.

"It has been the general practice of governments," said the late President Gompers, "to accord only to employers, the owners of capital, of the managerial side of commerce and industry, real participation in government and in deciding upon governmental policies. According to this custom the wage-earners belong to the class of the governed, never to the governing class." [1]

American labor believes, with Gompers, that there was a period in this country when we had a near approach to "class government." But however close we may have been, or may still be, to class government, American labor has at no time lost its faith in democracy. Nor has it proposed, as an alternative for capitalistic rule (whether real or merely alleged), to set up the rule of the working class. "National policies," American labor has always consistently declared, "must accord with broad democratic ideals that recognize all factors (in industry) and value each according to the service that it performs." [2]

It is true that American labor strives for power and in

[1] Address of January 18, 1916.
[2] *Ibid.*

58

this struggle it meets with resistance. But the struggle is in no sense a class war. It is a struggle neither for survival nor for power over others, but for self-development of the group and for recognition and increased influence in the body politic. This struggle is the very reason for the existence of the labor movement. "History is largely made up of the struggle of groups of people to overcome their environment and to overcome oppression by other groups." [1]

This irrepressible social conflict is not a class war. American labor does not regard any other social class as an enemy to be conquered; it demands only what it regards as its rightful share in industry and government. It sets up "enlightened self-interest"—not for itself alone, but for all classes—as the one great driving power that insures progress. "Initiative, aggressive conviction, enlightened self-interest, are the characteristics that must be dominant among the people if the nation is to make substantial progress toward better and higher ideals." [2]

Each social group must, first of all, look after its own interests—though in an enlightened spirit—and must expect other groups to do the same. The political ideal of American labor is self-government, or, as it has recently been called, self-determination, for each social group. Society as a whole, labor believes, can be controlled and effectively organized only through the co-operation of more or less autonomous groups, each contributing not a theory and program of universal welfare, but its own experience and point of view. Self-help, initiative, re-

---

[1] Reply of American Federation of Labor Political Committee to questionnaire of National Republican Advisory Committee, 1920.
[2] Samuel Gompers in *American Federationist*, February, 1919.

sponsibility, independence, all the strong and positive characteristics we have so long regarded as socially desirable in the individual, are held as having the same high social value when exercised by the organized group. These self-assertive qualities are no more anti-social in the group than they were in the individual. Social groups, however, are not arbitrarily instituted; they are genuinely representative only in so far as they are functional and the result of natural evolution and voluntary organization.

That, in a few words, is the basic social philosophy of American labor. It regards capitalists and employers, together with their economic dependents and their cultural kinsmen, not as enemies which labor is organized to fight and conquer, but as outsiders whose power over labor and opposition to labor organizations must be overcome if labor is to have its rightful voice in industry and government. There is no destructive hatred in American labor's attitude toward its economic opponents, no arrogant and autocratic tendency to pass final judgment on them or to decide arbitrarily, in the European Socialist manner, exactly what their proper and legitimate social function is to be. But there is a very clear and positive opinion as to their unsatisfactory attitude toward organized labor and an impressive determination not to remain under their power:

It is a serious and dangerous matter to intrust the determination of issues which concern the life, the happiness, the welfare and freedom of the workers into the hands of other men who do not and cannot know the toilers' world in which they live, move, and have their being.

There are many whose financial welfare is identical with

that of the employer, who are dependent upon his prosperity. There are many selfish and indifferent to the moral and ethical values of any issue that conflicts with their own comfort. There are some few with broader sympathies and keener and deeper understanding of human nature, who *try* to maintain the dispassionate attitude of justice toward both, but *upon some critical and vital issue can they completely overcome the formative, determining influences of environment, instruction, and the indefinable psychic influences of their own kind?"* [1]   (My italics.)

Labor does not expect or desire advancement through the altruism of other social groups. On the contrary, since it is seeking to extend its power and to get a larger share of the industrial product, it realizes that it must necessarily take the offensive, and that the strenuous opposition of certain social groups—the vested interests—is natural and inevitable. However just labor's claims may be, they are often to be won only at the expense of those who own and control industry.

This militant attitude is commonly misunderstood or misinterpreted. It is not the product of a revolutionary spirit. It is based upon a demand for ceaseless improvement and a realization that such improvement can be had only if labor keeps on demanding it and—in order to overcome inevitable opposition—backs up every demand by its collective power and by co-operation with other organized and functional democratic groups.

Labor expects to continue indefinitely its demands both for better wages and better conditions and for a larger and larger voice in industry and government—and it is prepared for the indefinite continuation of the resistance

[1] *American Federationist*, January, 1913.

of employers and profiteers and of those who take their standpoint.

> Because [said the late Samuel Gompers] employers as a class are interested in maintaining or increasing their share of the general product and *because workers are determined to demand a greater and ever greater share of this same general product, the economic interests between these two are not harmonious.* . . . There are times when, for temporary purposes, interests are reconcilable; but they are temporary only. . . .
> It [the wage-earners' struggle] is conducted against those who stand in the way, hostile to the advancement of conditions for the working people. It is conducted against those employers, whoever they may be—the employers who refuse to understand modern industrial conditions and the constant need for the advancement of the working people and who refuse to accede to the demands of the workers.[1] (My italics.)

The initial gains made are wrung from the employers through "collective bargains, strikes, and boycotts"; but in proportion as the employer is willing to recognize this new power and to make concessions to it there arises the possibility of industrial truces more and more prolonged —though only as long as owner and employer continue to make new concessions: *"The gains made by the organized labor movement in this country have generally been wrung from the employing classes. What workingmen of America have obtained in improved conditions, higher wages, shorter hours of labor, was not handed to them on a silver platter."* [2] (My italics.)

[1] Testimony of Samuel Gompers before United States Industrial Relations Commission, 1914.
[2] *Ibid.*

THE SOCIAL STRUGGLE

The preamble to the present constitution of the American Federation of Labor, adopted in 1886, begins as follows: "A struggle is going on in all the nations of the civilized world between the oppressors and the oppressed, a struggle between the capitalist and the laborer, which grows in intensity from year to year."[1] This phrase still stands in the Federation's Constitution. If a new Constitution were formulated by the Federation to-day, it is doubtful if labor's struggle would be described just in those words. But American labor has always taken an extremely serious view of its historic rôle and destiny and has abandoned ultra-radical ideas solely because it has felt that all the tremendous social changes needed to establish economic equality can be brought about through existing democratic institutions. It believes that "every movement of the working class itself that brings an increasing share of the wealth produced, every statute that loosens the monopolistic grip of the privileged classes on lawmaking, on the raw materials of nature, or on those forms of so-called capital which are but legalized tribute capitalized—all such steps picture an accelerating momentum of society in a movement away from Marx's prophesied necessity for an overturning of the fundamental principles of our existing social order."[2]

Nor does American labor feel that this great social change that is being brought about by the economic and political rise of the wage-earners is merely quantitative. It does not consist merely in a gradual transfer of income and power from the hands of capitalists into the hands of

[1] From preamble to the constitution of the American Federation of Labor, 1886.
[2] *American Federationist*, June, 1910.

63

wage and salary earners and other elements composing the masses of the population. It means, as labor never fails to insist, something vastly greater than this. It means that, as income and political power become more equitably distributed *the economic, political, and social policies of the old ruling class are gradually replaced by the policies of industrial and social democracy.*

It is a change that is bound ultimately to affect every part of our social structure. But there is no finality about it. American labor does not value it, on the ground that it will some day eliminate the employer or abolish profits, or that it may abolish or eliminate any other basic institution of the present society. American labor looks only for the ending of the *predominance* of the employer and profiteer in industry and politics. It recognizes the high social value of the private initiative and of the wage and profit systems to-day, and it may attribute a still higher value to these institutions when their power to control and dominate is ended.

Labor has expressed the belief that this conception of the social struggle is that of the *masses* of American producers of whatever category. It is a struggle to be carried on neither by a class nor for the benefit of a class. Even those few American labor unions that use the expression "class struggle" interpret it in a purely democratic and non-Socialist sense. Let me give an example:

After a thorough discussion the 1920 convention of the National Association of Machinists reaffirmed a paragraph of its constitution advocating "the class struggle along co-operative, economic, and political lines, with a view to restoring . . . our government to the people and using the natural resources and means of production and distribution for the benefit of all the people." [1] This declaration was not regarded as socialistic by the convention. The Socialists vehemently attacked it and wanted it to be made more radical. They wanted to recommend to the membership of the union not the "wisest use of our citizenship," but the "wisest use of our might as workers." And in place of asking the employment of the nation's wealth and means of production for the benefit of "the people" they wanted to make the clause read, for the benefit of "those who toil." When the convention rejected these changes—and by a large majority—Marxism was defeated, and the social and democratic faith of American labor was reaffirmed. On the other hand, the American labor point of view, as opposed to the vague and empty phrases of mere populism, was clearly defined when the word "people" was taken out of the draft as above quoted and the paragraph was made to close with the words "for the benefit of those performing useful service to society." This formulation avoids European socialism and laborism as positively as it avoids mere populism, since it recognizes the social function of all producers and not merely of wage-earners.

More and more frequently and consistently American labor is making definite appeal to all of the public that functions socially, with the sole exception of those capitalistic interests which oppose every social policy or political program leading to radical changes for the benefit either of society as a whole or of the producing masses.

The same standpoint was expressed by the Conference

[1] Amendment to preamble of constitution affirmed by 1920 convention.

of representatives of national Trade Unions in 1921, where nearly all of the unions, except the brotherhoods, were present: "Labor speaks from no narrow or selfish point of view. It speaks from the standpoint of American citizenship. And the indictment it lays is an indictment of the enemies of freedom and progress." [1]

Organized labor's conception of its relation to other social groups has been ably expressed by William Green, the present president of the Federation.[2] President Green makes no attack upon employers or upon capital. He admits willingly "the right of employers to control, direct, and manage industry and to receive a fair return upon invested capital," but he denies that ownership is the sole authority in industry and contends that they are under a social obligation to accept a right relationship with their employees and to recognize their employees' organizations. Many employers, he says, "believe that ownership in industry is supreme, superseding all other rights, and that this is the only authority in industry." Confronted by these hostile employers and their creed, which would leave non-owners no ground to stand upon, trade-unionism is "fighting for public acceptance of its creed and philosophy." [3] It is relying upon "the convincing power of logic, facts, and the righteousness of its cause and not merely upon its economic strength." In other words, even in its daily struggle with the hostile employer labor turns to the public for support.

[1] From American Federationist, April, 1921.
[2] Ibid., April, 1925.
[3] American Federationist, April, 1925.

THE SOCIAL STRUGGLE

There is scarcely a function of organized labor that is not inspired with this social struggle philosophy. Take as examples two of its activities most enthusiastically approved by conservatives. The new labor banks have been hailed as an approach to the existing business world as it stands and as being entirely freed from labor's ruling motive, the building up of a counter-force independent of the profit-takers. Yet there can be no question whatever that the labor banks were formed and are supported by labor largely "to balance the credit power now exercised by employing interests."[1] (See Chapter I.)

The purely educational activities of organized labor might also be imagined as freed from preoccupation with the social struggle. But it is not so. An investigation of social studies in the public schools made by the American Federation of Labor, under the president of the American Teachers' Federation and some of the most trusted and conservative of the labor chiefs, reaches the conclusion that "there are selfish and reactionary forces at work endeavoring to influence public-school education," that these forces, on the whole, are being successfully resisted by educators and educational authorities backed by progressive bodies, but that they have done considerable harm to the curricula and text-books and more harm by "the subtle prejudices they have created, especially in the minds of legislators and public education officers"—prejudices tending to affect the great body of teachers and to deprive them of independence of thought and action.

Among the national organizations listed by labor as attempting to influence education for ulterior purposes we find listed the American Bankers' Association, the Cham-

[1] Report Executive Council American Federation of Labor, 1923.

ber of Commerce of the United States, the International Association of Rotary Clubs, the National Association of Manufacturers, and the National Industrial Conference Board. The American Federation of Labor denies that it attempts to exert the same kind of influence on education "which reactionary organizations are attempting to exercise," and says that it opposes all influence by partisan bodies of any kind and merely wishes "to assist the educational profession and the general public to resist the encroachments of those who are attempting to use the schools in their own interests."

In reporting on text-books this labor investigation illustrated the sort of bias they complained of—and attribute to reactionary propaganda. One school text says dogmatically that the remedy for labor troubles is to be found in "compulsory arbitration." Another questions "whether there is, or ever has been, any real industrial occasion for trade unions in the United States." [1]

In the schools, as in the banking world and elsewhere, organized labor sees aligned against it powerful economic forces. Labor attacks these forces as "reactionary." But it claims it does not attack them from any narrow labor or class standpoint, nor from a standpoint that would regard them as having no social function and no right to existence.

Labor, as I have said, believes that its conception of the social struggle is democratic and American and has nothing whatever to do with intellectuals' sectarian theories or "proletarian" dogmas imported from Europe.

The first progressive and labor aim is—and must

[1] Survey of Social Studies in the Public Schools. American Federation of Labor, 1923.

68

be—to persuade the people to use their government for securing the upper hand over the complex of great corporations and allied business organizations that now overshadows it. In this aim organized labor can appeal effectively to the entire public, with the exception of the corporate interests and their satellites and dependents. It must be confessed that these forces of plutocracy compose a mighty host, not only in wealth and power, but even in numbers. Though this host is not so numerous as is sometimes claimed, it undoubtedly includes not only the overwhelming majority of business men and people of large or considerable incomes, but also those who confidently expect to rise into this class and those who look to it for promotion as salaried men, for assistance as small producers or for patronage as purveyors of goods and services to the rich and the well-to-do. But all these together do not constitute a very large minority—perhaps 5 or 10 per cent of the population, the other 90 or 95 per cent including all those of modest incomes and expectations not directly dependent on wealth. So that the labor and progressive campaign against the excessive power of concentrated and organized capital and for government supervision and control is an appeal to the people at large, regardless of civil or political status or economic function.

CHAPTER V

PROFITS—SOCIAL AND ANTI-SOCIAL

*Our Industrial Autocracy—Labor's Attack on Illegitimate Profits
—The Struggle Against the Financial Oligarchy.*

AMERICAN labor regards its struggle for better conditions as being of the highest social and democratic
significance. "Combined autocratic powers," says the
Federation, "are making every effort to destroy the freedom of workers to join together in defense of their interests. There may be conflicts that are more spectacular,
but there is none upon which, in the long run, human
progress will turn with greater effect."[1] "The greatest
force in American life capable of restraining predatory
capital and to that extent capable of maintaining the
democratic institutions of the country, is the trade-union
movement."[2]

A statement of the same import was signed also by
the railway brotherhoods. The social struggle is there
described as directed against reaction and autocracy in industry, the enemies not only of labor, but of democracy
and progress:

Labor understands fully that powerful interests to-day are
determined to achieve reaction in industry if possible. They
seek to disband or cripple the organizations of workers.

[1] From Report of Executive Council of the American Federation
of Labor convention of 1921.
[2] Declaration of presidents and officers of all unions of the American Federation of Labor, February, 1921.

They seek to reduce wages and thus lower the standard of living. They seek to keep free from restriction their power to manipulate and fix prices. They seek to destroy the democratic impulse of the workers which is bred into their movement by the democracy of the American Republic.

Labor must be and is militant in the struggle to combat these sinister influences and tendencies. Autocracy always insists upon restricting the income and the activities of workers.[1]

But labor holds that this fight to better wages and labor conditions, important as it may be not only to labor but to all society, is but the beginning of a larger struggle: "The effort to crush the voluntary organizations of the workers may be designed by employers as an effort to secure their own immediate enrichment, but no such effort can stop at that point. Whether its sponsors will it or not, it is an effort to bring upon our whole national organization of society unprecedented disaster and retrogression."[2]

According to Gompers, struggle against financial oligarchy is not a mere labor struggle: "There is a deep, vital issue to be solved. We have, not a class struggle, but a struggle between great, primary forces, between a group interest and a great, universal human interest. Labor is holding the line for humanity. . . . Labor is contending against the continued enthronement of Profit as the autocrat of our destinies. If labor's line is broken, the public welfare will be engulfed."[3]

The social struggle is largely a contest over the division of the product of the nation's industry. Labor gauges its

[1] *American Federationist*, June, 1921.
[2] *Ibid.*
[3] Samuel Gompers—International Labor News Service, July 29, 1922.

71

economic demands and develops its political program not according to any minimum standard of living, but according to the rising product of each industry and of the nation. (See Volume I, Chapter XII.) It notes the immense increase in the size and the number of large and "comfortable" fortunes and incomes, and it finds that their chief origin lies in profits—profits garnered largely from the very industries where organized labor has been most effectively stopped in its struggle for a larger share in the product.

While American labor does not attack profits as such, it by no means accepts the right of bondholders or stockholders to an undefined amount of interest or dividends, without further examination of the relative merit of their claims when compared with the claims of the other factors of industry. Its views are fairly and fully expressed in the following passage:

The full value of production does not go to the actual workingmen to-day. A portion goes to investment, superintendence, agencies for the creation of wants among people, and many other things. Some of these are legitimate factors in industry entitled to reward, but many of them should be eliminated. *The legitimate factors are superintendence, the creation of wants, administration, returns for investment in so far as it is honest investment* and do not include watered stock or inflated holdings.

The vast sums of money paid annually in dividends on stocks and interest on bonds by corporations managing and operating important industries constitute a very large proportion of the incomes of these industries. This is an unfair distribution of the incomes from industries. The owners, stockholders, or bondholders of modern corporations receive from this distribution an unearned income which is taken from the product of the labor of those who produce it.

The efforts of the American labor movement to secure

a larger share of the income are directed against all who illegitimately stand between the workers and the attainment of a better life. Employers, capitalists, stockholders, bondholders—the capitalist class generally—oppose the efforts of the workers in the A. F. of L. and in other organizations to obtain a larger share of the product. Very much of the opposition to the efforts of the working people to secure improved conditions has come from those who obtain what may be called an unearned share in the distribution. The beneficiaries of the present system of distribution desire to retain as much as possible of their present share or to increase that proportion.[1] (My italics.)

Here is a clear recognition of what some people would call a "class struggle," the capitalist class as a whole usually trying to get more profits and organized labor trying to restrict certain types of profit for the purpose of raising wages. But it is not the Socialist "class struggle," since the social expediency of profits and interest—when kept within certain broad and elastic limits—is not questioned.

American labor recognizes also a conflict of interests broader than that between employers and employed, that is the conflict between wealth possessors and wealth producers. This struggle, labor believes, is irrepressible and cannot be obviated; but it can be made less costly.

I believe [said Gompers] that as time goes on the wage-earners will continue to become larger sharers per dollar of the wealth produced. I have no fear as to the future of organized labor. I have no fear as to the future of labor. *There is a constant struggle which has been going on from time immemorial between the wealth possessors and those who produce wealth,* and that struggle has manifested

[1] Samuel Gompers's testimony before United States Industrial Relations Commission, 1914.

73

itself in different forms, at different times, in different countries. That struggle has continued up to date, and will continue so long as there are diverse interests between the two.
. . . There is something I want to obviate, that I am trying
to give my life's work to obviate, that the struggle shall
not be so bitter and costly.[1] (My italics.)

While labor recognizes the conflict of interest between
wealth producer and wealth possessor for the division of
each dollar produced, it does not deny the just claims of
the possessor. The position taken therefore, is not socialistic; but it is as far as possible from being capitalistic.
The organized labor of America does not strike either at
private capital or at private property; but it wishes to
subordinate both to the general welfare:

The eternal problem with which the labor movement has
to cope is control of property—to bring property into such
relations to human life that it shall serve and not injure.
It [the labor movement] was born out of efforts of workers
to think out modern phases of that world-old universal problem—property.

Trade unions regard property and the laws of property
as human institutions, intended for service in the development of individuality, giving each a feeling of security and
assurance and independence, which mean freedom to direct
and control his life.

It [the trade-union movement] does not seek to overthrow
private property. It regards private property as a necessary
agency for securing opportunity for individual independence
and resourcefulness, but it wishes to safeguard private property for use by preventing the perversion of property as an
agency purely for exploitation and individual aggrandize-
ment in order to establish an autocracy.[2]

[1] Testimony of Samuel Gompers before United States Industrial
Commission of April 18, 1899.
[2] American Federationist, November, 1916.

PROFITS—SOCIAL AND ANTI-SOCIAL

According to the theory of American labor, the entire product of industry belongs *primarily* to the "producers." The claims of "private property" or "possessors" are recognized, but only within limits set by the prior claims of producers and of the general welfare: "As producers, labor is interested in a fair distribution of the legitimate profits accruing from a business to which they contribute their energy and mental acumen—in fact, their lives—*as against the capital invested by others.*" [1] (My italics.)

The claims of private ownership and control, however legitimate within certain limits, are necessarily modified by the claims not only of the immediate producers, but of society! As President Gompers declared some twenty years ago, "The organized movement of the workers is to obtain more of the advantages which result not only from their labor, but from the combined genius of the past and present." [2] Society has its claims and labor has a right to share in these claims also.

Labor believes that the producers should determine in the main both the control of industry and the division of the product. But the national product owes its origin to producers of the past as well as the present. Our economic system and equipment are in large part the result of the labor of *society as a whole.*

In the declaration made in 1919, in which the railroad brotherhoods joined with the unions of the Federation— we find the same leading thought, namely, that industry must be operated not for profits *primarily* nor for improving wages *exclusively*, but for social service: "Labor is

[1] American Federationist, November, 1924.
[2] Samuel Gompers in *Organized Labor, Its Struggles, Its Enemies and Its Fool Friends,* 1903.

fully conscious that the world needs things for use and that standards of life can improve only as production for use and consumption increases. Labor is anxious to work out better methods for industry and demands it be assured that increased productivity will be used for service and not alone for profits."

How does this principle differ from the recent Socialist declaration "for a new social order based on production for use and not for profit?" (the "object" of the leading intellectual Socialist organization of America, the League for Industrial Democracy, formerly the Intercollegiate Socialist Society). The distinction is vital. American labor makes no proposal to *abolish* profits, but merely to *subordinate* them. American labor is not working for "production for use and *not* for profit." It is working for production based primarily upon social service and the welfare of producers, but allowing for profits in so far as they are consistent with and further this object.

Organized labor in this country would agree in part with Herbert Hoover when he says that private profits, even though they are often unjustified, are the high price we willingly pay for invaluable private initiative in industry. But American labor believes that there are already means at hand by which *excessive* and *unearned* profits can be controlled and largely eliminated.[1]

[1] I am discussing at this point not American labor's *program* of measures attacking unearned and excessive profits, but the *principles* by which it seeks to discriminate between profits that are social and profits that are illegitimate. (I have discussed the labor program elsewhere, in Volume I, Chapters X and XI and Volume II, Chapters VIII to X.)

However, I may mention here, as illustrative of the criteria adopted, one of the broadest measures of labor's program—the unearned increment tax on land valuations (approved by the Federation convention of 1920). That measure has the tendency to tax away profits due to

PROFITS—SOCIAL AND ANTI-SOCIAL

The labor movement of this country is not attacking profits. It is not attacking the active organizing capitalists who supply so much of the initiative in industry, except as their profits are excessive; it is attacking the speculator, the seeker for monopoly profits— and the non-producer, the parasite. "Adoption of the principles we here urge," declared the Federation convention of 1920, "will inevitably result in a rapid decrease of the number of non-producers who at present live by fastening themselves in one useless capacity or another upon the industrial life of the country. Proper absorption of non-producers into useful channels would be but a simple problem."

Labor attacks also the excessive and unearned *power* that so often accompanies profits, "the enthronement of profits as the autocrat of our destinies," and "the unchecked control of profits over industry and the dominating influence of profits over government." "Against an honest return and legitimate profits but few will protest. *We have yet to find an equal spur to initiative.* What labor maintains is that profit must not be the sole and dominating motive in industry, but that profit must come as the natural and logical result of service rendered and must constitute a reward for service instead of a reward for speculation, chicanery, exploitation, and autocratic domination." [1] (My italics.)

"Civilization and profits go hand in hand," says Pres-

---

monopoly as opposed to profits that would exist under free competition. This is by no means labor's sole method of discriminating between profits that are social and those that are anti-social. But it illustrates the spirit of the other criteria adopted.

[1] Article for the Wheeler Newspaper Syndicate, September 30, 1922.

77

ident Coolidge.[1] American labor does not question this
dictum. But the worst as well as the best of our civilization goes hand in hand with profits, and labor sees no
reason why we should not separate the evil from the good.
Labor opposes not the existence of profits, but the
enthronement of profits. There are many kinds of
profits. Profits, like interest, may be the legitimate payment for the use of capital, or they may be a legitimate
payment for management and initiative, but after all such
legitimate profits are paid, further profits may be taken
that have nothing whatever to do with the welfare of the
industry, and it is precisely those who look for such profits who control the great industrial corporations.[2]

"Banking houses in Wall Street dominate and even
elect the boards of directors of great industrial and transportation establishments. These in turn select managers
to suit the banking control, and these in turn are compelled to set up policies to suit the banking control."[3]

"Finance rules industry to-day. In the case of railroads Wall Street makes railroad policy in the interest of
profits. Railroad policy is not made in the interest of
transportation. A policy ordered by finance has profits
as its object."[4]

In so far as profits, in the form of dividends, are nothing more than a fair payment for capital, labor raises no
criticism. Such profits are needed for the welfare of the
industry itself; it must pay good dividends in order to be
able to borrow economically when it needs new capital.
Such profits are in accord with the welfare of the indus-

[1] Speech in New Haven, November 27, 1920.
[2] Samuel Gompers in The New York *Times,* July 23, 1922.
[3] The *Sunday Star,* Washington, September 10, 1922.
[4] Samuel Gompers in The New York *Times,* July 23, 1922.

try and the interest of the public. But an industrial policy directed mainly to obtain the maximum profits or aiming at profits exclusively does not stop at this point. It withdraws money from the industry without any corresponding benefit—and a large part of that money is devoted to purely private and often to anti-social purposes.

Labor reaches the momentous conclusion that to-day industry as a whole is organized *primarily* to produce profits and not to produce commodities, that finance controls industry with profits in view and with only a secondary consideration for the welfare of industry and those engaged in it or for the public interest. "Production is primarily for profit. That is the basis of the real issue to-day. That is why mine-owners, nationally organized, guard their secrets and refuse to agree upon terms with the workers. That is why railroad managements managing in the name of Wall Street refuse to come together with the workers and agree upon terms. Management is serving profit, not production needs, not the requirements of the people. This is the largest fact in the whole situation. It is the fact that is at the bottom of everything, and until people consider and understand that fact they are dealing with superficialities." [1]

It must not be supposed that organized labor sees the enthronement of profits as the arbiter of our destinies solely in our gigantic industrial corporations. The United States Chamber of Commerce speaks, legitimately, in the name of the "organized business" of America and the National Association of Manufacturers speaks for "organized industry." These organizations are just as strong exponents of the operation of industry for profits

[1] Samuel Gompers, International Labor News Service, July 29, 1922.

as are the great corporations. Of the United States Chamber of Commerce Gompers said: "The body is an organization of financiers and employers. *It is an organization of men who live by making profits.* It is an organization composed largely of men who perform *nonproductive service.* It is obvious that any position that may be taken by the Chamber on industrial questions is taken out of a sense of self-interest and that that sense of self-interest is one of the self-interest in behalf of the making of profit without contributing usefully to the industrial processes of our country." [1] (My italics.)

This is a strong expression; it is important to note, however, that Gompers recognized that a considerable part of the members of the Chamber are productive as well as selfish and that it was only the Chamber as a whole which he criticized as governed by "self-interest in behalf of the making of profit without contributing usefully to the industrial processes of our country."

Organized labor's attack on the operation of industry primarily for profit is not subversive or destructive; it has a very practical object in view, legislation directed not toward the operation of industry by government, but toward checking and controlling industry operated primarily for profit: "It might serve some purpose if legislators devoted their time to an effort to curb the piracy, the profiteering, and the ruthlessness of great financial powers in seeking to impose their will upon the world of industry." [2]

Labor is well aware that the freeing of industry from the exclusive or preponderant domination of the profit

[1] Samuel Gompers in *Labor*, May, 1922.
[2] Samuel Gompers in Wheeler Syndicate, September 17, 1922.

motive can be accomplished only by degrees. Mr. Gompers did not picture legislators as likely to do much in that direction at the present moment. But many of the chief measures of labor's political program have this object in view, and labor is entirely hopeful as to its ultimate accomplishment—for the reason that it feels that its standpoint is that of all society with the exception of a very small but very powerful minority:

There has never been a legislative proposal espoused by labor [said Gompers] that was not in the interest of all Americans except those who are aligned with special privilege and the great financial powers.

We cannot have prosperity and well-being for the wage-earners of our country without a consequent and coincident prosperity and well-being for our country as a whole. If this necessitates a curtailment of speculation and a curtailment of autocratic power and exorbitant, unearned increment for a few, I am sure that will cause no anguish except to the arrogant one-half of one per cent of our population which contributes neither intelligence nor initiative to our material, mental, or spiritual progress.[1]

[1] Samuel Gompers, article for Wheeler Newspaper Syndicate, September 31, 1922.

CHAPTER VI

THE GOVERNMENT OF INDUSTRY

Labor's Demand for a Voice in Industry—Self-determination for Industry—The New Social Structure.

THE labor unions, an organized democratic factor within industry, could scarcely have failed to develop a policy looking toward the democratic organization and government of industry. That policy would naturally emphasize the importance of *labor* in industry, of *industry* in the social structure, and of *democratic political government*.

Organized labor will undoubtedly contribute largely to shaping the political government of the future, but it will contribute still more largely to shaping the industrial government.

In developing its ideas of industrial government American labor does not aim at any political goal and is not under the influence of any political theory. Its industrial policy and ideals are drawn directly from its experience in industry. And, first of all, of course, from its experience in the organization of industrial labor.

In the labor-union view the organization of labor is, in itself, a primary and important step in the democratization of industry. As President Gompers said: "The agreement [the labor union contract with the employer] is the channel through which labor pours into industry its greatest effort, its most intelligent effort, its constructive thought. But more than that, it is the document through which complete revolution is wrought in the conduct of industry. From the moment in which workers and employers negotiate and agree upon terms, hours, conditions, and wages, the principle of autocratic domination gives way to the principle of democratic operation."

Organized labor works for the constant *extension* of this beginning of democratic government in industry. Here is the point of departure, and the unions do not advocate any theory or Utopia or any revolutionary principles except those that grow by a natural process of evolution out of its experience in regulating terms and conditions of employment in the workshop:

The trade-union movement, in co-operation with employers, has worked out machinery for the handling of industrial disputes and for the prevention of industrial disputes. This machinery, being the product of the normal and natural function of labor in its organized capacity, must stand and does stand as the proper and practical machinery for this purpose. *In its creation there has been expressed the sum total of the wisdom and experience of the industries in which it is applied,* and it is safe to say that there is within any given industry a greater knowledge concerning the operation and the needs of that industry than can be brought to bear from any outside agency. It is a matter of record that the machinery erected by organized labor in co-operation with the employers has enabled some industries to continue without interruption. without strike or lockout, for as long as forty years. As specific examples there may be cited the glass-bottle blowers, the stove molders and the newspaper printing trades. *The trade-union movement insists that there must be a constant extension of the principles of democracy in industry, but it contends that the practical appli-*

83

cation of this principle must be worked out within the industry itself.[1] (My italics.)

Having laid the foundations of industrial democracy through settlements of wages and labor conditions, by "collective bargaining" organized labor proceeds to work for the gradual enlargement of its functions.

Labor now participates more fully in the decisions that shape human life than ever before and more fully in America than in any other nation on earth; but our participation must be gradually brought to completion. *The purpose of this is not only the commanding of better wages and better conditions of work, vital as those are and have been.* The purpose that now unfolds is broader and nobler and filled with deeper meaning.[2] (My italics.)

Labor works to extend its sphere of action in two ways, it sets up an ideal and it specifies the first steps toward that ideal. It sets up an ideal of industrial democracy—the very reverse of a selfish partnership of capital and labor. But this is an ideal; that is, it is a goal to be approached by degrees and by the natural processes of evolution and it becomes sharply defined only in proportion as it is approached.

At present this "industrial democracy" is purposely defined only in broad and general terms. But some of its features are already clear. It is clear that labor recognizes that every useful element in society has its rightful claim to a share in the product and in the control of industry. Capital—or a part of capital—resists the fullness of these claims. Labor in fighting for itself must fight at the same time for all other useful citizens.

[1] Reply of American Federation of Labor to the questionnaire of the Republican Advisory Committee, 1920.
[2] Convention of American Federation of Labor, 1923.

THE GOVERNMENT OF INDUSTRY

American labor reviewed its ideals for industry a few years ago—at the time when the "super-power" and "giant power" projects first began to promise another great increase in our industrial product. "Finance," declared the *American Federationist,* "would send all of these great accumulating surpluses into profits. But humanity is entitled to a better distribution of this new-found production. The race as a whole has a stake in what the race achieves. Better methods, greater production, must mean more things for the working masses in the first place. It must then mean more freedom from toil. *And these things must be arranged with justice to every useful element in our citizenship. There can be no such adjustments unless there is within industry the machinery for running the affairs of industry. It is more than collective bargaining that is required. And labor has vastly more to give to industry than it can give through collective bargaining.*" [1] (My italics.)

"Labor has vastly more to give to industry than it can give through collective bargaining," and in order to make its full contribution it must have "a voice" in the shop, in the industry.[2] That is labor's proposed first step toward the democratic industrial government. The demand for "a voice" is not exorbitant, especially when we read labor's statement of the powers it leaves wholly in the hands of the management (see below).

Labor's demand for "a voice in the control of indus-

[1] *American Federationist,* May, 1924.
[2] This proposition in no way minimizes the importance of collective bargaining. Collective bargaining not only remains the foundation of the American labor movement, but as I have shown, all its newer functions depend upon the continued development of collective bargaining.

try" first became known to the nation during the war, when the labor unions were fully consulted in every one of the government's industrial boards, not only in the War Labor Board, but in the Shipping Board and all the others. After the war, employers sought, usually with success, to abolish this voice in control:

In so far as possible hostile employers have sought to reintroduce autocratic control into industry, making necessary a resistance on the part of the workers. Labor has enunciated the principle that the workers are entitled to an effective voice in the management and control of industry. To a larger degree than ever before, this principle was agreed to by employers during the war. It was found that it produced results of great value in the winning of the war. It made industry more productive.[1]

An "effective voice" in control does not mean control. For labor regards its demand for an effective voice as an implication of collective bargaining, and "collective bargaining in industry does not imply that wage-earners shall assume control of industry, or responsibility for financial management."[2] But once an effective voice is granted we have the beginning of a revolutionary change in the industrial structure—pointing toward further revolutionary change.

When Labor asks for "a voice in the management," it asks first, for union-management co-operation as now practiced to the profit of both parties and the public by the Baltimore and Ohio Railroad (see Chapter II). But it asks, further, that within certain sharply defined

[1] Samuel Gompers, from pamphlet, January, 1920, on "Collective Bargaining: Labor's Proposal to Insure Greater Industrial Peace."
[2] Samuel Gompers to American Federation of Labor convention at Montreal, 1920.

THE GOVERNMENT OF INDUSTRY

limits to be mentioned later organized employees should
be recognized *as equals in industry,* "with all of the rights
and privileges and all of the stature and standing of employers." The revolutionary importance attached by organized labor to this great social experiment (no longer
an experiment) can be gauged only by following closely
its own declarations on the subject. The first of these is
all the more remarkable since it was made at the Montreal
convention of the Federation in 1920, several years before the Baltimore and Ohio plan was inaugurated. I
shall quote some of its most salient passages:

There must be given to each individual a voice in the
shaping of his life and this right must extend to the workers in their organized capacity to be exercised through their
chosen representatives.

Industry to-day requires these remedial measures:

It requires greater democracy in order to give to the workers full voice in assisting in its direction.

It requires more intelligent management and acceptance
of the principle that production is for use and not for profit
alone.

The workers are appalled at the waste and ignorance of
management, but they are too frequently denied the chance
to offer their knowledge for use.

They decline to be enslaved by the use of their own knowledge and they cannot give of it freely or effectively except
as *equals in industry, with all of the rights and privileges and
with all of the stature and standing of employers.*

Autocratic industry kills incentive. It punishes brilliancy
of attainment. It warps the mind and drains the energy
from the body. We have repeatedly condemned the principle of autocratic control of industry and we now declare
that short of its complete removal from our industrial life
there is no industrial salvation and no hope of abundance in
our time.

87

LABOR AND GOVERNMENT

We urge the setting up of conference boards of organized workers and employers, thoroughly voluntary in character and in thorough accord with our trade-union organizations, as means of promoting *the democracy of industry through development of co-operative effort.*[1] (My italics.)

At the time it was formulated this pronouncement might have seemed somewhat theoretical: in view of the Baltimore and Ohio experiment initiated two or three years afterward it becomes quite definite and practical. What was proposed was not a new organization of labor or of industry, but that the existing labor organization should take on a new function, for which it knew it was fully prepared, and that the management should extend its organization so as to allow for that function.

Naturally the evolution of union-management co-operation within the shop and industry does not cease with installation. As it evolves it demonstrates the willingness of organized labor to co-operate and its ability to promote individual efficiency and the productivity of industry. Moreover, it gives organized labor and its experts a direct and accurate knowledge of at least one all-important side of finance, the mechanical cost of production.

The employers' movements for "employee representation" and "employee ownership" (already described) may be taken as rival or substitute plans to counteract and offset this rapidly spreading movement to give labor "a voice in control." For at the end of the war the movement had become formidable; strongly supported by public opinion, the labor demand and the wage-earners were

[1] Report of Executive Council of American Federation of Labor at Montreal, 1920.

ill-disposed to surrender voluntarily a power they had already effectively exercised. The employers often adopted the phrase "industrial democracy" to describe their own projects, and a part of the public, including many liberals who were genuinely anxious to look at things from the labor standpoint, followed the employers' reasoning. These liberals, starting out by adopting labor's premises, arrived unconsciously and unintentionally at employers' conclusions—greatly aggravating by their writings the difficulty now experienced by uninformed but fair-minded persons, however sympathetic with organized labor, in informing themselves on this question. A typical case of this reasoning is found in "The Industrial Code" of the Federal Council of the Churches of Christian America:

A deep cause of unrest in industry is the denial to labor of *a share of industrial management.* Controversies over wages and hours never go to the root of the industrial problem. *Democracy must be applied to the government of industry as well as to the government of the nation, as rapidly and as far as the workers shall become able and willing to accept such responsibility.* Laborers must be recognized as being entitled to as much consideration as employers and their rights must be equally safeguarded. This may be accomplished by assuring the workers, as rapidly as it can be done with due consideration to conditions, *a fair share in control, especially in matters where they are directly involved,* by opportunity for *ownership, with corresponding representation.*

The total effect of this pronouncement, because it concludes with a recommendation of "opportunity for ownership with corresponding representation," is damaging to organized labor. Labor may not object to such ownership and representation—in some cases may even approve of it—but not as *the* approach, or even as *an* approach, to industrial democracy. In its present form it is the employers' chief weapon against industrial democracy.

So American labor has demonstrated what it means by "a voice in industry." This first step toward industrial democracy has, in some instances, been taken—or rather, is in the process of being taken. What is the second step? Obviously it cannot be so clearly defined, since labor is not yet quite prepared for it. But as soon as one stage is in the process of being carried out, preparations necessarily begin for the following stage. The next stage labor calls "the self-determination of industry." This second stage looks beyond the shop to the formation of relations with groups of employees other than organized wage-earners and with ruling and controlling groups other than the operating management. Just as the first step consisted in the extension of the function of an existing organ (the labor union), so the next step contemplates a new organ or organs, namely new machinery for the co-operation of economic groups.

By "self-determination" for industry labor means, first, that each industry should enjoy a large measure of autonomy within the social structure, and, second, that industry should be operated largely through the co-operation of economic organizations representing all groups of producers within the industry.

There can be little question that this labor idea took its present shape partly under the influence of Herbert Hoover. Immediately after the war labor had urged "cooperation between the scientists of industry and the repre-

sentatives of organized workers." [1]   Shortly afterward
Hoover appeared before the Executive Council of the
American Federation of Labor to urge the same principle,
and relations have been cordial—and sometimes intimate—since that date.   It is also probable that Hoover
was influenced by the fact that labor's thought was moving
simultaneously along parallel lines.   But Hoover formulated the doctrine in a radically *anti-political* form, and at
moments, labor dropped into similar formulations.

Let me first summarize Hoover's position.   It seems
at all points in accord with the selfish interests of employers and capitalists—provided only that they are sufficiently farsighted.   It goes along with labor up to a
certain point.

Hoover presents "self-governing industry" as the great
revolution of the near future and almost as a panacea for
our economic ills.   The "organization of the voluntary
forces of our economic life" and the "co-operation of economic groups" if completed, he says, will provide us
with a "new economic system, based neither on the capitalism of Adam Smith nor on the Socialism of Karl
Marx." [2]

Though Hoover gave us the main lines of this thought
upon his return from Europe the year after the war (several years before labor's formulations) he developed it
fully only in a speech before the United States Chamber
of Commerce in 1924.

I believe [he said] we are in the presence of a new era in
the organization of industry and commerce in which, if
properly directed, lie forces pregnant with infinite possibil-

[1] Declaration of American Federation of Labor and railroad brotherhoods, December 13, 1919.
[2] Speech of November 19, 1920.

ities of moral progress. I believe that we are, almost unnoticed, in the midst of a *great revolution*—or perhaps a better word, a *transformation in the whole super-organization of our economic life.* We are passing from a period of extremely individualistic action into a period of associational activities.

Practically our entire American working world is now organized into some form of economic association. We have trade associations and trade institutes embracing particular industries and occupations. We have Chambers of Commerce embracing representatives of different industries and commerce. We have the labor unions representing the different crafts. We have associations embracing all the different professions—law, engineering, medicine, banking, real estate, and what not. We have farmers' associations, and we have the enormous growth of farmers' co-operatives for actual dealing in commodities.

We have perhaps 25,000 such associational activities in the economic field. Membership, directly or indirectly, now embraces the vast majority of all the individuals of our country.[1] (My italics.)

All this is almost identical with organized labor's conception of the evolution toward industrial self-determination. But Hoover does not stop at this point. He suggests that the chief function of government is "the stimulation of and co-operation with the voluntary forces of our national life" and urges that these organized minorities, though they now embrace "the vast majority of all the individuals of our country," should neither go against one another politically nor unite to influence or control government—that is, that they should not function politically at all. Government is regarded as a more or less separate entity which must, however, protect society from "domination" by any one of these groups.[2]

[1] Cleveland, May 7, 1924.
[2] November 19, 1920.

92

THE GOVERNMENT OF INDUSTRY

Hoover expects, in spite of all this new crystallization of economic organization, that it will be possible to prevent the conflicts of economic groups and, in spite of all this new structure, that it will be feasible to preserve at least that degree of "equality of economic opportunity" (or freedom to pass from one class to another) which characterized the old social structure! Assuming the perfect co-operation of economic groups, Hoover makes no allowance for economic conflicts.

"I do not believe," he says, "we can attain equality of opportunity or maintain initiative through crystallization of economic classes or groups arraigned against each other, expressing their interest by economic and political conflicts, nor can we attain it by transferring to governmental bureaucracies the distribution of material and intellectual products." [1]

The basic assumption of Hoover—and of those relatively liberal business leaders among whom he is the foremost figure—is that we are upon the threshold of a great revolution to industrial democracy through economic organization "if these agencies can be directed solely to constructive performance in the public interest." [2] In that event there would, indeed, be no conflicts and no need for governmental intervention at any point! It is labor's contention, however, that the great financial organizations cannot be directed "solely to constructive performance in the public interest" without the continuous and forceful pressure of the organizations of labor and of the producing and consuming masses, nor, in many instances, without the intervention of government.

[1] March 24, 1920.
[2] May 7, 1924.

93

LABOR AND GOVERNMENT

Labor's formulations on this subject at times seem to go all the way with Hoover's, but this is only in isolated passages, or temporarily, in passages written in 1923 and 1924, when the idea was new and not fully developed and when enthusiasm for it had not given labor time to bring forward reservations in accord with its policies and basic philosophy.

Labor's pronouncement on Industry's Self-Determination, passed unanimously by the Portland convention of the Federation, in 1923, has received high praise—though it has rarely been understood. Ex-Senator Beveridge, for example, wrote of it: "These short, clear paragraphs are statesman-like. They might have been written by either Jefferson or Hamilton, by Madison or Marshall, by Cleveland or Harrison—so fundamental are they and charged with public wisdom." [1]

Certainly the Portland declaration is one of the most able and significant ever made by American labor. It closes with the modest disclaimer that it presents "no new formula, no new philosophy," and, indeed, it is wholly in line with the evolution of American labor thought and policy. But, while it is true that even the newest ideas spring naturally from the old, the declaration's opening paragraph indicates quite definitely the degree and kind of novelty it contains:

We feel that the hour has struck *for a pronouncement of the aims of labor that shall more nearly express the full implications of trade-unionism* that has yet been undertaken in these annual reports. This we have had in mind in the preparation of previous reports, but we have preferred to follow the established practice of the American trade-union

[1] May, 1924.

94

movement, which is to allow expression of policy and program to proceed naturally from the life and needs of the people, giving voice from time to time only to such proposals and formulations as have been finally shaped out of experience.[1] (My italics.)

The document then shows that organized labor, in its quest of industrial democracy, has passed beyond the mere demand that labor should have "a voice" in the industry and is aiming at a broad and fundamental change in the social structure—to be brought about gradually and by natural process:

What we have observed is that the period ending with the beginning of the world war found political democracy in its fullest state of development, while the close of that period of overwhelming upheaval marked the opening of the period of intelligent demand and living need for industrial democracy. The close of the war marked for us a turning point in human relations and threw forth in bold relief the inadequacy of existing forms and institutions. Henceforth trade-unionism has a larger message and a larger function in society. Henceforth the movement for the organization of the workers into trade unions *has a deeper meaning than the mere organization of groups for the advancement of group interests,* however vital that function may yet remain.[2]

The keynote of the document is its advocacy of "the organization of all wage-earners and of all useful and productive elements" and the co-operation of these organizations for the government of industry. While labor's declaration does not reach all of Hoover's corollaries, it does go with him in accepting "organization" as being in itself almost a social panacea—though this position is

[1] Report of Executive Council, 1923.
[2] *Ibid.*

95

somewhat modified by later declarations, policies, and actions of labor, as I shall show.

The central thought is that the social structure must necessarily be organized along functional lines, subordinating merely geographical boundaries, and therefore also *present* political boundaries (which happen to be geographical) :

What is necessary is the perfection and completion of all the organizations that really function as a part of the industrial world. This includes not only labor, but those who are charged with the duties of management, those in the various engineering professions, those who serve in clerical capacities, those engaged in the various branches of distribution—in short all who contribute usefully in the making and distributing of the multitude of products by humanity.[1]

The second idea of the document is that, economic groups having been organized, there must be some organization of these organizations, some approach to nation-wide federation.

For the future industry must become something of which we have a national consciousness. It must cease to be a disconnected collection of groups, like states without a union. The future demands an American industry, in which it shall be possible for all to give of their best through the orderly processes of *democratic, representative organization.* (My italics.)

The manifesto goes on to say that it is not "the mission" of industrial groups to clash and struggle, that their "true rôle" is "to come together and legislate in peace." Its final paragraph calls for "the coming together in working bodies of all organizations through representatives who

[1] Article in Wheeler Newspaper Syndicate, by Samuel Gompers, September 20, 1923.

shall speak for organic groupings." This must seem to approximate the Hoover view. But the central thought of the Portland manifesto is such an organization of the relations between economic organizations as shall *facilitate* co-operation and collaboration—and not Hoover's wholly Utopian hope forthwith to *abolish* conflicts of economic interest and the struggles to which they lead.

The proposed "self-determination of industry" is not to be taken literally. While it implies a large measure of autonomy, it does not mean that industry is to be sovereign and absolute. It is important mainly as a further transition in labor's thought toward (1) the abolition of the control of industry by financial and profit-taking factors; (2) the effective governmental control of our great corporations and trade associations through new social organs differing fundamentally from those of our present government, and, possibly, (3) some form of industrial parliament or industrialized government (see Chapters VII to X).

The late President Gompers described two of these objectives:

The next step is organization of the shop, thus creating a trade council in which all factors in the industry have representation, and then organization of the whole industry along the same lines. This is a natural development which we see now in the making. *Ultimately, perhaps, those things which concern all industry may be determined by a national economic body, truly representative, competent to make decisions and to secure compliance, or political regulation must develop a new technique and more competent personnel.*[1] (My italics.)

This is a very accurate statement of labor's ultimate goal. There is no dogmatic certainty as to those steps

[1] *Seventy Years of Life and Labor*, p. 25.

of labor's policy that follow after labor has obtained a voice in industry, but there is little difference of opinion among labor leaders concerning them. The only addition that needs to be made to the Gompers statement is that, if we may develop *either* toward a national economic parliament *or* toward a new form of political regulation, *both* developments may take place simultaneously.

From the date of its foundation, Mr. Gompers was keenly interested in the development of the powerful and successful "industrial parliament" of Germany, the Reichswirthschaftrat, in which organized labor plays a subordinate but a very important part, and he repeatedly brought it to the attention of the Executive Council. In the summer of 1923 he commissioned the present writer to bring back from a visit to Germany what information was obtainable and he had from the beginning two reliable German labor-union correspondents informing him on the subject. When, in 1925, French labor persuaded the French government to inaugurate a similar scheme, the official weekly organ of the American Federation gave a sympathetic account which illustrates briefly and in a general way the idea as it takes shape in the mind of American labor.[1]

[1] The French government has created a national economic council whose object is "to consider questions concerned with the economic life of the country, and to find solutions for such questions, and to propose to the government the adoption of these solutions."

The council is composed of forty-seven members representing the various social and economic forces of the nation. "Labor" has thirty members, "capital" eight, and the "consuming" public nine. Members of the council are chosen in each category by the "most representative organization or organizations."

The labor group includes intellectual labor and education direction of labor, salaried work, and urban and rural crafts.

The capital group includes industrial and commercial capital, immov·

THE GOVERNMENT OF INDUSTRY

Neither the French nor the German "industrial parliaments" have been officially indorsed by American labor. But, at President Wilson's industrial conference in 1920 organized labor asked the federal government to encourage and promote the formation of national conference boards in each industry—somewhat similar to the British Whitley Councils. Quoting this action, Matthew Woll, one of the Vice-Presidents of the American Federation of Labor, wrote:

It is evident from the foregoing that the American Federation of Labor, including the railroad brotherhoods, has realized for some time the need for an *industrial congress* to aid our national government in dealing with industrial problems, and that the only possible method by which this could be accomplished, without conflicting with our present existing political form of organization, is through the formation of trade groups or trade associations on the part of employers, and trade unions on the part of wage workers, and by extending the principles of co-operation and co-or-

able capital (rural and urban property), banks, stock exchanges, insurance funds, and savings banks.

The consuming public group includes consumers' co-operative societies and purchasers' unions, associations of mayors and unions of towns, users of public services, fathers and mothers of families and mutual-benefit associations.

The council's functions are of an advisory nature. "It will in no sense be a parliament or even an industrial chamber, such as has been tried in certain neighboring countries," declares a statement by the prime minister. "It leaves intact the sovereignty of parliament and the authority of the government. It will form, one may say, a sounding-board for public opinion. It should also form a valuable center of economic information for the use of government departments, parliament, and all who are concerned.

Despite these deficiencies, the representatives of the Federation of Labor accept the council as a step in the right direction and will work for an enlargement of its powers.—(American Federation of Labor *Weekly News Bulletin,* April 20, 1925.)

dination to apply to both of these elementary and fundamental factors in our industrial society.[1]

The most important practical step taken by American labor toward securing "an industrial franchise comparable to the political franchise," as Gompers expressed it, was contained in a resolution of the Federation convention of 1925. This resolution called on Secretary Hoover to summon a conference of representatives of labor, farmers, and trade associations to discuss the elimination of legal obstacles "to the constructive organization of all essential factors in agriculture and industry." It also indorsed "the co-operation of all essential elements within industry" and urged, as a means of preventing the abuse of industrial organization, "uniform and public accounting at stated periods" as determined by the proposed conference. It was publicly stated (and not denied) that Matthew Woll had consulted with Secretary Hoover before introducing the resolution. The step contemplated would go a considerable way toward the voluntary organization of industry under government auspices.

A few months later Woll applied these principles to the federal boards and commissions that have now come almost to form a fourth branch of our government—in addition to the legislative, executive, and judicial branches. It is now more than a generation since Congress found that our primarily political government was ill adapted for the continuous performance of fundamental economic functions. The first of these economic boards, the Interstate Commerce Commission, was instituted nearly four decades ago, and for more than two decades has been endowed with such powers that it may

[1] New York *Evening Post*, April 11, 1922.

almost be called a co-administrator of our railroads. The
Federal Reserve Board has scarcely less power over our
banking system, and the Shipping Board, in view of our
nationally owned fleet, has been exercising an even
greater power over our ocean-going commerce. The
Federal Trade Commission was intended to cover a very
broad field of supervision over commerce and industry,
though with smaller powers. And these are but a few of
the more important instances. Governmental boards for
supervising our economic structure are expanding rapidly,
and when Woll proposes to reorganize and industrialize
them and to make them truly representative of all essential
economic factors he proposes to revolutionize, in an economic and democratic sense, the economically most important arm of our government. (See Chapter X).

He does something more than this; he applies the principle of an industrial parliament—still far off in all countries—to those existing institutions to which it is most
readily and scientifically applicable. And, above all, he
drops the impracticable and undesirable idea of a solidly
unified supervision of the economic structure (through an
industrial parliament or by any other means).

Vice-President Woll has brought together labor's
thought and policies concerning these boards and shown
that they amounted to a revolutionary modification of the
European experiment of an industrial parliament. For
American labor policy abandons the idea of a unified
control—through a body artificially instituted—for the
more modern idea of a plural control—through the industrialization and democratization of those various
boards and commissions that have naturally evolved out of
our economic needs, and therefore express them accurately.

The further process of industrialization and democratization, moreover, is also to follow the lines of existing economic structures and organizations.

Woll expounded this newest application of American labor policy upon taking Gompers' place as Vice-President of the National Civic Federation early in 1926. A few paragraphs from this address will give a fair idea of its principal features:

> Organized labor has declared against "the domination of industry by political bodies." It is opposed to domination and it is opposed to the political interference. But it favors control by bodies truly representative of industry and it realizes that such bodies can be organized only under the supervision of government.
>
> Here is a principle for the application of which our economic and political evolution is fully ripe. Yet it can have the most revolutionary significance. These boards have become an essential part of our political and economic structure—intermediaries between industry and government. As at present constituted they are attacked from both sides—as controlling too much and as not controlling enough. But from whatever side they are attacked it is agreed that their chief vice is that they are too political and not sufficiently economic in composition, structure, and function.
>
> Legislation should provide that every commission should be representative of each of the essential economic factors. The leading economic organizations should insist that their judgment should count in the selection of these representatives. They certainly would insist—and they could do it effectively, if they gave one another a measure of mutual support.[1]

[1] Address before National Civic Federation, January 9, 1926, quoted from International Labor News Service, February 6, 1926.

CHAPTER VII

THE ATTEMPT TO ISOLATE LABOR FROM GOVERNMENT

The Competence of Government in Industry Questioned—Simultaneous and Related Changes Contemplated in Industry and Government—Labor Refuses to Condemn Economic Functions of Government.

THE Portland manifesto—passed by the 1923 convention of the American Federation of Labor—arose largely as a protest against the intervention of governmental bodies in the internal management of industry, all recent instances of such intervention having tended to fix the status of labor, to determine wages and working conditions by law. and to deprive labor organizations of their rights and their powers.

The capitalist and business organizations, proving themselves stronger than the organizations of labor and agriculture, fell upon these boards and commissions, first to prevent them from controlling business and, second, to use them against organized labor and agriculture. Their publicity and fact-finding functions were first crippled by court decisions and then were radically reduced and in some cases all but abolished by President Coolidge's appointees on the boards.

At the same time certain of the boards were given judicial functions by Congress, permitting them to absolve capitalist combinations and to prosecute organizations of labor, to compel the enforcement of labor contracts to satisfy employers, and to furnish new grounds for judicial injunctions. These bodies had been originally instituted to control unfair profits and prices, but an extraordinary impression was deliberately created in the public mind that profits and prices could not be controlled without the compulsory fixing of wages.

Secretary Hoover, for example, has assumed that compulsory fixing of wages always accompanies every government intervention in industry and that any intervention whatever precludes industrial self-government.

I am sure [Hoover has said] you would, upon consideration, view the entry of the government on a nation-wide scale into the determination of *fair wage and fair profit* in industry, even if it could be accomplished without force, with great apprehension. There are some things worse in the development of democracy than strikes and lockouts; whether by legislative repression we do not set up economic and social repercussions of worse character is by means determined.

They have also the deficiency in that they undermine the real development of self-government in industry, and that, to me, is part of the growth of democracy itself. Courts and litigation are necessary to the preservation of life and property, but they are less stimulus to improved relations among men than is discussion and disposal of their own differences.[1]

In view of the perversion of some of the industrial commissions and boards from their original function into judicial bodies for the prosecution of organized labor and of other essential economic organizations, the Portland

[1] Speech of March 24, 1920.

convention of 1923 proposed "the rescue of industry from the domination of incompetent political bodies":

> The threat of state invasion of industrial life [the Federation declared] is real. Powerful groups of earnest and sincere persons constantly seek the extension of state suzerainty over purely industrial fields. Such ignorant encroachments as the Esch-Cummins Act, the Kansas Court of Industrial Relations, and the Colorado Industrial Commission Act, each a blundering gesture of government acting under the spur of organized propaganda or of political appetite for power, are examples of what all industry has to fear. The continuing clamor for extension of state regulatory powers under the guise of reform and deliverance from evil can but lead into greater confusion and more hopeless entanglements.[1]

There is unanimity among labor organizations that such bodies as the Federal Trade Commission have become so useless for their original purpose of fact-finding and the recommendation of constructive control legislation and completely and uniformly anti-labor in their judicial rulings, *subject to review by the regular courts* (no funds of labor), that their total abolition would be preferable to retaining them *in their present form and with their present personnel.*

So labor turned definitely against "the domination of political bodies." For years the unions had taken the position that "there is within any given industry a greater knowledge concerning the operation and needs of that industry than can be brought to bear from any outside agency."[2] This is the crux of labor's position on the

[1] Report of Executive Council, 1923.
[2] American Federation of Labor reply to questionnaire of National Republican Advisory Committee, 1920.

internal government of industry. The Portland convention declared "that there is no one so well qualified as those who are engaged in the industry to determine upon the institutions and agencies which will best meet the needs of those engaged in the industry," and that "the wisdom that exists outside of any industry concerning that industry is seldom worth taking into account." It went even farther, however, and launched a generalization so anti-political that, if literally taken, it would *seem* to amount to a declaration of the independence of industry from government, a proclamation of the absolute sovereignty of industry, a *laissez-faire* denial of the competence of government in industrial and economic matters.

But the manifesto by no means involved such an abandonment of political action; it was merely a turning point and "an expression of a new understanding of the rôle and value of political action," and we may quote as evidence in support of this statement the following paragraph from the manifesto:

Institutions try to perpetuate themselves. Political government seeks to retain all power and all functions. That this gives rise to incongruous situations is natural. That politicians should misunderstand the natural thing that is going on and should try to checkmate it is to be expected. It is no discredit to an institution that it cannot live forever. If it serves well in its time, that is honor enough. Our political government has served magnificently as the custodian of all power for a long time. It gave regeneration to the world. It will continue to serve nobly for no one knows how long, but it cannot serve in all capacities without strangling the very thing which it was devised to save— human liberty.

ISOLATE LABOR FROM GOVERNMENT

Here the attack is centered not upon political government as we know it and as it is, but upon "political government as the custodian of *all* power." And industry is made to ask not for all power for itself, but for a share of power. But what share? Industry, apparently, was to be assigned all power *over industry*. In this case the functions left to government would still seem to be relatively insignificant. For, as the manifesto says, "our national life to-day is becoming more and more industrial and the decisions that most vitally affect the intimate daily lives of our people are the decisions that are made in industry, in the workshops and factories, in the mines and mills, in the commercial establishments, on the railroads, and in the counting-rooms."

Unless political government is steadily to lose its importance the division of power between industry and government must be on another and broader basis than the assignment of the entire sphere of industry to industry, and I shall show that labor's position, taken as a whole, including the entire Portland manifesto and without excluding other preceding and subsequent formulations and actions, does very positively and definitely indicate this broader basis.

Industrial democracy may be developed both by a tendency away from outside political control within the workshop and within the industry and at the same time by an extension of outside political control over the economic and industrial structure at external points.[1]

---

[1] The probable twofold evolution of industry and government as stated by Gompers (see preceding chapter) contains a sentence which for convenience may be restated at this point: "Ultimately, perhaps those things which concern all industry may be determined by a national economic body, truly representative, competent to make deci-

Equally important is this further possibility—or probability—that the more or less autonomous control of industry from within will be gradually recognized and given an official status by the political government itself and so will gradually take on a semi-political character, while the evolution of outside governmental control will develop only in proportion as new governmental organs shake off their present purely political forms and take on a semi-economic character. Numerous positions taken by labor indicate that this twofold development is precisely the direction it expects industrial and political evolution to take.

Labor is undoubtedly seeking to prevent the *present state* from enlarging its encroachments in the field of industry, but in proportion as the state becomes further industrialized and as industry becomes further democratized a new relationship arises between industry and government. Labor is expecting precisely this twofold result from the new era of voluntary economic organization which, as Hoover points out, is already well on its way; this process, it is expected, will tend at the same time to industrialize the state and to democratize industry, and will pave the way for semi-official and official recognition of the economic organizations that will rule industry from within. This is the process which—although it is only in its earlier stages to-day—dominates labor's thought as to industrial government.

While this is the dominant note in American labor's

---

sions and to secure compliance, *or* political regulation must develop a new technique and a more competent personnel." (My italics.) It will be noted that there is no conflict between these two tendencies and every reason to suppose that both may develop simultaneously.

political and economic philosophy, it has been sometimes eclipsed since the Portland convention (in 1923), as I have said, by anti-political generalization so violent as to give a radically and wholly erroneous impression of labor policy.

In an editorial by Gompers we find the following absolute and exclusive contrast between political and industrial activity: "The gulf between politics and industry is as wide as the seven seas, and as deep. Also, politics breeds the demagogue, the emotionalist, the flatterer, the master of cajolery; industry breeds the master of knowledge. The realm of the one is a realm of abstraction and theory; the realm of the other is the realm of performance."

A number of other statements made by Gompers within a year or two of his death might seem to imply that the best thing government could do for industry was to do nothing. If we wish to explain these sweeping anti-political generalizations we must turn to the reasoning that underlies them. "Legislators know little of industry," said Gompers.[1] This is why both Gompers and organized labor reached the conclusion that legislators should be controlled by economic organizations and that industry should control its own internal affairs. That is labor's remedy. But labor has not concluded from the legislator's ignorance of industry that legislators and the bodies created by them should have no economic functions.

Gompers referred, on another occasion, to the profound truth that laws, in order to be effective, must be understood and consented to by those living under them: "The laws that are built as a result of organization are the laws that can be agreed to by those who must live

[1] Wheeler Newspaper Syndicate, September 17, 1923.

under them. This is important. There may be much crudeness, but in the end it is the way of democracy at work. In industry there can be no law unless there is almost universal recognition of its justice and practicability." [1]

This again points to the need for a decentralized government of industry, for self-government from within. But labor has shown that it fully realizes that such self-government cannot be absolute. It must be subject to a measure of control by society which, however general and flexible, must still be effective—that is, it must be subject to supervision or control by government—but of a government that is becoming gradually and increasingly industrialized. And in the external relations of industry—for example, in relation to credit, to power, to transportation and to raw materials—government (that is industrialized and democratized government) must not only have a voice, it must predominate—though, even in these matters, without interfering unnecessarily with industrial self-government.

"Economic law and necessity are stronger than legislation or police power," wrote Gompers.[2] This is true beyond question. It is on this ground that Gompers and the American labor movement have advocated the control of government by economic organizations that know economic law and necessity and not by an unorganized citizenry that can know only vague generalizations, arbitrary legislation, and police power.

But, as I have pointed out, it is not necessary to explain

[1] *American Federationist,* May, 1923.
[2] *Seventy Years of Life and Labor,* p. 24.

ISOLATE LABOR FROM GOVERNMENT

this series of Gompers's utterances in detail. Other more explicit statements of his, dealing with the precise constructive problem that lies before organized labor, leave no doubt that he realized fully (as the Federation has always realized) that government must play a certain part in the solution of the industrial problem. *"The great end to be desired,"* he said, for example, *"is the concentration of all efforts upon the improvement of our industrial processes and the perfection of our industrial organization."* But he immediately added that this necessitates *"the elimination of such abuses as profiteering, wasteful methods of manufacture and transportation, inefficient management, and financial manipulation."* [1] Against profiteering and financial manipulation, as both Gompers and the Federation have always understood, governmental as well as economic action is indispensable.

The attitude of American labor toward the economic functions of government was never more accurately stated than by Vice-President Woll when he said:

The opposition of organized labor to political interference in industry has been very widely misunderstood. It has been interpreted as meaning that labor accepts the business and industrial structures as they are, approves their practices, recognizes no fundamental evils, and does not believe government has any part to play in correcting such evils if they are recognized. Nothing could be more remote from the truth.

American labor has always recognized the fundamental evils in our industrial structure and has seen that government must play a part in curing them.[2]

[1] Article from Wheeler Newspaper Syndicate, September 30, 1923.
[2] Speech before the National Civic Federation, January 29, 1926, reproduced in International Labor News Service, February 6, 1926.

CHAPTER VIII

LABOR DEMANDS ITS SHARE IN THE BENEFITS OF GOVERNMENT

Capitalist Attempts to Restore Competition in Industry by Government Action—Labor's View of the Scope and Limits of Government Intervention—Capitalist Opposition to Government Control of Monopoly—Organized Business and Government.

WITHIN a few weeks after the Portland convention Gompers said, in his Christmas message : "The enemies of our movement say we are not in politics. The fact is we are in politics to the limit." He could scarcely have spoken otherwise. For it is solely organized capital that preaches that government shall have nothing to do with industry— often in the very manifestoes which attack organized labor.

"The function of our government is political—not economic," says the National Association of Manufacturers in its "Platform of American Industry" (1924). And the President of the United States Chamber of Commerce, which speaks—and with equal authority—for "American business," while conceding in the abstract that our vast increase in material wealth should be fairly and equitably distributed, says that this must be done "by the social system and the natural processes of trade" and not by "law and edict" and the "application of human judgment in authority." [1] Clearly these are the interested arguments

[1] Julius H. Barnes, Commencement address, University of Pittsburgh, June 13, 1923.

of large traders and capitalists, a political minority. This is not and cannot be the position of the political majority —the economic groups that suffer from the inequalities and injustices of the social system.

The opposition to governmental activity in industry is perhaps more ably and authoritatively voiced by Herbert Hoover than by any other person—and his position is especially important to us because no other person accepted as a spokesman by those who own and control industry has had so full a hearing with, or has exerted such an influence over, American labor.

Theoretically, Hoover opposes capitalism as much as he does Socialism:

Radicalism and reaction are, in fact, not an academic state of mind, but realize into real groups and real forces, influencing the solution of economic problems in this community. In their present-day practical aspects they represent on one hand, roughly, various degrees of exponents of Socialism who would directly or indirectly undermine the principle of private property and personal initiative, and on the other hand, those exponents who, in various degrees, desire to dominate the community for profit and privilege. They both represent attempts to introduce or preserve class privilege by either a moneyed or a bureaucratic aristocracy.[1]

Hoover also recognizes that it is precisely in the field of government and politics that capitalism is most menacing:

It is where dominant private property is assembled in the hands of the groups who control the state that the individual begins to feel capital as an oppressor.[2]

[1] Speech of September 16, 1919.
[2] *American Individualism*, p. 38.

He even describes how America has waged war on this capitalism:

Individual initiative was being throttled by the concentration of control of industry and service, and thus an economic domination of groups builded over the nation. At this time, particularly, we were threatened with a form of autocracy of economic power. Our mass of regulation of public utilities and our legislation against restraint of trade is the monument to our intent to preserve an equality of opportunity. This regulation is itself proof that we have gone a long way toward the abandonment of the "capitalism" of Adam Smith.[1]

Organized labor entirely agrees that "Government must keep out of the production and distribution of commodities and services"—but Hoover and the capitalist spokesmen generally interpret this to mean that there must be no real government control over industry (except public utilities). During the Presidential election campaign of 1924 the American Federationist pointed out that Hoover had passed from opposition to government ownership to opposition to government control, that he had put forward "the growth of the business conscience" as "far more precious than any amount of legislation."

There is some truth in his statement [answered the *Federationist*], but neither labor, the progressives nor the American people generally intend to rely on the business conscience to protect them from the dishonesty, inefficiency, and inhumanity which now mark their conduct of industry.

The able and well-informed Secretary of Commerce introduces other propositions of a similar character, all tending not to strengthen but to weaken the case for governmental control. He inveighs, for example, against that

[1] *American Individualism*, p. 53.

governmental centralization that would be necessary for thoroughgoing control, pointing out that our political system is decentralized. This is an absurdly illogical argument. The centralization of industry is a process which Mr. Hoover thoroughly understands and approves, as does American labor, as well as every forward-looking progressive. For those backward-looking pseudo-progressives who want to restore the industrial conditions of 1875 are only a minority now. *In so far as industry is centralized Mr. Hoover knows that government control will either have to be centralized or it will have to be abandoned.*[1] (My italics.)

The menace of "an autocracy of economic power" is not past, as Hoover implies, simply because we have regulated public utilities. (Surely it is infinitely *more* powerful than ever before.) And he admits that in so far as we have business "affected with monopoly" we must have regulation by law and "systematic prevention of domination of the few over the many."[2]

Yet this Herculean task must be accomplished without the government taking a single step in the field of industry!

To curb the forces in business which would destroy equality of opportunity and yet to maintain the initiative and creative faculties of our people are the twin objects we must attain. To preserve the former we must regulate that type of activity that would dominate. To preserve the latter, *the government must keep out of production and distribution of commodities and services.* This is the deadline between our system and Socialism.[3] (My italics.)

The principle italicized, if strictly interpreted, is precisely that of organized labor. But Hoover uses the

[1] *American Federationist,* November, 1924.
[2] March 24, 1920.
[3] *American Individualism,* p. 54.

phrase as meaning that government shall have no supervision and control over industry. He even insinuates (he
would scarcely flatly state it) that the menace of "capitalism" has passed, because it has been checked by the Sherman Act!

> The first phase of development on the business side [he
> says] was "pools" in production and distribution. They
> were infected with imposition upon the public and their
> competitors. In some parts they were struggles to correct
> abuse and waste. They were followed by an era of capital
> consolidations with the same objects, but also to create a
> situation of unbreakable agreements. *Both were against
> public interest and the public intervened through the Sher-
> man Act.*[1] (My italics.)

This is the position, then, of the most liberal and constructive faction of American capitalism and the most
friendly to organized labor. Government must not function in industry; any domination of organized capital over
industry and government is intolerable and must be "regulated," but government must not do anything about it.
"Industry"—*i.e.,* capital must heal itself. For the only
governmental remedy Hoover admits, the Sherman law,
which merely "forbids" combinations and monopolies to
exist and is admittedly based on the hope of restoring
competition by fiat, has had no tendency whatever either
to check the formation or growth of new giant corporations—whether a natural product like the Ford corporation or built out of combinations erected against the
letter or the spirit of that law—or to prevent their steady
progress in the direction of monopoly. While the point

[1] Speech before United States Chamber of Commerce, Cleveland,
May 7, 1924.

of absolute monopoly is not usually reached for all the commodities produced, the control of 90 per cent or even of 75 per cent of a product usually has the same practical effect. Hoover and the more advanced section of capitalists admit that "once we have business affected with monopoly we must have regulation by law." But they take refuge in the absurd apology that the monopolistic powers of our great corporations (except public utilities) are not absolute. We are, apparently, to wait until their control is 100 per cent complete before we do anything about it. Naturally that day will never arrive, though the time when they will have a 99-per-cent control—if they need it—seems not to be far away. But they may stop where they are, finding their present position more safe— and equally profitable.

There can be no doubt whatever that Hoover and all the leading spokesmen for capitalism uncontrolled by government are thorough masters of all these facts. They know that every great industry produces thousands of commodities and that when a single enterprise gets very large and represents a considerable proportion of the industry it has a practical monopoly, at least in a certain proportion of these commodities. Hoover confesses this knowledge when he says that "we do not want units so big or controls so wide that they destroy individual initiative or equality of opportunities," and that, accordingly, "we must maintain a sufficient number of independent units in any given industry to assure us that the fundamental competition is sustained." [1]

In other words, when the units in an industry are big enough and few enough, competition is destroyed and

[1] Speech before United States Chamber of Commerce, May 12, 1926.

monopoly has arrived and "the virility and strength of our whole economic system springs from spontaneous enterprise and the stimulation of competition."[1] And, finally to complete the thought, private monopoly, whether the result of legislative favor or a natural growth, is absolutely intolerable in a democratic republic.

Now what is the sole capitalist remedy? A continuation of "legislation to compel competition." This legislation is no longer advocated for public utilities, but it is still applied to "the manufacture and distribution of commodities," where "real," "effective," "constructive" competition is to be compelled by law![2] Government is to act to restore competition, but to do nothing whatever to deal with monopoly when it appears that competition cannot be restored. In a word there is an assertion of the practicability of governmental intervention in the field where it has proved the most ludicrously ineffective, namely "to unscramble the eggs" and opposition to governmental intervention in the only field where it is conceivable, constructive regulative legislation. *The result has been to establish one or more giant corporations as the dominant factor in each of our legally "stabilized" industries.*

Unfortunately, the study of labor's position as to industrial monopolies has been somewhat complicated through occasional statements which might indicate that it agreed, not only with the capitalist *premises,* as formulated by Hoover, but also with his anti-government *conclusions.* For example, the Gompers editorial above quoted goes on to say: "Labor declares that the question of controlling

[1] Speech before United States Chamber of Commerce, May 12, 1926.
[2] *Ibid.*

monopoly and conserving the public welfare against abuses by monopoly cannot be solved by the *political* state, and almost every attempt so to solve it will lead to more abuse than remedy." [1]

This is almost the Hoover, or liberal, capitalist viewpoint. But it is not a complete statement of the labor position. The labor position is that "the abuses of monopoly cannot be solved by the political state *alone*," especially as long as it remains purely political. This is shown not only in the great bulk of Gompers's writings and the official pronouncements of the Federation, but by the closing paragraphs of the same editorial:

The proper sphere of government in helping toward beneficial results is to find and furnish information, to get at and make known the facts, to encourage and insist upon development within industry of machinery which will take from invested wealth its dictatorial power over policies of production, employment, and public relations. There is a normal course which must be pursued, just as there always is where life and its perpetuation are concerned. The government may be helpful, but it cannot take over the task, without spoiling the whole effort.[2]

The foundation of labor's thought is undoubtedly that existing government should not and cannot "take over the task" of operating industry and must "keep out of the production and distribution of commodities and services." But even in the passage just quoted government is already assigned two immensely important industrial functions—publicity and encouragement of the organization and co-operation of all the human factors engaged in industry. Nor are these by any means the only

[1] *American Federationist*, September, 1924.
[2] *Ibid.*

119

industrial or economic functions labor desires and expects to be taken over by government, as I shall show.

Labor's position as to governmental action, especially in relation to the central problem, the means of checking, counterbalancing and restricting the power of organized capital in industry, has been more fully stated by Vice-President Matthew Woll. Vice-President Woll has made it clear that labor repudiates the fundamental capitalist proposition as to the function of government in relation to industry, namely that it has no function—except to help business. "The two major political parties," says Woll, "have heretofore approached the industrial life from the premise that to promote business will indirectly advance the interests of the wage-earners." That is, there has been a vast amount of political activity, of legislation, and of government aid in behalf of industry—but without interfering with the present industrial organization, or the present division of the product or the present distribution of power. As against this capitalist foundation principle that all governmental action in the economic field should be exclusively for the benefit of "business" as at present constituted, Woll shows that labor, though it favors this type of governmental action—if carefully circumscribed—demands also that "the interests of the wage-earning and farmer class must be conceived directly." [1]

In discussing his proposal at once to industrialize and to democratize the governmental economic boards and commissions, Woll gave an illustration of an application of this principle: [2]

[1] International Labor News Service. May 17, 1924.
[2] Speech before National Civic Federation, New York, January 29, 1926.

In their constructive policy for reforming these boards
[said Woll] organized labor, organized agriculture, and
every democratic economic organization are in accord. The
time has come in this country when these organizations must
and will be heard, and the time for purely business administration and a purely business man's government has just
about passed.

The economic boards and commissions of the federal
government have been constituted and have functioned to
serve business. Organized labor and agriculture agree that
this service is legitimate if carried on within the limits of
the public welfare. But they see no reason why these bodies
should not be so reconstituted that they will also function
to serve labor and agriculture and every essential economic
element.

Democracy means nothing, America means nothing, to the
farmers and wage-earners of this country, if their voices
cannot count for at least as much as business in our legislation and our government.

Woll's assertion as to the capitalists' own political attitude, namely that it leans freely on state capitalism or
governmental intervention on behalf of capital, needs no
proof. Nearly all our political campaigns are aimed,
avowedly and almost exclusively, at governmental stimulation of "business prosperity."

Many employers do not oppose state intervention
in industry, provided it is directed to the interest of
employers. American labor has taken due note of the
enthusiasm of leading American capitalists for the state
capitalism of Mussolini and for every similar experiment
in governmental economic despotism.

Judge E. H. Gary, president of the United States Steel
Corporation, has repeatedly declared that even governmental intervention in the labor question would not be

objectionable to capitalists if it were directed against employees as well as employers. In one of his speeches Judge Gary said that the reason many employers would not enter into collective bargains with the labor unions was that "they refused to be subjected to any kind of governmental supervision, investigation, or control, such as is required of employers." [1] It is true that American labor demands that governmental supervision, investigation, and control should be applied not against the citizens of the industrial state, but exclusively against those private interests which control and direct that state for private purposes.

Business often claims that it opposes governmental intervention in industry. But Woll points out that the truth is that business favors governmental intervention on behalf of business and opposes only governmental intervention aimed to benefit other economic groups. Other economic groups, according to organized business, must not aim directly at their own prosperity, but must get such prosperity as comes to them from the prosperity of business. If they imitate business and try to secure direct benefit, a tremendous agitation springs up immediately in the press against such "class legislation"—or, if they succeed in Congress, the cry is against "government by bloc."

An illustration may be taken from a speech of the recent head of the chief organization of American business. "There is no excuse," says Julius H. Barnes, president of the United States Chamber of Commerce, "for the formulation of political influence on the basis of trade or social position. Labor parties or farm blocs have no

[1] New York, May 21, 1926.

lasting place under the American conditions of national fair play."[1]   Hoover and all the other leading business spokesmen have expressed themselves in similar terms. And the late President Harding and President Coolidge have repeatedly voiced the same opinion.

Woll shows that, while demanding a certain extension of governmental activity in the economic field for the direct benefit of wage-earners and other popular groups, labor starts always from the premise that economic functions should be organized *as far as practicable* without governmental intervention.   His statement on this point is forceful and complete:

All other republics accept the doctrine that the state is the all-powerful being, and that the rights of the individual come from the state itself, as we choose to say all powers come from the individual, and the state and the nation have only such powers as the individual by his own volition and proper expression and manifestation has delegated to the government.

We recognize that if we accept the doctrine that labor is to seek its full reward in our industrial and social life through parliamentary action, we immediately discard the fundamental conception upon which our nation is founded, and accept the doctrine that the state is the all-powerful being. and we as individuals can only accept such freedom as the state will grant us.

The American labor movement believes that we are founded upon the proper philosophic basis—*absolute freedom of the individual,* the state being granted only such powers as become necessary and essential *to promote order, good will, and progress among those within society and within that government.*[2]

[1] Speech at Dallas. Texas, November 20, 1922.
[2] International Labor News Service, May 17, 1924.

LABOR AND GOVERNMENT

This proposed use of the powers of the state to promote "good will and progress in society" gives a wide scope to governmental action. What labor means by governmental action to promote good will in industry has already been sufficiently explained. Woll shows what labor means by asking for the state powers "essential to promote progress :"

First, the state protection of those "unable to exert voluntary action for self-protection." This clause refers to labor's indorsement of a large part of the so-called labor and social legislation—though by no means all of it, as American labor believes that voluntary action is effective in several of the fields covered by such legislation abroad.

Second, "legislation demanded by the economic interests of organized wage-earners, agriculturists, and other economic groups *in so far as these cannot be obtained by non-political action.*" The precedent for this principle lies in the special legislation and governmental aid so long extended and still extended to "business"—in so far as such aid has been recognized by other economic groups as legitimate.

Third, "to protect from the exploitation that has come by reason of the state having created artificial beings in law never contemplated by those who created our nation and never understood as having these great powers." Woll refers not only to the larger industrial and financial combinations, but to the smaller corporations and to "corporate institutions" generally. It is these corporations and their associations—which control such a large part of our economic structure and nearly all of our industrial structure—that constitute the menace of capitalism.

American labor surrenders nothing of the underlying democratic concept of American law and American government. It insists not only on individual freedom, but on freedom of contract. "In order that equality of contract may have full expression," says Woll, "it is the duty of the state to protect against this great corporate artificial person created by it"—that is, against the corporations.

American labor's position on fundamental governmental control of industry is sometimes misunderstood because it is opposed to the only legislation now standing on our statute books which ostensibly has that object in view, the Sherman Anti-Trust Act. American labor is opposed to the effort embodied in that statute, "to crush monopoly" by the perfectly futile attempt to restore and enforce competition by law. (See Chapter X.)

As early as 1899 the American Federation of Labor had already laid the foundation of its present position. It stood then, as it stands now, against the effort both to "restore" competition and to check the growth of the corporations, which were visibly carrying them toward monopoly; and it stood at the time against leaving these corporations free of all government control and in control of the government. However, labor had not yet reached the point of favoring the repeal of the anti-combination laws, even though it was aware that they had the reactionary and futile object of restoring competition, for the reason that it had not yet evolved any practicable alternative. The convention of 1899, therefore, protested against the campaign "to sweep away the present anti-combinations laws"—through the fear that by such repeal the trusts would have "at their command the judicial, executive, and military machinery of the political state."

When, after two decades, it was seen that the Sherman Act had not only failed—as labor had expected it would fail—to check the growth of the political power of the great corporations or to give the government any effective control over them, but was used against organized labor by the corporations and the courts, which regarded the unions as combinations in the meaning of the law, labor demanded, first the amendment, and, finally, when amendment proved ineffective, the repeal of all the anti-combination laws.

Vice-President Woll was a leader in the movement for repeal. After the Portland convention adopted the demand for *repeal,* in 1923—in place of the clauses of the Clayton Act which had attempted, unsuccessfully, to *exempt* labor from these anti-trust laws—Woll was asked if labor had reversed its attitude toward the great corporations, and if the unions had reached the conclusion that there was no trust problem. "I did not say that we have no trust problem," Woll replied; "I merely declare that we cannot solve it by enforcing the Sherman Act:"

I don't think it was ever capable of practical enforcement. It was so rigid that no serious attempt was made to enforce it. The economic fallacy underlying the Sherman law was recognized by the Supreme Court when it laid down the "rule of reason" in its interpretation of the law in 1910. Competition is in its very nature self-destructive. Perfect and enduring competition would mean that units of business would have all to be kept the same in size and power. As soon as one unit gets larger than another the larger unit can effect economies which enable it to undersell the rival. This leads to trusts. Big business can't be kept down by enforcing competition. Competition ends in big business and consolidation is a natural consequence.[1]

American labor believes that the great corporations should not be destroyed (even if that were practicable) and that they should not even be attacked as such. *"Labor's fight is not against combination in industry as such, but is against the evil influences which control great combinations and which are all too often exerted in our political, judicial, and economic life."* [2] (See Chapter X.)

The need of gaining influence over government in the interest of organized labor and of other popular economic organizations is not a theory, but a principle upon which these organizations have always acted and are acting increasingly from year to year. The reason why this practice of economic democracy is objected to by "organized industry" is not far to seek. Any economic class or interest that is already getting what it wants from government is likely to regard the attempt of other groups to get what they want as "class legislation." To organized labor this accusation—so popular with the interests just now in control of the American government—is pure hypocrisy. As President Gompers said,

What is any legislation but class legislation or the formulation by one group of people of what they deem a policy in their interest? Few laws are passed by unanimous consent. It follows, then, that tariff legislation is "class legislation" in the interests of manufacturers; that free trade is "class legislation" in the interests of consumers; that our laws protecting "property" are class legislation handed down from

[1] Interview in New York *World*, November 29, 1925.
[2] *American Federationist*, September, 1924.

the middle ages when the property-holding classes controlled the government.[1]

It is recognized even by the most conservative of labor leaders that capitalistic interests are ever present—actually in control, or attempting to gain control, of government. John H. Donlin, for many years president of the Building Trades Department of the American Federation of Labor, for example, has fully described the governmental activity of the capitalistic interests, and the urgent need for combating it and securing for labor its due voice in government.

These interests are powerful influences [says Donlin] in the selection of those who represent the people in government, and while it is the great masses who elect, it is the few who dictate elections.

The people are not organized and have no way to force a government, but moneyed interests are organized and alert. They swagger through legislative halls, administrative mansions, dictate to professors, preachers, and editors; they dominate with an iron hand the affairs of society.

But there must be some law to protect that multitude unable to keep step and who really suffer in a land of plenty. Are not all the bankers of this country, all the great corporations, all the forms of business, controlled by the same principle and susceptible to the command of the voice of the interests?[2]

The great business organizations, labor points out, have either established headquarters at Washington or have numerous representatives on the spot all the time. The greatest of them all, the United States Chamber of

[1] Quoted from Mr. Gompers in *Labor and the Common Welfare*, by Hayes Robbins. p. 52.

[2] Report of Building Trades Department, American Federation of Labor, 1921.

Commerce, has erected a building there at the cost of several million dollars to serve as headquarters—and Washington is certainly not our commercial capital. The United States Chamber of Commerce, the National Association of Manufacturers, the Association of Railway Executive, the Coal Dealers' Association, the American Mining Congress, the National Oil Bureau and the Petroleum Association—to say nothing of the Steel Corporation and other great corporations—are permanently "on the job," in touch not only with all legislation, but with every single governmental bureau that affects their interests.[1]

Charles S. Barrett, president of the National Board of Farm Organizations, the group of agricultural associations that has most closely and consistently co-operated with organized labor, has given close attention to and made a careful study of the *modus operandi* of these capitalist organizations and giant corporations at Washington and has written a book on the subject, the observations and conclusions of which tally completely with those of organized labor. Replying to the President's attacks on government by blocs, as applied to the nonpartisan alignment of Congressmen by *popular* organizations, Barrett shows that the "lobbies" of capitalist organizations, operating quietly but efficiently, have long been fulfilling exactly the same function, and says that, ac-

[1] These militant and political functions of trade organizations were referred to by Herbert Hoover (speaking to the National Association of Manufacturers' convention in 1922) as the protection of their rights "in relation to other economic groups" and by the Federal Trade Information Service as their *"co-operative management of legislative questions and Litigation"* and their *"co-operative action to promote closer relations with the government."* (My italics.)

cording to the President himself, "party government is all right and even surreptitious lobbying may be tolerated, especially if carried on by famous lawyers who are able to make their approach through exclusive social or financial avenues." [1]

Barrett describes in some detail how the lobbies of such organizations as the United States Chamber of Commerce and the National Association of Manufacturers function—giving names and copious illustrations. The former organization, he says, is really a national association of lobbyists of the various business organizations and with the assistance of the National Association of Manufacturers and similar bodies, is "trying to dictate the entire policy of the administration and Congress":

Operating behind closed doors and approaching members of both branches of Congress through camouflaged highways, the *assistant government* and the social lobby are gradually but surely undermining the confidence of the members in the ability of the people to govern. They are surely coming around to the idea that there must be some kind of a supergovernment, keeping its identity forever under the rose.

The right of commerce to organize is fundamental. It cannot be properly questioned. The right of labor, of finance, and of agriculture to do the same thing has been established by law and no right-minded person will question it. But none has a right to attempt to acquire by force, by subtlety, by camouflage, or by any other means a virtual proprietorship of the government of the United States. [2]

These are broad generalizations, but they do not exaggerate the views of progressive farmers' organizations

---

[1] *Uncle Reuben in Washington*, p. 15.
[2] *Uncle Reuben*, pp. 19, 88.

and labor unions as to the means by which our government is at present operated.

The popular economic organizations do not contend that the great corporations and business organizations have secured a complete control of the government in all its branches. Some legislation has been passed against their bitter and united opposition—and many of their favorite measures have been defeated. The passing of the soldiers' bonus and the defeat of the Mellon tax plan by Congress in 1925 are recent illustrations. The amendments to the federal Constitution allowing a federal income tax and establishing the direct election of Senators, the postal savings banks, and the parcel post, were all passed against the almost solid opposition of "the interests" (see Volume I, Chapters IV to VI).

There is, therefore, no hopelessness as to the future. But all the legislative achievements of the popular economic organizations up to date are regarded by labor as no more than a drop in the bucket when compared with the legislation, the appointments, the contracts, the administrative favors secured by the financial, industrial, and commercial interests.

CHAPTER IX

GOVERNMENT OPERATION WEIGHED AND FOUND WANTING

Labor Favors Government Operation of Certain Public Utilities Only: The Water Power Question—The Plumb Plan for the Democratic Operation of Railroads—The Coal Miners and Governmental Intervention in the Coal Industry.

BEFORE the European war governmentalism or state socialism had an enormous following—outside of the organized labor movement. State socialism was most highly developed in Germany; the Fatherland was hailed by state socialists throughout the world as the most advanced of the nations, in spite of the rule of the "junkers," and was spoken of as an "economic democracy." A book appeared by a well-known American radical progressive under the extraordinary title of *Socialized Germany*.[1]

Organized labor nowhere shared those illusions. The labor unions and Socialists of continental Europe were almost unanimous in declaring their opposition to state socialism; the German Socialists were especially pronounced in this opposition, and only a minority of the British laborites, following the lead of non-labor "intellectuals," idealized the "Socialism" of Kaiserist Germany.

[1] See *Socialized Germany*, by Frederick C. Howe.

OPERATION WEIGHED AND FOUND WANTING

But even the governmentalism advocated by British labor did not propose the indefinite extension of all the functions of government. It did not favor the extension of the political functions of government, but solely the extension of governmental economic functions. And this is still the only form of governmentalism which has any large numerical following in the labor movement of any country of the world (outside of Russia) to-day.

Indeed, opposition to state socialism or state capitalism is decidedly stronger in labor than in capitalist circles. Vice-President Woll, of the American Federation of Labor, referring especially to speeches made on a single occasion by two pre-eminent international bankers of this country, said:

American labor is in total disagreement with those American and international bankers and captains of industry who defend the Soviets at some points and the Fascists apparently all along the line. American labor is American; it does not believe that the opposite economic and political system can bring good to any people—and least of all in the economic sphere. It is opposed to the governmental operation of industry—even under a democratic government. American labor is opposed to state socialism not only because it destroys democracy and individual liberty, the foundations of our economic as well as our political system, but because it does not work. It does not and cannot promote efficiency, initiative, individual or group responsibility, or voluntary organization.[1]

There is no longer a strong demand by organized labor in any economically advanced country for government ownership irrespective of its form.

The final lesson was learned during the war. Every-

[1] Speech before the National Civic Federation, January 29, 1926, reproduced by International Labor News Service, February 6, 1926.

where governments had entered into the field of industry. But when labor began to ask for "a voice" or some measure of control within the industry, it was soon made to realize that its difficulties were the same whether the industry was governmental or in private hands. Within a few months after the close of the war organized labor everywhere began to formulate its new position in accord with this not altogether unexpected discovery—and especially in Great Britain and Germany. In Great Britain some of the Socialists, surprising as it might seem, were among the first to lead in the new direction. At the annual convention of the Miners' Federation in 1918, its secretary, Frank Hodges, said:

> For the last two or three years a new movement has sprung up in the labor world which deals with the question of joint control of the industry by representatives from the side which represents, for the most part, the consumer, and representatives of the workmen, who are the producers. *Nationalization in the old sense is no longer attractive. As a matter of fact, you can have nationalization, but still be in no better position than you are now under private ownership.* That is the experience of institutions which have been state owned and state controlled for many years. . . .
>
> Now is it any good to have these mines nationalized unless we are going to exercise some form of control as producers? If not, the whole tendency will be toward the power of bureaucracy. We shall be given no status at all in the industry, except to be the mere producers, as we have been in the past years. Under state ownership the workmen should be desirous of having something more than mere wages or mere employment; the workmen should have some directive power in the industry in which they are engaged. Now, how are we going to have this directive power under state control? (My italics.)

It will be seen that this opinion of an advocate of government ownership is close to that of those labor-union leaders who had *opposed* government ownership. For example, compare it with the opinion of Vice-President Woll:

> The American Federation of Labor, the only organization able to speak for the workers, is opposed to the government owning all means of production and distribution and is against the state regulating all our industrial relations and activities. It holds that to convert private and individual ownership of property and free and voluntary service into government ownership and compulsory labor is not to create industrial democracy, but to establish governmental bureaucracy and state slavery.[1]

The first impulse of labor democracy in America, as in other countries, was to attempt to control capitalism through government ownership and operation of railroads, mines, public utilities, and industrial monopolies. But the present tendency in this country, both with organized labor and with other progressives, is almost wholly in favor of government control rather than government ownership and operation. Government ownership and operation may or may not be viewed as the ultimate outcome. Those labor-unionists and progressives who do regard it as the probable outcome admit that, before we can afford to experiment with government ownership, government and governmental organs for the control of industry must undergo a transformation quite as complete as industry itself would undergo in the process of being taken over by government.

In arguing for "ultimate government ownership," the

[1] *Publications of American Sociological Society*, vol. xiv, p. 54.

late Senator Ladd of North Dakota pointed out that "we must grow up to the job," and continued:

We must have good government before we have much government ownership. So we must go slowly and endure some of our present ills until we are strong enough for the task. Yet there is no hope for the future if government can't be improved according to its growing responsibilities. Community life has become too vast and complex for the continued discharge by private agencies of some functions, and if government cannot be made honest and efficient enough to handle them we are in a bad way.

Private ownership is no longer equal to the commonly beneficial administration of public utilities, railways, coal mines, and forests. The only hope for utilization in the common interest is in public ownership—but, as I said, *we must improve government before it can take up all these gigantic tasks.*[1] (My italics.)

This is as much an argument against, as for, government operation *at the present moment.* What is demanded by this school of thought now is not government operation so much as a government fit for government operation—not so much the governmentalization of industry as the industrialization of government.

The platform upon which La Follette was a candidate for President in 1924 declared for government ownership of railroads "with definite safeguards against bureaucratic control" as "the only final solution of the transportation problem." The Progressive campaign text-book explained that this was "a remedy to be applied only when the time is ripe." Clearly one unripe condition is that effective "safeguards against bureaucratic control"—in other words, the special government machinery and ad-

---

[1] *Magazine of Wall Street*, December 9, 1922.

ministrative experience and ability required—have not yet been devised.

Far from urging *immediate* government operation of railroads, La Follette and his progressive and labor supporters urged an entirely different kind of reform; the repeal of the Cummins-Esch law then governing the railroads, that repeal involving, first, railroad rates "not on present inflated capital values, but on prudent investment and cost of service," and, second, the determination of wages by voluntary conciliation boards instead of the semi-compulsory Railway Labor Board. Neither measure is a preparation for government ownership, any more than it is a re-enforcement of private ownership.

Nor are organized labor and the allied progressives traveling at present in the direction of government ownership and operation of the coal mines. The United Mine Workers actively agitated for nationalization in 1920; they say little about it to-day. This demand was in the La Follette Wisconsin platform in 1923; it had disappeared in the year following. The Wisconsin platform, as well as the National Progressive platform, struck the new note—government control, instead of government ownership—and President Coolidge and the other spokesmen of capitalism took up the issue in that form and answered that we already have too much government control.

The progressives of 1924 demanded the conservation and "public control" also of the nation's natural resources, including coal, iron, and other ores, oil, timber, and water power. This meant government ownership in some cases, but not usually government operation. A common plan widely favored was a lease either to a semi-public corporation especially instituted for the purpose, or to a private corporation with direct or indirect public participation in profits and numerous conditions limiting and controlling the management.

In its first pronouncement on this subject after the war American labor demanded the continuation at least for a two-year trial period of the war-time government ownership and operation of railroads. But while labor was positive in its indorsement of government ownership, it was already uncertain about government operation, and advocated it only as a test: "It is essential that a thorough test be given all phases of railroad control and operation before a definite peace-time policy be finally concluded." In the following year the railroad organizations indorsed the so-called "Plumb plan," providing for "democratic operation," while the Federation of Labor as a whole also indorsed "democratic operation" as a general principle.

The most important of the fields in which labor has long favored government control is in banking and credit. Government ownership of public utilities had been indorsed in the Federation of Labor program of 1919. "Public and semi-public utilities should be owned, operated, *or* regulated by the government in the interests of the public," said the Federation statement, avoiding the crucial question. In addition to this position as to government intervention in the field of credit, transportation and public utilities, labor in its "reconstruction program" favored the continuation of the wartime government control of the American merchant marine (which included government operation) and government ownership and operation of wharves and docks, and of water power.

OPERATION WEIGHED AND FOUND WANTING

The water-power question came to the foreground in 1923, not only in view of the combination of plants into super-power and giant power projects, but specifically because of the federal project at Muscle Shoals and the California Water and Power Act. The convention of the Federation held in that year voted unanimously for "public development and control of water resources for the service of the people at cost" and for "the withdrawal and curtailment of special privileges to private interests controlling this natural resource for incomplete and costly development for private profit" in order to "relieve the people of exploitation and the burden of the extravagance, waste, and costly financing of private development and ownership." [1]

In regard to the Muscle Shoals question James Noonan, president of the Electrical Workers and Vice-President of the American Federation of Labor, expressed the view that "the practicability of public ownership or governmental ownership in operating power plants" had been demonstrated and that "this project built with the money of the public and for their use should be retained and operated by the government." [2] Mr. Noonan held that private operation with supervision by public-utility commissions had proved unsatisfactory, even when these were honest, because commissioners were appointed on political and geographical grounds and with insufficient salaries, their powers and duties circumscribed not only by law but by the high-paid corporation lawyers hired by the operating corporations to accomplish that object.

In his 1926 message, accepted as exceptionally

[1] Convention of the Federation, 1923.
[2] *American Federationist*, July, 1925.

139

satisfactory by labor, Governor Smith of New York, in opposing private operation, referred to the success of the water-power development already undertaken by that state and continued: "We have allowed nearly all of our natural resources to fall into private hands for private development and private profit. Water is the last great one still in the hands of all the people." [1]

I say to the state [continued Governor Smith a few weeks later], develop it without cost to our taxpayers through the water power authority which will enable them to earn from its use a sufficient amount to amortise and retire the bonds. In view of our past experience, the ultimate consumer, the man on the farm, in the home, and in the workshop, will be infinitely better off when he purchases the finished product under the scheme of the state water-power authority than he would be in the hands of private corporations organized for private profit. [2]

Governor Smith advocated, first, "the development of these water-power resources under state ownership and state control" through a special public corporation with the right to issue tax-exempt securities, and second the distribution of power through private corporations which could be controlled effectively by the state because of its ownership and control of the power plants. This plan was overwhelmingly and enthusiastically approved by the organized labor of the state.

So, by 1923, several services and utilities which labor held to be liable to and ready for governmental intervention had been definitely marked either for "governmental" or for "democratic" operation. But no sooner was the idea of governmental intervention generally accepted than

[1] The *World,* January 7, 1926.
[2] February 3, 1926.

the entire argument within the movement was transferred to this question as to what kind of operation was desirable.

The defeat of the few advocates of government operation (as a general principle) was soon complete. The question for labor is: "Under government operation what becomes of the rights of labor and what changes take place in the legal position of employees?" The danger was fully recognized by each and every group of labor affected. There is little doubt that under government operation there would be an attempt to fix wages through a government board, and at the same time to prohibit or to penalize heavily the collective cessation of work on the part of labor organizations. On the matter of compulsory fixing of wages by a governmental board there is no difference of opinion in labor circles. At a meeting held in New York on January 30, 1922, Plumb himself, the leader of the governmentalists, speaking for the railway labor unions, declared that the Railway Labor Board should never have been established, since it left wage awards in the hands of the so-called "public" members of the board. In contrast to this plan, which undoubtedly is the one that it would be attempted to force upon labor under government operation, the plan for "democratic operation" proposed by Plumb and adopted by the railroad unions provided for the decision of these questions by a tri-partite board on which the technical administrative staff of the railroads would hold the balance of power between labor and the public.

But even these provisions for "democratic operation" were unsatisfactory to some of the unions. Andrew Furuseth, leader of the seamen's union, objected to the application of the resolution for "government ownership with democratic operation" to "transportation systems" and moved that the words "railway systems" be substituted. The seamen were strongly opposed to anything even approaching governmental operation of ships, since it threatened restoration of the conditions of serfdom which prevailed until recently in the merchant marines of the world, and in particular before American labor secured the passage of the Seamen's Act.

Daniel J. Tobin, treasurer of the American Federation of Labor, national head of the Teamsters and Chauffeurs, supported Furuseth with the statement that the war's depressing effect on the occupations he represented had come largely from the governmentally controlled express companies.

The street railway unions in many cities have taken the same position; they are opposed to municipal ownership except in so far as it is accompanied by clauses protecting organized labor. One illustration may suffice:

The defeat by the labor unions of the proposed municipal street-car system in Detroit has puzzled and taken aback the "intellectual" group of advocates of public ownership of utilities in general. They have been in the habit of hastily going ahead with their theories without taking into account the lessons the wage-workers have learned thereon, sometimes at a dear price. . . . No municipal ownership scheme, with trade-unionism left out, can be acceptable to trade-unionists and liberty-loving citizens.[1]

But while organized labor in all countries has clearly lost any interest it may have had in government ownership *as such,* its new demand either for democratic operation or for labor representation in control has not yet

[1] *American Federationist,* February, 1916.

reached a definite form. Almost all the factions of organized labor throughout the world are now standing for a *mixed* control in which labor shall play an important part. Some labor programs demand an *equal* division of control between organized labor and other industrial factors. In others (like the Plumb plan) a deciding voice is to be left in the hands of a technical or administrative staff. Still another plan gives to organized labor plus the technical force a voice equal to the other economic or governmental factors. In no important instance, apparently, does labor now advocate leaving the controlling voice in the hands of labor on the one side, or, on the other, in the hands of the government or of a governmentally selected body representing the "consumers" or the "public." [1]

The principle underlying the Plumb plan, officially indorsed by all the railway unions, was summarized in a pamphlet issued by the Plumb Plan League:

Substitute for the present Wall Street control the unhampered management of trained officials and employees—the most intelligent and efficient transportation organization in the world.

Pay capital a fair and fixed return on the dollars actually invested in railroad property, and divide savings effected by economy and efficiency between the public and the operating organization—share and share alike.

Under this plan the consumers were given a still stronger protection than mere minority representation on the board of directors. For the rate-making power was to remain as at present in the hands of the Inter-

[1] British labor favored the plan of the government coal commission, known as the Sankey report, providing for joint control by workers, consumers, and the technical and commercial side of the industry. The official German coal commission made similar recommendations.

state Commerce Commission, a wholly governmental body: "The rate-making power remains with the Interstate Commerce Commission, and if wages were raised so high that rates had to be increased, the commission could refuse to change them and shippers might appeal to the courts for redress. If the operation by the directors results in a deficit Congress can revoke their charter."

Without specifically endorsing the Plumb plan, the Federation of Labor twice voted (in 1920 and 1921) for the principle of "democratic operation" which would cover the Plumb plan—on the second occasion by a majority of 29,000 to 8,000. The opposition to "democratic operation" was expressed by President Gompers at the convention of 1920:

The tendency is to prevent the men of labor in all activities in all forms of employment from exercising their economic as well as their political rights, and particularly the employees of the government of the United States; and government ownership simply means that the workers in these industries become government employees.

I believe there is no man to whom I would take second position in my loyalty to the Republic of the United States, and yet I would not give it more power over the individual citizenship of our country.

There was no inclination on the part of any responsible delegates at either of these conventions to deny the cogency of this argument. It was merely asserted by Frank Morrison, secretary of the Federation, and by other advocates of government ownership with democratic operation, that railway employees were *already* treated, or were about to be treated under the new Cummins-Esch

Railway Act, practically as government employees, a
prediction which was fully borne out by later events, in
particular by the extraordinary federal injunction of September 1, 1922, which had been especially provided for
by the Cummins-Esch Act. Indeed, it had been asserted
by President Gompers himself that the purpose of that
Act was to deprive labor of all rights. A similar opinion
was expressed by J. A. Franklin, head of the boilermakers:

> You will be told that we are taking a great risk, that we
> are liable to be deprived of our citizenship, that we are
> liable to be denied the right of American citizens; but I want
> to submit to you the question whether there can be any more
> stringent orders issued than those contained in the Cummins-
> Esch bill. We are denied almost every right that men can
> be denied.

Another important labor-union group which has advocated government ownership—though within similar
limits—was the coal-miners. This union resolved in 1919
"that the coal-mining industry be operated by the federal
government and that the mine workers be given *equal
representation* upon such councils or commissions as may
be delegated the authority to administer the affairs of the
coal-mining industry or the authority to act upon the
question of wages, hours of labor, conditions of employment." The plan involved *equal representation* of organized labor in the operation of the industry, although
the indorsement of the Plumb plan on the same occasion
indicates that there was also approval among the miners
of its more moderate principle.

It is the miners' view that the government will be
forced to intervene in the industry. There is no anxiety

[1] American Federation of Labor Convention, 1922.

to delay that intervention; the aim is to prevent the establishment of such a plan of governmental operation as would destroy the rights of labor organizations, and to obtain, if possible, a plan of democratic operation.

President Lewis of the miners has stated his opinion that "sooner or later the government will be obliged to intervene in the coal industry, and either take it over outright or else regulate and restrict the mining of coal in such a way as to eliminate gradually the over-development of the industry and thus bring about a regularity of operation that will insure greater possible earnings to the coal-worker, greater possible legitimate profits to the mine-owner, and cheaper coal to the consumer." He continued: "If the owners will not set their houses in order the public will step in and enforce order, because in a democracy such as this no set of men, whether in the ranks of labor or of capital, can be allowed permanently to maintain a public nuisance." [1]

The miners took a similar position during the anthracite coal strike of 1925 and 1926—except that the question was no longer one of nationalization or government operation, but of government regulation, supervision, and control of profits and prices—which, by implication, might be extended in some form or some degree to wages. At the outset of the strike President Lewis indignantly rejected the proposals of John Hays Hammond, chairman of the Coal Commission of 1923, because they went so far as "semi-regulation" by the federal government. The chief constructive recommendations of that commission had been for the permanent supervision of the anthracite industry through federal licenses and a Coal Division of

[1] Congressional hearing, April 3, 1922.

146

the Interstate Commerce Commission, mainly with a view to giving permanent publicity to costs, profits, wage rates, and prices. But the commission had also declared the coal industry "a public service" and was for giving the President extensive and arbitrary "emergency powers," laying a new foundation for sweeping and mandatory anti-union injunctions; it proposed also to give the new "coal division" semi-judicial functions.

But during the progress of the strike the mine-owners gained the ear of the public for their proposal for the arbitration of wages by some public or semi-public body to be appointed by the President. President Lewis replied by urging the simultaneous arbitration of *profits and prices*. There was at least as much ground, he said, for "the arbitration of property rights" as for "the arbitration of human rights." But this thorough-going species of public intervention, if made permanent, would mean something more than "semi-regulation" and an approach to the supervision and control proposed by the Federal Coal Commission—though not necessarily with those features objected to by organized labor.

So that the miners finally themselves proposed regulation. The union statement after one of the conferences with the mine-owners said:

The mine-workers proposed that both sides join in a request to Congress to enact legislation providing for complete regulation of the entire anthracite industry, inasmuch as it appeared to be impossible for the miners and operators to adjust their differences. This would mean regulation of profits and the selling price of coal, as well as every other phase of the industry. Under this plan it would be necessary to open the books of the coal companies, and again they refused.

147

LABOR AND GOVERNMENT

The fact that organized labor protested against all the regulatory measures proposed in the Congress of 1926 does not mean that the miners have turned against all regulation. All of these measures tended directly or indirectly to fix wages as well as prices in an "emergency" [1]— a strike or lockout. For example, the Copeland bill proposed to revive the powers of the war-time "fuel administrator," who forced a reduction of real wages and ordered the miners' leaders arrested for refusing a "mandatory" court injunction (based upon the war-time law) ordering them to call off a coal strike!

Government control or supervision, as distinguished from government operation, is that form of governmental intervention upon which American labor is most united, since it does not necessarily involve government wage-fixing. Government control, moreover, is applicable not only to railroads, mines, water power and public utilities, but, in widely varying degree, to all the great industrial corporations. And it involves a status for labor which is that neither of private nor of government employees.

American labor's advocacy of government supervision and control in preference to government operation was clearly brought out in one of Gompers's last and most important editorials—written in reply to a weighty campaign statement of Secretary Hoover on the subject. In this editorial Gompers said:

Organized labor stands for the most thoroughgoing kind of governmental control to stop the corruption and abuses which monopoly has developed. It wants industry honestly and fairly conducted, with freedom for the workers and room also for normal, natural economic development and

[1] *American Federationist*, May, 1924, p. 611.

change. It is the enemy of autocracy and bureaucracy alike and it sees in government ownership no necessary remedy. Yet in all affairs the people must find a way to make their voice effective as the source of all final decisions.

Mr. Hoover says, It is a question of whether it shall be government ownership or private ownership under control. To organized labor and to the great majority of the progressives this is not at all the main issue. *The main issue is the question of control and operation, whether there is government ownership or private ownership.* Labor's opposition to governmental operation, which, as Mr. Hoover points out, might interfere with the right collectively to cease work, is so unqualified that there is no section of the labor movement, no matter how radical, which does not oppose it. In so far as government ownership means government operation, labor is unanimously against it.[1] (My italics.)

American labor is not opposed to government operation in every instance. The unions are willing to accept government operation when they believe the public welfare demands it, but they are then subordinating the interest of the wage-earners in that particular industry or service to the interest of wage-earners generally—or of all citizens including wage-earners. For example, the labor unions undoubtedly favor Governor Smith's plan (see above) for government operation of water-power plants, as a strategic means for the effective public control of the distribution of power by publicly regulated though privately operated corporations, and not for the sake of the plant employees. They expect to gain as citizens—and as citizen-wage-earners in industries based largely on the use of this public water power.

[1] *American Federationist*, November, 1924.

CHAPTER X

THE SOLUTION: SOCIAL SUPERVISION AND CONTROL

The Movement to Democratize and Industrialize the Economic Boards—Labor and Big Business—Economic Decentralization vs. Political Decentralization.

CONTROL over the great corporations that administer industry and dominate government is the foundation of the labor and progressive program. I have shown that labor regards the shifting of the control of industry in the democratic direction as a gradual and natural process that is already proceeding both within the industry and from without. The labor and progressive object is "not to rebuild the foundation of business overnight," but, in recognition of the fact that "the gigantic combinations in basic industry could, if properly controlled, be very valuable servants of the public, to take practical measures to bend these great powers to genuine public service, and install government control of big business in the place of big business control of government." [1] That is a correct statement of the position of organized labor— as it was of the position of the majority of the progressives allied with labor in the 1924 election.

While the control of corporations and of trade associations—which have the same monopolistic tendencies—

[1] Progressive Campaign Book, 1924.

must be semi-governmental, it does not need to be carried out by means of the existing machinery of government. On the contrary, labor would first "industrialize" and democratize all existing governmental boards and commissions that are empowered to regulate corporations, trade associations, and business, and would make them representative of all important economic organizations and of all essential factors of industry. I have referred to the national economic conference proposed by labor with the object of furthering the constructive organization and co-operation of the essential elements of agriculture and industry and to the fact that Vice-President Woll, who fathered this resolution, proposes that all our national boards and commissions should be composed on that principle. (See Chapter VI.)

These boards and commissions, when reorganized to represent finance, management, technicians, labor, agriculture, consumers, and all the major economic groups, would, first and above all, favor the maximum of self-government and self-regulation of industry. But they would also stand as intermediaries between industry and government, and their second most important function would be to keep the government and the general public informed as to the basic facts of industry—with a view both to prevent unnecessary and destructive legislation and to promote constructive legislation and social control. Majority and minority recommendations would be laid before Congress, and the members of the boards would be peculiarly effective in educating the organized and socially effective sections of the public by the reports they would send back to their organizations.

Complete and efficient publicity would require "uni-

form and public accounting at stated periods." Such
thorough and permanent publicity would in itself constitute a remedy for many industrial ills, inviting and encouraging their cure through non-governmental economic
organizations. But further governmental action would
follow where necessary, even against some of the economic organizations—one of the objects of publicity being to serve as "a basis for policies preventing the misuse of industrial organizations" [1]—a principle that applies
to corporations as well as associations. (See Volume I,
Chapter XI.)

Woll shows that labor demands publicity as a basis
for *effective action to prevent extortionate practices
leading to extortionate prices and profits:*

It is true that large combinations may use their power
to exact extortionate prices. I believe, however, that if
large businesses were required to give a public accounting
of their business, public opinion would soon exert pressure
upon those concerns who were holding up the public. The
function of the Federal Trade Commission should be to
investigate the profits and cost of production of big business
combines rather than to prevent consolidation.

We must stop thinking of big business concerns as being
national goblins simply because they are large in size. Let
them be as big as they want to. The public's alarm should
be in the profits that they make and not in the size of the
agency that makes the profits.[2]

Labor's strong and persistent outcry for the publicity
of profits cannot be interpreted as a belief that mere continuous investigation, however effective as a partial remedy, will *in itself suffice* to cure profiteering or unre-

[1] American Federation of Labor Convention, 1925.
[2] Interview in New York *World*, November 29, 1925.

stricted capitalism. So great, however, is the weight attached to publicity and so strong is labor's opposition to unscientific governmental interference in industry that it might appear that publicity is accepted as sovereign and sufficient. Woll writes:

The recommendation of the Federal Trade Commission is that the greatest good will comes not through prosecution or driving combinations to operate under cover of some seemingly legal device, but by making public all vital statistics of basic industry, including ownership, production, distribution cost, sales, and profits. It is by permitting trade associations and by disclosing their activities to full public view that we shall restrain those combinations that may attempt to harm the public good for selfish and personal gain.[1]

That is, publicity is the first remedy, and must first be given a fair trial. Yet Woll goes on to show that publicity, after all, is to be regarded largely as a means. The government is indispensable both "to promote and to encourage co-operation and combination" and to "equalize the advantages as well as prevent the possible abuses of this collective power."[2]

The great corporations, moreover, follow the same policies as the trade associations, but with impunity, since under the Supreme Court's "rule of reason" they are practically immune from the Sherman Act. They developed on a large scale before the trade associations and they are even more important in the American economic structure. Labor's view as to the means by which they can and should be controlled shows its underlying principles as to the whole question of the governmental supervision of industry.

[1] New York *Evening Post*, April 11, 1922.
[2] *Ibid.*

LABOR AND GOVERNMENT

At the time of the anti-trust movement in the last decade of the twentieth century, as I have pointed out, American labor had already formulated its opposition to legislation directed against the development of large industrial units or "trusts" and against the attempt to restore competition by law ("to unscramble the eggs"). But labor fully recognized the overwhelming economic and political power of these new industrial combinations and the necessity of subordinating them by one means or another to some superior power. The Federation convention of 1899 declared that "organized labor is deeply concerned regarding the swift and intense concentration of the industries and realizes that unless successfully confronted by an equal or superior power, there is economic danger and political subjugation in store for all." [1]

American labor realized, as the general public never has realized, that there was no power in the community great enough to cope with the trusts without the co-operation of organized labor. Not that organized labor could hope to accomplish much when acting alone, but it saw that it would necessarily be one of the main factors in the militant democratic movement necessary to deal successfully with the growing and solidifying industrial and financial powers. The experience of all countries had shown that the only resistance to the control of industry and government by high finance that has been even half effective has been where labor has taken a prominent and active part in the militant democratic movement. American labor put forth this claim to natural leadership in the early stages of the trust movement:

[1] Annual Report to convention of 1899.

THE SOLUTION

Experience will demonstrate that there is a power growing wholly unnoticed by our superficial friends of the press which will prove itself far more potent to deal with the trusts, or, if the trusts inherently possess any virtue at all, to see that they are directed into a channel for the public good, and that growing power is the much-despised organized labor movement of our country and our time. Wait and see.[1]

Labor did not propose, however, to join in with any of the destructive and reactionary measures that were brought forward at this time by small producers, competitors, and business victims of the trusts: "We cannot [labor declared] if we would, turn back to the primitive conditions of industry which marked the early part of the last century. It is therefore idle chatter to talk of annihilating trusts. The trust is, economically speaking, the logical and inevitable accompaniment and development of our modern commercial and industrial system. For our own part, we are convinced that the state is not capable of preventing the development—or the natural concentration, of industry." [2]

Labor rejoiced that the state could not be used by competitive producers to destroy the trusts; but it also felt the utter hopelessness at that time of using the state effectively for the purpose of constructive control. (See Chapter VIII.) Labor saw that it must wait:

The great wrongs attributable to the trusts are their corrupting influence on the politics of the country, but as the state has always been the representative of the wealth possessors, we shall be compelled to endure this evil until the toilers are organized and educated to the degree that they

[1] *American Federationist,* December, 1896.
[2] Annual report, A. F. of L. convention, 1899.

shall know that the state is by right theirs, and finally and justly come to their own, while never relaxing in their efforts to secure the very best possible economic, social and material improvement in their condition.[1]

Two decades later, that is in 1919, the year after the termination of the European war, organized labor felt that working with its progressive allies it had become strong enough to make an effective demand for the first constructive step. As we read in its "reconstruction program" of that year: "It is essential that legislation should provide for the federal licensing of all corporations organized for profit. Furthermore, federal supervision and control should include the increasing of capital stock and the incurring of bonded indebtedness, with the provision that the books of all corporations shall be open at all times to federal examiners."[2]

In other words, organized labor felt that in these two decades a great advance had taken place both in the economic strength of labor movement and in its political strength—the latter due largely to the fact that other social groups, equally strong numerically and similarly placed economically, had by this time come to take similar views as to the necessity and feasibility of a certain degree of government supervision of industry, in the form of corporation control.

Labor and its progressive allies now feel that the great industrial corporations, creatures of the law which wholly overshadow the government in wealth and power, must and can be controlled, from the foundation up, through

[1] Annual report of A. F. of L. convention, 1899.
[2] Labor's reconstruction program, 1919. See Volume I, Chapter X.

publicity, through federal incorporation[1] or licenses, through profit taxation, through control of credit, transportation, power, and raw materials.[2]

The Executive Council of the Federation in the year 1921 made the following declaration on this subject:

We have reached a time in our financial, commercial, and industrial history which demands a careful review of existing corporate tendencies, the sources of their power, influence, and strength, and the advantages, rights, privileges, and immunities they have secured, and which are denied to all other groups of people in our land.

The 1923 convention of American Federation of Labor voted for the repeal of the Sherman Anti-trust law. By moving to control excessive profits and corporations and not against monopolies or combinations[2]—that is, by ignoring the presence or absence of commercial competition—labor has placed the struggle against plutocracy on an altogether more solid and permanent foundation than it had occupied before labor took a leading part among the progressive forces. Every corporation being the creature of the law, and practically every large concern now being incorporated, labor can see no fundamental limitation in the possibilities of this form of legal control.

But all effective governmental control of industry, whether by federal incorporation, licenses, or any other plan, would have to be guided by federal boards and commissions representative of the essential economic factors. These boards are already in existence, and in spite of their present obsolete and political structure and the over-ex-

[1] Federal incorporation was proposed by President Taft in an able message to Congress in 1911.
[2] See Volume I, Chapter XI.

tension or undue limitation of their powers, some of them are more or less effective. A considerable degree of efficiency would nowhere be denied to the oldest of them all, the Interstate Commerce Commission nor to the Federal Reserve Board. The Tariff Commission, the Federal Trade Commission, and the Shipping Board are in a more difficult position and their functions are less clearly marked, but they have been indispensable, whatever their present defects may be. If we consider all these boards together we realize at once that such bodies, intermediate between our governmental and industrial structures, are bound to grow in importance—and it takes little imagination or speculation to see that, if they are reorganized and put on a democratic and an economic instead of a political basis, they may go far to solve the problem of the democratic and social administration of industry.

"Once these boards are made truly representative—that is, representative of working America and not of politics —they will become efficient," says Woll. "Once they become efficient they will be intrusted with further powers. And when they are intrusted with further powers they will soon find a way to put an end to the bi-partisan political and financial oligarchy that is now running this country." [1]

The gradual extension of such new forms of governmental supervision and control is what labor as well as the progressives are looking toward in this country. The Interstate Commerce Commission already has a large measure of control over the railroads—and it is increasing year by year. A recent Supreme Court decision declared that the Cummins-Esch Transportation Act of

[1] International Labor News Service, April 10, 1926.

1920 has "put the railroads more completely than ever under the fostering guardianship and control of the commission, which is to supervise their issue of securities, their car supply and distribution, their joint use of terminals, their construction of new lines, their abandonment of old lines" as well as fixing all interstate and some intrastate rates.[1]

Changes in function invariably produce changes in structure. We shall surely witness soon either an enlargement and reorganization of this commission or the development of new instruments for transportation control.

In the field of credit, progressives and organized labor approve the principle of the Federal Reserve Board, by which the government in theory dominates the credit system of the country, but in fact dominates it only nominally, since the board has always been firmly in the hands of the very bankers who are supposed to be under its supervision. Organized labor and the progressives would give labor, agriculture, and other economic groups proportional representation on this and all similar boards. As the Progressives of 1924 said, "the government now has in this board an instrument by which the injurious use of the power of private bankers could be *checked* if this instrument were properly employed." That is true, but it is a negative expression; it is equally obvious that the power of this board could be used in large measure *to control and direct* the credit of the nation, and without the government entering into the banking business.

The joint declaration of the American Federation of Labor and the railroad brotherhoods of December, 1919, urged "the organization and use of credit to serve produc-

[1] Northern Pacific case decided May 22, 1926.

tion needs and not to increase the incomes and holdings of financiers." "Control over credit," it added, "should be taken from financiers and should be vested in a public agency, able to administer this power as a public trust in the interests of all the people."

The attitude of organized capital and organized business to these boards and commissions, on the whole, is naturally hostile. The railroads for twenty years fought successfully against the foundation of the Interstate Commerce Commission, the bankers opposed the inauguration of the Federal Reserve Board and the industrial corporations opposed the Federal Trade Commission. This opposition disappeared when these bodies fell into the hands of the railroads, the banks, the industrial corporations and trade associations. But there can be no question that the capitalists fear that the personnel of the boards may change again and that they may be used in the future for real and effective supervision or control— as is proved by a ceaseless capitalist campaign to restrict their powers.

The capitalists naturally resist every effective form of corporation supervision and control. I have mentioned their pretended cure of monopoly by compulsory restoration of competition, the unscrambling of the eggs by governmental fiat.[1] I have mentioned their revival of the state-rights doctrine in order that all corporation legislation may remain in the hands of the states.[2] This doctrine, if accepted would give an absolute guaranty of non-regulation to every great corporation that is federal in its scope and cannot either legally or practically be regulated by state action. A third capitalistic argument is that

[1] See Chapters VI to VIII.
[2] See Volume I, Chapter XI.

there must be less federal supervision and control, fewer federal boards and commissions, because they tend to build up a great centralized bureaucracy. President Coolidge says:

No plan of centralization has ever been adopted which did not result in bureaucracy, tyranny, inflexibility, reaction, and decline. Of all forms of government, those administered by bureaus are about the least satisfactory to an enlightened and progressive people. Being irresponsible, they become autocratic, and being autocratic they resist all development. Unless bureaucracy is constantly resisted it breaks down representative government and overwhelms democracy.[1]

American labor agrees with every word of this as applied to bureaus in the strict sense, but not as applied to the new commissions. No social group has suffered more from bureaucracy or fought harder against it than the labor unions. But what is President Coolidge's remedy for centralization? Merely "local self-government."[2] This emphasis on local self-government means nothing more nor less than capitalist self-government—and the abandonment of all hope of social supervision and control over the corporations and the industrial structure.

The great industrial corporations and combinations will never regulate themselves, nor can these great centralized and nation-wide industries be regulated by the states. When opponents of all general regulation, like Coolidge and Hoover, attack the only practicable regulation by an appeal to states' rights as against the agencies of the federal government, former Secretary of the Treasury, William G. McAdoo, like labor, regards this as a very obvious subterfuge. "These people," he

[1] Speech before William and Mary College, May 15, 1926.
[2] Ibid.

LABOR AND GOVERNMENT

points out, "are not interested in states' rights because they
honestly desire to see the powers of the state governments
protected or extended." [1] What they want is merely to
see the federal economic agencies abolished or restricted.

Labor understands thoroughly that the remedy for centralization is decentralization. But it sees no reason whatever why this decentralization should be political, traditional, and geographic, and every reason why it should be
along economic, modern, and industrial liens.[2]

[1] Mr. McAdoo has pointed out that economic liberty must be protected "through the only agency competent to deal therewith—the
federal government." The federal economic boards and commissions,
he believes, are absolutely indispensable.

"Mr. McAdoo said it was deceiving to imagine that by abolishing
governmental agencies the rights of the people would be delivered
from the keeping of great organizations of clerks and secretaries and
department heads and left secure in their own serene strength.

"We shall simply be transferring them from a governmental
bureaucracy employed by the people to a host of private bureaucracies
employed by the corporations," he said, "for in the bad sense, as in
the good sense, every great modern corporation has a tendency to be
a bureaucracy, just as the government has."—(Speech in Des Moines,
May 25, 1926.)

[2] Both the historic significance of the national economic commissions and the revolutionary possibilities that lie in their further industrialization and democratization have been clearly recognized by
Mr. Silas Bent. Shortly after the above-quoted expressions of Mr.
Woll and while the present volume was in press, my attention was
called to his accurate analysis of the commission development in the
Century Magazine (July, 1926) concluding with the following significant and convincing paragraphs:

"*Commission government at Washington is an attempt to reconcile
the formula of democracy with the fact of an industrial autocracy.*
Democracy won its triumphs in the escape from a feudal servitude to
land-holding overlords. Primarily it satisfied an aspiration to own
and till the soil. The right to vote meant liberation from agricultural
peonage. The industrial civilization which has grown up since the
framing of our constitution comprises a system of overlordships
based on the market and the factory. No longer is a right to the
land our problem: *the new problem involves equal suffrage in commerce and industry.* We have endeavored to cope with the transforming influences of a gigantic and highly integrated oligarchy by inte-

THE SOLUTION

The government must be controlled, in the main, by economic organizations rather than by political parties or sectarian bodies; Congress must be organized by the great economic groups representing the entire population, or at least every economic function; the government must be divided mainly into economic bodies, representing the chief

---

grating governmental powers in a group of commissions, and we have achieved, palpably, but indifferent success. *Upon the outcome of our gropings, it is not too much to say, depends in large measure the fate of the democratic experiment.* (My italics.)

"The most interesting and significant thing in the situation is the demand that there be regional representation on the Interstate Commerce Commission. This is not partisan; it has come from men in both the major parties, speaking for the East as well as the South. Nor is it without precedent. A bloc representing Western farmers demanded and got representation on the Federal Reserve Board. It was argued that this powerful agency, dealing with questions potent in the financial welfare of the whole country, should be free of sectional or class influences; on the other hand, it was contended, and with success, that our banking system was commercial in its origin and growth, that its structure was such as to result in discriminations against agricultural industry, and that the Reserve Board should hear a voice capable of explaining the needs of the farmer. *The demand for regional or industrial representation may be extended to other commissions.* We may have, in time, farm representation on the Tariff Commission, sectional or mining or manufacturing representation on other commissions and boards. It is not impossible that through the extension of this process, and through the erection of safeguards against inequities in the practices of the agencies (many must be the safeguards!), *they may become, after a fashion, democratized.* That is to say, they may come in time to embody a sort of delegated authority from the electorate, either through an elective process, or through limiting the field of appointment." (My italics.)

Surely "the indifferent success" we have so far achieved through these commissions has a greatly improved prospect of becoming a real success—and democracy has a greatly bettered chance of winning over industrial autocracy—as organized labor and organized agriculture, realizing the possibility of making them representative of economic democracy, rally increasingly to their support. And organized labor and agriculture can make their support infinitely more effective through their new discovery of the efficacy of organized non-partisan voting and the congressional bloc.

163

economic activities of the nation rather than the largely antiquated and often unworkable executive, legislative, and judicial departments; and, finally, these new governmental bodies must be representative of economic groups rather than political parties or geographic sections. If it is said, for example, that the West and the South should have equal representation, along with other sections, in any federal body affecting agriculture, the answer is that sections should not be represented, but cotton and wheat and corn, fruit and cattle and hogs.

Governmental decentralization must be fostered and accelerated along those very economic lines upon which it is proceeding in fact—and in spite of the Hamiltonian-Jeffersonian, Græco-Roman, pre-industrial theories upon which our governmental structure has been so largely developed in the past. The chief branches of government are becoming and must increasingly become not the legislative, judicial, and executive, but industry, commerce, agriculture, finance, transportation, and the export and import of goods and capital. The further subdivisions of government are following and must increasingly follow the same economic lines, dealing with each of the manufacturing, extractive, and agricultural industries and with each of the branches of commerce, transportation, finance, and international economic relations.

Already artificial municipal, county, and state lines have become absurd for the regulation of transport and public utilities, and agreements between governmental bodies along natural regional lines are the order of the day. Already 80 per cent of our legislation is economic, according to the careful estimates of a leading business organization, and the proportion is steadily increasing. Our executives

THE SOLUTION

and our courts are more and more occupied with problems of business and production. Our government took its political form before the industrial era. It is being transformed steadily to correspond to the economic reality. That reality has little to do with the more or less imaginary boundaries between the states and bears almost no relation to the theoretical divisions of government.

Every breath of modern development in every country on earth is working in this direction. Obsolescent political organizations and purely political institutions are maintained and defended to-day almost exclusively by anti-progressive, politically retrogressive, and selfish business interests which have learned to use them for their purposes. Inefficient and ancient political and governmental forms suit these interests infinitely better than those modernized forms of economic government which are learning how to control industry—under the influence of increasingly efficient popular economic organizations that are gradually learning how to control politics and government.

Nor does American labor base its social program wholly upon the newer forms of government. It has also adopted a new political method and a series of political and economic policies that would go far toward reconstructing society independently of fundamental changes in government.[1] But all three of these developments are closely related and should be regarded as parts of a single whole.

[1] See Volume I.

INDEX

(Italic letters denote volume)

Adamson Act. *See* Railroads

Administrative Staff. *See* Management

Agreements. *See* Collective Bargaining

Agricultural Conference, National, *i*, 87–90

Agricultural Exports. *See* Haugen Bill

Agriculture. *See* Farmers

Aluminum Trust, *i*, 164

Amalgamated Clothing Workers, *i*, 77, 104, 106, 109

Amendments, Constitutional. *See* Child Labor; Senators, Direct Election of; Tax, Federal Income

America, *i*, 1, 2, 7, 14, 17

Anthracite. *See* Coal

Anti-Injunction Acts. *See* Injunctions

Anti-Trust Laws. *See* Big Business; Clayton Act; Sherman Act

Arbitration, *i*, 57, 62, 96, 101, 181, 214–216; *ii*, 60

Arizona, *i*, 99

Atkeson, *i*, 87

Autocracy in Industry, *i*, 232; *ii*, 40, 48, 62, 69–73, 107, 150

Bailey, Senator, *i*, 53

Bakers, *ii*, 6

"Balance of Power," *i*, 159

Ball, Senator, *i*, 131

Baltimore and Ohio Railroad, *ii*, 30, 33–38, 79–81

Banks—

Against Governmental Credits, *i*, 193

Control and Supervision of, *i*, 21, 74, 81, 102; *ii*, 152

Control over Industry, *i*, 11, 184; *ii*, 46

Governmental, *i*, 69, 71, 78

Hostile to Organized Labor, *ii*, 4, 5

Labor Banks as a Remedy against, *ii*, 8–14

See also Capital; Credit; Federal Reserve Board; Finance; Home Loan Banks; Labor Banks; Postal Savings Banks

Banks, Labor, *i*, 21, 25; *ii*, 3–5, 7–10, 38, 50, 152

Bankers' Association, American, *i*, 159; *ii*, 59

Barnes, *ii*, 104, 105, 114

Barrett, *ii*, 121

Bent, *ii*, 154, 155

Berry, *ii*, 37, 38

Beveridge, Ex-Senator, *ii*, 89

Beyer, *ii*, 34, 36

"Big Business"—

And Competition, *ii*, 106–110, 117, 118

Control of, *i*, 173, 194; *ii*, 49, 118, 140, 152–157

Development in the United States, *i*, 10–14

Hostility of Organized Labor, *i*, 17

Legislation Against, *i*, 34

"Big Business"—(*Continued*)
Lobby and "Bloc," *i*, 163
Organized Labor and Progressives United Against, *i*, 117
See also Banks; Business; Capital; Competition; Credit; Finance; Profits
Bill of Grievances, Labor's, *i*, 34–36, 51, 52, 64
Blacksmiths, International Brotherhood of, *i*, 77
Blaine, Governor, *i*, 99
Bloc, Congressional—
and Organized Minorities, *i*, 155, 160–163
and Parties, *i*, 159, 163–165
Attacked by the President and Organized Business, *i*, 129–132, 155, 157–159; *ii*, 114
Blocs and the Federal Boards, *ii*, 155
Blocs Successful, *i*, 166, 167
Contrasted with European Blocs, *i*, 154, 157, 161
Controls Congress with Opposition Aid, *i*, 129
Popular and Business Blocs and Lobbies, *i*, 155, 157, 158; *ii*, 120–123
Preferred to a Party Re-alignment, *i*, 142, 151, 167, 168
Progressive Democratic-Republican Bloc Supported by Labor, *i*, 123
See also Non-partisan Policy
Boards and Commissions, Federal—
Ex-Secretary of the Treasury McAdoo Defends, *ii*, 154
Interference of, in Industry Opposed by Labor, *i*, 95–97
Labor Proposes Industrialization and Democratization of, *i*, 172, 173; *ii*, 92, 94, 112, 113, 149, 151, 155–157
Organized Business Opposes Extended Power of, *ii*, 152

Boards and Commissions, Federal—(*Continued*)
President Coolidge Opposes, *ii*, 153
Publicity and Fact-finding through the Boards, *i*, 183, 184; *ii*, 144, 145
See also Federal Reserve Board; Federal Tariff Commission; Federal Trade Commission; Interstate Commerce Commission; Shipping Board
Boilermakers, *ii*, 137
Bonus, Soldiers', *i*, 14, 100, 101; *ii*, 123
Borah, Senator, *i*, 172
Boycott. *See* Consumers
Brady, *ii*, 49
British Labor Party and Laborites, *i*, 64, 104, 106, 107, 110, 125, 126; *ii*, 124, 125
Brookhart, Senator, *i*, 73, 75, 99, 103, 108, 125
Brotherhoods, Railroad. *See* Railroad Labor
Bryan, Governor Charles, *i*, 171
Bryan, William Jennings, *i*, 39, 111, 171
Building Trades Dept., A. F. of L., *ii*, 120
Bureau of Labor, U. S., *ii*, 17
Bureaucracy, *ii*, 153
Business, Organized—
and Farmer-Labor Entente, *i*, 90, 91
Campaign against Congress, *i*, 128, 130
Domination over Government, *i*, 76–78, 79, 83; *ii*, 120, 123
Hostility of, to Progressive Legislation, *i*, 69, 72, 73
Industry Operated for Profits Only, *ii*, 71, 72
Lobby and "Bloc," *i*, 155, 160–165
Opposition to Federal Boards

INDEX

Business, Organized—(*Continued*)
   and Commissions, *ii*, 95, 152
   Opposition to Governmental Economic Activity, *ii*, 104, 105
   Opposition to Labor Organization, *ii*, 4, 5, 46
   Political Opposition to Labor, *i*, 98, 133, 135
   See also Capital; Chambers of Commerce; Class; Manufacturers' Associations; Profits

Calder, Senator, *i*, 99
California Water and Power Act, *ii*, 131
Campbell, *i*, 99
Canals. *See* Waterways
Cannonism, *i*, 42, 164
Capitalism—
   Against Governmental Action, *ii*, 104–108
   Can It Be Divorced from Management? *ii*, 43–49
   Capitalists Opposed to Governmental Credits, *i*, 193, 204
   Co-operation of Labor with, *ii*, 21–39
   "Democratic," *ii*, 3–20
   Domination of, Challenged by Labor, *ii*, 40–49
   Excess Profits Attacked, *ii*, 62–73
   Labor's Struggle Against, *ii*, 50–61
   See also Autocracy; Banks; Big Business; Business; Class Rule; Credit; Finance; Profits
Capper, Senator, *i*, 61, 62
Caraway, Senator, *i*, 147
Carpenters, *i*, 118
Carter, *i*, 77
Carver, Prof. Thomas N., *ii*, 15, 20

Catholic Hierarchy, *ii*, 30
Catholic National Welfare Council, *i*, 203, 208; *ii*, 16, 17
Centralization. *See* Structure
Chambers of Commerce, *i*, 12, 17, 25, 98, 127
Chicago Tribune, *i*, 51, 154; *ii*, 22
Child Labor, *i*, 16, 21, 45, 57, 115; *ii*, 4, 59, 71, 72, 104, 114, 120–122
Churches of Christ in America, Federal Council of, *ii*, 81
Cigarmakers, *ii*, 6
Civic Federation, National, *ii*, 93
Civil War, *i*, 7, 39
Class Legislation, *ii*, 114, 119
Class Rule, *ii*, 50, 105, 106, 120
   See also Autocracy; Capital and Business Organized
Classes and Class-Struggle, *i*, 7–10, 13; *ii*, 50–61, 84, 85
Clayton Act, *i*, 43–46, 51, 52, 68; *ii*, 118
Clerical Employments, *i*, 10, 11
Cleveland Conference. *See* Conference for Progressive Political Action
Coal, *i*, 12, 20, 21, 48; *ii*, 27, 28, 121, 128, 129, 135–141
Coal Commission, Federal, *i*, 181–183; *ii*, 30, 138
Coal Miners. *See* Miners
Coal Strikes, *i*, 181, 214, 215
Cold Storage Regulation, *i*, 176, 178
Collective Bargaining—
   Anti-Trust Acts and, *i*, 68
   Employers Opposed to, *ii*, 24–32, 39
   Expansion of the Principle of, *ii*, 74–79
   Its Relation to Other Phases of the Labor Movement, *i*, 18–24, 25, 26
   Legislation Necessary to Supplement, *i*, 31

Collective Bargaining—(*Cont.*)
   Progressives for Right to, *i*, 71,
      115
   Right to Recognized by Gov-
      ernment and Public, *ii*, 22,
      23, 24
   See also Defensive Politics;
      "Employee Representa-
      tion"; Legal Status;
      Union-Management Co-
      operation
Colorado, *i*, 70, 71
Colorado Fuel and Iron Co., *ii*,
      27, 28
Combinations. *See* Big Business
Commissions, Federal. *See* Boards
Commodities, Government Pur-
      chases and Sales of, *i*, 177,
      186
Company Unions. *See* "Em-
      ployee Representation"
Compensation. *See* Insurance
Competition, *i*, 12, 25, 68, 74,
      178, 179, 185. *See also* Big
      Business
Concentration of W e a l t h. *See*
      Division of Income
Conference for Progressive Po-
      litical Action, *i*, 97, 103–
      109, 124, 125, 146
Congress—
   Attack Against, *i*, 128–133
   Congressional and Presidential
      Elections, *i*, 113, 114, 118,
      121–135
   Election of 1920, *i*, 53, 54, 61, 67
   Election of 1922, *i*, 95, 98–102,
      108, 109
   Election of 1924, *i*, 144–153
   First Nation-wide Attempts to
      Elect Friendly Congress-
      men, *i*, 34–42
   Labor-Progressive Co-operation
      in, *i*, 113, 114, 118, 121–135
Consolidation, Industrial, *i*, 11–14
Constitution of American Federa-
      tion of Labor, *i*, 137; *ii*, 55

Constitution of United States, *i*,
      131, 151, 166. *See also*
      Amendments
Consumers—
   Are They Adequately Protected
      by a New Kind of Manage-
      ment? *ii*, 14–17, 85
   Remedies for High Cost of Liv-
      ing, *i*, 57, 175–189
   Representation of, *ii*, 135, 138,
      143
   Taxation of (Indirect Taxes), *i*,
      200
   Versus Middlemen, *i*, 73, 163
   Versus Profiteers, *i*, 20
   Wage Earners as, *i*, 18, 19, 175
   Wages and the, *i*, 230
   See also Prices; Publicity; Tax-
      ation
Convict Labor, *i*, 52, 57
Coolidge, President—
   And Congress of 1922, *i*, 130
   Defeat of Coolidge Senators,
      i, 79
   Nomination of Charles B. War-
      ren, *i*, 74
   No Opposition to Business Lob-
      bies, *ii*, 121, 122
   Opposition to Government Con-
      trol, *ii*, 129, 153
   Opposition to Government Ex-
      penditure for National De-
      velopment, *i*, 183, 209, 210
   Opposition to Organized Agri-
      culture, *i*, 78, 81
   Opposition to the Progressive
      Bloc, *i*, 155, 158–163; *ii*,
      115
   Opposition to Progressive Can-
      didates, *i*, 108
   Opposition to Taxation to Re-
      duce Wealth, *i*, 197–200,
      202
   Says the People Own This
      Country, *ii*, 10
   Soldiers' Bonus Passed over
      Veto of, *i*, 100

INDEX

Coolidge, President—(*Continued*)
  Tax Plan Defeated, *i*, 101
Co-operation—
  Co-operative Credit System, *i*, 74
  Farmers', *i*, 68, 178, 179
  Governmental Aid for, *i*, 185, 186
  of Business Units, *i*, 12, 26, 145
  of Labor and Capital, *ii*, 30–38, 78
  of Organized Social Groups, *ii*, 25, 82–94
  See also Consolidation and Big Business; Organization; Self-determination; Union-Management Co-operation
Copeland, Senator, *ii*, 140
Corporations, Giant. *See* Big Business Corporations, *i*, 11–13, 21, 173–175; *ii*, 10, 11, 61, 116, 140, 143, 149. *See also* Industry, Control of
Cost of Government, *i*, 203
Cost of Living. *See* Consumers and Prices
Cost of Production, Monthly Government Statements, *i*, 177
Cotton States Board, *i*, 53
Couzens, Senator, *i*, 200
Cox, Governor, *i*, 59
Credit—
  Control of, *i*, 173, 177; *ii*, 130, 151, 152
  Public, Expansion of, *i*, 21, 190–194
  See also Banks; Capital; Federal Reserve Board; Finance
Cummins-Esch Railroad Act, *i*, 53–59, 72, 74, 81, 100–103; *ii*, 129, 150
Cummins, Senator, *i*, 53
Current History, *i*, 3

Daugherty, Attorney-General, *i*, 74, 101

Daugherty Injunction, *ii*, 137
Davis, *i*, 108, 111, 118
Dawes, Vice-President, *i*, 155, 158
Debt, National, *i*, 195, 201–204
Decentralization in Industrial Control, *i*, 163, 208–210; *ii*, 153, 156
Decentralization in Labor Organization. *See* Structure
Defensive Politics, *i*, 29–33, 115
Democracy, *i*, 1, 2, 7–9, 14, 23, 173, 174, 195, 205; *ii*, 62. *See also* Industrial Democracy
Democratic Operation, *ii*, 133, 138
Democratic Party and Democrats—
  Administration Turns Against Labor, *i*, 48
  Candidate for President Endorsed (1920), *i*, 55
  Controlled by Reactionaries, *i*, 118
  Democratic Administration Endorsed by Labor, *i*, 47
  Democratic Friends of Labor, *i*, 125
  Democratic Governor and Republican Senator Elected in Nebraska, *i*, 71
  Endorsed by Labor as Opposition Party, *i*, 36, 37
  Governors Elected, *i*, 98, 99
  Is It Becoming the Progressive Party? *i*, 134, 135, 167, 168
  Its Effort to Control Organized Labor Politically, *i*, 28
  Labor Democratic in Democratic States Only, *i*, 147
  Labor Rebuffed as to National Candidates and Platform, *i*, 111, 112
  Labor's Hope of Capturing, *i*, 141, 142
  Minnesota Party Destroyed by Labor, *i*, 70
  Must It Choose between Liber-

Democratic Party and Democrats—(*Continued*)
alism and Progressivism? *i*, 171–173
Party Condemned by Labor, *i*, 39, 142
Presidential Candidates and Platforms Preferred, *i*, 38
Pro-Labor Democratic Group in Congress, *i*, 134
State Organizations Captured, *i*, 53, 70, 72
Supports the Clayton Act, *i*, 46
Department of Labor, U. S., *i*, 51, 185
Detroit, *ii*, 134
Dial, Senator, *i*, 131
Dill, Senator, *i*, 103
Distribution of Wealth. *See* Division of Income
Division of National Income—
A Better, Desired for National Prosperity, *i*, 212
A Better, through Governmental Action, *i*, 171–174
A Better, through Taxation, *i*, 196–211
Efficiency Dependent Upon Better Division, *i*, 218–220, 232
Higher Wages Restricted by Excessive Profits, *ii*, 63, 64
Labor Demands a Proportionate Share in Increase, *i*, 224–227
Labor Not Obtaining Proportionate Share in Rising Industrial Production, *i*, 227–228
Labor Not Securing Proportionate Share of Rising National Income, *i*, 220–222
Labor's Income Advancing Relatively as to Other Groups, But Not as to Profit-takers, *i*, 229–231

Division of National Income—(*Continued*)
Labor's Share Increased by Immigration Restriction, *i*, 222–224
Divorce of Ownership and Management, *ii*, 13–15, 43–48
Donlin, *ii*, 120
Dues, Labor Union, *i*, 15. *See also* Finance; Labor Union

Economic, Labor's New Economic Activities. *See* Banks; Insurance; Union Management Co-operation
Economic Research, National Bureau of, *i*, 216
Edgerton, *i*, 159
Education, *i*, 10, 25, 50, 195, 204–210; *ii*, 59, 60
Efficiency, *i*, 86, 196, 216–220, 225, 231–233; *ii*, 32–39
Eight-hour Day. *See* Eight-hour Law; Shorter Workday
Eight-hour Law, *i*, 51, 57
Electrical Workers, *i*, 104; *ii*, 7, 31
Eliot, *i*, 205
Elkins, Senator, *i*, 131
El Paso Convention, A. F. of L., *ii*, 47
Emergency Fleet Corporation, U. S., *i*, 210
Emerson, *i*, 205, 206
Emmett, *ii*, 17, 18
"Employee Ownership," *ii*, 3, 7, 9–20, 80, 81
"Employee Representation," *ii*, 3, 7, 21–39, 80
Employers, *ii*, 53, 54, 65. *See also* Banks; Business; Chambers of Commerce; Corporations Credit; Employee; Finance; Management; Manufacturers; Profits
Engineers. *See* Technical Staff

INDEX

Engineers, Locomotive, *i*, 77, 78. *See also* Railroad Labor

"Equal Opportunity," *ii*, 79, 106, 107, 109

Equity, American Society of, *i*, 79

Europe, *i*, 7, 10, 28, 93, 223; *ii*, 60

Excess Profits Tax. *See* Taxation

Executive, *i*, 121. *See also* President

Expenditures, Governmental. *See* Taxation and Credit

Experts, *i*, 25

Exports, Marketing of Agricultural. *See* Haugen Bill

Express Companies, *ii*, 134

Fall, Attorney-General, *i*, 101

Farm Bureau Federation, *i*, 86

Farm Exports, *i*, 194. *See also* Haugen Bill

Farm Labor Union, *i*, 71

Farm Loan Board, *i*, 210

Farm Organizations, National Board of, *i*, 80

Farmer-Labor Party, *i*, 105, 112

Farmers and Agriculture—
  Agricultural Policies Favored by Labor, *i*, 193, 194
  Conference for Progressive Political Action, *i*, 104, 105, 108
  Effort to Separate Labor and Farmers, *i*, 75, 89–91, 162, 163
  Evolution of American Agriculture in Relation to Labor, *i*, 8–10
  Farm and Labor Blocs, *i*, 153
  Farm Bloc, *i*, 155
  Farm Loan Act Supported by Labor, *i*, 50
  Farmers' Economic Troubles Recognized by Labor, *i*, 228, 229
  Farmers' Right to Government Aid, *ii*, 83, 112, 113, 116

Farmers and Agriculture—(*Cont.*)
  Federal Representation on Economic Boards, *ii*, 143, 155, 156
  Labor's Attitude to Farmers, *i*, 76–79
  Organized Agriculture *versus* Organized Business, *ii*, 121, 122
  Political Co-operation with Labor, *i*, 53, 65, 95, 98, 138, 163
  Relation to Capital, *i*, 13
  Voluntary Organization for, *i*, 170

Farmers' International Congress, *i*, 85

Farmers Non-Partisan League, *i*, 68, 72

Farmers Union, *i*, 71, 79, 86, 88

Federal Employees, *ii*, 6

Federal Reserve Board, *i*, 74, 81, 102; *ii*, 94, 150–152, 155

Federal Trade Commission, *i*, 97, 178–181, 184, 193, 194, 210; *ii*, 94, 97, 144, 150, 152, 155

Federation, Labor Union. *See* Structure

Federation Bank of New York, *ii*, 4

Federation of Economic Groups. *See* Self-determination

Federationist, The American, *i*, 3, 26, 29, 31, 32, 51, 59; *ii*, 59, 170–173

Fess, Senator, *i*, 157, 158

Finance and Financiers—
  Can It Be Divorced from Management? *ii*, 43–44
  Control of, *i*, 186; *ii*, 48
  Control over Industry, *i*, 11, 12; *ii*, 40, 41, 70–73
  Labor's Resistance to Financial Control, *ii*, 41, 42, 73
  Opposition to Labor, *ii*, 6–10
  See also Banks; Credit; Capital

Finance, Labor's Political, 127

173

INDEX

Financial Oligarchy. *See* Autocracy, Industrial
Firemen, *i*, 77. *See also* Railroad Labor
Florida, *i*, 199
Foreign-born, *i*, 16, 49, 91. *See also* Immigration
Foreign Policies, *i*, 3, 4, 18, 74, 110, 116
Forestry, *i*, 192; *ii*, 128
Franklin, *ii*, 137
Frazier, Senator, *i*, 99, 125
Freedom of Contract, *ii*, 117
Free Speech, *i*, 19, 57, 115
Frelinghuysen, Senator, *i*, 99
French Industrial Parliament, *ii*, 90, 91
Frey, *i*, 224
Friends—"Reward Friends and Punish Enemies" Slogan, *i*, 36, 138–141

Garrett, *i*, 135
Gary, *i*, 130, 158, 164, 165; *ii*, 19, 20, 113, 114
German Economic Council, *ii*, 90
German Socialists, *i*, 107
Germany, *ii*, 124, 126, 135
Gompers, Samuel—
Against Class-Rule, *ii*, 50
Against Excessive Political Action, *i*, 29; *ii*, 99–104
Against Financial Control of Industry, *ii*, 39–43, 103
Against Government Operation, *i*, 140, 141
Against Government Ownership, *i*, 136, 137
American Labor and American Democracy, *i*, 1, 2
A Reactionary Congress Denounced, *i*, 36
Author's Association with, *i*, 3
But for Legislation for Labor, *i*, 30, 34
But Many Political Enemies Vanquished, *i*, 61

Gompers, Samuel—(*Continued*)
Claims Non-partisanship, *i*, 40, 41
Class Legislation, *ii*, 119
Conflict of Interest with Employers, *ii*, 51, 54; with Finance, *ii*, 63–66; with Organized Business, *ii*, 72, 73
Co-operation with Farmers, *i*, 76, 88–90
Democratic National Platform and Candidate Endorsed, *i*, 37, 38
Employee Representation, *ii*, 25, 26
Endorsement of Independent Presidential Candidate (La Follette), *i*, 112, 113
For a National Economic Body, *ii*, 89, 90
For a Voice in Control, *ii*, 78
For an Industrial Franchise, *ii*, 92
For Economic Self-determination, *ii*, 51
Foreign Politics Temporarily Dominating the Federation, *i*, 49
For Government Control over Finance, *ii*, 49
For Political Action, *ii*, 104
For Political Regulation in a New Form, *ii*, 89, 90
Government Has Ceased to Represent Property Only, *i*, 2
Labor's Platform in 1924, *i*, 114, 115
Nation's Economic Loss from Unemployment, *i*, 112
Political Defeat Acknowledged (1920), *i*, 54
Political Failure Turned to Success, *i*, 43, 44, 46
Political Victory Again, *i*, 99, 100

INDEX

Gompers, Samuel—(*Continued*)
Profit Sharing (U. S. Steel
Corp. Plan), *ii*, 18, 19
Rebuffed by Democratic Party,
i, 111
The Congressional Bloc, *i*, 121,
122
The Non-partisan Policy, *i*, 145,
147
Gore, Senator, *i*, 53
Government Control of Industry.
See Industry
Government Employees, *ii*, 133–
141
Government Ownership and Oper-
ation—
and Employees, *ii*, 133–139
"Employee Ownership" *versus*,
ii, 17
Government Control Preferred
to, *ii*, 129, 139–141
Government Operation Reject-
ed, *ii*, 133–141
Labor for, of Public Utilities, *ii*,
130–132, 141
Labor Not for (1924), *i*, 110
Opposition to, Becomes Opposi-
tion to Government Con-
trol, *ii*, 106
Progressivism Accused of Lean-
ing Toward, *i*, 171
Progressives for Ultimate, of
Public Utilities, *ii*, 127–129
State Bank, Insurance and Ele-
vator (North Dakota), *i*,
68–71
World Labor Opposed to, *ii*,
124–127
See also Democratic Operation;
Government Employees;
Socialism
Governmentalism. *See* Boards
and Commissions; Federal;
Government Ownership;
Portland Manifesto; Social-
ism

Government of Industry. *See*
Boards and Commissions,
Federal; Industry, Control
of and Self-determination
for; Voice in Control of In-
dustry, A
Grange, National, *i*, 86, 87
Green, William—
Against an Independent Politi-
cal Party at the Present
Time, *i*, 150
Against Independent Candida-
tures (as a Rule), *i*, 123
Against Industrial Autocracy,
ii, 58
Against Mere Political Opposi-
tionism, *i*, 97, 98
Co-operation with Farmers, *i*,
84, 228, 229
"Employee Ownership," *ii*, 20
"Employee Representation,"
(Colorado Fuel and Iron
Co. Plan), *ii*, 28, 29
Endorsement of La Follette, *i*,
110, 145
Food Prices, *i*, 84
For Appeal to Public Opinion,
ii, 58
For Non-partisan Policy, *i*, 151
Government Ownership, *ii*, 20
The New Wage Policy, *ii*, 226,
227

Hammond, *i*, 138
Harding, President, *i*, 59, 60, 87,
90, 178, 190, 192, 213; *ii*,
115
Haugen Bill, *i*, 74, 75, 78, 97, 100,
153, 162, 171
Health, Public, *i*, 195, 202, 208
Heflin, Senator, *i*, 162
Hillman, *i*, 77, 106, 108
Hillquit, *i*, 108
Hodges, *ii*, 126
Holland, *i*, 119
Home Loan Bank, Governmental,
i, 7, 188, 189, 192

INDEX

Hoover, Herbert—
Against Government Intervention, *i*, 210; *ii*, 96, 106–111, 140, 141, 153
Against Popular Blocs, *ii*, 115
And Organized Agriculture, *i*, 75
Changes in Real Wages, *i*, 221, 222, 226
Distribution of Wealth, *i*, 196, 220
Divorce of Management and Finance, *ii*, 13–15
Economic Conflict Recognized, *ii*, 121
For Co-operation of Organized Social Groups, *ii*, 25, 82–85, 92, 100
For High Wages, *i*, 212
For Low Prices, *i*, 212
For Private Profits, *ii*, 68
For Shorter Hours, *i*, 231
For Union-Management Co-operation, *ii*, 33, 34
Graduated Taxation to Level Excessive Incomes, *i*, 196, 197
Inheritance Tax and Capital Expenditure, *i*, 197, 198
Labor for Increased Productivity, *i*, 222, 225
Legislative Restriction of "Strong and Dominant," *i*, 196; *ii*, 105, 106
Second Industrial Conference, *ii*, 24
Unemployment Conference, *i*, 192
Hours. *See* Shorter Workday; Eight Hours
Housing, *i*, 187–189, 192
Houston, *ii*, 15
Howe, *i*, 124
Huddleston, *i*, 125
Hunt, Governor, *i*, 99
Hutchinson, *i*, 118

Illinois, *i*, 147, 148
Illinois Federation of Labor, *i*, 147, 148
Illiteracy, *i*, 16. *See also* Education
Immigration, *i*, 16, 47, 50, 52, 57, 101, 116, 117, 222–224
Income, National, *i*, 13. *See also* Division
Incomes, High, *i*, 13
Income Tax. *See* Taxation
Independents. *See* Third Party
Individual Freedom, *ii*, 109, 115, 125
Individual Initiative, *ii*, 113, 115, 116
Industry—
A Voice in Control of. *See* Voice
Control of, *i*, 172, 173; *ii*, 61, 74–77, 99, 100, 106–110, 113, 117–120, 134–141
Organized. *See* Business, Organized
Self-Determination for, *ii*, 84–94
Industrial Conference Board, National, *ii*, 29, 60
Industrial Conferences, U. S., *ii*, 21–25, 91
Industrial Congress. *See* Industrial Parliament
Industrial "Democracies" and "Republics." *See* "Employee Representation"
Industrial Democracy. *See* Boards and Commissions, Federal; Industry, Control of and Self-determination for; Voice in Control of Industry
Industrial Parliament, *ii*, 89–94
Industrial Relations Commission, U. S., *i*, 220
Inheritance Tax. *See* Taxation
Injunctions, *i*, 19, 57, 96, 102, 115; *ii*, 137, 140. *See also* Legal Status

INDEX

Insurance, *i*, 21, 25, 57, 68, 69; *ii*, 6, 7, 38
"Intellectuals," *ii*, 124, 134
Integration, Industrial. *See* Consolidation
Interlocking Directorates, *i*, 11–13
International, *ii*, 40
International Federation of Trade Unions, *i*, 3
International Questions. *See* Foreign Policies
Inter-State Commerce Commission, *i*, 164; *ii*, 94, 135, 136, 139, 150, 152
Iowa, *i*, 71–75, 101
Irish Question, *i*, 49
Irrigation. *See* Land

Jackson, *i*, 7, 8
Jefferson, *i*, 7, 8; *ii*, 156
Jewell, *i*, 219; *ii*, 35, 36
Johnson, Senator Hiram, *i*, 99
Johnson, Senator Magnus, *i*, 112, 123
Johnston, Wm. H., *i*, 77, 108, 124
Judges, Direct Election of, *i*, 115. *See also* Judiciary
Judiciary, *i*, 130. *See also* Defensive Politics; Injunctions

Kahn, Otto, *ii*, 125
Kellogg, Senator, *i*, 99
Kenyon, Senator, *i*, 192
King, Mackenzie, *ii*, 27
King, Wilfrid I., *i*, 220
Kline, *i*, 77

"Labor," *i*, 126, 135, 146
Labor Capitalism, *ii*, 320
"Labor Legislation," *i*, 18–22, 31; *ii*, 116
Labor Party, *i*, 28, 126, 147; *ii*, 114. *See also* British Labor Party
Ladd, Senator, *ii*, 127, 128
Ladies' Garment Workers, *i*, 104; *ii*, 7

La Follette, Robert M.—
Accused of Pandering Localities, Groups and Classes, *i*, 162
Accused of Standing for Progressivism Against Liberalism, *i*, 171, 172
Endorsed for President by Labor, *i*, 39, 110–125, 142–147
For Non-Partisan Tactics, *i*, 129
Government Ownership of Railroads, *ii*, 128, 129
La Follette Platform, *i*, 114–117
La Follette Progressives in Congress, *i*, 47, 99–103
See also Progressivism
La Follette, Robert, Jr., *i*, 76, 123
"*Laisser-faire*," *ii*, 98–105
Lamont, *ii*, 125
Land, *i*, 8, 180
Experimental Farms, *i*, 180
Graduated Tax on Unused, *i*, 180; *ii*, 68, 69
Ownership, *i*, 180
State and Municipal, *i*, 180
Leasing of Public Utilities, *ii*, 130
Legal Status of Labor, *i*, 18–20, 57, 96. *See also* Clayton Act; Sherman Act; Defensive Politics; Injunctions; Supreme Court
Legislative Achievements, *i*, 40, 49–63
Lewis, John L., *i*, 77, 118, 181, 214–217, *ii*, 138, 139
Liberalism, *i*, 171, 172
Licensing of Corporations, Federal, *i*, 175; *ii*, 138, 148
Lincoln, *i*, 7, 8, 9
Lobbies, *i*, 121, 122. *See also* Bloc; Business
Locomotive Engineers. *See* Engineers
Lodge, Senator, *i*, 122
Longshoremen, *i*, 118
Longworth, *i*, 166

INDEX

Machinists, International Association of, *i*, 77, 124; *ii*, 6, 34, 56, 57

Maintenance of Way Employees, *ii*, 6

Management, *ii*, 64, 71, 135, 143. *See also* Union Management; Divorce

Manufacturers' Associations, *i*, 12, 17, 25, 127, 159, 199; *ii*, 4, 27, 60, 71, 72, 104, 121, 122

Marketing of Agricultural Exports. *See* Haugen Bill

Marx, Karl, *ii*, 55, 57, 83

McAdoo, *i*, 111, 141, 171, 172; *ii*, 153

McCormick, Senator, *i*, 131

McNary-Haugen Bill. *See* Haugen

Meat Packers, Regulation of, *i*, 97, 178-180, 193

Mellon, *i*, 74, 75, 100, 101, 135, 136, 164, 199, 200, 202, 210; *ii*, 122

Membership, Labor Union, *i*, 14, 15

Merchants' Associations. *See* Chambers of Commerce

Mexico, *i*, 57

Middlemen, *i*, 176-178

Miners, *i*, 71, 77, 118, 214, 215; *ii*, 129, 137-141. *See also* Coal Strikes

Mines. *See* Coal

Minnesota, *i*, 70, 71, 103, 105, 112

Mondell, *i*, 99

Monopolies. *See* Big Business

Montana, *i*, 70, 71

Montreal Convention, *ii*, 79

Morrison, *i*, 136

Municipal Ownership, *ii*, 134

Muscle Shoals Power Plant, *i*, 164, 192; *ii*, 131

Musicians, *ii*, 6

Mussolini, *i*, 132; *ii*, 113

Nationalization. *See* Government Ownership; Power; Public Utilities; Railroads

Natural Resources, *ii*, 129, 131

Nebraska, *i*, 71, 101, 103

Newberry, Senator, *i*, 74

New Jersey Chamber of Commerce, *ii*, 22

New Jersey Federation of Labor, *i*, 119

New Parties. *See* Third Parties

Newspapers, *ii*, 37, 38

New York, *i*, 98, 99, 103

New York City, *i*, 209

New York City Federation of Labor, *i*, 119

New York City Merchants Association, *ii*, 22

New York *Times*, *i*, 3

New York *Tribune*, *i*, 3, 133, 162

Non-Partisan Policy, Labor's—
Applied Against Labor, *i*, 49
"Balance of Power," *i*, 138, 139
Concentration in Single Primary, *i*, 69-74, 141, 142
Effective Both on Legislative and Executive Branches (1916), *i*, 46, 49, 50
Independent Candidatures Frowned upon, *i*, 146-148
More Applicable to Congressional than Presidential Elections, *i*, 122, 133
New Party not Imperative, *i*, 149-151
Not Violated by Endorsement of Presidential Candidates, *i*, 39-41, 111, 114, 143-147
Party in Power Primarily Responsible, *i*, 50
"Reward Friends, Punish Enemies," *i*, 139-140

Non-Voting Stock, *ii*, 11, 12

Noonan, *ii*, 131

Norris, Senator, *i*, 103

North Dakota, *i*, 68, 69, 105, 147

178

INDEX

Occupational Representation. *See* Decentralization

Oil, *ii*, 121, 129. *See also* Teapot Dome

Oklahoma, *i*, 67, 71, 72, 196

"Open Shop," *i*, 19; *ii*, 4

Oppositionism, *i*, 56, 97, 98

Organization of Economic Groups. *See* Self-determination

Organization, Voluntary, *i*, 171–173; *ii*, 116, 125

Organize, the Right to. *See* Collective Bargaining

Organized Agriculture. *See* Farmers

Organized Capital, *i*, 17. *See also* Big Business; Business, Organized; Finance

Organized Minorities. *See* Bloc

Ownership. *See* Divorce of Ownership and Management; Employee

Palmer, *i*, 221

Parcels Post, *i*, 50, 51; *ii*, 123

Party Government. *See* Bloc; Non-partisan

Party Re-alignment, *i*, 134, 135, 148–151

Peace Negotiations, *i*, 3

Peek, *i*, 74

Pennsylvania, *i*, 67, 98, 99

Pennsylvania Railroad, *ii*, 26, 27, 30, 34

Perkins, *ii*, 6

Philanthropy, *i*, 195, 196

Philosophy, Labor's Social, *i*, 18, 20, 22

Photo-Engravers, *ii*, 6

Pinchot, *i*, 88, 98, 99

Plant Councils. *See* "Employee Representation"

Platforms, Labor, *i*, 57, 63, 110–120

Platforms, Party, *i*, 58, 61, 158

Platforms, Progressive, *i*, 68–75, 114–116

Plumb, *i*, 218; *ii*, 130, 133–137

Plumb Plan. *See* Plumb

Plumbers, *ii*, 6

Plutocracy. *See* Autocracy; Class Rule

Poindexter, Senator, *i*, 99

Politics and Industry, *ii*, 101–103

Portland Manifesto, *ii*, 43–48, 86–89, 95–101

Postal Savings Banks, *i*, 50, 51; *ii*, 123

Post-Office Clerks, *ii*, 6

Post-Office Employees, *i*, 51, 101

Power, *i*, 191; *ii*, 102, 131, 132, 141

President, the, and the Presidency, *i*, 36, 130–133, 168

President, Direct Election of, *i*, 115

Presidential Elections, *i*, 37–39, 53–60, 109–120, 142, 153

Presidential Primaries, *i*, 168, 169

Prices—
  Agricultural, and Labor, *i*, 83, 84
  Are They Voluntarily Lowered? *ii*, 14–16
  Control of, *i*, 175–189; *ii*, 96, 139, 144
  Monopolistic or Privately Fixed, *i*, 12, 175
  Prices and Taxes, *i*, 199, 200
  Publicity, *i*, 57, 173
  See also Consumers

Primaries (Direct Primary Elections)
  Key to American Labor Politics, *i*, 126, 147
  Labor Driven Out of Minnesota, *i*, 112
  Labor Participation in, *i*, 41, 53, 54, 61, 68–77, 131, 134, 141
  Organized Business and Reactionaries Opposed to, *i*, 128, 129, 159
  Presidential, *i*, 169
  To Interest of Progressives in General, *i*, 21
  See also Bloc, Congressional; Non-partisan Policy

INDEX

Printing Pressmen, *i*, 118; *ii*, 6, 37, 38

Privileges, *i*, 172

Producers, *ii*, 57, 66, 67

Productivity. *See* Efficiency

Profits and Profiteering—
Are They Being Automatically Reduced? *ii*, 14–16
Control of, *i*, 175–189; *ii*, 139, 144
Excessive, and Profiteering, *i*, 175, 176; *ii*, 62–73
Industry Operated Solely for, *ii*, 40–49
Monopolistic, *i*, 12
Publicity of, *i*, 57, 181, 182; *ii*, 139, 144
Taxation of, *i*, 48, 173
Versus Wages, *i*, 19, 232; *ii*, 39
See also Banks; Big Business; Capital; Credit; Finance; Publicity; Taxation

Profit-sharing, *ii*, 17, 18. *See also* "Employee Ownership"

Profits Tax. *See* Taxation

Progressivism and Progressives—
Against Capitalist Control of Government, *ii*, 61
A Progressive Congress, *i*, 101–109
A Progressive-Conservative Re-Alignment, *i*, 142, 149–151
Co-operation with Labor, *i*, 23
For Democratization of Federal Economic Boards and Commissions, *ii*, 151
For Government Control, *ii*, 142
For Ultimate Government Ownership, *i*, 127, 128, 129
Is It Opposed to Liberalism? *i*, 171–174
La Follette Progressives, *i*, 47
Old Party Progressives, *i*, 60, 67, 70–76
Pre-War, *i*, 2
Progressive Party, *i*, 41, 47, 67
The Progressive Bloc, *i*, 122, 128

Progressivism and Progressives—
(*Continued*)
Will the Democratic Party Become the Progressive Party? *i*, 134, 135, 167, 168
See also La Follette; Progressive Platforms; Roosevelt; Wilson

Prohibition, National, of Alcoholic Beverages, *i*, 91, 92, 116

Property, *i*, 2; *ii*, 66, 67, 105, 139

Public Buildings, *i*, 192

Public Labor Appeal to, *i*, 64, 65; *ii*, 58, 61

Public Utilities, *i*, 11; *ii*, 106, 107, 109, 128–137

Public Works, *i*, 190–193

Publication, Labor's Book, *ii*, 25

Publicity—
As a Remedy and Weapon against Profiteering, *i*, 175–185
of Corporation Accounts, *i*, 176, 185; *ii*, 92, 139, 143–145, 149
of Cost of Production, *i*, 177, 181, 182
of Meat-Packers Accounts, *i*, 179
of Prices, *i*, 177
of Tax Returns, *i*, 176
Through Federal Licensing, *i*, 175
Through Price-marking, *i*, 176

Race Question, *i*, 91, 92

Radicals and Radicalism, *i*, 174. *See also* Socialism

Railroad Department, A. F. of L., *i*, 54; *ii*, 23, 34–36

Railroad Labor Board, *i*, 96, 115, 218, 219; *ii*, 22, 23, 129, 133. *See also* Cummins-Esch Act

Railroad Labor Organizations, *i*, 14, 22, 54, 71, 72, 77, 78, 104, 109; *ii*, 62. *See also*

180

INDEX

Union-Management Co-
operation
Railroad Rates, *ii*, 135, 136
Railroads—
Adamson Eight Hour Act, *i*, 47
Governmentally Aided, *i*, 75, 82
Government Control, *ii*, 102, 129
Government Ownership, *i*, 70, 171; *ii*, 128, 130
Railroad Labor and the Railroad Question, *i*, 20, 21
Railway Executives, *ii*, 121, 152. *See also* Cummins-Esch Act; Railroad Labor Board; Plumb Plan
Railway Carmen, *ii*, 7
Reclamation. *See* Land
Rents, *i*, 87, 88, 189
Republican Party and Republicans—
Anti-Labor Republicans Defeated, *i*, 131, 147
Contains Majority of Labor's Opponents, *i*, 36
Coolidge Administration Attacked, *i*, 101, 130
Denounced by Labor, *i*, 39
Effort to Capture Organized Labor, *i*, 28
Labor Driven Out of Primaries in Minnesota, *i*, 112
Labor Rebuffed by, *i*, 111
Platforms Denounced, *i*, 55, 58–61
Progressive Republicans Supported, *i*, 47, 69–72, 98, 99, 103, 125, 146, 147
Progressive Republican Vote in Congress of Considerable Size, *i*, 202.
Pro-Labor Republicans Reduced in Numbers, *i*, 134–136
Republican Congress Anti-Labor, *i*, 37

Republican Party and Republicans—(*Continued*)
Republican Presidents Friendly, *i*, 37
Will It Become the Conservative Party? *i*, 167, 168
See also Coolidge
Revolution, *i*, 2, 10
Ripley, *i*, 184, 185, *ii*, 11-13
Ritchie, Governor, *i*, 171, 172, 209
Rivers, *i*, 192
Roads, *i*, 191, 192, 198, 204
Rockefeller, *ii*, 27
Roosevelt, *i*, 39, 41, 43, 47, 102, 129, 141, 149, 196, 197
Root, *i*, 158, 161, 165
Rotary Clubs, *ii*, 60
"Rule of Reason," The Supreme Court's, *ii*, 118, 145
Russia, *ii*, 125

Sage Foundation, *ii*, 27, 28
Salaried (Lower) and Minor Professional Groups, *i*, 10, 15, 20, 228–230
Salaries, High, *i*, 13
Sales Tax. *See* Taxation
Sankey, *i*, 135
Savings, *i*, 213
Schools. *See* Education
School Teachers, *i*, 15, 207; *ii*, 59
Seamen, *ii*, 133
Seamen's Act, *i*, 45, 57, 59; *ii*, 134
Searles, *i*, 181
Selekman, *ii*, 28
Self-determination in Industry. *See* Industry
Semi-skilled. *See* Unskilled
Senators, Direct Election of, *i*, 14, 50, 128, 159; *ii*, 123
Sherman Anti-Trust Act, *i*, 34, 67, 116; *ii*, 108, 117, 118, 145, 149
Shields, Senator, *i*, 131
Shipping, *i*, 210; *ii*, 130

INDEX

Shipping Board, U. S., *i*, 110; *ii*, 78, 94, 150

Shipstead, Senator, *i*, 103, 112, 113

Shop Unions. *See* "Employee Representation"

Shorter Work Day, *i*, 85, 86. *See also* Collective Bargaining

Small Capitalists, Producers and Traders, *i*, 9, 229; *ii*, 147

Small Investors, *i*, 20, 184, 204; *ii*, 10, 12, 16

Small Taxpayers, *ii*, 20

Smith, Adam, *ii*, 83, 106

Smith, Governor Alfred E., *i*, 98, 99, 111, 119, 141, 171, 172, 189, 202, 203; *ii*, 132, 141

Smith, Frank L., *i*, 147

Smith, Senator Hoke, *i*, 153

Social Democracy, League for, *ii*, 68

"Social Justice." *See* Labor Legislation

"Social Reform." *See* Labor Legislation

Social Struggle, *ii*, 50–61, 62, 63

Socialism and Socialists—
  American Labor Free from Socialist Doctrine, *i*, 23
  "Class Struggle" Doctrine Rejected, *i*, 93; *ii*, 52, 56, 57, 65
  Coolidge Calls Radical Taxation Socialism, *i*, 197
  European Socialists in America Attempt to Capture Unions, *i*, 28
  Government Control as Remedy Against, *i*, 172
  Hoover Against, *i*, 196; *ii*, 41, 83, 105, 107
  Socialist View of Capitalism Rejected, *ii*, 40
  Socialist View of Profits Rejected, *ii*, 68
  Socialists in the Progressive Conference, *i*, 104–107

Socialism and Socialists—(*Cont.*)
  Socialists Refuse to Follow Labor Leadership (1924), *i*, 124
  The New Progressivism Not Socialist, *i*, 102

"Socialized Germany," *ii*, 124

Soviets, *ii*, 125

Speculators. *See* Middlemen

Stabilization, *i*, 12

Standardization. *See* Stabilization

State Socialism Rejected by Labor in Europe and America, *ii*, 124, 126. *See also* Governmentalism

States' Rights. *See* Decentralization

Steel Corporation, U. S. *See* U. S. Steel Corporation

Stone, *i*, 77

Street Railway Employees, *ii*, 134

Strikes, *i*, 9, 86; *ii*, 96, 141

Structure, Labor Union, *i*, 18, 22, 23

Subsidies, *i*, 96

Supreme Court, *i*, 20, 58, 62, 115; *ii*, 118, 145

Sutherland, Senator, *i*, 99

Sweet, Governor, *i*, 125

Switchmen, *ii*, 7

Tariff Commission, Federal, *i*, 210; *ii*, 150, 155

Tariff, Customs, *i*, 82

Tax, Federal Income, Amendment, *i*, 14

Taxation—
  Direct (Income and Inheritance), *i*, 116, 117, 194–203, 209, 210
  Graduated Land Tax, *i*, 180
  Mellon Plan, *i*, 74, 101, 164; *ii*, 123
  of Profits, *i*, 48, 102, 173
  Publicity of Returns, *i*, 57
  Sales Tax, *i*, 96

INDEX

Taxation—(*Continued*)
Taxation for Development, *i*, 190–193, 204–206
See also Land; Mellon
Teachers. *See* School
Teachers, Federation of, American, *ii*, 60, 61
Teamsters and Chauffeurs, *ii*, 134
Teapot Dome, *i*, 74, 130
Technical Staff, *ii*, 135, 143
Texas, *i*, 67, 78
Textile Industry, *i*, 17
Third Party Movements, *i*, 28, 103–109, 112–114, 122, 131, 142–146, 151
Thomas, Norman, *i*, 119
Times. See New York
Tobacco, *i*, 206
Tobin, *ii*, 134
Townsend, Senator, *i*, 99
Trade Associations, *ii*, 4, 143, 145, 152
Trade Commission. *See* Federal
Trade Union Candidates, *i*, 138, 139
Trainmen, Railway, *i*, 118
Tribune. See Chicago; New York
Trusts. *See* Big Business

Underwood, Senator, *i*, 53
Unearned Income, *ii*, 62–73
Uniform Public Accounting. *See* Publicity
Union Co-operative Life Insurance Company, *ii*, 6, 7
Union Label. *See* Consumers
Union Labor Life Insurance Company, *ii*, 6, 7
Union-Management Co-operation, *ii*, 32–39, 78
United Mine Workers of America. *See* Miners
United States Steel Corporation, *ii*, 18–20. *See also* Gary
Unskilled Labor, *i*, 16, 17

Van Kleeck, *ii*, 28

Versailles Treaty, *i*, 102
Veterans' Bureau, *i*, 101
Voice in Control of Industry, *ii*, 74–82

Wadsworth, Senator, *i*, 210
Wages—
A Constantly Rising Wage, *i*, 216
Against Fixed Wages, *ii*, 95, 96, 133. *See also* Arbitration; Collective Bargaining
A Saving Wage, *ii*, 213
A Wage Based on *Industrial* Productivity, *i*, 224, 225
A Wage Based on Productivity, *i*, 215, 216, 219, 220, 224, 225
Certain Farm Organizations Oppose High Wages, *i*, 87, 88
High Wages and National Prosperity, *i*, 212, 213
High Wages *vs.* Labor Unionism, *ii*, 21
Labor for Wage Increases at Expense of Profiteers, but Not of Other Social Group, *i*, 228–231
Labor Opposed to Levelling, *i*, 217
National Productivity Must Be Raised, *i*, 217, 218
Real Wages Rising Because of Immigration Restriction, *i*, 222, 223
The Living Wage, *ii*, 213, 214
The Wage Needed to Raise It, *i*, 218, 219, 232
Wages and Collective Bargaining, *i*, 18
Wages Not Rising with National Productivity, *i*, 221, 222
Wages Not to be Fixed by the Inefficient Establishment, *i*, 215
War-Time Wage Boards, *i*, 48

INDEX

Walker, *i*, 147, 148

Wall Street Journal, *i*, 130

Wallace, *i*, 77

War Boards, Labor on, *i*, 48; *ii*, 79

War Labor Board, *ii*, 22, 79

War, World, *i*, 13, 14, 26, 49. *See also* Foreign Policies

Warren, *i*, 74

Warshow, *ii*, 12

Washington, *i*, 71

Waste of Government, *i*, 203. *See also* Bureaucracy

Waterways, *i*, 191

Wealth. *See* Division

Wharves and Docks, *ii*, 130

Wheeler, Senator, *i*, 103, 110, 123

Whitley, Councils, *ii*, 91

Willard, *ii*, 33–35

Wilson, William B., *ii*, 24

Wilson, Woodrow—

for Anti-profiteering Policies, *i*, 176, 179, 181

for Control of High Prices, *i*, 176, 178, 181

for Corporation Publicity, *i*, 176

for Federal Licensing of Corporations, *i*, 176

for "Reconstruction of Economic Society," *i*, 170

for Reduction of Large Fortunes by Taxation, *i*, 197

Immigration Act Passed over Veto of, *i*, 51

Industrial Conferences, *ii*, 22, 24

On Capitalism, *ii*, 41

Praises Labor's Efforts Against Reactionaries, *i*, 47

Regarded as Pro-Labor, *i*, 47

Signed Cummins-Esch Act, *i*, 59

"The Trusts Are Our Masters Now," *i*, 117

versus Partisan Politics, *i*, 129, 159

Wilson and La Follette Progressivism. Compared, *i*, 103

Wilson-Roosevelt Progressivism, *i*, 141, 149

Woll, Matthew—

Against Anti-Trust Laws, *ii*, 117, 118

Against Dividing Town Against Country, *i*, 78

Against Fascism, *ii*, 125

Against Government Ownership Operation, *ii*, 125, 127

Against Organized Business Control of Government, *i*, 82, 83

Against Sectionalism, *i*, 78

Against Socialism, *ii*, 125

Against Sovietism, *ii*, 125

A New Social Grouping Against Big Business, *i*, 78, 83

For an Industrial Congress under Government Auspices, *ii*, 91, 92

Labor Assumes Progressive Leadership in Congressional Campaign, *i*, 124

Labor for Government Aid Against Industrial Ills, *ii*, 103

President, Union Labor Life Insurance Co., *i*, 67

Price Control, *ii*, 145

Profit Control, *ii*, 145

Proposes to Industrialize and Democratize Federal Economic Boards, *ii*, 112, 113, 143, 150

Publicity for Corporations, *ii*, 145

Women, *i*, 16, 21

Woodlock, *i*, 124

World. See New York

World Court. *See* Foreign Policies

Young, Owen, D., *i*, 233; *ii*, 20

184